Endorsements for *Placemaking with Children and Youth*

This wonderful book recognizes that sustainable development calls for highly participatory local communities, including children and youth, who can cooperatively plan for and flexibly respond to environmental change. Based on this engaged view of citizenship, it offers a comprehensive range of practical methods for everyone who would like to better involve young people in this effort.

> —Roger Hart, Professor of Psychology and Geography at the Graduate Center of the City University of New York, and author of *Children's Participation: The Theory and Practice of Involving Young Citizens in Community Development and Environmental Care*

. . .

Placemaking provides an essential resource for anyone hoping to give the youngest among us a voice. The wealth of knowledge and experience contained within this book comes together with compelling clarity and purpose and needs to be read by everyone working with communities and their environments.

> —Sam Williams, Co-author of *Cities Alive: Designing for Urban Childhoods*, Arup

. . .

Placemaking with Children and Youth makes a valuable contribution to the growing body of literature that focuses on the practice of place-based education. Even novices to this approach will find simple and straightforward tools capable of opening up the world of local inquiry and action to both themselves and their students.

> —Gregory A. Smith, Professor Emeritus, Graduate School of Education and Counseling, Lewis & Clark College, co-author with David Sobel of *Place- and Community-Based Education in Schools*

. . .

This is the most helpful guidebook I have read regarding our work with children! Insightful and well-structured, this guide provides a holistic and comprehensive approach to genuine participation, providing valuable tools and methods that can be adjusted to different contexts and project types. It has also helped me to understand why some methods didn't work for our team in past projects. Chapters 5 and 6 provide succinct explanations that can help easily communicate with a team what needs to be done, and Chapter 11's case studies justify the purpose and necessity of actual tools. Best practices are always great to read, but very hard to replicate without the explicit instructions this guide provides.

> —Maria Sitzoglou, Architect and Urban Designer; City of Thessaloniki Urban Resilience Consultant; Child Friendly Cities Advisor for 100 Resilient Cities

. . .

This book presents the most thorough and comprehensive discussion of all facets of participatory design and planning with children and youth that I have ever read. The team of authors has been at the forefront of innovative participatory urban planning and design with children and youth for many years, and it is a boon for all of us that they have decided to give us insight into all they have learned along the way. This fully illustrated book has the capacity to become a bible for design professionals and researchers, whether they are new to this approach or seasoned advocates.

> —Dr. Kate Bishop, Senior Lecturer, Faculty of Built Environment, University of New South Wales, Sydney, Australia

. . .

This guide presents an extraordinarily rich compilation of traditional and innovative engagement and participatory methods to develop projects with children and young people creating sustainable cities. This book is essential for researchers, practitioners, and anyone interested in including young people in local research and action.

—Tuline Gülgönen, Associate Researcher, Center for Mexican and Central American Studies, author of *Jugar la Ciudad*, and co-director of the documentary *Ciudad Grande*

• • •

Derr, Chawla, and Mintzer's book gathers from around the world useful methods and experiences of engaging youth in the design of their environments. When youth have a say in the design, their alienation turns into a sense of responsibility to society. As the authors quote a teen, "I learned that my voice is important. Our community cares for its youth." And as Driskell and Van Vliet write in their foreword, having youth see their ideas built has enduring impact. This book shows us how a place good for youth is good for us all.

—Stanley King, President, The Co-Design Group, Vancouver; co-author with Susan Chung of *Youth Manual: The Social Art of Architecture Involving Youth in the Design of Sustainable Communities*

• • •

To work with children of different ages, social circumstance, and cultural environments requires knowledge and competence. In this book a great number of examples from urban and community projects of different size and ambition from all parts of the world give the reader expert knowledge and wide practical advice. Collaboration between children and planners makes cities more enjoyable to live in, communities socially more closely knit, and the environment more sustainable.

—Maria Nordström, Ph.D., Associate Professor and Senior Researcher, the Swedish University of Agricultural Sciences, Alnarp, Sweden

• • •

Placemaking with Children and Youth is an inspiring, fresh addition to the hallowed library of human habitat design! I am so grateful that this book has been written, with its guidance on how to engage kids, how to work in diverse urban environments, and its numerous case studies that can be replicated. Now, many more children can be assisted to grow into their full potential as community leaders and changemakers!!

—Mark Lakeman, Founder, The City Repair Project

Placemaking
with Children
and Youth

Placemaking

with Children

and Youth

Victoria Derr,

Louise Chawla,

and Mara Mintzer

PARTICIPATORY

PRACTICES

FOR PLANNING

SUSTAINABLE

COMMUNITIES

New Village Press • New York

Published in the United States by
New Village Press
bookorders@newvillagepress.net
www.newvillagepress.net
New Village Press is a public-benefit, not-for-profit publisher.
Distributed by New York University Press
newvillagepress.nyupress.org

Paperback ISBN: 9781613321003
Available also in hardcover and digital formats
Publication Date: September 2018
First Edition

Library of Congress Cataloging-in-Publication Data
Names: Derr, Victoria (Victoria Leigh), author. I Chawla,
     Louise, author. I Mintzer, Mara, author.
Title: Placemaking with children and youth : participatory
     practices for planning sustainable communities / by
     Victoria Derr, Louise Chawla, and Mara Mintzer.
Description: First edition. I New York : New Village Press,
     2018. I Includes bibliographical references and index.
Identifiers: LCCN 2018035831 (print) I LCCN 2018039690
     (ebook) I ISBN 9781613321027 (ebook trade) I
     ISBN 1613321023 (ebook trade) I ISBN 9781613320945
     (ebook institution) I ISBN 1613320949 (ebook institution)
     I ISBN 9781613321010 (hardcover) I ISBN 1613321015
     (hardcover) I ISBN 9781613321003 (pbk.) I
     ISBN 1613321007 (pbk.)
Subjects: LCSH: City planning—Environmental aspects. I City
     planning—Social aspects. I City planning—Citizen partici-
     pation. I Sustainable development—Citizen participation.
     I City children. I Urban youth.
Classification: LCC HT166 (ebook) I LCC HT166 .D384 2018
     (print) I DDC 307.1/216—dc23
LC record available at https://lccn.loc.gov/2018035831

Cover design: Lynne Elizabeth
Interior design and composition: Leigh McLellan
Front cover photo credits: Top: Osa Menor and Lunárquiqos.
Bottom (clockwise from top left): Speelwijk, Lynn M. Lickteig, Lynn M. Lickteig, Gabriela Gonzalez and DaVinci Camp Summer Institute.
Back cover photo credits: Top: Lens on Climate Change.
Bottom: Growing Up Boulder

*We dedicate this book
to young people
around the world*

CONTENTS

LIST OF BOXES

LIST OF FIGURES

LIST OF FORMS
AND TABLES

ACKNOWLEDGMENTS

Writing a book requires the expertise and ideas of many people. Writing a book on participatory practices with young people amplifies this scope enormously. This book draws on more than 40 years of collective practice, to foster a society where all people are valued, included, and listened to. From the initial values and lessons drawn from the early work of Kevin Lynch and Roger Hart to the contemporary practices of people around the globe, many inspiring and committed individuals have made this work possible. We gratefully acknowledge the inspiration that this early work continues to provide. We have been fortunate to draw on people who revived the Growing Up in Cities project of Kevin Lynch and who have long personal histories of work to improve the quality of cities for children: in particular, David Driskell, Karen Malone, Jill Kruger, Robin Moore, and Nilda Cosco have contributed case material, reflections, and images to this book.

When the principles of Growing Up in Cities came to Boulder, Colorado, many other hands began to influence the work included in this book. Willem van Vliet, founder and former director of the Children, Youth and Environments Center at the University of Colorado is foremost among them. When Willem van Vliet and David Driskell converged in Boulder, they conceived the Growing Up Boulder program, which was launched in 2009 and which has involved all three authors of this book. Without their vision and early leadership, this book would not be possible.

The list of partners and supporters in Growing Up Boulder's work is very long and grows with every project. Former Colorado State Senator Dorothy Rupert believed in Growing Up Boulder from the beginning and helped secure financial support for it. Within the City of Boulder, some who have made this work possible include David Driskell, Tracy Winfree, Jeff Dillon, Kathleen Bracke, Jane Brautigam, Natalie Stiffler, Jean Sanson, David Kemp, Anna Nord, Marnie Ratzel, Caitlin Zacharias, Sam Assefa, Jean Gatza, Lesli Ellis, Jennifer Korbelik, Deryn Wagner, Halice Ruppi, Mark Gershman, Jeff Haley, Tina Briggs, Doug Godfrey, Nick DiFrank, Alex Zinga, Alexis Moreno, and Allison Bayley. Within the schools, our steadfast partners have included Deidre Pilch, Leslie Arnold, Kiffany Lychock, Sam Messier, John McCluskey, Peter Hegelbach, Jennifer Douglas Larsson, Lester Lurie, Jacqueline Esler, Cathy Hill, Tamar van Vliet, Lisa O'Brien, Cheryl Spears, Kate Villarreal, Alysia Hayas, Vicki Oleson, Lauren Weatherby, Ellen Hall, and Jasmine Bailon. At the University of Colorado, Boulder, we thank Brian Muller, Nate Jones, Alea Akins, and the Outreach and Engagement team. Also, Lynn Lickteig and Stephen Cardinale have brought many of Growing Up Boulder's projects to life through their skilled and artful photography. Many students and volunteers have contributed directly to the projects featured in this work, including Katherine Buckley, Kate Armbruster, Pier Luigi Forte, Ilaria Fiorini, Flaminia Martufi, Nathalie Doyle, Gianni Franchesci, Erin Hauer, Maggie Fryke, Anna Reynoso, Nathan Brien, Ildikó Kovács, Alessandro Rigolon, Simge Yilmaz, Erica Fine, Corey Lunden, Jake Accola, Emily Tarantini, Steve Sommer, Morgan Huber, Alyssa Rivas, JoAnna Mendoza, Sarah Bartosh, Aria Dellepiane, Erika Chavarria, Jason Green, Will Oberlander, Hannah Sullivan, Jackie Cameron, Claire Derr, Darcy Varney Kitching, Danica Powell, Ann Moss, Andrea Rossi, Aileen Carrigan, and Lori Carlucci.

Through our work promoting children's participation around the world, we have found many kindred spirits, whose work and ideas also are featured in this book: Giovanni Allegretti and Marco Meloni, Jorge Raedó Álvarez of Osa Menor and Fabiola Uribe of Lunárquiqos, Jackie Bourke and Dorothy Smith, Sudeshna Chatterjee, Yolanda Corona Caraveo and Tuline Gülgönen, Corrie Colvin and Kelly Keena, Illène Pevec, Omayra Rivera Crespo and her team at Taller Creando Sin Encargos, Patsy Eubanks Owens, Stanley King and Susan Chung, Matt Kaplan, Isami Kinoshita, Merrie Koester, Angela Kreutz, Janet Loebach, Beth Osnes, James Rojas, Marjan Verboeket and Marjan Ketner, Sue Wake, Karen Witten, and Penelope Carroll.

Former GUB intern Emily Tarantini directly contributed to the book through graphic design of many images. Ben Harden helped generate maps for Chapters 4 and 7. Hope Arculin at the Carnegie Library for Local History, Boulder, Colorado, and Nathalie Andrews at the Portland Museum in Louisville, Kentucky, were instrumental in helping secure images from their archives. The oral history in Chapter 4 was accessed from Carnegie Library for Local History, Boulder, Colorado, with thanks to Cyns Nelson.

The idea for writing this book began when Victoria (Tori), Louise, and Mara all were working together in Boulder, as part of the Growing Up Boulder program, and when Tori planned to start a new position at California State University Monterey Bay, which would provide the space and time for completing a work of this kind.

Tori thanks Louise, Willem and Mara, for inviting her into the fold; Georgia Lindsay for her friendship and scholarly encouragement; Emily Tarantini for her good humor, can-do attitude, and graphics support; Jordin Simons for her smiles, interest, and helpful suggestions; and Yolanda Corona Caraveo and Tuline Gülgönen, for their friendship and enriching collegiality from Mexico. Tori also thanks the students from California State University Monterey Bay's environmental studies' research methods course and the participants at the children's participation workshop at the National Autonomous University of Mexico for their enthusiasm and thoughtful feedback as we developed this book. And finally, Tori especially thanks Jeff and Eli for their understanding, patience, and encouragement—I write so much better with the fullness of heart that comes from having you in my life.

Louise thanks Roger Hart and Leanne Rivlin for their influence and support ever since she embarked on the study of children's environments long ago, her doctoral students from whom she has learned so much, and the many dedicated activist academics and child advocates who have made this an inspiring path to follow, including my coauthors on this book. It is also a privilege to be surrounded by the large Growing Up Boulder network of design faculty and students, city staff, local teachers, and community volunteers who are constantly inventing new ways to bring children's voices into city planning and design. To Gene, my appreciation for his steadfast encouragement as I pursue my fused commitments to children, nature, and cities. With this book completed, I am happy that he and I will have more time to enjoy the nature and city around us together.

Mara thanks David, Willem, and Louise for including her in the creation of Growing Up Boulder from the beginning; and, she thanks Tori for helping take the program to the next level of possibility during her time in Boulder. Mara is grateful to Cathy Hill, current Growing Up Boulder education coordinator and past GUB teacher, for her friendship, vision and collaboration, and for formalizing some of the GUB procedures and documents shared in this book. Lastly, Mara thanks Kaya for her child-friendly analysis of the world, Harry for his unconditional support, Barry for his wisdom, and all three for their love. This village allowed me the time to work on the book.

Collectively we thank Lynne Elizabeth at New Village Press, for sharing our vision for a brighter, more inclusive world where children are actively involved in shaping it.

FOREWORD

The creation of sustainable cities is synonymous with the creation of a sustainable future for our planet. Knowledge, political will, and behavior change are as critical as clean technology and resource efficiency in altering our currently unsustainable course. This endeavor requires cultivating both awareness and agency; to develop a deep understanding of the world around us and our symbiotic relationship with it, while becoming increasingly adept at identifying and taking effective action.

This may seem too large a mission in which to situate a practical guide concerned with young people's engagement in local research and action. However, the future depends on the nurturing of new generations to become environmentally aware and to commit themselves to the restoration of a world they have inherited in such a degraded state.

As the examples in this guide demonstrate—drawn from experiences across continents, cultures, and community contexts—young people have insights and perspectives that adults, habituated to their environment, too often don't see. As these youth research their communities, develop ideas for change, and speak out, they learn how to put principles of local democracy into practice, collaborating with others to identify concerns, develop recommendations, and prioritize actions. They experience the value of diversity and inclusiveness, and discover that they can be effective agents of change, not only by engaging with their local government, but also independently, on their own. For a 12-year-old to present recommendations at a public meeting or to point to a trash bin, a community mural, or a more child-friendly transit stop that resulted from their efforts, has enduring impact.

Like the authors, we have been working for many years to understand, facilitate and advance meaningful youth engagement. We believe in its transformative potential because we have seen it in action. We have heard the hope and determination in young people's voices as they gain confidence in their knowledge, ideas, and actions; we have seen how young people's participation can change the course of contentious adult conversations (always for the better!); and we have witnessed the pride and respect that grow as young people feel heard and find adult allies in their schools, youth programs, local government, and elsewhere who are willing to work with them to implement change.

When we met nine years ago over beer at The Hungry Toad, a local bar, to plot how we might initiate a new youth engagement effort in Boulder, Colorado, we envisioned a partnership between the city government, the university, and the local school district, committed to both a long-term vision and more modest short-term goals.

Our long-term aspiration was to implement principles of the UN Convention on the Rights of the Child at the city level—an ambitious endeavor given that the US government had not ratified this treaty (and still hasn't), leaving local efforts without a high-level platform to legitimize the work and help direct resources to it. Our more immediate goal was to get a few projects underway and secure a two- to three-year funding commitment. By demonstrating young people's competence and the value of their contributions to local planning and development, we hoped to kindle a culture change in which youth participation in local affairs would no longer be extraordinary, but mainstreamed and routine.

Since then, thanks to the hard work and determination of the three authors and their many allies, supporters, co-facilitators, colleagues, and enthusiastic youth participants, the Growing Up Boulder partnership has flourished and matured. In the process, they have innovated new engagement methods, learned the "secret sauce" of making projects and partnerships work, and gained deep insight into working with young people in a manner that stays true to the principles and ethics of meaningful participation. They have also affected the outcome of dozens of city projects, policy initiatives, and studies, engaging nearly two-thousand young people who are now more familiar with their local government, have new understandings of local issues, and are better prepared to shape a more sustainable future.

This guide to engaging young people is impressively comprehensive, deeply grounded in practical experience and decades of research, and broad in both its project examples and potential application. The authors have drawn on their international networks, professional knowledge, and direct experience to deliver a youth-engagement toolkit that is unprecedented in scope and depth.

You, the reader and user of this guide, are now charged with the role of master craftsperson: you must determine how best to put this kit to use, tailoring it to community needs, your group's skills, and the specifics of your situation.

As you do so, have fun! The great project of sustainability of which you are a part is daunting; and pulling off a successful youth engagement initiative isn't easy either. But the joy of working with young people is that they demand that we pause, play, and laugh along the way, as we create, *with them*, a world worth sustaining.

Cheers.

—*David Driskell*
Deputy Director, Planning
and Community Development,
City of Seattle, Washington

—*Willem van Vliet*
Professor Emeritus, Program
in Environmental Design,
University of Colorado Boulder

ORIENTATION TO THE CHAPTERS

This book is designed to be a guide for people new to participatory practice as well as a resource for practitioners who seek new approaches or ideas. It also offers many innovative methods for researchers who primarily want to understand how young people experience their communities, and many curriculum ideas for educators who want to make class activities relevant to their students' lives. It is organized in a sequential flow, from foundational frameworks for children's rights and ethical practice to methods, analysis, and case examples. We anticipate that readers can use chapters in any order, turning to salient methods or projects of interest, and we have written with this in mind. Throughout the book, examples from six continents illustrate participation in practice.

Chapter 1 provides an overview of policy and supportive frameworks for children's rights, discusses the current contexts of child friendly cities and urban planning, and shares insights into the value of young people's participation for sustainability and inclusion. Chapter 2 shares frameworks and steps for establishing programs and projects. Chapter 3 discusses the ethics of participation, grounded in the Convention on the Rights of the Child and subsequent documents that have defined ethical principles for participation. It also provides an overview of the ethics of conducting research with children and youth.

Chapter 4 moves into the details of developing projects, with an emphasis on methods for understanding community environments and issues before establishing a new project or when a project needs to be re-evaluated midstream. While this book's focus is participatory methods, many projects begin with background research featured in Chapter 4 that can establish a solid foundation for work with young people. Chapters 5 through 7 provide the core of participatory methods featured in this book. Chapter 5 presents arts-based methods, as a way for young people to access the heart and express their values and ideas. Methods include drawing, murals, collage, photography, video, and drama. Chapter 6 describes interviews, focus groups, questionnaires, and related methods. While these methods are also used in traditional research, our focus is on how they are employed with young people as integral parts of participatory processes. Chapter 7 provides a range of methods for taking young people into the city and enabling them to record their experiences, including child-led tours, learning expeditions, photo-framing, photogrids, bioblitzes, and mapmaking.

Chapter 8 includes a range of ways to share ideas in a community context. Charrettes and co-design, participatory budgeting, child and youth presentations, and other community events demonstrate that young people and other community members can develop ideas together. Chapter 9 focuses on ways of analyzing and presenting information, including annotations, coding and sorting qualitative data, and child- and adult-generated reports that honor young people's perspectives. Chapter 10 moves into methods for evaluation, with an emphasis on formative assessment, which can be used to modify and improve programs and projects. This chapter includes methods for evaluation *with* young people, in keeping with the tenets of participatory practices. Chapter 11 features eight case studies of participatory projects from five countries and four continents: a schoolyard transformation in Canada, neighborhood design in Australia and the United States, long term care settings in South African hospitals, revitalization of public space for mobility and play in Puerto Rico and the Netherlands, increasing safety on the streets of Bhopal and Mumbai, India, and open-space planning in the United States. Chapter 12 concludes by revisiting elements of participatory practice, as illustrated throughout the book, weaving in the voices of young people who were part of some of the case examples.

A Word about the Instructions and Time Allocations in this Book

Regarding the lengths of time suggested for methods in this book, such as 30 minutes for one part of a method and 15 minutes for another part: they are approximate. Robert Chambers, known for his development of methods to engage local people in development planning and assessment, noted that one of the main lessons that he learned in his long career is to be "optimally unprepared."[1] That means being well prepared to lead a method or workshop session, but not so tightly scheduled that there is no flexibility for exploring, experiencing, and learning. "Good participatory processes," he concluded, "are predictably unpredictable."[2]

The allocations of time suggested in this book are just that—suggestions based on our own experience and the experience of others familiar with these methods. They are general guidelines, but feel free to adapt them to the context of your work. If young people are deeply engaged in a method and your schedule allows it, let their enthusiasm carry you longer. If you work within tight timeframes and need to break a method into several brief steps, experiment with this approach.

The critical orientation, Chambers noted, is to be open to questions, reflections and recommendations as they arise. One of his other lessons is to "hand over the stick."[3] Don't feel that you need to be the expert on every part of every method that you introduce. Partners, other staff in your organization, interns, volunteers, and young people themselves may have ideas for ways to vary and extend these methods. That, for the most part, is how these methods developed in the first place. Someone had the idea of trying a participatory approach, found like-minded associates, and over time, people learned what worked through trial and error and openness to experimentation. Embark on these methods with the same open attitude! If it turns out that a new technique could benefit from changes, remember Chambers' other counsel: "Fail forwards."[4] We learn by doing.

---

1. Robert Chambers, *Participatory Workshops*. (London: Earthscan, 2002), xiv. His approach that began as Participatory Rural Appraisal is now commonly called Participatory Learning and Action.
2. Ibid.
3. Ibid.
4. Ibid., 1.

Growing Together through Participatory Placemaking

For three months, 60 eight-year-olds researched model neighborhoods for density and walkability and identified child friendly design recommendations for the City of Boulder, Colorado. In a culminating event, city staff and officials visited their school to hear children's visions for housing design, increased inclusivity and sustainability, and ways to integrate flood protection with opportunities for play. During a discussion period, one of the city leaders asked students to identify their favorite aspects of the project. Dozens of hands shot into the air. In different ways, students shared their excitement about exchanging information and ideas with professional designers to inform the project. After one girl described her high points in this community-based design process, she concluded, "Doing this was heaven! I want to keep doing this all my life!"

· · ·

In Johannesburg, South Africa, children in a downtown squatter camp collaborated with the mayor's office to document their lives and identify ways to improve living conditions for children in informal settlements like theirs. At first, as they made drawings and shared stories about their homes and daily routines, they did not want their names on any of their work for fear that people in the city would discover their marginal status. But when the day arrived for them to present their recommendations in a workshop for staff from the city, nonprofit organizations, and aid agencies, they had elected representatives from their group who spoke for them, and they had hung their pictures around the room with their names included. As the workshop unfolded, one of the boys later confided, "I felt so proud for all of us."[1]

· · ·

This book presents programs and methods that are intended to offer young people experiences like these and embed child and youth participation in the culture of urban decision-making.[2] It provides an introduction to the history and principles of participation, a framework for developing projects, and useful tools and approaches to engaging children and youth, ages 2–18, from project conception to completion and celebration. Case studies come from cities

---

1. Jill Swart-Kruger, "Children in a South African squatter camp gain and lose a voice," in *Growing Up in an Urbanising World*, ed., Louise Chawla (London: Earthscan Publications, 2002), 111–133; and personal communication by Jill Kruger to Louise Chawla.

2. This book uses "children" as the term is defined by the United Nations to include all people under 18. The term "young people" is used synonymously. "Youth" includes older teens in addition to young adults.

in both developed and developing countries and illustrate both small and large scale projects, using a variety of methods that range from those that require very few resources to those that incorporate the latest technological innovations.

You can use this manual to help you plan a single project, such as involving students in renovating a park or improving pedestrian safety in their city. Even if you have ambitions to do more, a commitment to a single project can be a good way to begin, to try out new ways of working and identify partners who also believe in the value of young people's ideas. If you want to go further, this book invites you to pursue the larger aim of creating an institutionalized program for participatory design and planning that can include a variety of individual projects over time and make young people's contributions to city decision-making a distinctive part of your city's identity and culture.

While this book draws from a wide range of projects and practices throughout the world, it is rooted in the authors' experiences of coordinating participatory programs with young people, through UNESCO's Growing Up in Cities work internationally and the Growing Up Boulder partnership based in Boulder, Colorado, USA. Together, we bring to our writing more than 50 years of combined experience in participatory practices with children and youth.

A theme that runs through all the methods described in this book is the importance of young people's voices—in expressing their lived experiences, their playfulness and imagination, and their practical solutions for realizing sustainability within cities. In a recent resilience planning project with children in Boulder and Mexico City, a partner teacher asked students what they saw in common between the children in both cities. We were not surprised when one eight-year-old said, "We are all trying to make the world a better place." It has been our collective experience that young people have much to offer to the fields of urban planning and design and to our society at large: they creatively solve

problems and inspire positive solutions, consider the needs of diverse people as well as animals and ecosystems, and want to actively contribute to making their communities better places in which to live.

Placemaking is the participatory act of imagining and creating places with other people. It cultivates a sense of hope and possibility. Not only are children's perspectives important in their own right, but their positive outlook is infectious for adults as well as an inspiration for intergenerational action. No one knows what the future is going to bring, but it is certain that we will have to live more sustainably. Toward this end, everyone's wisdom and skills matter. As part of this transformation, we can choose to move toward a world that reveals a spirit of community and shared resourcefulness. And we can create openings for children and youth to be part of these efforts, to be part of strong democracies.

An International Framework for Children's Participation

In the 1960s, in reaction to massive postwar urban renewal in Europe and North America, some urban planners and designers concluded that vital and inclusive cities could never be achieved by distant top-down decision-making: urban professionals need to work with communities, understand residents' perspectives, give them a voice and speak for them in planning and design processes. These "advocacy planners" improvised new participatory methods to engage with adult groups.[3]

In 1970, in response to the cresting wave of the environmental movement, UNESCO (the United Nations Educational, Scientific and Cultural Organization) convened a group of environmental professionals to discuss people-

---

3. Paul Davidoff, "Advocacy and pluralism in planning." *Journal of the American Institute of Planners* 31, no. 4 (1965): 331–338.

centered solutions to environmental problems. They believed that people could form positive relations with the environment if they were supported in the pursuit of beauty in their surroundings and dignity in human relationships.[4] One member of this group was Kevin Lynch, who had pioneered the use of walks, interviews, and map-making to understand how adults experience urban districts and how places function for them.[5] Wanting to understand how people's relations with their cities develop over time, he proposed a new UNESCO program, Growing Up in Cities, to apply similar methods with small groups of children in early adolescence in low-income urban areas faced with rapid change.

Lynch succeeded in assembling teams of geographers, social researchers, architects, urban planners, and designers in Mexico, Argentina, Poland, and Australia. Children shared how they used local places, resources they valued, their constraints, and fears. They had thoughtful suggestions for how to make their localities better places for all ages.[6] But in the 1970s, Lynch discovered, city officials showed no interest in young people's ideas. He published his team's methods and findings and went on to other ventures.

In 1989, the United Nations' adoption of the Convention on the Rights of the Child (CRC) created new conditions for young people's participation. The most rapidly accepted human rights document in history, it has been ratified by all member nations of the United Nations with the current exception of the United States. It contains 41 articles that are designed to ensure children's protection from harm, provision of basic needs, and participation in decisions that affect their lives, followed by 13 articles related to implementation.[7] Ratifying nations commit to submitting regular five-year reports to the United Nations Committee on the Rights of the Child to document the progress they have made toward realizing children's rights, and these reports attract scrutiny by the media and child advocacy organizations. The Committee on the Rights of the Child has ruled that children's rights to participation include a voice in decisions that shape their environments.[8]

This principle was extended by Agenda 21, the framework for action that was generated at the United Nations Conference on Environment and Development (the Earth Summit) in 1992. It includes a chapter on children and youth as a major group whose protection and health need to be central to goals for sustainable development, and who need to be included in participatory processes to improve the environment.[9] The Habitat Agenda, the plan of action from the United Nations Conference on Human Settlements in 1996 (Habitat II) specifically addressed the importance of participatory processes with children and youth to create better conditions in cities and towns and "to make use of their insight, creativity and thoughts on the environment."[10] Habitat III, which brought urban actors together from across the globe in 2016, affirmed the principles of sustainable development and the inclusion of people of all ages, genders, ethnicities, and income levels in urban decision-making.[11]

In response to the United Nations adoption of the CRC, UNESCO revived the Growing Up in Cities program in 1995, with an initial focus

4. Chawla, *Growing Up in an Urbanising World*, 22.

5. Lynch, Kevin. *The Image of the City.* (Cambridge, MA: MIT Press, 1960).

6. Lynch, Kevin. *Growing Up in Cities.* (Cambridge, MA: MIT Press, 1977).

7. UNICEF, "Convention on the Rights of the Child." UNICEF.org. http://www.unicef.org/crc (Retrieved June

29, 2016).

8. Rachel Hodgkin and Peter Newell, *Implementation Handbook on the Convention on the Rights of the Child.* (UNICEF, 1998).

9. United Nations, *Agenda 21.* United Nations.org. https://sustainabledevelopment.un.org/outcomedocuments/agenda21. (Retrieved June 29, 2016).

10. United Nations, *The Habitat Agenda*, UN Conference on Sustainable Development, Habitat II. http://www.un-documents.net/hab-ag.htm. (Retrieved July 27, 2016).

11. United Nations, *The New Urban Agenda.* Habitat III.org. https://www.habitat3.org/the-new-urban-agenda. (Retrieved July 27, 2016).

in eight countries,[12] and UNICEF (the United Nations Children's Fund) launched its Child Friendly Cities Initiative in 1996.[13] This initiative provides a template to help governments integrate children's rights into policies and programs across sectors. In countries that have ratified the CRC, governments at every level have a responsibility to make efforts in good faith to support children's rights, and this has inspired the funding and implementation of many participatory projects. In the United States, progressive cities can independently choose to advance children's rights. This is one of the motives behind the establishment of Growing Up Boulder, one of the main programs that this book features.

In Europe, initiatives to involve young people in urban planning and design are shared by the European Network of Child Friendly Cities through blogs and biennial conferences.[14] In the United States, the Children, Youth and Environment Network of the Environmental Design Research Association organizes a strand of sessions on child and youth participation at annual conferences. Currently there is a dynamic global field of practice in participatory urban design and planning with children and youth. This book draws on this international network for case studies that illustrate effective methods and approaches to participation.

Changing Contexts of Urban Planning

Sustainability, resilience and climate adaptation have come to the forefront of social and environmental issues that urban planning needs to address. Planning for sustainability seeks to balance The Three E's—environmental quality, economic development, and social equity and vibrancy.

Cities seek to achieve these goals through a wide range of means, including cleaner, more efficient energy usage; compact and connected development; sustainable modes of transportation; integration of nature into the urban fabric; and an inclusive city, with opportunities for people to actively shape the places where they live through placemaking and participatory governance.

Increasingly, humanity lives in cities, and therefore cities are prime sites for the search for a sustainable balance between human needs and the planet's finite resources. In 1975, when participatory research with children was emerging, 37% of the world's population lived in cities. In 2014, this figure was 54%.[15] The United Nations projects that 66% of the world's population will be urban dwellers by 2050.[16] In 1975, the majority of urban residents lived in China, Europe and North America.[17] By 2014, more than half of all urban residents lived in Asian cities. Whereas approximately half of the world's population lived in "less developed" countries in 1975, this number has grown to 75% of the world's population in 2015. These population shifts are projected to continue, with the highest rates of urban growth anticipated in Asia and Africa, especially in lower resourced countries.[18]

As a result of growing population pressures, rising resource consumption, and climate change due to increasing atmospheric concentrations of greenhouse gases, the world is also facing un-

12. Chawla, *Growing Up in an Urbanising World.*
13. UNICEF, "Child Friendly Cities." UNICEF.org. http://www.childfriendlycities.org. (Retrieved June 28, 2016).
14. Ibid.

15. United Nations, "World Urbanization Prospects: The 2005 Revision." United Nations.org. http://www.un.org/esa/population/publications/WUP2005/2005WUP_FS1.pdf. (Retrieved July 26, 2016); United Nations, "World Urbanization Prospects: The 2014 Revision." United Nations.org. https://esa.un.org/unpd/wup/Publications/Files/WUP2014-Highlights.pdf. (Retrieved July 26, 2016).
16. United Nations, "World Population Prospects: The 2017 Revision." United Nations, Department of Economic and Social Affairs. http://www.un.org/en/development/desa/population/. (Retrieved December 27, 2017).
17. United Nations, "World Urbanization Prospects: The 2014 Revision." United Nations, Department of Economic and Social Affairs, Population Division. Custom data acquired via website. (Retrieved July 26, 2016).
18. Ibid.

precedented environmental change. Cities have a large ecological footprint as they draw resources from all over the planet to meet urban dwellers' basic needs as well as the many desires of a global consumer culture. Yet cities also offer efficiencies such as public transportation and dense housing near accessible services. Financial and human capital are concentrated in cities, with many creative and educated people who can work together to move society in more sustainable directions.[19]

Environmental degradation affects human settlement patterns, as rural families move to cities to escape drought and declining soil quality, and families leave coastal regions threatened by rising sea levels. Political instability adds to these population shifts, as families flee violence in Central America, the Middle East, Africa, and other regions of the world. Families also disperse across cities and nations as they seek employment in a globalized economy. With urban migration comes the imperative to understand the shifting terrain of cities from the perspective of all citizens who live and work, struggle and play there.

Since the 1970s, we have also seen the increasingly inequitable distribution of resources, from growing concentrations of wealth in the hands of a few, to government disinvestment in public services.[20] While many urban shifts can be seen and assessed at large scales, inequities are directly felt at local levels, in the "finely grained differentiations" experienced in informal settlements, slums, ghettos, and public housing sites.[21] Scholars who consider the city a site for social transformation, where people can be active agents of change, call for participatory processes as an important aspect of urban governance. Through this means, decision-makers can seek out the perspectives of marginalized, immigrant, and lower income residents within a city, who may be geographically and politically isolated.

Resilience planning seeks to prepare for natural disasters, such as flooding or earthquakes, but also examines chronic stresses that impact the everyday lives of people in cities, such as poverty, unemployment, and inequality. It is compatible with other urban planning initiatives, including the development of green infrastructure, which increases a city's wildlife habitat and flood protection while providing cleaner air and water and lowering summer temperatures. Mounting evidence demonstrates that urban green spaces benefit human health and wellbeing in many ways, for all ages and across all social classes.[22] For children in particular, regardless of family income, vegetation around homes and schools and nearby parks is associated with better concentration and impulse control; better academic achievement; better coping with challenges; reduced stress, depression and aggression; greater physical activity; more imaginative and socially cooperative play; and a stronger sense of connection and care for nature.[23]

Resilience as an emerging field in planning recognizes that a city's people are the best source of resilience, and so understanding and planning for resilience involves understanding people's strengths and resourcefulness as well as their concerns and vulnerabilities. Resilience planning is thus a natural arena for participatory practices with young people.[24]

19. Sheridan Bartlett and David Satterthwaite, eds., *Cities on a Finite Planet.* (London: Routledge, 2016).

20. Faranak Miraftab and Neema Kudva, eds., *Cities of the Global South Reader.* (London: Routledge, 2015).

21. Ibid., 2

22. Terry Hartig, Richard Mitchell, Sjerp De Vries, and Howard Frumkin. "Nature and health." *Annual Review of Public Health* 35 (2014): 207-228.

23. Louise Chawla, "Benefits of nature contact for children." *Journal of Planning Literature* 30, no. 4 (2015): 433-452; Diana Younan, Catherin Tuvblad, Lianfa Li, Jun Wu, Fred Lurmann, Meredith Franklin, Kiros Berhane et al. "Environmental determinants of aggression in adolescents." *Journal of the American Academy of Child and Adolescent Psychiatry*, 55, no. 7 (2016): 591-601.

24. Victoria Derr, Louise Chawla, and Willem van Vliet, "Children as natural change agents: Child friendly cities as resilient cities," in *Designing Cities with Children and Young People: Beyond Playgrounds and Skateparks*, ed., Kate Bishop and Linda Corkery. (New York: Routledge, 2017), 24-35.

Child Friendly Cities

Concurrent with these new contexts of city life, children's experience of cities has changed since participatory research with young people emerged in the 1970s. Children in many developed and developing cities spend less time on the street and more time in structured activities, less time outside roaming independently with friends and more time indoors with technology. The cities in which children live can be more dense, with fewer and more manicured parks, or more sprawling, with greater distances to amenities. At the same time, parents' fears of strangers, traffic and crime have increased. The loss of free movement outdoors to meet friends and explore the local environment can have negative impacts on the health and wellbeing of urban children and youth.[25]

How young people communicate with each other has also shifted dramatically in the past 30 years. Social media, internet resources, and cell phones have enabled many young people to connect virtually and share their lives with their friends and peers. These media allow young people much greater access to communication and information, but these same technology users may never have taken a civics course or participated in meaningful dialogue about their cities. Some youth, nevertheless, are more politically active through digital media, and digital media are a critical aspect of political mobilization.[26] For better or worse, technology and media communications are a part of young people's lives. They can hold young people captive in front of screens indoors, but they can also connect friends and families, and play a positive role in participatory practices. Many participatory projects now integrate technology in a range of ways,

including the production of graphic renderings to illustrate potential designs, design alternatives experienced through three-dimensional virtual environments, and digital voting in participatory budgeting.

While many large-scale, systemic factors are changing the nature of urban planning and children's lives, children's visions for good places in which to grow up have remained relatively consistent over time, and they align with the goals of a sustainable city. In many countries, from affluent to less resourced, young people have expressed a desire for cities that include:

- Peer gathering spaces
- Places where they feel socially integrated and accepted
- Varied, interesting activity settings
- Freedom of movement and feelings of safety
- Community identity
- Green spaces for informal play, sports, and nature exploration
- The ability to contribute to their community, through participatory processes, volunteer actions, and stewardship
- For older youth, opportunities for employment.[27]

Already in the 1970s, Kevin Lynch noticed "some human constants in the way children use

25. Claire Freeman and Paul Tranter, *Children and their Urban Environment: Changing Worlds.* (London: Earthscan Publications, 2011).

26. Ben Kirshner and Ellen Middaugh, eds., *#youthaction: Becoming Political in the Digital Age.* (Charlotte, NC: Information Age Publishing Inc, 2014.)

27. Chawla, *Growing Up in an Urbanising World*; Freeman and Tranter, *Children and their Urban Environment*; Victoria Derr and Ildikó G. Kovács, "How participatory processes impact children and contribute to planning: a case study of neighborhood design from Boulder, Colorado, USA." *Journal of Urbanism: International Research on Placemaking and Urban Sustainability*, 10, no. 1 (2017): 29–48; Victoria Derr, Yolanda Corona, and Tuline Gülgönen, "Children's perceptions of and engagement in urban resilience in the United States and Mexico." *Journal of Planning Education and Research* (2017): doi: 0739456X17723436.; Lynch, *Growing Up in Cities*; Karen Malone. "'The future lies in our hands': Children as researchers and environmental change agents in designing a child-friendly neighbourhood." *Local Environment 18*, no. 3 (2013): 372–395.

their world" when he compared findings across Growing Up in Cities sites.[28] Decades of work to understand child friendly cities reveal basic needs for healthy child and youth development that cities can serve.[29] Although young people across time and space may assess city features in similar ways, how resources can be provided varies site to site, and participatory collaborations to improve local environments have intrinsic value in themselves.[30]

Methods of Participation

When Kevin Lynch and his colleagues initiated Growing Up in Cities in the 1970s, they applied a core set of methods: observations, mapping, drawings, photography, interviews with young people, interviews with adult community members and decision-makers, and guided tours led by young people.[31] When the program was revived in the 1990s, these methods were supplemented with surveys and questionnaires, focus groups, workshops and other community events, and greater use of the arts.[32] Since that time, many people have tested, adapted, and developed new methods and approaches to participation. Some of these innovations have included new forms of technology, such as the use of Geographic Information Systems (GIS), graphic design programs, and interactive media. Other innovations have embraced low technology methods. For exam-

ple, the City as Play method, pioneered by James Rojas in East Los Angeles, uses found objects to "scramble the brain and awaken creativity" with people who otherwise do not interact with urban planning processes.[33] His use of everyday objects, such as hair curlers and salvaged toys, has opened the door for participation with marginalized people, providing opportunities for storytelling and visioning.[34]

In recent years, when we shared our work with Growing Up Boulder at conferences and in meetings with representatives from other cities, people repeatedly told us that they wished we would produce a book that would cover methodological innovations as well as lessons learned in developing effective approaches that sustain participatory practice over time. We present this book to you with the hope that it will serve this purpose. What child and youth advocates have known since Growing Up in Cities was introduced in the 1970s, and what we know now, is that young people are valuable contributors. Effective participation provides opportunities for young people to share their perspectives as experts on their own lived experiences, to deepen their understanding of cities and the processes that shape them, and to contribute their creative thinking to broader planning processes. We know that effective, sustained participation has to be bottom up and grassroots, but also top-down (Figure 1.1), with people from all levels of the city working together—from city agencies, to university programs, to youth organizations, to environmental and cultural organizations, to teachers in classrooms—all of us working with young people.

28. Lynch, *Growing Up in Cities*, 12.

29. Louise Chawla and Willem van Vliet, "Children's rights to child friendly cities." *Handbook of Children's Rights*, ed., M. Ruck, M. Peterson-Badali, and M. Freeman (New York, Routledge, 2017), 533–549.

30. Victoria Derr and Emily Tarantini, "'Because we are all people:'" Outcomes and reflections from young people's participation in the planning and design of child-friendly public spaces." *Local Environment: International Journal of Justice and Sustainability* 21, no. 12 (2016): 1534–1556.

31. Lynch, *Growing Up in Cities*.

32. David Driskell, *Creating Better Cities with Children and Youth*. (London: Earthscan Publications, 2002).

33. Rojas, James. "Place It!" Talk given to Environmental Design Program, University of Colorado Boulder on September 22, 2014. Available at: https://vimeo.com/106818561. (Retrieved on July 28, 2016).

34. Rojas, James. *Interactive Planning Manual*. Growing Up Boulder.org. http://www.growingupboulder.org/uploads/1/3/3/5/13350974/interactive_planning_manual.pdf. (Retrieved on July 28, 2016).

Figure 1.1. Frameworks for participation span all levels of governance, from international agreements to local initiatives. Image credit: Emily Tarantini

Why it Matters

Regardless of the issues to be explored, from planning a small playground, to introducing policies for greater equity, to filmmaking for climate adaptation, young people have an important role to play in shaping the development of cities. Many support the idea that young people should participate in urban planning and design because they will inherit the outcomes. However, many children's rights advocates, including ourselves, believe that children and youth are not just in the process of *becoming* adults: they are a unique group that already has much to contribute to society, just as they are. This principle underlies the Convention on the Rights of the Child, Agenda 21, the Habitat Agenda and other international agreements to advance cities and sustainable development.

Young people themselves want to be seen as valued contributors, and to be included in urban decision-making and public places within their communities. Social inclusion is particularly significant in the context of adolescent development. Our research with Growing Up Boulder has shown that at the beginning of projects, young teens aged 11–16 frequently state that they do not feel that their government cares about their ideas. While we have seen teen perceptions shift during processes of engagement, without widespread mechanisms for participation, many teens will continue to feel excluded from society. When teenagers are separated from society, they express greater feelings of social exclusion, indifference, and antagonism.[35]

Social inclusion matters not only in participatory realms, but also in public spaces. Some in urban planning have expressed concern that public spaces are becoming less inclusive, with less mixing across ages, income levels, and ethnic groups.[36] Teen girls, in particular, are isolated from public spaces in many parts of the world.[37] While many assume that teens want to be separated from other ages, child friendly cities research has not found this to be true. Participatory processes reveal that teens want to be integrated into public spaces, and they want spaces to be well designed and developed for people of all ages, abilities, ethnicities, and interests.[38]

35. Melvin Delgado, *Community Practice and Urban Youth: Social Justice, Service-Learning and Civic Engagement.* (New York: Routledge, 2015).

36. Ali Madanipour, ed., *Whose Public Space? International Case Studies in Urban Design and Development.* (Abingdon: Routledge, 2013).

37. Anastasia Loukaitou-Sideris and Athanasios Sideris. "What brings children to the park? Analysis and measurement of the variables affecting children's use of parks." *Journal of the American Planning Association* 76, no. 1 (2009): 89–107.

38. Jackie Bourke, "'No messing allowed': The enactment of childhood in urban public space from the perspective of the child." *Children, Youth and Environments* 24, no. 1 (2014): 25-52; Myrna Marguiles Breitbart, "Inciting desire, ignoring boundaries and making space," *Education, Childhood and Anarchism: Talking Colin Ward*, ed., Catherine Burke and Ken Jones (Abingdon: Routledge, 2014), 175–

For all of us working with Growing Up Boulder, "seeing is believing." Many adults and city staff were initially skeptical that young people could positively contribute to planning processes until they heard young people's thoughtful considerations. They learned that plans for physical improvements, policies, regulations, education, and programming could be more effective when they included young people's recommendations. As a result, city staff have become advocates for greater inclusivity in planning processes. For example, a city staff person recently concluded her presentation about youth contributions to open space planning with a slide that asked, "What did we learn about engaging Junior Rangers in planning? . . . They care; they think expansively; they can dialogue well . . . we want to engage them more often!"[39] The results not only impact city staff, but also higher levels of leadership, from advisory board members for city departments to city councilors, who now hold staff accountable for integrating young people's ideas into their final plans.

Finally, participation matters because it can significantly contribute to the sustainability of cities. Education for sustainability calls for holistic thinking that invites children and youth to play an active role in conceiving a sustainable future.[40] Through their creativity and genuine concern for creating better places to live, young people readily consider issues of sustainability—from desirable modes of transportation, to renewable energy production, to city greening, to the integration of diverse residents into the urban fabric. Participatory processes with young people cultivate citizens who know how to work collaboratively to create a more sustainable future. This is the heart of placemaking with children and youth.

185.; Derr and Kovács, "How participatory processes impact children and contribute to planning: a case study of neighborhood design from Boulder, Colorado, USA."; Derr and Tarantini, "Because we are all people."

39. Victoria Derr, Halice Ruppi, and Deryn Wagner. "Honoring voices, inspiring futures: Young people's engagement in open space planning." *Children, Youth and Environments* 26, no. 2 (2016): 128–144.

40. Peter Blaze Corcoran and Philip M. Osano, "Young people, education, and sustainable development." *Exploring Principles, Perspectives, and Praxis.* (Wageningen, the Netherlands: Wageningen Academic Publishers, 2009)

"Cities have the capability of providing some-thing for everybody only because, and only when, they are created by everybody."[1]

How do we engage young people in crea-ting places they will care for and love? As discussed in Chapter 1, participation is a right of all people, no matter their age, and many cities and countries have developed provisions to facilitate it. Yet there is no one-size-fits-all tem-plate for every city and every goal. Approaches should be tailored to project and partner needs, from short-term and small-scale projects to longer-term, institutionalized programs for par-ticipation that may include a variety of different projects over the years.

The heart of participation is actively involv-ing local people in decisions that affect them. Participation shifts the emphasis from govern-ment action and decision-making to democratic engagement, where all members of a community have expertise on the places where they live, and can meaningfully contribute to shaping their physical structure and policies. Characteristics of effective participatory planning include:[2]

Local and place-based. People are most inter-ested and engaged when they can speak about their own lived experiences and influence de-cisions that will directly affect their lives. Place-based participation makes sense because young people want opportunities to shape where they live. Local contexts also influence how a project is conceptualized, influence partner selection, methods employed, and final deliverables.

Transparent. Throughout a project, all partic-ipants should understand who is participating,

Supporting Young People's Engagement

participant roles, and project expectations. It is important to communicate the practical limits for a project. For example, in designing a park, participants can learn to work within a budget or limitations on the types of features that can be included. In this way, everyone shares realistic expectations. Sometimes adults are concerned that if young people do not get what they ask for in a project, they will become disengaged. Our experience has been that young people un-derstand and accept limitations and appreciate transparency.

Inclusive. All people have a right to participate. It is not always possible to include everyone in a project, so it is important to think about partners that can help facilitate the greatest inclusion. Children from marginalized communities, such as recent immigrants, are not likely to participate in political or social systems. It is important to make a special commitment to include young people who are least likely to be heard, due to immigration status, ethnicity, income, language, physical barriers, or disabilities.

---

1. Jane Jacobs, *The Death and Life of Great American Cities* (New York: Random House, 1961).
2. Adapted and expanded upon from David Driskell, *Creating Better Cities with Children and Youth.* (London: Earthscan Publications, 2002), 32–34.

Relevant. For *participation* to be relevant, it should focus on local issues that have significance for those involved. A project should be relevant to the city leaders, community members, and staff of child- and youth-serving organizations who participate. Special attention also should be given to developing projects and methods that are culturally relevant. Many issues of relevance at a local scale also have significance at regional, state, national, or global scales. It can be helpful to think about issues as they are experienced locally, but also draw from examples of best practices at multiple scales, to inspire participants' thinking, develop expertise, and generate meaningful recommendations.

Educational for all parties. Participation is not a one-way street. In effective participation, all parties learn from each other. Children and youth learn from experts and also each other. They develop their capacity for listening, expressing ideas, working in teams, and solving problems—essential components of a democratic society. Project leaders, community members, city staff, and officials also can learn, when they bring open minds and attitudes to how young people's ideas can shape their thinking and work. Reflection is an important means of learning from each other—with young people and adults reflecting together not only on the project topic, but also on the process, with the goal of continual learning and improvement.

Sustainable. Participation is a means to achieving an initiative's long-term continuation, through the personal investment, understanding, and sense of stewardship it fosters. Programs are easier to sustain when all parties share in the investment and see personal relevance. At a larger scale, participation is a means to achieving social, economic, and environmental sustainability. When young people develop a sense of personal responsibility, have opportunities to develop and express their voice, share ideas with city leaders, and develop a sense of stewardship and invest-

ment in their community, they are contributing to a more sustainable society.

Voluntary. For participation to be meaningful, as well as ethical, it should be voluntary. Children and youth should be able to choose whether they participate, and positive options should be provided in school or after-school settings so that no one feels pressured to join.

Playful. It is important to remember the importance of play and humor in participation. Young people want to contribute their perspectives to urban planning, but they also want to enjoy themselves. Methods that use multiple senses, integrate arts and creativity, and allow flexibility and freedom of expression are more effective in sustaining young people's interest. Playfulness can influence the methods we choose, ideas we generate for design (Figure 2.1–2.2) or simply the way we think of participation—enjoying each other, and each other's ideas, can be part of participatory processes.

Establishing Programs and Partnerships

What are key elements to consider in setting up a new program or partnership? Engagement of young people may look different in the varied contexts in which it develops, yet there are some consistent factors necessary to establish programs and projects.[3] In this section we consider key processes for establishing programs and provide examples of sustained participation. While one-time projects help increase young people's perspectives for a particular place or time, sustained participation, through institutionalized programming, helps shift the balance of power by normalizing young people's inclusion in decision making. In this chapter we pro-

---

3. A "program" supports on-going participatory practice whereas a "project" is a one-time or short-term initiative.

Figure 2.1. Children on a walking tour in the Netherlands climbed on electrical boxes along their route. (See Chapter 7 for a discussion of walking tour methods.) Photo credit: Speelwijk

Figure 2.2. Play on electric boxes served as inspiration for design along play routes, to designate areas in the neighborhood where children like to play. (See Chapter 11 to learn more about this case study.) Photo credit: Speelwijk

vide a framework for developing more enduring, participatory programs with the recognition that cultural and institutional shifts take time and may not always be possible or appropriate.[4] To begin, we identify three steps for the early stages of program establishment:

Step 1 Identify a **local leader**—someone who will lead a project and facilitate early legwork.

Step 2 Establish **program partners** from municipal governments, schools, nonprofits, and universities.

Step 3 Establish **agreed-upon goals** and strategies for engagement.

Figure 2.3. Steps in establishing a program or partnership.

Steps in Establishing a Program or Partnership

Identify a local leader

Step 1 To get started, a program will need a local leader who understands the community context as well as the values and potential of engaging young people in participatory planning—a local "champion." This could be someone in a municipal agency, university or local nonprofit,[5] or an interested community member. Early leadership is essential to developing a program that fits the community, to identifying a network of interested and potential partners, and to providing consistency in establishing structures for participation. Drawing from case material in Chapter 11, the examples below illustrate diverse forms of leadership:

- As a Ph.D. student, landscape architect Janet Loebach responded to a school's interest in greening their school garden and coordinated diverse partners, from university faculty to school administrators, teachers, and youth themselves to facilitate planning and design that would transform the school grounds.

4. A useful guide with additional resources for building strong community partnerships to improve environments for children and other ages is: North American Association for Environmental Education, *Community Engagement: Guidelines for Excellence*. North American Association for Environmental Education, http://naaee.org/eepro/resources/community-engagement-guidelines. (Retrieved January 8, 2018).

5. Nonprofit organizations, as they are termed in the United States, are synonymous with non-governmental organizations (NGOs) in much of the rest of the world. Both terms refer to organizations whose work benefits the general public and is not conducted for profit or shareholder benefits.

- The design firm *taller Creando Sin Encargos* organized a series of workshops to engage young people in transformations of public spaces in Puerto Rico. They involved young people in all stages of the design process, from initial site assessments, to design, and building a variety of amenities in public spaces.

- In the case of the Open Space and Mountain Parks (OSMP) case study, newly hired OSMP Planner Deryn Wagner approached Growing Up Boulder because she wanted to initiate youth engagement practices in her position with the city. She led her agency in taking seriously the potential of young people's engagement as a standard practice.

Establish program partners

Step 2   Municipal governments, schools, nonprofits, and universities all will have different goals and contributions to a participatory program. In order to sustain partnerships over time, each party must benefit *and contribute* in some way. Governments may choose to partner because they value and support inclusive citizen participation. Primary or secondary schools may be most interested in how participatory projects can facilitate curricular goals. University faculty and staff may want to support the professional development of their students or provide opportunities for campus-community partnerships for their courses. A youth-serving nonprofit might seek opportunities to enrich their after-school services. Regardless of the specific motivations, all partners should support mutual learning. Box 2.1 illustrates some of the benefits partners describe from participatory programs.

Municipal governments are a central partner in establishing authentic programs that can contribute to lasting community change. Potential municipal partners include:

Box 2.1. Benefits of Participation

- Authentic connection with other partners

- Opportunities for dialogue and learning between peers and among diverse partners

- Opportunities to learn about and integrate diverse ideas into urban planning and policy processes

- Enhanced resources—both financial and in-kind

- Contributing to a cultural shift— a mindset in which children and youth are seen as active agents in creating community change

- A stronger, more inclusive local democracy

- Places that better serve people of all ages

- Parks and recreation
- Youth services
- Community planning
- Public housing authorities
- Libraries
- Arts and culture
- Transportation
- Health and human services
- Designers who staff or consult with city departments

City councils and city manager's offices can be important in supporting and sustaining participatory programs. Municipal departments benefit from engagement because young people can make their projects better, more lively, and more directly relevant to the community members who will use these places and services. They also benefit by increasing community goodwill toward their projects and from increased opportunities to leverage resources. Through partnerships, municipalities are able to reach more children, youth, and community members than they could engage directly on their own.

Schools and organizations that serve children and youth are essential to a participatory process. For one, they are a source for consistent access to young people and promote educational development. But they also provide in-depth knowledge of the specific groups of young people they serve and can provide valuable ideas about how to best engage them. Potential partners include:

- Primary and secondary schools (including individual teachers)
- Preschools
- Before- and after-school enrichment programs
- Family resource centers
- Public health and recreational programs focused on children and youth
- Programs that serve migrant or immigrant children and families
- Nonprofit organizations that serve children and youth

These partnerships can provide schools and nonprofits with access to "real-world" projects that enhance student learning or create more meaningful after-school programs. Young people benefit from opportunities to shape their communities; to learn from their peers, adult community leaders, and elders; and to feel heard and empowered through participatory practices. Schoolteachers also benefit when students engage in creative processes that help them build skills—including writing, public speaking, or art—and learn specific content, such as civics, sustainability, or urban planning.

Universities can be significant partners in establishing and maintaining programs. Potential partners within the university setting include:

- Service-learning and community engagement institutes and centers
- Architecture, landscape architecture, and planning departments
- Environmental studies departments
- Health and human services departments
- Child and youth development departments
- Education departments
- Political science departments

Universities can provide many in-kind resources, including students and faculty who bring knowledge of best practices in urban planning, child and youth development, and participatory action research as well as the ability to disseminate this work through presentations and publications. University students can gain important skills by helping to conceptualize and implement projects, and they can make valued contributions to programs which may have limited resources. University faculty can find opportunities for research and publications, service to the community and university, and enriched teaching practices.

Step 3 — Establish structures and strategies

Once initial partners are established, it is important to collaboratively identify processes and goals to support program implementation.

✔ Identify program goals. Program goals identify and help to institutionalize explicit values for young people's participation. These can include a mission statement, guiding principles, and expectations that create a supportive culture for participation (Box 2.2). UNICEF's Child Friendly Cities Initiative and UNESCO's Growing Up in Cities projects provide frameworks and useful models for this. However, each program will want to tailor its goals to the specific context of project partners. Partners may want to revisit their own goals over time, to adapt to the changing context of participatory practice in their community.

✔ Identify a program leader. Early on, it is important to identify a dedicated staff person, faculty member, or community member, who can take leadership of communication and coordination. This role might be filled by the same person who was an initial champion or by someone new, but our experience is that implementing and sustaining participatory programs requires someone who is dedicated to this work and can coordinate meetings and engagement events, research best practices or new methods for engagement, and communicate among all partners and the community at large. Co-leaders with close communication may share this role.

✔ Develop an organizational structure. Organizational structures help identify roles, time commitments, and budget priorities for program partners. They establish a framework for how organizations will participate, and the roles and processes by which young people will also participate in decision-making and management (Box 2.2 and 2.3).

✔ Identify physical spaces. Programs will need to identify spaces for program administration, meetings, planning, and youth gathering. Ideally, these spaces are accessible and

---

Box 2.2. **Growing Up Boulder's Structure**

Growing Up Boulder is a partnership for child and youth participation in city planning and design in the city of Boulder, Colorado. Since its inception, it has employed an iterative approach to participation—adapting to new circumstances, new community issues, the changing needs of partners, and the ideas and input from thousands of young people. Yet it also has held a consistent structure, guided by goals, structures, and principles that help sustain the program.

Mission Statement

Growing Up Boulder's mission is "to empower Boulder's young people with opportunities for inclusion, influence, and deliberation on local issues that affect their lives."

Organizational Structure

Growing Up Boulder (GUB) established both an executive committee and steering committee, which meet at regular intervals. The executive committee is comprised of leaders from municipal government, the school board, and the nonprofit sector and meets twice annually to set the general direction for GUB. The steering committee is a broader mix of university faculty, staff and students; municipal staff members; and a wide range of nonprofit staff and schoolteachers who work directly with children and youth. The steering committee meets about five times per year and discusses current and proposed projects. It is a source of innovation and networking for GUB projects as well as for best practices in working with young people in urban planning. While the structures have remained relatively consistent, the individuals and organizations represented tend to vary by project relevance and shifts in employment, allowing for adaptation needed to sustain projects over time.

Initial program partners included community planning and health and human services departments within the city. Over time, as parks and transportation departments also became partners, GUB's emphasis shifted to engagement in city planning and design. As GUB reflected on its own processes, partners developed a model for participation that reflected the values and approaches to effective engagement (see Box 2.7).

Box 2.3. **No One Size Fits All**

There is no single way to institutionalize child friendliness. When the City of Salinas, California was thinking about how they could increase community participation and increase trust between community members and city leaders, a focus group of community non-profit workers envisioned a strategy with youth allies at the heart. These youth allies would be trained and supported by university faculty and students, interact with city leaders to identify goals, and networked with community partners that serve specific neighborhood hubs. These youth allies would lead participatory activities in partnership with adults in the community. While the strategy is still under consideration, the model shows one example of many possible means of envisioning an institutionalized framework for young people's participation.

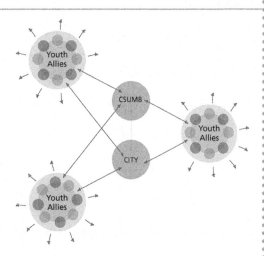

Figure 2.4. A series of neighborhood networks put "youth allies" in the center of community organizing for participation. Image credit: Jordin Simons

comfortable for young people as well as project leaders and community members. These spaces should also contain room for storage of project supplies (such as paints, markers and papers) and project artifacts (such as models, murals, or presentation boards).

✔ Identify resources and funding. All communities have limited resources for participatory processes. The value of a strong partnership is that it can help leverage existing resources to achieve participation goals through in-kind contributions and resource sharing. However, funding is also important for the long-term sustainability of a program.

✔ On-going funding for paid staff (full- or part-time, depending on program demands) will ensure long-term program management and nurturing of network connections. This role may be provided through an existing position in which these roles and responsibilities are articulated in a job description,

or by funding a specific position. Additional funds may be needed to support acquisition of resources such as project supplies, printing costs, cameras, or design services (Table 2.1). Funding helps sustain on-going staff, provides continuity, and integrates young people's participation into the culture of the city.

✔ Put agreements into writing. Written agreements can contribute to transparency and can help avoid misunderstandings. A Memorandum of Understanding (MOU) is a formal agreement between two or more organizations (Figure 2.5). An MOU is not legally binding but does identify agreed upon roles and communicates serious intent. Many large institutions, such as universities or local governments, involve their internal legal advisors when developing an MOU.

In addition, programs should identify processes for taking, distributing, and storing meeting notes. Just as with formal MOUs, meeting notes help to provide clarity,

Table 2.1. Potential Sources and Expenses for Program Administration

Potential Sources	Potential Expenses
Municipal operating funds	Coordinating staff salaries
School district operating funds	
Universities	• University salaries or fellowships
	• Operating expenses (computers, office space, administrative support services)
	• In-kind donations of faculty time and space
	• Supplies such as cameras, paints, markers, paper
	• Outreach grants for projects
Grants or donations from foundations, corporations, local businesses, government, or private donors	• Supplies such as cameras, paints, markers, paper
	• Some salaries or administrative costs
	• Stipends for teachers
Community	Adult volunteers to assist with project implementation
Design firms	Pro bono or fee-for-services for limited consultations

Memorandum of Understanding

This Memorandum of Understanding (MOU) is made on [DATE] by and between [PROGRAM PARTNER 1 and MAILING ADDRESS, "P1"], [PROGRAM PARTNER 2 and MAILING ADDRESS, "P2"], and [PROGRAM PARTNER 3 and MAILING ADDRESS, "P3"], collectively referred to as "parties."

WHEREAS [PROGRAM NAME] is an initiative created through a partnership between [P1], [P2] and [P3], along with other organizations such as [ANY ADDITIONAL PROGRAM PARTNERS THAT WILL BE LESS FORMALLY ENGAGED]; and

WHEREAS [PROGRAM NAME] focuses on building meaningful connections between young people, local community leaders, and decision-makers in an effort to address issues of concern and make [COMMUNITY NAME] a better and more inclusive place for young people;

NOW THEREFORE, in consideration of the mutual promises contained herein, the Parties agree as follows:

1. [Services and resources P1 will provide]
2. [Services and resources P2 will provide]
3. [Services and resources P3 will provide]

The Parties pledge to collaborate in good faith to attempt to informally and amicably resolve any disputes that may arise between them concerning this MOU. Any notices to be given by one Party to the other Parties under this MOU shall be in writing.

This agreement will be effective on [DATE] and shall renew annually unless further modified.

[NAME, TITLE, SIGNATURE, DATE of SIGNING for PARTNER 1]
[NAME, TITLE, SIGNATURE, DATE of SIGNING for PARTNER 2]
[NAME, TITLE, SIGNATURE, DATE of SIGNING for PARTNER 3]

Figure 2.5. A sample Memorandum of Understanding

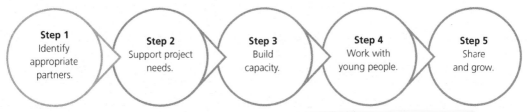

Figure 2.6. Steps in implementing projects.

advance projects in a timely way, and avoid misunderstandings in complex projects. Meeting minutes should identify:

- The date and location of the meeting
- Who attended
- Agenda items (the topics discussed in the meeting)
- General notes for each agenda item
- Action items that identify who will complete specific tasks after the meeting
- Items to carry forward to future meetings

In summary, key elements in establishing programs include:

- Identifying a local champion, who understands the local community and can establish partnerships
- Identifying partners whose mission and purpose align with child friendly cities and participatory practices
- Identifying leaders within each partner institution, who will serve as on-going champions and advocates both within their respective institutions and the community at large
- Establishing a set of agreed upon goals, strategies, and structures for achieving young people's participation, including the resources (financial, human, physical, or other) to support the program, and
- Putting these agreements into writing.

Implementing Projects

Once an initial structure is established, there are a number of additional factors to consider when implementing projects. Primary among these are:

Step 1

Identify appropriate partners

Effective participation requires both bottom-up and top-down decision making and dialogue (Figure 1.1). Once initial partners are identified for a program as a whole, it also is important to consider how each group will engage, how often, and for which projects. One approach to deciding this is to complete a stakeholder analysis, such as in the sample table for a parks planning project (Table 2.2). Stakeholders are any individual or organization who can influence or be impacted by project outcomes. Stakeholders may be different for transportation projects than for a climate action project, so thinking through appropriate partners is important for every project.

Partner identification should ensure that the project engages children, youth, and community members for whom the project is personally relevant and meaningful. Partner identification should also ensure that marginalized populations are included, as much as is possible and relevant to the project. Questions to strategically guide project partner selection include:

- Can young people provide insights about issues of key importance?
- Is success likely with these partners?

Table 2.2. Sample Stakeholder Analysis

Stakeholder Name/Affiliation	How is the stakeholder connected to the project?	What does the stakeholder value about the project?	How can the stakeholder contribute to the project?	How can the stakeholder engage with the project?
Municipal parks planners	Project lead	Parks for healthy communities	Organizing meetings, directing designs, providing funds for implementation	Focus groups and community meetings
Neighborhood residents (children, parents, elderly)	Current users and users of the end result	Play, community, mental and physical well-being	Generating ideas, helping with appropriate aspects of building and maintenance	Participatory design workshops, some installations, stewardship
Adjacent primary school (teachers, students, administration, facilities staff)	User of the end result	Education and play, connecting with community	Generating ideas, helping with appropriate aspects of building and maintenance	Participatory design workshops, ecology curriculum, garden planning, long term stewardship
Retirement community center	Current park users	A sense of history and belonging, a place for nature connection, exercise, and relaxation	Generating ideas, intergenerational stories and sharing	Participatory design workshops
Consulting landscape architects	Contractor for design services	Designing a beautiful and functional park	Translating and integrating community ideas into design language and safety standards	Attending interim and final workshops, drafting plans for feedback

- Are these young people representative of the population that needs to be understood?

- Do these young people reflect relevant marginalized communities?

Support project needs

Step 2

We discussed resources and funding in the "Establishing Programs" section of this chapter (Table 2.1).

At project outset, a work plan and budget can identify existing resources and how additional needs might be funded or provided (Box 2.4). Early planning can provide opportunities to write grants or solicit donations to assist with material costs for specific projects. In-kind contributions include those items that someone is contributing to the project without expecting remuneration. In-kind contributions can include a person's time and services—through existing employment or volunteer work—as well as materials, equipment, or space.

Build capacity

Step 3

Effective participation requires many different types of skills and understandings. Capacity building can greatly enhance the effectiveness of project implementation, in the beginning of a project or when new partners become involved. Examples of areas for capacity building include:

- Learning how to use new methods of engagement

Box 2.4. **Sample Project Budget Items**

10-Week Photovoice Project

In-Kind
City recreation staff
Staff coordinator
University students
University printing and computers

Arts Council Grant
10 cameras
Photo paper and printing
Exhibit display materials
Contracted professional photographer

16-Week Park Design Project

In-Kind
City planning and parks staff
Staff coordinator
University printing and computers

University Outreach Grant
Model-making materials
Teacher stipends
University students

Box 2.5. **Training Municipal Leaders in Quebec**

Natasha Blanchet-Cohen and Juan Torres worked with municipal leaders in the early stages of child-friendly city initiatives in Quebec to demonstrate methods and procedures for working with children. They enhanced existing initiatives by showing city staff how participation occurs, modeling processes for city staff to learn by example. In one case, Blanchet-Cohen and Torres worked with city staff to facilitate a festive evening, with hot chocolate and music, during which they interviewed youth about how they use public spaces. In another, they facilitated dialogues between city staff and youth to identify more effective structures for communication between youth and municipal government. After these workshops, municipal staff were more comfortable with participatory practices, recognizing that approaches can be relatively simple and that results could generate new ideas for their work.[1]

1. Natasha Blanchet Cohen and Juan Torres, "Accreditation of Child-Friendly Municipalities in Quebec: Opportunities for Child Participation." *Children, Youth and Environments* 25, no. 2 (2015): 16-32.

- Understanding approaches to positive communication with children
- Increasing cultural sensitivity
- Attending city leadership workshops

While these capacities may be a part of many professionals' training, not everyone may have experience working within particular contexts, understand the nuances of a particular population, or feel comfortable with participatory methods. Training is also important for uni-

versity students, faculty members, community volunteers, and youth who want to move into leadership positions (Box 2.5).

Work with young people

Subsequent chapters of this book will focus specifically on methods for working with young people; we highlight some core principles of effective practice here:

Box 2.6. Setting Priorities for Coastal Stewardship in Monterey Bay, California

In an engagement process designed to inform a school's long-term coastal stewardship program in Monterey Bay, California, children began by drawing a favorite place or activity in their community. Responses varied: a climbing tree, a biking spot, a particular beach, a climbing gym. This initial activity helped children feel their ideas and experiences had value. It also provided facilitators with important insights into the children's lived experiences. Some children, who lived in an impoverished neighborhood, said, "Well, in our neighborhood there is nothing to draw." In response, facilitators encouraged these students to draw a place or activity that was meaningful to them, even if it was not in their neighborhood. Students then drew a special animal, Disneyland, and a climbing gym. These children began talking more about their experiences and sharing stories with their peers. Approaches to stewardship may be different for children with different experiences of the local environment, yet whatever their experiences may be, children feel validated when their ideas are heard.

✔ Build trust by working with established partners. Participatory processes often bring together new faces and groups of people. By drawing from established networks of organizations who already have built trust with children and youth, participatory processes can capitalize on existing relationships. This can create a context in which young people are more comfortable and willing to share their ideas.

✔ Go to the locations where young people already are. Through existing partnerships, you should be able to engage children and youth in places where they feel comfortable, such as a school, community center, after-school program, or public space. Young people are much more likely to participate if you go to places where they already are than if you ask them to come to an unfamiliar place in their free time.

✔ Begin by learning about young people's interests and questions about a topic. It can be tempting to jump into the details of finding out what people would like to see in a project, rather than building community capacity to make informed recommendations. As part of project initiation, it is important to identify what kinds of ideas, connections, or interests young people already have regarding a project topic (Box 2.6). Taking the time for such processes builds confidence for children to move into less familiar terrain, such as urban planning, and also enriches adults' understanding of the experiences young people bring to a project.

✔ Allow opportunities for young people to learn and develop their ideas through diverse and creative approaches. Children (and adults) learn best when they use their brains and bodies in diverse ways. Using a range of methods enables young people to deepen their knowledge through diverse learning pathways. Some children love to draw, while others are more comfortable building models, and still others thrive when they go outside.

When projects integrate multiple methods, they provide opportunities for all children to contribute to and learn from each other's strengths. Young people become especially engaged with playful methods. Creativity can take many forms, from an artistic representation of "who I am and what I love about my community" (Chapter 5, Box 5.7) to creation of graphics for a public presentation or poster (Chapter 9), to the expression of ideas through theater or puppetry (Chapters 5, 6, and 11).

✔ Be open to experimentation, trial and error. The growing movement of community placemaking is a rich source of innovation in methods for engagement. But innovation can only happen in environments where people understand that learning happens through trial and error. Children and youth should be supported in learning and exper-

imenting, but so should all project partners. Some of the most exciting project outcomes arise from times when partners are open to exploring new ideas as a part of a participatory process, thus embracing the idea that participation is educational for all parties involved.

Many of these ideas are emphasized in Growing Up Boulder's model for engaging young people (Box 2.7).

Box 2.7. **Growing Up Boulder's Evolving Approach to Participation**

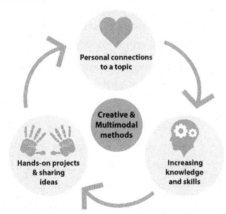

Figure 2.7: Heart, head, hands model for participation. Image credit: Emily Tarantini

Phase 1: Build on Children's Initial Connections to a Topic. This is typically the time when project leaders introduce a project—for example, how should the city redevelop its civic area? What does it mean to be resilient? They identify appropriate partners and suggest approaches to learn about the experiences and expertise that young people can bring to this topic. Many of the art-based methods in Chapter 5 facilitate these early expressions.

Phase 2: Increase Children's Knowledge and Ability to Contribute. Participation is an educational process. Growing Up Boulder exposes young people to a topic through diverse methods, such as slideshows of exemplary precedent projects, field trips, films, independent research

and conversations with experts. Young people learn about a local issue, while exploring how other people have addressed this same issue in other parts of the world. (See Chapters 5-7 for examples of these methods, and the Chapter 11 case of neighborhood design in Boulder.)

Phase 3: Synthesize Ideas and Share. Young people develop ideas and recommendations, and make these concrete through means such as three-dimensional models, drawings, digital presentations, posters, table displays, and photo exhibits. They share these ideas with city and community partners, who listen and exchange ideas. Young people might present their ideas at a city council meeting or at an event in their school. Growing Up Boulder prefers to provide opportunities for young people to initially share their ideas in spaces that are comfortable—their after-school studio space, their school, or community center. (See Chapter 8 for examples of this in practice.)

This model is supported by creative and multimodal methods of engagement, committed partners, and customized deliverables that meet the needs of participants. When time and project goals permit, many of these stages are revisited, with city leaders sharing interim plans for feedback, or students receiving feedback and then further developing their ideas (Chapters 9 and 10 suggest ways to report on and evaluate projects).

Share and grow

Step 5

Participatory projects can only remain relevant and educational when all parties are engaged in an on-going process of sharing and learning from each other.

✔ Create contexts for dialogue and reflection at multiple points of the process. Reflection is critical to learning and adaptation. While reflection at the end of a process is essential to identifying improvements, it is also important along the way. Critical issues for communication include how projects should be conceived and developed (discussed above), but also how projects should adapt and evolve over time. As a project nears completion, it is also important to discuss how young people's ideas will be communicated to multiple audiences, and how planners will share back with youth how they are applying their ideas. These ideas are discussed in depth in Chapters 8-10. Reflection processes can be integrated into a project in multiple ways:

- Young people reflect on what they liked or did not like about the project, in writing or orally in group formats
- They share their favorite methods and reasons for their choices
- They give feedback at the end of each session
- They complete a pre- and post-project assessment
- Project leaders, teachers and youth leaders reflect on a project together
- Participants in committee or community meetings provide structured or informal feedback
- Time for reflection is scheduled into partner meetings

✔ Develop customized deliverables. Most projects warrant a report that outlines who was involved, when, and how, as well as the outcomes and ideas of the project. These documents are particularly helpful for city planners or design consultants who may be integrating multiple perspectives into a single plan. Project reports also provide a long-term record that is helpful for city staff as they work on new initiatives, as well as for outside entities interested in learning from previous experiences. (See Chapter 9 for diverse examples of reports.) In addition to project reports, however, other deliverables might include:

- An annotated map, plan or graphic
- A powerpoint presentation for use by city leaders or community members
- Three-dimensional models that are displayed at a library
- A website that serves as a repository for project data
- A newsletter or newspaper article written by youth
- A public photography exhibit
- A mural that hangs in a community center or public space

✔ Communicate how ideas were used. The implementation of planning and design projects often extends beyond a participatory project's timeline by months or even years. It is important for project partners to identify the longer term process and how they will communicate back to participants the ways that their ideas were integrated (Chapters 8, 9, and 11). Some examples of how this might happen include:

- Sending a letter to participants showing how their ideas were translated into a plan
- Posting young people's ideas on municipal websites and highlighting how they influenced a project

* Holding a celebration event after a park is built and inviting all project participants to attend

In summary, key elements in implementing programs and projects include:

* Identifying appropriate partners for every project, using stakeholder analysis to help identify appropriate roles

* Funding programs and projects through a diverse stream of resources, including municipalities, school districts, universities, community resources, and private foundations

* Building capacity for methods and approaches to sensitive and culturally relevant engagement

* Working with young people by establishing trust, going where young people already are, learning about young people's interests and concerns, using creative and varied methods, and remaining open to experimentation, and

* Sharing and growing through frequent dialogue, customized deliverables, and communicating about how ideas impacted a project.

Sustaining Programs

Partners are more likely to provide the support necessary to sustain programs when they see the relevance and benefit to their own work. Sustaining programs thus requires a continual process of adaptation, to maintain relevance among all parties. This requires flexibility and an awareness that while the specific partners, projects, or approaches may evolve over time, adherence to the core value of including young people in participatory processes will remain consistent. People and partners may play different roles in different project contexts. Some partners may fade out as their organizational needs shift. And other partners emerge as new opportunities arise. This is a normal part of the process.[6] At any point in a program, it is important to remember that change takes time.

At a larger scale, participation is also an essential component of sustainability. The process of participation is itself part of developing a more sustainable society. Because sustainability means different things to different people, communication and respectful consideration of different program partners is essential to long-term success. Sustaining programs—and making strides toward sustainability—is akin to a dance in which each partner responds to others in cycles of exploration and growth.

Key aspects of sustaining programs over the long term are that the program be institutionalized in some way; that partners communicate, learn and adapt regularly; and that all parties hold each other accountable and celebrate successes.

Principles for Sustaining Programs

Principle 1 **Create supportive institutional structures**

Programs can be more easily sustained when they are supported by a strong institutional framework that is flexible enough to accommodate shifting contexts and goals. As discussed in this chapter's section on "Establishing Programs," long-term institutional structures identify and support program goals and values, partner roles and responsibilities, and dedicated resources. Supportive structures also help to integrate participation into municipal decision-making and cultural practice, so that it is not seen as special or separate from other aspects of participation but becomes a part of institutional culture (Box 2.8).

---

6. Peter Plastrik, Madeleine Taylor, and John Cleveland, *Connecting to Change the World: Harnessing the Power of Networks for Social Impact* (Washington, DC: Island Press, 2014).

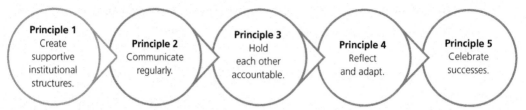

Figure 2.8. Principles for sustaining programs.

Communicate regularly

Principle 2

Regular communication can take many forms—recurring partner meetings, project planning meetings, email and phone communication, and newsletters, websites or annual reports. Recurring partner meetings—once a month or every other month—help to build the supportive structures needed to sustain a program. Additional meetings may also be needed with a subset of partners to implement particular projects. Project leaders should be aware that many professionals experience "meeting fatigue," and therefore seek a balance of communication modes—so that regular, face-to-face communication is productive and purposeful. Occasional meetings that contribute to shared learning—through partner presentations, workshops, or guest lectures by visitors from other cities—can also help to fuel motivation and sustain program interest. Presentations and digital or print media are also important in communicating to wider audiences how young people's ideas are integrated into city planning. An annual report or newsletter can celebrate accomplishments and communicate to a broader audience of city leaders and partners who may be interested but not regularly involved in a program (Figure 2.9).

Box 2.8. Institutionalizing Participation in Quebec

The nonprofit *Carrefour Action Municipale et Famille* (CAMF) based in Quebec, Canada created a structure for accrediting municipalities as child-friendly in 2009. To receive certification, municipalities must demonstrate commitment to the rights of young people and must integrate young people into decision-making processes. Accredited cities develop an action plan, prepare annual reports, and celebrate National Child Day. In their evaluation of this process, Natasha Blanchet Cohen and Juan Torres found that accreditation "set the stage for valuing and actualizing child participation." The accreditation process served as a marketing tool for attracting families to the city; led to additional financial resources; strengthened collaboration among municipal departments; and created a sense of obligation to carry out participatory practices with children.

Accreditation contributed to greater awareness and openness for young people's participation. Blanchet Cohen and Torres suggest that accreditation can be an effective way of initiating and sustaining young people's participation in a city.

In their evaluation of municipalities in Quebec that applied for accreditation, Blanchet Cohen and Torres identified accountability as an important criterion for certification renewal: municipalities that had not actually engaged young people in participatory practices, or that had not integrated young people's ideas into practice, could not gain renewal.[1]

---

1. Blanchet Cohen and Torres, "Accreditation of child-friendly municipalities in Quebec: Opportunities for child participation," 26.

<table>
<tr><td>Principle 3</td></tr>
</table>

Hold each other accountable

An important factor in any participatory program is that each partner be accountable to agreements, projects, and children (Box 2.8). Accountability is particularly important in sustaining the morale of all project partners. It is also important in reducing the risk that young people might become disenfranchised, if their ideas are voiced but not respected or acted upon. Being accountable does not necessarily mean that all children's ideas will be included in a final park design or transportation policy. However, it does mean that young people are included in discussions about their ideas, other factors that influence a project, and how their ideas will influence the final outcomes of a process.

<table>
<tr><td>Principle 4</td></tr>
</table>

Reflect and adapt

Frequent reflection is important for project and program improvements, as discussed in the "Implementing Projects" section of this chapter. Reflection about projects and the program as a whole can occur at scheduled meetings, in written feedback, or anonymous surveys. As a program, partners can identify successes, areas for improvement, and means to adapt the program in the short- and long-term. Reflection is thus an important part of a cycle of adaptive learning, in which program partners embrace the idea of "education for all."

<table>
<tr><td>Principle 5</td></tr>
</table>

Celebrate successes

Creating and sustaining a culture of participation requires the dedication of many people. In order to sustain people's commitment, it is important to build opportunities for celebration and recognition of achievements into a project or program. Such moments help all project partners pause from daily work and recognize a project's

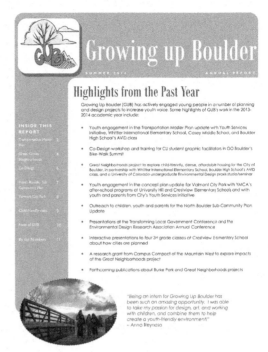

Figure 2.9. Sample front page of an annual report. Image credit: Growing Up Boulder

or year's accomplishments. This can enhance motivation and provide opportunities for reflection and renewal. From press releases to pizza, "celebration" can take many forms, depending on the scope, timing, and accomplishment (Chapter 8).

In summary, key principles for sustaining programs include:

- Communicating regularly through recurring meetings, guest speakers or workshops, and print or digital media
- Holding each other accountable to the goals, principles, and actions established by the partnership
- Reflecting and adapting program approaches to participation, and
- Celebrating successes at regular intervals and through varied means.

*"Where after all do human rights begin?
In small places, close to home . . .
Unless these rights have meaning there,
they have little meaning anywhere."*[1]

3

Ethics of Participation

Ethical principles are guides to determining right and wrong conduct. When young people participate in community planning and design, there are two realms of ethical concern.

The quality of human relationships. One realm concerns the quality of relationships among everyone involved. The following questions need to be considered, from the highest levels of city and organizational leadership, through the adults who work directly with young people, to each group of children and youth:

- Do people treat each other with respect and fairness?

- Do they cooperate in good faith to put ideas into action?

- Does collaborative work include time to discuss ethical principles together?

The collection and use of information. Participation in city decision-making typically involves the collection of information about existing places and how to make them more suitable for people's needs and aspirations. Therefore another realm of concern relates to how information is gathered and used:

- Do participants understand research goals and share information voluntarily?

- Is information collected and used in ways that provide benefits while avoiding harm?

Although each of these realms of project activity has its own rules of conduct, the underlying principles overlap. People are more likely to share valid information about their communities and themselves when they feel that they are treated with respect and fairness. Using information according to participants' wishes helps maintain relationships of respect.

Ethical Relationships among Participants

Much has been written about ethical relationships between adults and young people during the practice of participation. Two documents in particular form a useful framework of key principles that guide this book. One, the United Nations Convention on the Rights of the Child, applies to all people under the age of 18 and addresses all areas of government influence over children's lives. The second, the Wingspread Declaration of Principles for Youth Participation in

---

1. Eleanor Roosevelt, "Remarks at the United Nations, March 27, 1953." Cited in Ellen Hall and Jennifer Kofkin Rudkin, *Seen and Heard: Children's Rights in Early Childhood Education,* (New York/London, Ontario: Teachers College Press/ The Althouse Press, 2011), 21.

Box 3.1. **Selected Articles of the United Nations Convention on the Rights of the Child**

The Convention extends to children several basic civil rights held by adults in democratic societies, and recognizes that rights need to be combined with responsibilities. Key articles that apply to ethical planning and design with children are summarized here.

- Article 2: Programs should avoid discrimination of any kind, and treat all participants with respect regardless of race, color, sex, language, religion, opinions, nationality, ethnicity, disability, family income or wealth, or other status.

- Article 3: In every action concerning children, advancing children's best interests must be a primary goal.

- Article 12: Children should be given opportunities to express their views freely and be heard in all matters that affect them, when they speak directly for themselves and when adults represent them.

- Article 13: The right to freedom of expression includes opportunities to seek, receive and share information and ideas, using different media, with due respect for the rights of others.

- Article 14: Children have a right to freedom of thought, conscience and religion, and to express their beliefs freely as long as they show respect for the rights of others.

- Article 15: Children have rights to freedom of association and peaceful assembly.

- Article 23: Mentally or physically disabled children need to be provided conditions that promote their dignity, self-reliance, and active participation in their community.

- Article 29: Education (which can be interpreted to include participatory planning and design with children) should help children:

  - Develop their personality, talents, and abilities to their fullest potential

  - Develop respect for human rights

  - Develop respect for their own culture and the cultures of others

  - Prepare for responsible life in a free society, in a spirit of understanding, peace, tolerance, equality of sexes, and friendship among all people

  - Respect the natural environment

- Article 31: Children have rights to rest and leisure, play, and participation in cultural life and the arts.

Community Research and Evaluation, applies to adolescents and young adults and focuses on the quality of participatory processes. Although these documents are very different in their scope and authority, together they cover all ages that this book is intended to serve, and their principles are consistent with each other.

The Convention on the Rights of the Child contains articles that speak directly to children's rights to participation in decisions that affect their lives, as well as underlying values that should guide participatory programs and activities[2] (Box 3.1). Since the Convention's adoption by the General Assembly of the United Nations in 1989, it has been ratified by every member nation with the exception of the United States, where it has been signed by the U.S. Ambassador to the United Nations but never ratified by

---

2. UNICEF, "Convention on the Rights of the Child." UNICEF.org. http://www.unicef.org/crc (Retrieved June 29, 2016).

Congress. In countries that ratified the Convention, governments at every level are required to make efforts in good faith to apply its principles, and to document progress every five years in a national report to an international Committee on the Rights of the Child. In the United States, city governments, schools, and community or-ganizations may voluntarily commit to adhere to the Convention's principles.

In the year 2000, activist academics and international development experts who worked with children gathered for a symposium in Oslo, Norway to seek consensus on rights-based principles for Children's Participation in Community

---

Box 3.2. **Conditions of Effective Projects for Children's Participation**

Conditions of project or program establishment

- Whenever possible, the project builds on existing community organizations and structures that support children's participation.

- The project is based on children's own issues and interests.

Conditions of entry

- Participants are fairly selected.

- Children and their families give informed consent.

- Children freely choose to participate or decline.

- The project is accessible in scheduling and location.

Conditions of social support

- Children are respected as human beings with essential worth and dignity.

- Participants show each other mutual respect.

- Children support and encourage each other.

Conditions for competence

- Children have real responsibility and influence.

- They understand and have a part in defining the goals of activities.

- They play a role in decision-making and accomplishing goals.

- They are helped to construct and express their views, and are provided with the information they need to make informed decisions.

- There is a fair sharing of opportunities to contribute and be heard.

- The project creates opportunities for the graduated development of competence, enabling children to continue unfolding their potential for achievement.

- The project sets up processes to support children's engagement in issues they initi-ate themselves.

- The project results in tangible outcomes.

Conditions for reflection

- There is transparency at all stages of decision-making.

- Children understand the reasons for outcomes.

- There are opportunities for critical reflection.

- There are opportunities for evaluation at both group and individual levels.

- Participants deliberately negotiate differ-ences in power.[1]

---

1. Adapted from Louise Chawla, "Evaluating children's participation: Seeking areas of consensus." *PLA Notes* 42 (October 2001), 9-13.

Box 3.3. **Principles that Guide Participation with Very Young Children**

Very young children, age six and under, face many barriers to participation in their communities that are similar to barriers faced by children of all ages with disabilities—from physical barriers such as windows that are too high to see through and doors that are too heavy to open, to social and attitudinal barriers such as expectations that they should be seen but not heard and beliefs that they have no views to express. When the Committee that oversees implementation of the Convention on the Rights of the Child took up the subject of "the right of the child to be heard," they stated that even preverbal children form views that merit serious attention, and therefore adults need to sensitively attend to what infants and young children communicate.[1] This is also the position of a report on *Building Better Cities with Young Children and Families* issued by the Bernard van Leer Foundation and 8 80 Cities, a Canadian organization that advocates attention to the perspectives and needs of vulnerable residents, such as children, older adults and disabled people.[2] The report argues that attending to these groups, including children under six and their families, is the most effective way to create cities that work well for everyone.

Growing Up Boulder began its work with preschools through a partnership with the Boulder Journey School, a school for children from six weeks old to six years old, inspired by the Reggio Emilia tradition of infant and preschool education.[3] Reggio Emilia infant-toddler centers and preschools were built from the rubble of World War II in northern Italy by mothers and educators who were motivated to prevent a return to fascism by encouraging young children to

---

1. Committee on the Rights of the Child, *General Comment No. 12: The Right of the Child to be Heard*

2. 8 80 Cities, *Building Better Cities with Young Children and Families*. (The Hague, The Netherlands: Bernard van Leer Foundation, 2017), https://bernardvanleer.org /publications-reports/building-better-cities-with-young-children-and-families. (Retrieved January 2, 2018).
3. Ellen Lynn Hall and Jennifer Kofkin Rudkin, *Seen and Heard: Children's Rights in Early Childhood Education* (New York/London, Canada: Teachers College Press/The Althouse Press, 2011).

Settings.[3] With attention to the Convention on the Rights of the Child, they agreed on basic conditions for participatory projects that translate children's rights into action (Box 3.2). Several members of the symposium were experts in child development, so they ensured that these are also conditions that promote children's competence, self-respect and prosocial behavior. This list of conditions can be used both to guide the organization of a new project or program and to evaluate its effectiveness in promoting rights-based goals.

Several participants at the Oslo symposium worked with very young children, as they believed that the foundation for democratic practice is laid in infancy and early childhood, when young children learn to expect respect for their needs and interests—rather than domination that primarily treats them as an object to control. There have been controversies about when Article 12 of the Convention on the Rights of the Child begins to apply, as it states that governments "shall assure to the child who is capable of forming his or her own views the right to express those views freely in all matters affecting the child, the views of the child being given due weight in accordance with the age and maturity of the child."[4] Some people have read these words

---

3. Louise Chawla, ed. Special issue on children's participation—evaluating effectiveness. *PLA Notes (Participatory Learning and Action)* 42 (October 2001).

4. UNICEF, "Convention on the Rights of the Child." UNICEF.org. http://www.unicef.org/crc (Retrieved June 29, 2016).

Figure 3.1. Children's rights to participation in their communities include freedom to explore and investigate the world around them. When children at Boulder Journey School wrote their own Charter of Children's Rights, they included the statement that "children have a right to touch everything, but gently"—such as this sheet of ice. Photo credit: Boulder Journey School

think for themselves and work together collaboratively. A founding principle of this approach is that young children express themselves through "100 languages."[4] They engage with the world with all their senses and with their emotions as well as their curiosity and intelligence. Corre-

4. Ibid. This idea of the "100 languages of children" was coined by Loris Malaguzzi, prime author of the educational philosophy of the Reggio Emilia approach.

Figure 3.2. The 100 languages of children include drawing, painting, and other expressions through the arts. Photo credit: Boulder Journey School

spondingly, they express themselves through their bodies and behaviors, play, and art, as well as speech (Figures 3.1 and 3.2). This means that the realization of children's rights is as much about cultivating "adult ears" to listen and hear what children say through different media, as it is about "children's voices."[5]

5. Roger Hart, "The developing capacities of children to participate," *Stepping Forward: Children and Young People's Participation in the Development Process*, ed., Victoria Johnson, Edda Ivan-Smith, Gill Gordon, Pat Pridmore and Patta Scott (London: Intermediate Technology Publications, 1998).

as implying that below a certain age, children are incapable of forming individual views or saying anything that deserves serious attention. Article 12 raises the question: At what point are children old enough and mature enough to have their views given significant weight?

When Gerison Lansdown was commissioned by UNICEF to assemble research and legal opinions that could help answer this question, she concluded that children's capacities to form views and develop maturity depend on the respect and opportunities that they are given from early childhood to the threshold of adulthood.[5] If barriers to participation are lowered

and appropriate assistance is provided, children can share significant views from an early age. Citing Lansdown's review, the Committee on the Rights of the Child concluded that, "Research shows that the child is able to form views from the youngest age, even when she or he may be unable to express them verbally."[6] This conclusion is consistent with evidence that even infants are finely attuned to others around them and "speak" responsively with their eyes, bodies, and vocalizations.[7] Research also shows that even

5. Gerison Lansdown, *The Evolving Capacities of the Child* (Florence, Italy: UNICEF Innocenti Research Centre, 2005).

6. Committee on the Rights of the Child, *General Comment No. 12: The Right of the Child to be Heard* (2009), www2.ohchr.org/english/bodies/crc/docs/AdvanceVersions/CRC-C-GC-12.pdf

7. Daniel Stern, *The Interpersonal World of the Infant* (New York: Basic Books, 1985).

> **Box 3.4. Wingspread Declaration of Principles for Youth Participation in Community Research and Evaluation**
>
> 1. Youth participation in community research and evaluation transforms its participants. It transforms their ways of knowing, their activities, and their program of work.
>
> 2. Youth participation promotes youth empowerment. It recognizes their experience and expertise, and develops their organizational and community capacities.
>
> 3. Youth participation builds reciprocal partnerships. It values the resources and assets of all age groups, and strengthens supportive relationships among youth and between youth and adults.
>
> 4. Youth participation equalizes power relationships between youth and adults. It establishes common ground for them to overcome past inequities and collaborate as equals in institutions and decisions.
>
> 5. Youth participation is an inclusive approach to diverse democratic leadership. It increases the involvement of diverse groups, especially those who are traditionally underserved and underrepresented.
>
> 6. Youth participation actively engages young people in real and meaningful ways. It involves them in all stages, from defining the problem, to gathering and analyzing the information, to making decisions and taking action.
>
> 7. Youth participation is an ongoing process, not a one-time event. Participants continuously clarify the purpose, reflect upon the process, and use the findings for action and change.

very young children are capable of empathy and a sense of fairness that form a foundation for democratic ideals of equality and social justice.[8] Implications of these conclusions for the participation of very young children are discussed in Box 3.3

To engage young children in the participatory design and planning of cities, helpful steps include:[9]

---

8. William Damon, *The Moral Child* (New York: Free Press, 1988); Martin Hoffman. *Empathy and Moral Development* (New York: Cambridge University Press, 2000).

9. These points draw on Priscilla Alderson, *Young Children's Rights: Exploring Beliefs, Principles and Practices.* (London: Jessica Kingsley, 2000); Hall and Rudkin, *Seen and Heard*; and Vicky Johnson, Roger Hart and Jennifer Colwell, eds. *Steps for Engaging Young Children in Research: Volume 1, The Guide.* (Brighton, UK: Education Research Centre, University of Brighton, 2004), 21–34, https://bernard vanleer.org/publications-reports/steps-engaging-young -children-research-volume-1-guide/

- Partner with existing programs for young children and their caretakers, such as child-care centers, preschools, and children's libraries, where teachers and staff are already attuned to young children's forms of self-expression.

- Take time to build relationships of trust with young children and their families.

- Don't rush. Learning to hear the 100 languages of children takes time.

- Create settings for "supportive social learning," where a sense of community is valued as an achievement in itself, caring relationships between community members are nurtured, and children are encouraged to solve problems and develop ideas in groups as well as individually.[10]

---

10. Hall and Rudkin, *Seen and Heard*, 55.

- "Amplify children's voices," which means not only bringing young children's views to the attention of decision-makers, but also translating children's expressions in ways that help others appreciate the profundity that often characterizes young children's thought.[11]

- Understand the needs of caretakers as well as their children.

Be prepared that young children may suggest cities that are more playful and full of art and nature. Research shows that from an early age, children extend their developing sense of morality to other animals and living things in addition to human beings.[12] In our work with preschools and elementary schools in the Growing Up Boulder program, we have found that young children are more likely than older age groups to express concern for other species. (For evidence of young children's capacities to contribute to their cities, see Figure 5.14 in Chapter 5, Box 7.5 in Chapter 7, Box 8.12 in Chapter 8, Image 9.10 in Chapter 9, and the profile of Open Space Planning in Chapter 11.)

For adolescents and young adults, a guide to ethical practice is the Wingspread Declaration of Principles for Youth Participation in Community Research and Evaluation, drafted at a symposium on Youth Participation in Community Research held in Wisconsin in 2002[13] (Box 3.4). Representatives from organizations for community research and development, youth advocacy organizations, universities and private foundations, as well as many youth leaders, gathered from across the United States. During three days of sharing good practices, they drafted and adopted the Declaration. Although its principal purpose is to guide participatory research to improve conditions for youth and their communities, it is relevant to many forms of community engagement, including the implementation of ideas.

Everyday Ethics in Action

The urban planners David Driskell and Neema Kudva have argued that ethical principles need to pervade five dimensions of a program's functioning (Figure 3.3).[14]

- **Normative dimension:** An organization's expression of values related to young people and participation, which should be stated publically in the organization's mission and goals ("what we believe")

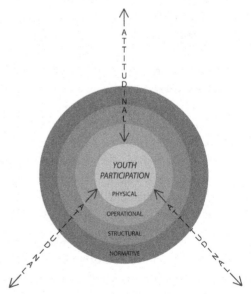

Figure 3.3. Ethical principles that should guide participatory programming. Image credit: Emily Tarantini

11. Ibid.

12. Olin Eugene Myers, Jr., *The Significance of Children and Animals: Social Development and Our Connections to Other Species*, 2nd edition. (West Lafayette, IN: Purdue University Press, 2007).

13. Wingspread Symposium. *Wingspread Declaration of Principles for Youth Participation in Community Research and Evaluation.* University of Michigan. ssw.umich.edu /sites/default/files/documents/research/projects/youth-and -community/SymposiumII.pdf. (Retrieved September 23, 2016).

14. David Driskell and Neema Kudva, "Everyday ethics: framing youth participation in organizational practice." *Les Ateliers de l'Ethique*, 4, no. 1 (2009): 77–87. (A journal of CREUM: Centre de Recherche en Ethique de l'Université de Montreal)

- **Structural dimension:** An organization's programs, staff positions and budget priorities, which need to demonstrate that "child and youth participation" are not hollow words, but something that the organization actively supports ("what we are doing")

- **Operational dimension:** The organization's everyday practice that includes mechanisms for giving young people a meaningful say in decision-making ("how we do things")

- **Physical dimension:** The provision of physical spaces where participation takes place. This includes an office or desks where youth leaders and adult facilitators can work, space to store program materials, a meeting space, and in some cases, an entire youth center. It extends to spaces in the community where participation regularly occurs, such as a service-learning class.

- **Attitudinal dimension:** The attitudes toward young people and their participation manifested in day-to-day program interactions, between adults and young people and between young people themselves. When it functions well, it is expressed in a general culture of acceptance, support and understanding which encourages young people to believe that they have a right to participate and feel committed to doing so.

These five dimensions are interactive and, at their best, support each other and sustain participation over the long term. Together, they constitute "everyday ethics" in action. For each of the questions for self-reflection that follow, it is useful to go through each dimension as a checklist. Is this area of ethical practice embedded in each dimension of my organization's functioning? Build time for reflection on these questions into meetings with project leaders and partners and the training of project staff and volunteers.

**Self-reflection 1
Power**

Am I sensitive to the imbalance in power between adults and young people, and do I strive to avoid acting as if adults always know best?

In most community settings, adults have controlling power. Indeed, adults in power know more about the constraints and possibilities that govern city decision-making, such as budgets, elections, flood plains, and state and national regulations. Nevertheless, the basic premise of participation is that the people who live and work in cities are experts about their own lives and how well places serve them—and this expertise extends to young people. Some adults acknowledge this principle and some do not, and even those who do need to regularly review what they communicate when they interact with young people. "Adultism" is deeply entrenched in societies around the world: the belief that adults are superior to children and that childhood is defined by gradually diminishing levels of weakness and incapacity as children grow toward the end state of adulthood. For this reason, it is radically innovative when any program values children for who they are and what they can do at each stage of their lives and showcases their capabilities rather than their weakness.

Basic principles of respect for children as unique individuals, what children know, and what children can do need to be clearly communicated to everyone who enters a project setting.[15] These principles need to be shared and discussed explicitly, and as Driskell and Kudva note, they need to penetrate every dimension of

---

15. For a useful training manual and activities for facilitators and child participants to increase awareness about children's rights and ensure that children's rights are upheld, see: Plan International, *Bamboo Shoots: A Training Manual on Child-Centred Community Development/Child-led Community Actions for Facilitators Working with Children and Youth Groups.* (Bangkok, Thailand: Plan Asia Regional Office, 2010), https://plan-international.org/publications/bamboo-shoots. It includes an activity to write child-made rules for respectful collaboration. (Retrieved January 2, 2018).

Box 3.5. **Rules for Working Together**

When children in long-term care in King George V Hospital in Durban, South Africa began a series of activities to identify how hospital settings and treatment programs can promote children's resilience and healing, they first agreed on ways to work together harmoniously. Together they established the following set of rules, which were written on a large sheet of paper hung on the wall.

Figure 3.4. Children sign their rules for fair and ethical practice with their handprints. Photo credit: Monde Magida

Rules

1. If I talk, you must listen.
2. Say your words/ideas without fear.
3. Help each other.
4. Listen to each other.

Each child signed the list with a colorful handprint (Figure 3.4).[1]

(For a profile of the Phila Impilo program, see Chapter 11.)

---

1. Jill Kruger, *Live life! Children Advocate Best Practices for Healing.* (Overport, South Africa: Young Insights for Planning, 2008).

---

a program's work. (For an example of children's role in identifying principles, see Box 3.5.) At the same time, it is important to recognize that internalizing these principles in community and city decision-making may be a long-term process of education for everyone involved. Young people are learning skills of active and responsible citizenship, while adults are learning how valuable their contributions can be.

| Self-reflection 2 Respect | Does this project embody a climate of respect among all partners? |

Power imbalances permeate all levels of society. They are inherent in relationships between city leaders and the citizens they are appointed to serve; agency and organization directors and staff; those with more and less money, privilege and education; those with and without citizenship. In many societies, they pervade relations between people of different colors and ethnicities, men and women, boys and girls. Children occupy positions of gender, ethnicity, and social class as well as age, and for each child to be treated without discrimination, adults who facilitate participation need to create relations among themselves where each person's perspective and skills are valued. This creates a context in which similar respect can be extended to each child.

Even when this is done, it does not follow that each person will feel equally comfortable speaking up or taking leadership for an activity. In some cultures, girls may feel more confident sharing their ideas in a group of their own sex, or children of immigrants may feel more free to share their experiences among others like themselves. Equal respect among all does not mean that everyone needs to do everything in the same way. Projects flourish when participants at every age have options, when they can elect to work with others who put them at ease, and when they can choose activities where they feel competent or where they will develop new skills.

Does this participatory process involve a genuine sharing of influence and voice between adults and young people?

As citizen participation became popular in city planning in the 1960s, the planner Sherry Arnstein observed that the term "participation" was used in widely varying ways, ranging from approaches that she considered nonparticipation, that were really intended to "educate" or "cure" participants so they would accept what people in power proposed, through tokenism, to genuine citizen power.[16] The geographer Roger Hart adapted Arnstein's ideas in a much-cited "ladder of children's participation."[17] He began with three forms of nonparticipation: manipulating children to carry adults' own messages, using children merely as decoration to support an adult cause, and tokenism when children appear to have a voice but they are given little opportunity to form their own opinions and influence the subject and style of communication. (These problems are often evident at high-level events, as Box 3.7 shows.)

Genuine participation, Hart argued, begins when children have genuine choices: to participate or not, to choose the level at which they feel comfortable participating, to take positions of leadership when they feel ready for it, and to decide not only what they want to do and say but how they want to communicate. Even at the initial level of taking assigned roles, children can experience authentic participation if they understand the activity's purpose and they are free to join or decline. Choosing to be part of an adult-organized march against the closure of a community school, for example, can be a valuable experience of citizen action. Often, adults want to consult children about adult-designed projects, through surveys or group interviews, and if children understand the decision-making process and their opinions are taken seriously, this is also legitimate.

At increased levels of participation, decision-making is shared, whether projects are initiated by adults or children themselves. This reflects Hart's belief that the ability to work with others for the common good is a higher level of development than decision-making by a single individual. (For an example of shared decision-making in the realm of research about children's lives, see Box 3.7.) In the field of urban planning and design, where people of all ages use public spaces, shared decision-making by children and adults is the most realistic goal. Yet one outcome of this process may be to increase young people's access to spaces that they can control, where they can both initiate and direct activities, such as fort-making by younger children or organizing and staging a dance concert by teens.

Hart's ladder of participation forms a useful rubric for adults to reflect on how they are working with young people and discuss issues of power, through conversations among partners in a project and dialogues with children and youth. Hart cautioned, however, that the intention of the ladder is to show that different forms of genuine participation apply to different contexts.[18] One is not intrinsically "higher" than another.

Like the urban planner David Driskell in his book *Creating Better Cities with Children and Youth*, we consider increasing interaction and collaboration among children and other community members a goal in itself, as important as shared power to make decisions and affect

16. Sherry R. Arnstein, "A ladder of citizen participation." *American Institute of Planners Journal* 35, no. 4 (1969): 216–224.

17. Roger Hart, *Children's Participation*. (London: Earthscan Publication, 1997).

18. Roger Hart, "Stepping back from 'The Ladder': Reflections on a model of participatory work with children," in *Participation and Learning*, ed. A. Reid, B. B. Jensen, J. Nikel and V. Simovska (Guildford, UK, Springer, 2008), 19-31.

Box 3.6. **Child Speakers at High-Level Events**

With preparation and practice, children can speak confidently and eloquently on their own behalf at adult-organized meetings, conferences and other high-level events. Without careful attention to ethical principles, however, it is easy to use young people as decoration or in tokenistic or manipulative ways. Are the young people who speak representative of those they claim to speak for? Were they selected by their peers? Did they develop the ideas that they are sharing in cooperation with their peers so that they are truly speaking for the group they represent? Will they report back to their peers, and will the adults they address send a report about how they have taken the young people's ideas into account?

At an international conference on children in cities, one of this book's authors witnessed what can go wrong if these ethical questions are ignored. Organized by an international development agency in partnership with a charity that works with slum children, the conference took place at a luxury hotel, and it was opened by the Minister of Urban Development for the host country, with members of the press in attendance for the minister's speech. The minister congratulated the charity and development agency for bringing people together from all over the world to generate ideas for how to improve cities for children, and he announced that he looked forward to sitting down with the conference organizers when the gathering was over to discuss how to upgrade cities for children's well-being. When the minister finished speaking, the head of the development agency noted quietly to those around him that his agency had already gotten everything it wanted from the conference in these opening ten minutes (press attention, the minister's commitment to a meeting).

Later on that day, a group of older children and young teens, selected from the slums where the charity was working, spoke about the miseries they faced in their unhealthy environments. Each child went to the microphone to give what sounded like an adult-scripted speech: a list of the burdens of living without sewers, toilets, trash collection, enough clean water pipes, adequate housing or play spaces. (Some people in attendance said that they had witnessed the children memorizing their speeches the evening before under the direction of charity staff.) Each child concluded with a plea for adults to save them from these conditions. On the closing day of the conference, the children came back on stage to repeat their pleas.

These slum conditions are all too real for millions of children around the world, but the speeches were an uncomfortable display of words that appeared to have been assigned by adults, that exhibited the children as victims rather than as dignified agents with ideas of their own. Despite all these outer problems, they came from places where residents with creativity and resourcefulness could work as partners in problem-solving. Whereas some of the children appeared to relish their turn at the microphone, others appeared terrified, and mortified if they failed to remember their words.

change.[19] As long as both of these vectors of action are present, different forms of participation can be authentic. Appropriate forms of interaction and influence may not only vary from project to project, but also at different stages of a single project. Existing youth groups, for example, can serve as valuable partners in establishing a project, and even young children can help select, or improvise, participatory methods to accomplish shared goals (Box 3.3).

19. David Driskell, *Creating Better Cities with Children and Youth.* (London: Earthscan Publications, 2002).

Box 3.7. **Children and Youth as Researchers**

Children and youth play the role of researchers when they document their cities through methods like photovoice, mapping, or interviewing others. With training, they can often gather information about other young people's city experiences and aspirations with particular effectiveness because they understand youth cultures better than most adults, and this can help them establish rapport. Beyond gathering data, young people can contribute to designing and analyzing research, gaining skills and sharing valuable suggestions at each stage of the research process.

For example, when Julia McMillan wanted to know how children journeyed to school in Gateshead in the United Kingdom, she imagined that she would use questionnaires, photography, and travel diaries: but she decided to begin by asking the 54 children, ages 10-11, in her sample which methods they thought would best enable them to record their journeys. The children divided into groups of their own choosing and wrote their suggestions on large sheets of paper. The only

method from her list that appeared on theirs was photography. The majority of boys wanted to write rap songs. Girl-only groups preferred poetry, play-scripting, filmmaking, mapping, drawing and PowerPoint presentations. Two mixed-sex groups wanted group discussions and interviewing. As a result, the project was enriched by a variety of alternative research choices that allowed children to develop methods that best suited their skills and learning styles. Young people also felt greater ownership of the project.[1]

_____

1. Catherine Alexander, Natalie Beale, Mike Kesby, Sara Kindon, Julia McMillan, Rachel Pain, and Friederike Ziegler, "Participatory diagramming: A critical view from North East England." *Participatory Action Research Approaches and Methods: Connecting People, Participation and Place*, ed., Sara Kindon, Rachel Pain, and Mike Kesby (Abingdon: Routledge, 2007), 122–131.; Jane Higgins, Karen Nairn and Judith Sligo, "Per research with youth." *Participatory Action Research Approaches and Methods: Connecting People, Participation and Place*, ed., Sara Kindon, Rachel Pain, and Mike Kesby (Abingdon: Routledge, 2007), 104–111.

**Self-reflection 4
Diversity**

Are efforts made to ensure that participants represent the diversity of different groups that are affected by city decisions, including marginalized populations?

To answer this question, it is first necessary to gather basic information about children and youth in the city. How many young children, children of school age and teenagers are there? Where do most of them live? What ethnic and socioeconomic groups do they belong to? How many are citizens or come from families where citizenship is an aspiration? In many communities, the Department of Child and Family Services or a social-service nonprofit compiles this infor-

mation from census reports and other sources. The goal is not that participants in every project must exactly reflect the statistical composition of young people in the city, but to ensure that young people from different population groups have opportunities to present their views whenever planning and design decisions affect them.

Young people from groups that have limited political power often speak up less in public groups than young people from families that take privilege for granted. Therefore it is critical to work with adult partners and advisors who are trusted members of these communities, who can bring these young people in or open doors to go where they are, and to ensure that they feel comfortable in the participatory settings that they join. (See Chapter 8.)

One of the groups most likely to be marginalized is children with disabilities. Article 23 of the Convention on the Rights of the Child requires governments to "recognize that a mentally or physically disabled child should enjoy a full and decent life, in conditions which ensure dignity, promote self-reliance, and facilitate the child's active participation in the community."[20] Article 7 of the United Nations Convention on the Rights of Persons with Disabilities adds that governments "shall ensure that children with disabilities have the right to express their views freely on all matters affecting them, their views being given due weight in accordance with their age and maturity, on an equal basis with other children, and to be provided with disability and age-appropriate assistance to realize that right."[21] As with young children, opportunities to participate in their communities depend not only on their own capacities but also on whether their societies place social, cultural, attitudinal, and physical barriers in their way or offer assistance and support. According to this "social model" of disabilities, a disability is not an inherent property of an individual alone, but the consequence of interactions between individuals with impairments and the barriers that they encounter[22]

A slogan of the disability rights movement is "nothing about us, without us." In planning for inclusive participation, consult children and youth with disabilities. Other useful advisors may be their service providers and organizations that advocate for their rights. Representatives of these groups are best prepared to identify solutions to overcome barriers and the types of support and adaptations that will help young people engage in activities. As projects unfold, ask young people with disabilities to give frequent feedback to ensure that they find interventions effective. Because the type of assistance needed depends on the nature of impairments, include young people with a variety of disabilities in project planning and evaluation.

As you need to do when working with young children, learn to listen in diverse ways. Remember that assistance does not mean doing things for young people that they can do for themselves; the goal is to enable young people to express their competence. Remember also that the standard of success does not necessarily mean complete independence. Participation and community are about interdependence. Finding cooperative ways of working together has value in itself.

There are guidebooks with specific suggestions for working with young people with different types of impairments, including impairments in hearing, sight, communication, physical mobility, mental health, intellectual ability, and cognitive processing.[23] Because young people's conditions can range from mild to severe and can be compounded by more than one impairment, there are no "one size fits all" recommendations.

20. "Convention on the Rights of the Child," www.unicef.org/crc

21. United Nations, *Convention on the Rights of Persons with Disabilities*, United Nations.org, www.un.org /development/desa/convention-on-the-rights-of-persons -with-disabilities.html. (Retrieved January 2, 2018).

22. Ralph Sandland, "A clash of conventions? Participation, power and the rights of disabled children." *Social Inclusion* 5, no 3 (2017): 93-103.

23. Helpful guides include: CBM, *Inclusion Made Easy* (2012), http://www.cbm.org/Inclusion-Made-Easy-329091. php; Nilda Cosco, "Extending the participatory process to children with disabilities," in Driskell, *Creating Better Cities with Children and Youth*, 58-59; Elena Jenkin, Erin Wilson, Kevin Murfitt, Matthew Clarke, Robert Campain and Lanie Stockman, *Inclusive Practice for Research with Children with Disability: A Guide*. (Melbourne: Deakin University, 2015) http://www.voicesofchildrenwithdisability.com/wp-content /uploads/2015/03/DEA-Inclusive-Practice-Research ACCESSIBLE.pdf. (Retrieved January 3, 2018); Joseph Rowntree Foundation, *Consulting with Disabled Children and Young People*, 2001, https://www.jrf.org.uk/report/consult- ing-disabled-chidlren-and-young-people. (Retrieved January 3, 2018); Kuper, Hannah, Frank Velthuizen and Gwen Duffy, *PLAN International Guidelines for Consulting with Children and Young People with Disabilities*, 2016, https://plan -international.org/publications/guidelines-consulting -children-and-young-people-disabilities. (Retrieved January 3, 2018).

In general, however, visual cues and games work well for children who face hearing, cognitive, and communication challenges; and auditory cues engage children with visual impairments. Children with autism and sensory processing disorders may benefit from quiet "cool down" spaces where they can withdraw if group activities become overstimulating. For an example of a project to lower physical barriers to disabled children's play while educating all children about the handicaps and strengths of people with disabilities, see Box 3.8.

Box 3.8. **Leveling the Playing Field**

Access to playgrounds and parks for children with disabilities depends on a welcoming social environment as well as the elimination of physical barriers and the construction of play equipment and settings that invite "play for all."[1] After Boulder Valley School District in Boulder, Colorado issued bonds to improve school grounds, 10- to 11-year-olds at Mesa Elementary School took on the project of redesigning their school ground for accessibility. To understand the human face of disabilities, they learned about how people with disabilities experience the world and surmount challenges. Called "Leveling the Playing Field," the semester-long project brought all fifth grade classes in the school together with classes of undergraduate students in environmental design from the local university.

The design students began by leading the younger students through an evaluation of their school building and grounds based on the regulations of the Americans with Disabilities Act—measuring, for example, the slope of ramps and tension of doors. With their mentors, fifth graders studied materials for ramps and playground surfaces that children could maneuver in wheelchairs. They took a field trip to a playground for all abilities in a neighboring town. A man who was blind from birth, a deaf woman, and a father with a daughter confined to a wheelchair visited

the school to explain how they experienced the world. A doctoral student in design arranged to provide a wheelchair, crutches, a tapping stick, blindfolds, and a walker in the school library so that students could check out this equipment and practice moving around the school and playground with these devices (Figure 3.5).

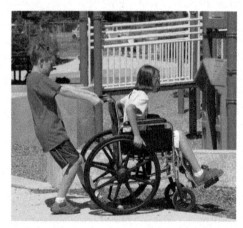

Figure 3.5. During a project to redesign a schoolyard for children of all abilities, students took turns navigating the space with different mobility devices, including wheelchairs, walkers, and tapping canes. Photo credit: Lynn M. Lickteig

The fifth graders divided into small groups and each group took a section of the schoolyard to study closely and redesign. Each group made a model that exhibited their proposed ideas. At the end of the term, each group presented its model to representatives of city government, the school district, their school's playground committee, and faculty and students from the design program.

1. Robin C. Moore and Susan M. Goltsman, *Play for All Guidelines*, 2d edition. (Berkeley, CA: MIG Communications, 1997).

Self-reflection 5
Identify Strengths

Does this project emphasize the identification of community strengths rather than weaknesses?

Planning and design aim to improve places: to make them safer and more inviting, functional, lively, beautiful, health promoting, and ecologically sustainable. To reach these goals, it is necessary to identify problems that need to be addressed as well as a vision to be achieved, but it is important to stress community strengths rather than primarily compiling a list of problems. This is particularly the case when a project focuses on children's own community. Children are quick to read signs of disinvestment, crime, and decay in their surroundings as evidence that they are not valued.[24] Otherwise, why wouldn't their society provide them and their families with a clean and safe environment and why wouldn't their neighbors take pride in maintaining their homes and streets? Even with teenagers who are able to investigate historical and systemic answers to these questions, it is important to recognize resourcefulness, resilience, and other strengths in themselves and their community.

Eliud Ngunjiri calls these two options for community evaluation and development positive self-discovery versus negative discovery.[25] The first approach begins by engaging people in identifying resources—in themselves, their families and their communities. What strengths and talents do they bring to the project? What are their culture's strengths? What positive features of their environment need to be protected or enhanced? What local institutions and local leaders could be allies? How does their vision for their locality reflect positive elements of its identity? In a process of positive self-discovery, when the

time comes to consider problems, problem-solving begins from a position of strength rather than weakness.

Self-reflection 6
Expectations and Outcomes

Does this project raise realistic expectations and deliver valued results?

The answer to this question is connected to the identification of strengths and weaknesses. In our own practice, we encourage young people to think creatively about how to make their community, nearby park, after-school center, or other location a better place—without restricting the free flow of ideas. After all possibilities are proposed, the group reviews suggestions together, and invariably children themselves introduce some practical constraints. In our experience, young people are open to realities like budgets and flood plains, and willing to consider the feasibility of ideas.

When a project intersects with areas of government authority, adult facilitators can help participants sort their ideas into three categories.

1. What improvements can they themselves, their families, and friends accomplish together? The community strengths that the group has already identified help fill out this list. Which of these aims can they begin on right away?

2. Which improvements would be possible with external support, such as resources or expertise from a local organization, non-profit, or foundation? For example, could advisors from an environmental organization help draw up a plan for tree planting with species that are adapted to survive local conditions? Is there a nursery that might donate trees?

3. Which improvements are the responsibility of the government, such as a new traffic light at a dangerous intersection or better

---

24. Louise Chawla, ed. *Growing Up in an Urbanising World.* (London: Earthscan Publications, 2002).

25. Eliud Ngunjiri, "Viewpoint participatory methodologies: double-edged swords." *Development in Practice* 8, no. 4 (1998): 466-470.

waste collection? Which departments of government have jurisdiction over this issue and how can they be reached?

The wheels of government tend to turn slowly, but even if a government response comes after this particular group of young people has moved on, a plan that includes immediate as well as more distant objectives ensures that participants will see some results from their actions. Experiencing results contributes to an individual and collective sense of self-efficacy: the belief that as an individual and as a group, we can achieve goals that matter to us.[26] Otherwise, participation can be a lesson in futility and disempowerment. (For examples of ways to inform young people about how their ideas are applied, see Chapter 9.)

This point highlights a facet of participation that can be easily overlooked. Outcomes can be both tangible—like new trees planted—and intangible—like new feelings of confidence to affect change. Both types of outcomes are important, and as the importance of mastery experiences for the development of a sense of efficacy shows, the two are related. Seeing tangible outcomes strengthens intangible feelings such as confidence in oneself and the group. Yet it is possible for a project to fail to achieve a difficult tangible goal but still succeed in instilling citizenship skills and values, if young people feel that adults worked with them in good faith, their contributions were significant, and they learned means of collective action that they can apply with better chances of success in the future.[27] Studies of people who take action for social justice and environmental protection reveal that they saw their actions yield results at least some of the time, and this

fortified them to persist when they encountered challenges.[28]

| Self-reflection 7 Safe Spaces | **Do the adults who facilitate this project create safe spaces where young** |

people are protected from harm?

Although the ethics of participation requires a sharing of power and an emphasis on young people's capabilities, under conditions of risk young people expect adults to show moral authority. A fundamental obligation for program leaders is to protect young people from harm. This begins with moving quickly to ensure that conditions of mutual respect are maintained by preventing any sign of bullying among peers and any condescending treatment by adults. In many programs, it includes formal procedures for screening staff and volunteers who work with children.

Participation can open controversial topics, such as the rights of adolescents to gather in public places or the rights of children of refugee or immigrant families. Program leaders need to make certain that if young people speak up in public, they and their families will not be put at risk of retaliation. Sometimes it is safer not to be visible. In this case, other ways of improving children's lives need to be found.

Although participatory planning and design focus on evaluating and improving physical places, sometimes children share social confidences with program facilitators, and sometimes these confidences involve incidents of violence and abuse. In countries with strong social services, authorities who can protect the child need to be informed. When child services are weak or unavailable, community advisors may be able to help. During Growing Up in Cities action re-

26. Albert Bandura, *Self-Efficacy* (New York: W. H. Freeman, 1997).

27. Louise Chawla, "Participation as capacity-building for active citizenship." *Les Ateliers de L'Ethique* 4, no. 1 (2009): 69-76. (Journal of CREUM, Centre de Recherche en Ethique de l'Université de Montréal)

28. Bandura, *Self-Efficacy*; Louise Chawla and Victoria Derr, "The development of conservation behaviors in childhood and youth." *Oxford Handbook of Environmental and Conservation Psychology*, ed. Susan Clayton (New York: Oxford University Press, 2012).

search in a squatter camp in South Africa, for example, it became evident that a young girl was being abused by her father. In the absence of social services, a respected older woman in the community was consulted, and she met with the mother to work out a plan for the girl's protection. It is important for adults working with children to know the limits of their own training and resources to help in cases of special need, as well as to know community services and allies who can step in.

Children may have concerns about participation. It is good to check in at different points in a project, especially when there are any signs of discomfort or disinterest. If children are encouraged to share what they feel in an atmosphere of trust, it may be possible to resolve problems through open discussion. There can also be a suggestion box or website link where children can drop suggestions or concerns with anonymity. In the Growing Up in New York City program that had five sites for participation in four boroughs, a child ombudsperson was appointed who was independent of any site, whom children knew they could turn to if they felt this need.[29]

Ethical Methods of Gathering, Sharing and Using Information

In addition to embodying ethical relationships among all participants, projects need to follow ethical practices in collecting, communicating and using information. Many activities that involve young people in classrooms or out-of-school groups in investigating their local environment can be considered forms of place-based learning that do not require formal research consent from parents or assent by the children involved. Nevertheless, it is wise in all cases to keep parents informed about any special project their

child is engaged in and to ensure that children understand how their work will be used. Project partners need to agree to gather and share information in ways that will respect everyone involved.

When a project involves college or university partners, any research that they conduct must be approved by their Institutional Review Board. School districts, city agencies, community development agencies, and child-advocacy organizations are likely to have related rules. Because children have limited autonomy, many of these rules are intended to give them special protection.

Ethical review boards are formally bound by three principles: respect for persons, beneficence, and justice. People's autonomy to make decisions about participation in research needs to be respected. All participants should be treated equally, and benefits and risks should be fairly distributed. In practice, review boards typically apply limited interpretations of these principles, with an emphasis on ensuring that research does no harm.[30] They usually work with a model of research that involves a team of objective and unbiased researchers who pre-design all stages of data collection and analysis, and then apply this design to research "subjects," who often respond without initially understanding what the research project is about. For this reason review boards tend to view research as an intrusion into people's lives, with an impact that should be minimized.

As the preceding discussion of ethical relationships among participants has shown, participatory research begins with a much broader field of ethical concerns. Everyone is expected to learn from each other, adults and children alike, and the process of gathering information about a city or community together is seen as an activity with intrinsic value, in which everyone gains

29. David Driskell, personal communication with Louise Chawla, 2008.

30. Lynne C. Manzo and Nathan Brightbill, "Toward a participatory ethics." *Participatory Action Research Approaches and Methods*, ed., Sara Kindon, Rachel Pain and Mike Kesby (London: Routledge, 2007), 33-40.

new knowledge and competencies. Rather than beginning with a completed research plan with all details predetermined, project partners plan the research together and adapt it according to needs and opportunities that arise. Whenever possible, children and youth help identify what the community needs to know and how this information can be collected, communicated, and analyzed. It is important to discuss these broader aims of participatory research with review boards in advance.[31] Within this context, basic rules of ethical research should guide all projects.[32]

| Self-reflection 8 Benefits vs Harm |

At every step, is the collection, analysis, application and storage of information designed to maximize benefits and avoid harm?

In sequence, the following steps should be followed:

1. Clearly define the purpose for which information is being gathered, confirm that all partners understand and support this goal, and make sure that there are adequate resources in terms of time, money, materials and human skills to complete planned activities.

2. With partners and community advisors, discuss in advance any possible adverse consequences. Could this research make information public that children, their families, or their communities have reasons to keep private? In countries where the status of immigrants, refugees, or certain ethnic groups is politically controversial, it may be safer not to attract attention. Children who live in poverty, or who

face disabilities, could feel embarrassed if conditions of their lives are made known. Do children live in a culture where they are not expected to speak up with ideas of their own, where adults may get angry if they see this happen? Is this risk especially serious for girls? Plan in advance how to avoid potential harm, working with community leaders who can anticipate problems and who can communicate a project in ways that encourage local support rather than opposition.

3. Confidentiality provides that information revealed by a person will not be disclosed to others without his or her permission. When research focuses on a particular neighborhood or a particular group in a community, it can be difficult to assure confidentiality. This is especially true when children and youth speak in public. Fortunately, participatory planning and design usually gather information at a community level, with minimal possibilities of risk for individuals. In this case the appropriate level of disclosure can be negotiated with ethics review boards, parents, and children themselves. Students may be assigned nicknames—which can be names they choose to give themselves—or they may want to be known by their real names. When information is controversial, anonymity—a stronger level of protection—may be appropriate; it assures that if someone gains access to stored records, the identity of individual participants cannot be traced.

4. If a question might evoke difficult memories, identify in advance people who can step in with appropriate skills to counsel and support an individual child or a group.

5. As the project unfolds, continue to check in with partners, community advisors, and children themselves. Are they finding the research process beneficial? Enjoyable?

31. Ibid.

32. Katie Schenk and Jan Williamson, *Ethical Approaches to Gathering Information from Children and Adolescents in International Settings* (Washington, DC: Population Council, 2005).

Box 3.9. **Sample Parent's Consent Form**

This example includes typical components of a parental consent form, but if you are working through a university review board or the research office of the school district or other institution, follow the format that they prescribe. Older youth (in the United States, youth aged 18 or older) can sign a form like this for themselves, if written to them directly. Many consent forms for youth aged 12–18 include both a parental signature and youth signature line on the same document.

Form 3.6. Sample text for a parental consent form. The boxes to the left of the consent form are for explanatory purposes only and would not be included in the consent form. The sample text is designed to be modified based on the specific context of your project.

Consent to Participate in Research
Children's Views about Transportation in the City of Alameda

Title and Purpose of Study	The purpose of this study is to identify the opportunities and barriers to active transportation that youth (ages 11-15) experience in the City of Alameda. Specifically, this study aims to understand from young people's perspectives where the barriers are geographically located and how can planning help eliminate or mitigate them.
Description of project	We invite your child to participate in this study through his/her participation in the Alameda After School Program. Participation will include a mapping activity, a walking tour in which youth take photographs of transportation features, and to discuss these experiences with other youth. The research will be conducted over 4 sessions: 3 to gather perspectives, and 1 in which youth develop recommendations for action or change.
Benefits & Risks of Participation	This study will inform Alameda's transportation master plan update. Your child's participation will directly benefit many other children, youth, and families who may benefit from transportation planning that includes young people's perspectives. Improvements may provide benefits in the form of increased safety and increased ability to move about the city independently. There are no identified risks to participating in the study. We will follow all of Alameda After School Program's Safety Policies for the walking tour, including an adult-child ratio of 1-4, safety vests, and observing all traffic signals.
Guarantee of Anonymity	Your child's responses will be anonymous. We will collect information about walking routes, biking routes, locations of homes, schools, and neighborhoods, as well as locations that are easy or hard to get to. This information will be mapped, but no names will be attached to the data that youth provide. The results of the research will be published in a report that will be provided to the City of Alameda, and may be published in academic papers. Your child's name will not be used in these publications unless we seek explicit written permission to do so.
Voluntary Participation	Your child's participation is voluntary, based on your consent and your child's assent. Your child may discontinue participation at any point in time. If your child chooses not to participate, there will be no penalty, and an alternative activity will be provided at Alameda After School Program.
Formal Agreement	If you have any questions about this research or your child's participation in it, please feel free to contact me at 555-111-7777 or myemail@mywork.org. You will be given a copy of this form after you have signed it.

Sincerely,
[Insert signature]
My Name
My Affiliation

Child's Name _____

Parent or Guardian Signature _____   Date _____

Parent or Guardian Name (please print) _____

Box 3.10. **Sample Assent Form**

This example includes typical components of a child assent form, in which a child agrees to participate. This form can be used with children under 18. For youth aged 12–18, the assent may be added to the parental consent form (Box 3.9) rather than creating a separate document.

Form 3.7. Sample text for child assent form. The boxes to the left of the consent form are for explanatory purposes only and would not be included in the consent form. The sample text is designed to be modified based on the specific context of your project.

Assent to Participate in Research
Children's Views about Transportation in the City of Alameda

Title and Purpose of Study	My name is [Insert First and Last Name]. I invite you to participate in a project to understand how you move around the city, for example by walking, biking, scootering, or taking the bus. We are interested in how people your age (ages 11-15) get around the City of Alameda so that we can make changes to better support your ability to move about.
Description of project	We invite you to participate in this research during your Alameda After School Program. If you agree, you will be a part of a mapping activity, a walking tour in which you take photographs of transportation features, and a discussion about these experiences with other youth in your after-school program. We will have 3 days of activities, and 1 day in which you can make recommendations for action or change.
Benefits & Risks of Participation	The City of Alameda is working on its plans that guide how transportation is built or changed in the city over time. Your views may directly benefit many other children, youth, and families who may have similar experiences moving around the city. We will follow all of Alameda After School Program's Safety Policies for the walking tour, including an adult-child ratio of 1-4, safety vests, and observing all traffic signals.
Guarantee of Anonymity	While we value your perspectives, we will not use your name with any work we write or share with others.
Voluntary Participation	Your participation is optional, and you can change your mind about participating at any time. If you choose not to be a part of these activities, there will be no penalty, and an alternative activity will be provided at Alameda After School Program. We encourage you to discuss this research with your parents, who will also receive a permission form to sign.

If you have any questions about this research you can ask me or your after school program leaders at any time. If you want to contact me with questions, you may do so at 555-111-7777 or myemail@mywork.org. You will be given a copy of this form after you have signed it.

Sincerely,
[Insert signature]
My Name
My Affiliation

Formal Agreement	_____ YES, I want to be a part of the study. I understand that even if I check "Yes" now, I can change my mind later and choose not to participate. _____ NO, I do want to be a part of the study.

Your Name _____

Your Signature _____ Date _____

Do they feel comfortable with all of its parts? Safe in all settings?

Self-reflection 9
Informed Choice

Is everyone who participates well informed and do they choose to participate voluntarily?

- Because children have limited autonomy in society and may have limited capacities to understand research, a parent or legal guardian needs to give initial consent to participation. This means there needs to be a channel to inform parents and guardians about research aims and approaches and to answer questions, typically through letters or an open meeting. Consent needs to be guaranteed in writing. (See Box 3.9 for a sample consent form.)

- For successful relations with a community, it is important to identify other gatekeepers and local leaders who should also be informed and consulted.

- Youth who have reached legal majority can sign consent forms for themselves. (This age varies country by country and for different areas of decision-making.) Anyone younger needs to give assent after their parents or guardians have given consent. This is usually done with a signed form, such as the example shown here, although agreement by young children may be oral. The research needs to be explained in terms that a child can understand, with time for children to discuss the project and ask questions. Because children are taught to see adults as authority figures whose demands they must obey, it is critical to stress that their participation is voluntary, they can choose not to answer any question that makes them feel uncomfortable, and they can withdraw at any time. (See sample assent form in Box 3.10.)

- Make sure that when consent or assent are not given, alternative activities are provided.

Because participatory projects often involve multiple partners, it is important to comply with each partner's rules for collecting and using information. For example, when Growing Up Boulder staff work with the local school district, they follow its requirements. They begin by consulting the district's list of parents who do not want their children's names or photographs made public. Even when parents have consented to having photographs of their children or their children's words used in public presentations, reports or media releases, program staff get young people's permission before including their names. Although they may use photos of children's drawings or models freely without names, they ask children if they want their names shared. Partner organizations provide one level of rules for the use of information, but program leaders may choose to provide added levels of protection.

*"We are the children of the world,
and despite our different backgrounds,
we share a common reality."* [1]

4

Understanding Communities through Background Research

Prior to initiating participatory processes with children and youth, it is important to gather information about their community. This helps ensure that activities will accurately represent the people who live in a place and the resources and constraints of the place itself. This chapter describes methods for collecting this information, drawing on four main approaches:

- secondary sources of data that have already been gathered by others
- interviews
- observations
- photo documentation

These methods can help you understand the place where you are working. They can answer key questions. What groups live here? What is their social and economic status? How many residents are children and youth? Can the project area be divided into neighborhoods with distinct identities? How did these places come to be the way they are? How are the communities that live here represented in city decision-making? What are this area's distinctive environmental features? Who is using public spaces, and what are they doing?

You will need beginning answers to these questions in order to determine which groups of children and which places are best suited to your project's goals and to find strategic partners and allies. The methods in this chapter are presented as ways to gather background about a project site; but as a project unfolds, it may be helpful to revisit some of these methods. For example, as issues that children and youth face become

more clear, are there additional local experts who should be interviewed? Are there places of special importance to children and youth where additional observations would be useful? Would a search of historical documents shed light on the origin of issues that people are discussing?

This chapter describes the purpose of each method, gives directions for how to apply it, and offers examples of its practice. This material is designed to help you gather and communicate knowledge about a site and its people during initial planning stages; but once a project is underway and local children and youth have become engaged, you may want to share these methods with young people as co-researchers to deepen understanding of the site. (See Chapter 6 for examples of this.) Later in a project, you, your community partners, and young people themselves may raise new questions that make a return to these methods useful. Therefore many of the methods presented here will appear again in later chapters as participatory processes, including mapping, interviews and photo documentation.

---

1. Gabriela Azurday Arrieta (age 13) and Audrey Cheynut (age 17): 2002 representatives of the Children's Forum, addressing the U.N. Special Session on Children.

Secondary Sources

Demographic data tell who lives in an area and characteristics of this population. *Historical documents* suggest the forces that have shaped the environment and its people. *Maps* show key features of the physical environment. Geographic Information Systems (GIS) have opened new ways to embed data such as population characteristics and local history within physical maps. Local universities or planning agencies may provide relevant expertise in accessing these data, and may have experts who can help you access these sources.

Demographic data

Demographic data are helpful in understanding populations at all scales: from a city as a whole, to districts and neighborhoods, to small sites such as a school. In the United States, demographic data are accessible through the U.S. Census Bureau and local school district websites. The Census Bureau's Quick Facts provides easily accessible basic information, such as overall population and percentages of the population by age, sex, race and Hispanic origin, housing and family arrangements, health, transportation, income level, and poverty.[2] School districts typically also provide data about their student population, including ethnicity, free and reduced meal enrollment (a measure of low-income families who need food assistance), attendance, English language learners, and youth in foster care. Municipalities, counties, and regional districts compile similar information. These data will

exist in high resourced cities and countries, but are much less likely to be available, or accurate, in communities comprised of many low income or immigrant families, where people may be living without documentation or with such high mobility rates that data are not easily gathered or maintained. In such cases, the survey interview method may be a more appropriate means of gathering this information.

You may not need to gather demographic data for every project. However, these data can provide a quick snapshot of a neighborhood or community as a whole. Even if you are already familiar with the neighborhood where you intend to work, these data can help you think about appropriate participatory processes and project partners. If, for example, a large number of students are English language learners, then their English teachers and support staff may be important partners. These data may also indicate

---

Box 4.1. **Oral History Guides Participatory Design: 10 Walks of Burke Park**

At the beginning of a participatory design process, undergraduate environmental design students explored a city park's history—its past land uses as a ranch, its geology and ecology. Students also interviewed long-time local residents to document the park's history through their words. The result—*10 Walks of Burke Park*—was a 44-page guide to discovery with self-guided tours, information to identify local birds and trees, and stories that not only documented a sense of place but also helped to generate new design ideas to enrich park experiences for future users.[1]

1. Program in Environmental Design, *10 Walks of Burke Park*. The University of Colorado, Boulder. https://www.colorado.edu/envd/10-walks-burke -park. (Retrieved December 27, 2017).

---

2. Quick Facts can be accessed from https://www.census.gov /quickfacts. Once at this web page, enter the state, county, city, town, or zipcode for the location. You may browse all data by scrolling through category options, or select for a specific fact that you wish to find from the dropdown menu "select a fact" or the menu for "all topics." For example, each of these menus has a category for Age and Sex that will provide "Persons under 5," "Persons under 18," and "Persons over 65." Data can be generated in table, chart, or map form by using the interface buttons to the right of the location.

Box 4.2. **Historical Photographs Can Influence Participatory Processes**

When Growing Up Boulder began a visioning process for its Civic Area Redesign, young people visited the Boulder History Museum in order to learn about the site's history, which included Chief Niwot and the Arapaho people, immigrants and gold-miners in the 1800s, and greenway planning by Frederick Law Olmsted, Jr. in the early 1900s. This visit inspired Boulder teens to think about designing "a place for everyone," with ideas that included cultural quotes along walkways, memorial flags, and wildlife corridors.[1]

_____

1. Victoria Derr and Emily Tarantini, ""Because we are all people:" Outcomes and reflections from young people's participation in the planning and design of child-friendly public spaces." *Local Environment: International Journal of Justice and Sustainability* 21, no. 12 (2016): 1534-1556.

Figure 4.1. Historical photos showed that the bandshell was used to host powwows in the 1930s. Photo credit: Daily Camera Collection of the Carnegie Branch Library for Local History, Boulder, Colorado

Figure 4.2. A boy dancing in a 1930s pow-wow at the bandshell in Boulder's Civic Area.
Photo credit: Daily Camera Collection of the Carnegie Branch Library for Local History, Boulder, Colorado

that the parents of many students may not speak English at all. Engagement processes with bi- or multi-lingual facilitators or translators may be needed in these cases. Or, if a large percentage of youth are in foster care, relevant organizational partners may be social service departments that oversee foster care enrollment and support services. It could also indicate that youth in foster care, who are likely to experience higher rates of mobility and displacement, may have limited familiarity with their neighborhood. Initial participatory methods may thus focus on building knowledge of a particular place.

Historical documents

Historical documents—from recent times as well as centuries past—can provide important background to participatory processes. Historical sources include newspapers, photographs and oral histories, which may be stored online, in books, or as artifacts in local history museums. One of the benefits of participatory research is that it draws on local knowledge as a strength of communities. This may include understanding the history of a place prior to, or as part of, a participatory design process. Oral histories, for example, may help you understand people's relationships to a place in the past, or think about new possibilities for intergenerational design (Box 4.1). Historical photographs show past

Box 4.3. Creating a "Treasure Map" for the Boulder Civic Area

Growing Up Boulder intern Emily Tarantini wanted to create a map that young children could read, using simple graphics, street names, and easily recognized landmarks. The goal was to create a map that primary students could take to the site to understand place features and that they also could use back in the classroom to recall places where they wanted to begin their own designs. Her process drew inspiration from children's treasure maps, which only show basic orienting features. Emily drew these features in a pop-up style to help orient younger children, who might not recognize building footprints or understand birds-eye view maps.

The specific steps used to create this "treasure map" include:

1. Download a Google map for the site being planned

2. Use GIS to frame the area and to trace streets and building footprints

3. By hand, trace the elevations of the key buildings or architectural features

4. Scan hand tracings

5. Polish drawings in Adobe Photoshop

6. Overlay onto the original map using Adobe Illustrator

7. Provide final coloring and polishing of images in Adobe Illustrator

Similar maps could be generated using watercolors overlain on a base map.

Figure 4.3. A treasure map designed for children ages 8–9. Image credit: Emily Tarantini. This map initially appeared in the Derr and Tarantini, "Because we are all people."

Figure 4.4. Children used the "treasure map" in the classroom as a way to try out spatial locations for their design ideas. Photo credit: Emily Tarantini

uses of a place and may inspire ideas for ways to commemorate a site's history (Box 4.2). Reports from government agencies or civic organizations may reveal previous studies and prior community engagement initiatives that should inform current planning processes. Libraries and local historical societies can be important resources for learning about the documents that are available. They may also provide guided history walks or connect you to local experts, and inspire ideas for methods or materials that will be useful for engagement (Box 4.2).

Maps

To understand how a place has changed over time, historic maps are invaluable. Many historic maps are now readily available through image and map searches on the Internet.[3] They may also be available through a local history society, history museum, library, or university programs in geography or history. There may also be maps for your region that highlight information such

3. See, for example, http://maps.yahoo.com and www.historicmapworks.com.

Figure 4.5. An example of a topographic map that can be used to generate a base model. Image credit: Ben Harden

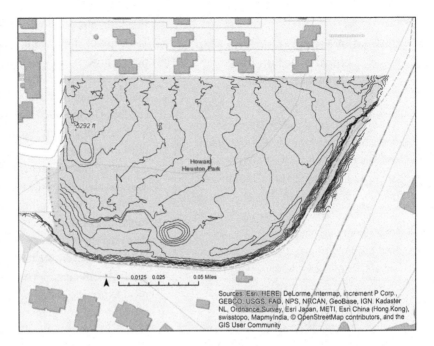

as population density, biodiversity, cultural sites, transportation routes, and businesses.

Easy access to objective land surface data has given new vitality to community mapping, which adds social and cultural meanings of the landscape to geographic features. Community maps are produced through participatory processes that share local knowledge, history, and experiences.[4] Although community maps may be simple hand-drawn sketches or even drawings in the dirt, easy access to base maps on the Internet makes it possible to overlay community stories and images on this spatially accurate foundation. Overlays can be made from tracing paper or acetate to layer different types of knowledge or stories. These maps may also be used as a platform on which to build models and draw visions for change (See Boxes 4.3 and 4.4).

Transect maps represent a path through the environment, showing changing environmental conditions along the way. Although maps are sometimes generated by university departments, municipal planning departments, and planning firms, they can alternatively be simple hand-drawn maps that members of a community make as they walk a route together.[5]

Satellite images of the earth that are now available for every continent through Google Earth have revolutionized the information available to everyone with access to Internet.[6] For every location, it is possible to zoom in to a small scale that makes it possible to identify individual buildings, trees, and other landmarks, or zoom out to see a site in relation to its larger setting. These aerial photos, and the Google Maps option that highlights streets and landmarks, can be printed out as resources for discussion during project planning. Satellite image maps can also be modified to create simpler maps that are easy for children to understand and use (Box 4.3).

---

4. Alix Flavelle, *Mapping our Land: A Guide to Making Your Own Maps of Communities and Traditional Lands*. (Greenwich, CT: Lone Pine Foundation, 2002); for a local mapping system that focuses on sustainability, see www.greenmap.org.

5. For directions about how project team members can use transects as a tool to identify and draw issues of concern and possibilities for improvements in a community, see Catalytic Communities, catcomm.org/transect-walk/.

6. See www.google.com/maps. In this site it is possible to select either Google Earth, to display aerial photos of a location, or Google Maps, for maps that highlight streets and landmarks.

thinking about how the steepness of land or direction of slope might be thought about in a design process (Box 4.4).

In addition to the wealth of aerial photo and map information that computers have made accessible, Geographic Information Systems (GIS) have revolutionized the possibilities for information that can be overlaid on maps. GIS are computer-based systems to collect, store, manage, and analyze spatial information and related "attribute data" or information about map features. (See Box 4.5 for an example of oral-history data referenced on a city map.) Local universities or planning agencies may provide relevant expertise producing GIS maps. GIS requires technical expertise, and it can serve as a method to store information gathered during initial investigations of a project site. But it has also opened up a new world of community activities in the form of Participatory GIS (or PGIS).[7] (See Chapter 7). With some technical support, even children and youth can be taught basic processes for entering map information, as later examples of participatory map-making in this book will show.

An assemblage of maps not only helps you understand a site better, but it can be shared with children and youth when you explore a site together. Existing maps can also form the basis for critical discussions about what they represent and what they omit. This can motivate young people to create new maps of their own that feature previously undocumented information.

Interviews

Key Informant Interviews

Key informants are people who can help you better understand the community where you are

Topographic maps show features of the land using contour lines to indicate elevations above sea level and surface slope (Figure 4.5). They can be obtained using GIS software or from geological survey offices and websites, planning departments, university map libraries, and sometimes local libraries. Topographic maps are useful in

7. See special issue: Giacomo Rambaldi, J. Corbett, R. Olson, M. McCall, J. Muchemi, P. K. Kyem, D. Weiner, and R. Chambers, *Participatory Learning and Action 54: Mapping for Change: Practice, Technologies and Communications.* International Institute for Environment and Development, www.iied.org, 2006.

Box 4.5. **Mapping Memories of the City**

In preparation for the 150th anniversary of the founding of the City of Boulder, Colorado, undergraduate students researched the content of oral history interviews with elderly residents, available from the local history museum. From the transcripts, they extracted residents' memories about growing up in the city and their favor-

ite places. On an historic Sanborn Fire Insurance Map, quotations from the transcripts were linked to the places that people recalled. Using Flash technology, people could click these "hotspots" and open up windows with the quotations and related historical photos.

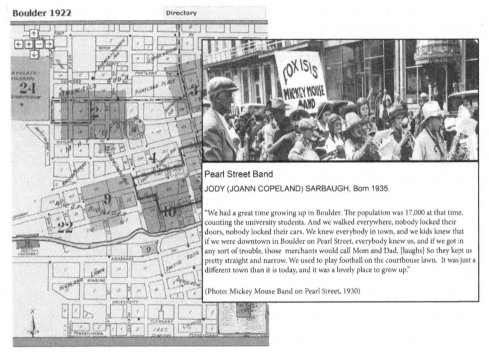

Pearl Street Band

JODY (JOANN COPELAND) SARBAUGH, Born 1935.

"We had a great time growing up in Boulder. The population was 17,000 at that time, counting the university students. And we walked everywhere, nobody locked their doors, nobody locked their cars. We knew everybody in town, and we kids knew that if we were downtown in Boulder on Pearl Street, everybody knew us, and if we got in any sort of trouble, those merchants would call Mom and Dad. [laughs] So they kept us pretty straight and narrow. We used to play football on the courthouse lawn. It was just a different town than it is today, and it was a lovely place to grow up."

(Photo: Mickey Mouse Band on Pearl Street, 1930)

Figure 4.8. A screen shot of the Boulder oral history map, with a link to a woman's recollection of growing up in the 1930s and 1940s, and a photograph of the Mickey Mouse children's band parading down Pearl Street. Image credit: Photograph from the Boulder Historical Society Collection, Carnegie Branch Library for Local History, Boulder, Colorado. Transcript of Oral History Interview with Jody (Joanne) Copeland Sarbaugh, OH1411, Carnegie Branch Library for Local History, Boulder, Colorado. Map assemblage courtesy Children, Youth and Environments Center, University of Colorado.

working. They may include community leaders (including youth leaders), municipal staff, staff in youth-serving organizations, university experts, architects and urban planners, other environmental professionals, school administrators, and teachers—or anyone else with local expertise. Early on in project establishment, they can help you determine appropriate participatory

methods and identify who to include as project partners and participants. Before you talk with these people, gather background information about them in order to understand their experience and role in the community. Chapter 6 discusses youth interviews with adults during a participatory project.

Materials. A notepad, a pencil or pen for recording notes, a pre-determined list of questions, and an optional audio recorder

Key informant interviews are usually conducted individually and focus on the following types of questions:

- In your experience, what key issues do young people face in this environment?

- Has this environment changed for young people since you first came here?

- How do you think this could be made a better place for young people?

- Which staff people from partner organizations should be involved in this project? What roles do you anticipate they would play?

- Given the topic and scope of this project, are there particular types of participants you think should be involved?

- What types of methods would you suggest using?

- Do you know of similar projects that have been conducted elsewhere that would serve as good models?

- Are there community members who could lend expertise to this project?

- Are there particular outcomes that would be useful?

- Is there existing information that would help to inform this project?

Interviews can be informal, lasting approximately 30 minutes. Sometimes it can be helpful to go back to a key informant at various points in the project, at a new phase, or when questions arise, to gain new clarity or insights for how to move forward. Occasionally, a key informant interview might be with a professional outside the community. For example, if you are employing a specific method that you know another city or organization has used, you might conduct a key informant interview to understand the details and nuances of this method.

Survey Interviews

Secondary sources of information are the most efficient means of gathering basic knowledge about a community. However, sometimes these data do not exist. For example, in low-income or informal settlements, there may not be accurate information about how many children live in an area. This information can be gathered by taking a household survey door-to-door (Box 4.6) or surveying young people and their caretakers in places where they gather. Before beginning, make sure that these data are essential to the project, as this method can involve significant investments of time and money. (See Chapter 6 for instructions to creating survey questionnaires.)

The Child Friendly Cities program of UNICEF provides a comprehensive set of tools to collect community assessment data, structured by key provisions of the Convention on the Rights of

---

Box 4.6. Gathering Household Survey Data

Promoting Safe Communities, a program led by UNICEF (United Nations Children's Fund), ACE (Action for Children's Environments) and other organizations in India, aims to create safer, more resilient and more inclusive communities for children in slums and squatter settlements in the Indian cities of Mumbai and Bhopal. To understand how these communities function for children and to learn children's priority needs, ACE trained local nonprofit organization partners to conduct household surveys door to door. For more information, see the profile of this program in Chapter 11.[1]

1. ACE, "Promoting Safe Communities: Improving child protection in slums through a convergent approach in Mumbai and Bhopal." Action for Children's Environments. http://acetrust.net/project/promoting-safe-communities. (Retrieved January 2, 2017).

the Child that can enable decision-makers in city government or leaders in youth-serving organizations or community-based organizations to identify priority areas for improving living conditions for children and youth. It offers surveys for children, adolescents, their parents, parents of infants and preschool children, and community service providers and local authorities to evaluate the quality of young people's access to education, play and leisure, health services, safety and protection, and participation and citizenship.[8] The questions can also be used as the basis for interviews with key informants. A facilitator's guide explains how to bring decision-makers, community leaders and child advocates together to review results, identify other available sources of information, and discuss implications for action. Although the toolkit is primarily intended to prepare an overview of how well a community, or city as a whole, is meeting requirements of the Convention on the Rights of the Child, action steps may include further participatory research to understand community conditions for children and youth more deeply.

Observations

Informal Observations and "Hanging Out"

Much social research begins with observation—of ways that people interact with physical spaces and with each other. Informal observation typically occurs in the settings where participatory activities will take place, such as a playground, park, street, or school ground. Observations can reveal who uses an area, how they use it, and how these uses vary by time of day, day of the

week, and season of the year. This information might lead to:

- More focused questions to explore
- Identification of specific groups for participation (e.g., ages, ethnicities)
- Identification of effective methods for participation
- New insights that would otherwise not be revealed. Informal observations may confirm initial assumptions about how a place functions, or suggest new project directions.

Materials. A notebook, pen or pencil, camera (optional, see Box 4.7)

Informal observation involves visiting a place, making observations as unobtrusively as possible, and taking notes. Typically, the place will be one targeted for future participatory planning or design; however, it could also be a place that supports similar activities. If, for example, a group of children are going to create a design for a playground on what is now a parking lot, observing a park or two makes much more sense than taking detailed notes at the parking lot. Most typically, however, observations gather information about existing conditions and behaviors at a site where design changes are planned. Observations should include:

- The date, time, and weather
- The types of activities taking place
- The people involved
- Interactions with the physical environment
- Interactions between people
- Sketches of specific patterns, places, or activities
- Any ideas that emerge from the observations—insights, questions, special places

In addition to making notes, you may want to take photographs or draw sketches of key site

8. UNICEF, *Child-Friendly Cities Assessment Toolkit.* UNICEF.org. http://childfriendlycities.org/research/final-toolkit-2011/. (Retrieved June 30, 2017). To see case studies of these tools in action and learn how they can be adapted for different settings, see: CERG, "Child Friendly Places," http://childfriendlyplaces.org. (Retrieved January 11, 2018).

Box 4.7. To Click or Not to Click?

Cameras can feel intrusive—to the people being observed, and sometimes for the person observing. A camera can change the nature of people's behaviors if they are aware of it. A general rule of thumb is that it is okay to take pictures of people, when the setting and activities are the focus. However, if you are taking pictures with individuals as the focus, then permission is required in advance. Because the purpose of informal observations is to broadly understand how people use spaces, photographs should focus on the settings for activities. Because some cultural groups or individuals do not welcome photog-

raphy, observers should use good judgment and ask permission or refrain from taking pictures if it feels intrusive. Sketching is an equally valuable way of recording activities and settings and can often suffice.

However, a picture *can be* worth a thousand words—it contains rich visual information that can be hard to collect otherwise. When young people are involved in hanging out, it is a useful communication tool. Photographic methods for participation will be discussed in greater detail in Chapters 5 and 7.

elements and people's activities. If people ask questions about what you are doing, explain your project. After making observations, you may want to approach a few people to ask them how often they come to this place and why it attracts them. You can share your notes with other members of your project team early on, to engage in discussions about what these observations mean and how they might inform project development.

"Hanging Out" is a variation of informal observations, when observations occur with young people and they are invited to participate.[9] It involves spending time with small groups of young people in a chosen space, and it can occur in a variety of ways. In one variation, an adult facilitator spends time playing, chatting, and getting to know the young people who visit a space (Box 4.8). Through repeated visits, as relationships become established, young people may share ideas and secrets that would otherwise not emerge in a more structured activity. A second variation is to ask young people themselves to become the observers of a site. Armed with notebooks and

cameras, young people can take pictures, make notes, and identify not only the types of activities and people at a place, but also their own concerns and ideas for the site (Chapters 5 and 7).

Behavior Mapping

Systematic observations of public life began in the 1960s when anthropologists, urban sociologists, and design researchers began to closely examine how people interact with city spaces. While much attention had focused on the design of buildings, transportation, and parks, much less attention had been given to understanding why some places "work" for people and others do not. Jan Gehl's studies of Copenhagen and William H. Whyte's Street Life Project in the city of New York were seminal in shaping the methods and understanding of how people use city spaces.[10] The study of public life recognizes that our assumptions about how people use spaces may be incorrect, and systematic observations

---

9. David Driskell, *Creating Better Cities with Children and Youth* (London: Earthscan Publications, 2002), 99-102.

10. Jan Gehl, *Life between Buildings* (Washington, DC: Island Press, 2011) (originally published in 1971); William Hollingsworth Whyte, *The Social Life of Small Urban Spaces* (New York: Project for Public Spaces, 1980).

Box 4.8. "Hanging Out" with Young Children

At the beginning of a long-term public park planning process for the Boulder Civic Area, the Boulder Journey School took young children on a picnic to the existing park with families and teachers. While the children and families played, teachers took notes and photographs. Teachers made observations about children's activities and places of play, and also noted specific ideas and expressions the children shared during their time at the park. Teachers made a digital slide show, with photographs and annotations about children's activities. These included:

- Running
- … and Running
- … and Running
- Investigating a bridge
- Tossing leaves
- Examining trees
- Sharing treasures
- Playing in the dirt and sand
- Wishing it were possible to build with these coolers behind the Farmers' Market, like giant building blocks

These notes provided early understandings about how children engaged with the site. The purpose was simply to explore and get to know the site. Later in this process, children participated in more depth: conducting their own research, making their own recommendations, and sharing them with city council members and city planning staff. (See Chapter 8.)

---

can help us understand what is actually happening. The methods and materials involved are similar to informal observations, but they involve more systematic recording. In addition to answering questions about *who* uses a space, *where* and *how*, these methods also help answer *how many people* and *for how long*. Young people can also be involved in behavior mapping. See Chapter 11 for a participatory example of behavior mapping in schoolyard design.

Systematic observations include field notations of people's behavior in a public space and behavior mapping, which makes repeated records of behavior over time.[11] Young people can also be involved in behavior mapping. Although behavior mapping was originally done as a paper-and-pencil measure on base maps—and can still be done this way for simple assessments—handheld digital coding devices are now available that can instantaneously analyze and represent data as it is gathered.[12]

Materials. Digital wristwatch with timer (or phone), clipboard, base maps, and pencils or fine-point permanent markers, access to GIS or Adobe Creative Suites if you wish to compile observations in a digital map.

Behavior mapping involves the systematic observation of a designated area. The area is typically divided into zones that can be observed for a set amount of time, usually 10–15 minutes. Specific types of behaviors are recorded using a

---

11. For a history of systematic city observations and an overview of different methods, see Jan Gehl and Birgitte Svarre, *How to Study Public Life* (Washington, DC: Island Press, 2013).

12. Nilda Cosco and Robin Moore, "Using behaviour mapping to investigate healthy outdoor environments for children and families." *Innovative Approaches to Researching Landscape and Health*, ed. Catherine Ward Thompson, Peter Aspinall and Simon Belm (London: Routledge, 2010), 33-72; Nilda Cosco, Robin Moore and Mohammed Islam, "Behavior mapping." *Medicine and Science in Sports and Exercise* 42, no. 3 (2010): 513-519.

Box 4.9. Sample Coding Instructions for Behavior Mapping

Codes to identify person's age (best estimate):

Adult alone (not with child)	A
Child (infant 0-2)	I
Child (3-5)	C3
Child (6-11)	C6
Early Adolescent (12-15)	A12
Adolescent (16-18)	A16

Other identifying characteristics to note:

- Homeless
- Gender (M/F/O)
- Race/Ethnicity (White, Latino, African American, Asian, South Asian, mixed, or unclear)

Behavior codes

Direct interaction with the space		Movement through the space	
Watching creek	Cr	Walking	W
Watching wildlife	Wi	Wheelchair	Wh
Playing along creek edge	Eg	Running	R
Playing in the creek	Ck	Biking	B
Fishing	F	Skateboarding	Sk
Playing with loose parts	L	Scootering	Sc
Imaginative play	I	Sitting	Si
Sleeping	Sl	Kayaking	K
Playing with natural elements (grasses, rocks)	NP	Tubing	T
Climbing	Cl		
Facilitating Play	FP		
Picnicking	Pi		
Other play (none of the categories above—please note type)	P		

pre-determined set of codes. Typically behavior mapping records all behaviors within the site during the time of recording. In addition to behaviors, characteristics of people can be recorded according to age, ethnicity, and group composition (Boxes 4.9 and 4.10).

Behaviors are mapped repeatedly over a series of times. This can be done at different times of day, on weekends as well as weekdays, and across seasons to reflect changes in use. Once behaviors are recorded, the data can be compiled and presented in a single map, or series of maps that focus on specific behaviors, times of day, or user groups (Figure 4.10).

Figure 4.9. Sample data sheet for recording behavior observations. Image credit: Emily Tarantini

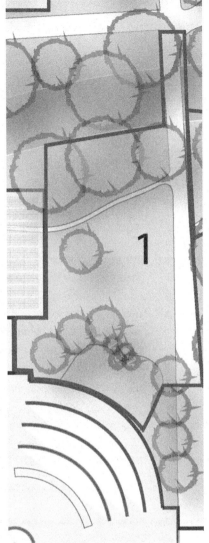

Play Area 1 🕐

Date	
Observer initials	
Zone (1-4)	
Temp & weather conditions	
Time (start/stop)	

*Attach additional sheets per zone if more than 15 groups observed.
* Complete all basic data. Use data code to locate locations on map.
  Draw arrows to indicate movement patterns/directions
* Use notes to record additional behaviors or group dynamics,
  new observed behaviors.

Map Code	People/Activity Description (Record by Group)	Notes
1		
2		
3		
4		
5		
6		
7		
8		
9		
10		
11		
12		
13		
14		
15		

Figure 4.10. Compiled behavior map showing all observations, using symbols to denote different types of activities. Image credit: Emily Tarantini

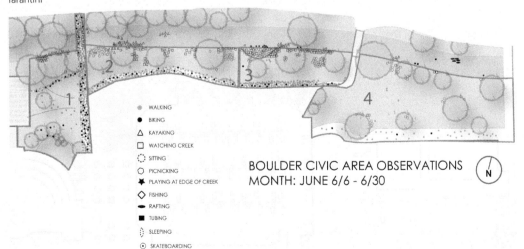

⊙ WALKING
● BIKING
△ KAYAKING
□ WATCHING CREEK
⋯ SITTING
○ PICNICKING
✹ PLAYING AT EDGE OF CREEK
◇ FISHING
➤ RAFTING
■ TUBING
⸰ SLEEPING
⊙ SKATEBOARDING
⸗ USING INFORMAL PATHS

BOULDER CIVIC AREA OBSERVATIONS
MONTH: JUNE 6/6 - 6/30

N

Box 4.10. **Behavior Mapping to Understand Community Park Use**

with Corrie Colvin Williams and Kelly Keena,
Blue Lotus Consulting and Evaluation

The Nature Kids / Jóvenes de la Naturaleza (NKJN) project is designed to increase Latinx children, youth, and family members' access to nature within the City of Lafayette in Boulder County, Colorado. NJKN is a multi-partner collaborative project initiated by a local nonprofit, Thorne Nature Experience, and funded by Great Outdoors Colorado, which seeks to support a safe, ten-minute walk to nature for everyone in the Lafayette community, particularly Lafayette's lower income neighborhoods. The collaborative is working to accomplish this through environmental education programming and infrastructure improvements to existing and potentially new parks, playgrounds and trails.

As a starting point, NKJN supported a series of workshops with young people and their families to understand how the community currently connects with nature. Blue Lotus Consulting and Evaluation, LLC was asked to gather this information prior to NKJN implementation so that the project would be able to track changes over time. Blue Lotus designed a behavior mapping protocol to understand the extent to which parks and open space were being used in Lafayette prior to any changes to infrastructure. The protocol included five sites in the city. Observations sought to explain:

- If the parks were being used
- Who was using the parks
- What users were doing in the parks

The behavior mapping protocol included observation periods in the morning, lunchtime, afternoon, and evening, and it included three scans over 30 minutes for each location. The protocol also called for taking photographs of the location that may help explain the design, use, or potential barriers to use of each site.

To identify types of use, the protocol identified users by age (adult, adult+child, youth) and activity. Activity codes included: running (R), walking (W), biking (B), birding (BR), exploring (E), playing (P), sitting (S), or other (O).

Figure 4.11. A behavior map showing average numbers of child visitors to the parks observed (See Box 4.10). Image credit: Blue Lotus Consulting and Evaluation, LLC

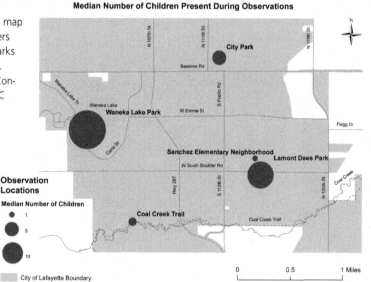

Maps presented the median number of visitors to each park, with separate maps for each age group (adult, children, youth) based on the target audiences of NKJN programming: children, youth and families (Figures 4.11–4.13). Observations showed that people were using the parks in a variety of ways, spending time under the trees, and mostly unplugged. Many youth were spending time together outside, hanging out with their friends. Children played on existing structures or creatively in the surrounding areas. This initial data will help NKJN monitor use of these spaces over time, including those spaces slated for improvement through the project.

Nature Kids I Jovenes de la Naturaleza: http://naturekidslafayette.org/

Blue Lotus Consulting and Evaluation: https://www.bluelotuseval.com/

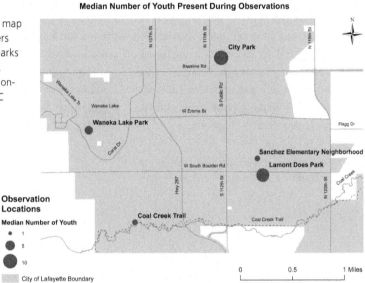

Figure 4.12. A behavior map showing average numbers of youth visitors to the parks observed (See Box 4.10). Image credit: Blue Lotus Consulting and Evaluation, LLC

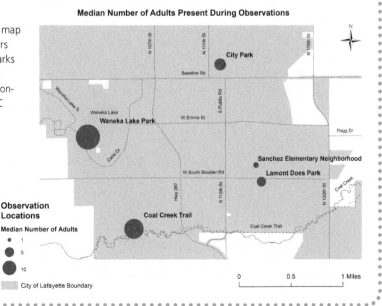

Figure 4.13. A behavior map showing average numbers of adult visitors to the parks observed (See Box 4.10). Image credit: Blue Lotus Consulting and Evaluation, LLC

Photo Documentation

Photogrids

A photogrid, or visual survey of a site, forms a systematic way of moving across a site and recording its features.[13] When you are getting to know a site, it can provide a comprehensive overview that gets you to move beyond familiar landmarks. It also creates a historical record of a place at one point in time, and therefore a valuable means to monitor how a place changes, if photos are taken again at the same grid points at a later time. You may create a photogrid as a way to identify and record site elements during initial project planning, or you may do this later with children and youth as a participatory process. For instructions for making photogrids and its participatory examples, see Chapter 7.

13. David Driskell, *Creating Better Cities with Children and Youth*. (London: Earthscan Publications, 2002), 188–190.

Before and after photos

Before you contemplate changes to a site, it is useful to record the site's original condition. Make a photographic record of what is there, moving through the site and taking photos in all directions. Include evidence of how people use the site.

During participatory design processes, these photos can be posted on the wall as a catalyst for discussions, and suggested changes can be drawn directly over the photos. After changes have been made, photograph the site again. Before and after photos can form a dramatic way to show what participants have accomplished together. Continuing to photograph a site over time forms a way to evaluate how new features are used by a community. See Chapter 10 for an example of effective before and after photographs.

5

Art-Based Methods

Self-expression through the arts is included in Article 13 of the Convention on the Rights of the Child as one of children's civil rights: "The child shall have the right to freedom of expression . . . either orally, in writing or in print, in the form of art, or through any other media of the child's choice." Article 31, which affirms a child's right to rest, play, and leisure, also recognizes the right "to participate freely in cultural life and the arts." [2] In our experience, when we enable young people to express their feelings and ideas through methods of their choice, they gravitate to the arts—to music, poetry, painting, and digital arts. This was also true in the example from the United Kingdom of children choosing their own methods to document their travel to school: most of their choices were arts-based (Box 3.7).

Art-based methods provide an excellent starting point for participatory processes. They allow young people to access their hearts: they are methods that allow young people to explore themselves, their world, and their values. In the words of a young Native American of the Tewa people, "Art is important because it describes people's feelings and what they think about their people and their own ways." [3] From this perspective, art is important in developing personal connections to a topic. Art-based methods help all members of a participatory project understand: What is important to me as an individual? What is important to our community? What experiences and perspectives do we have for a place? For an activity? This chapter will explore methods that help students identify connections and values to a place or urban issue.

Art-based methods can also be important in the analysis and synthesis of ideas. They can provide creative means of summarizing discoveries during a participatory project, in a way that resonates with young people's interests. They can help a community express its history and identity and come together around a shared vision.

This chapter provides examples of methods that help young people express their values and synthesize and present their ideas through creative means:

- Drawings
- Murals
- Collage
- Nicho boxes
- Photographic methods
- Storytelling and writing
- Role plays, drama, and puppet shows

---

1. Bruce Hucko, *Where There is No Name for Art: The Art of the Tewa Pueblo Children.* (Santa Fe, New Mexico: School of American Research Press, 1996), 8.

2. UNICEF, "Convention on the Rights of the Child." UNICEF.org. http://www.unicef.org/crc. (Retrieved March 12, 2017).

3. Hucko, *Where There is No Name for Art*, 1. Quotation from Pauline Bourdon when she was age 12.

- Video and film
- Three dimensional models
- City as Play

It is important to remember that children and youth are the experts on what their creations mean. With every method, allow time for young people to interpret their work: in writing, if they are old enough, or by asking open-ended questions about what they have made and recording their answers. Remember also that young people own their creations. Ask them if they want their name on their work (unless you are collaborating with a university where rules of confidentiality prohibit this). If you want to take their work for your records or an exhibit, ask for their permission. If they want to keep what they have made, ask if you can take a picture or make a copy for yourself.

This chapter describes the purpose of each method, gives directions for how to apply it, and offers examples in practice. For each of the methods presented, remember that participatory processes are about generating and sharing ideas. The artifacts generated can be significant in themselves, but often they are tools for identifying interests, setting priorities, and making recommendations. This is helpful in taking the pressure off the methods themselves, especially if young people are concerned whether their art is "good enough." Everyone's voice matters, and the methods are simply media to help young people express themselves.

Drawings

Drawing is a simple method that children can readily use to express ideas, describe an experience, and communicate with each other. For the drawing method to be most effective, it is helpful to have prepared in advance the *purpose* of the drawings, to have a pre-written prompt to get children started, and to allow time to share and discuss ideas. The drawings themselves can pro-vide important information, but it is the sharing and discussion that allow rich understandings of children's perspectives. These discussions promote an understanding for the *significance* of the picture—why children drew what they did.

Never assume that you know what a child's drawing means without asking. Jill Kruger, who has done a lifetime of participatory advocacy with children in South Africa, illustrates this point vividly with a story about a child's drawing of a smiling clown. What else could it be but a happy clown? The child explained, however, that it was a witch disguised as a clown to capture children for their body parts.[4] With very young children, ages 2–6, try to record their utterances as they draw. Otherwise when they show the final product and you ask what it is, you risk getting the answer, "It's a picture."[5]

Drawing is an excellent way to begin one-on-one interviews about children's place feelings and experiences. Even shy children tend to open up when attention is focused not on them but their explanation of their drawing. When you want to use drawings in this way, ask for the child's permission to take notes by hand or with a recording device, and label different elements of the picture that the child discusses.

Ages. While this method may be used with any age, we have found it to be most effective with children ages 4–11. Children 12 and older are often self-conscious of their drawing abilities, and this can inhibit expression rather than serve to develop it.

Materials. Paper, pencils, crayons, colored pencils or markers, clipboards or hard surfaces (if drawing will be outside or there will be no tables)

---

4. Jill Kruger to Louise Chawla, personal communication.
5. Elizabeth Coates, "I forgot the sky! Children's stories contained within their drawings." *International Journal of Early Years Education*, 10, no. 1 (2002): 21–35. Reprinted in *The Reality of Research with Children and Young People*, ed. Vicky Lewis et al. (Thousand Oaks, CA: Sage Publications, 2003), 5–26.

Time to Complete. About 45 minutes total—10 minutes for introduction; 15 minutes for drawing; and 20 minutes for sharing and discussing.

Method

- Introduce the activity—tell children what it is you plan to have them do and why

- Provide the materials for the activity—paper and drawing implements

- When everyone is settled with their materials and actively listening, tell children the details of what you want them to do—use the prompt that you have prepared.

- Check in with participants. Do they have questions? Do they understand what they are supposed to do?

- As children begin, wander around the room or place where they are drawing. Children will ask questions for clarification and will begin to share their ideas. Ask questions that are general: Can you tell me more about this? What is special to you about this place? In this way, you can encourage them to continue but will not overly direct their drawing.

- If children are able, ask them to clearly label their drawings in their own words. Or a facilitator can write key words on the drawing.

- Once the work is nearing completion, give a 2- to 3-minute warning that the drawing time is coming to a close.

- Ask each participant to share his or her drawing. This can be done in small groups with a single facilitator, or with the whole group, depending on the number of facilitators and amount of time available. If possible, record the main points of the children's ideas on flipchart paper for all to see. Children are welcome to offer edits to the recorder's words if their ideas are not captured correctly.

- **Possible Extension:** Depending on the size of the group and amount of time available, ask each child to make a connection to something they heard another child say or draw that also resonated with them. This is a way to build group cohesion but also to help children process ways that they have shared interests and experiences with others in the group.

Space use

Some children may look at others' work to get ideas about what they "should" draw and make copycat drawings. If you want to be sure that you get children's original ideas, work in a big space where everyone can spread out, or with small groups where each child can have his or her own space and undisturbed focus. Emphasize that there are no wrong ideas—every contribution is valuable.

Paper size

Some children get immersed in this activity. Provide large sheets of paper and have extra sheets available in case some children want to extend their drawing beyond the margins of one page. Otherwise the scale of their response is constrained by the size of the paper.

Sample Prompts

- To understand the types of places that are important to children in their community:

  Today we are going to draw a special outdoor place. I want you to begin by thinking about a place where you like to spend time. It can be a favorite place, an exciting place, a hiding place, an exploring place, or any kind of place that is special to you. Think about what you like to do in this place and who you go there with. Think about what you see, smell, feel or remember about this place. When you are ready, you may begin to draw this place. (If the children are old enough, ask them to label the most important parts of their drawings.)

- To understand how children use or experience their local area:

Box 5.1. **Using Drawings to Initiate and Evaluate Participatory Research**

In the city of Pachuca de Soto, Hidalgo, Mexico, children and adolescents participated in a project over eight months to identify issues of concern in their community, to gather information about these issues from their peers, and to develop recommendations.

Drawings were used as a means of both identifying initial concerns and as a means of evaluating what they learned as a result of the project. Initially, a group of young people in youth councils drew pictures of the issues that most concerned them in the community. These drawings were used to determine issues of interest, problems they saw in their communities, and as a means to identify a priority area of focus for further work.

From these drawings, young people identified themes of bullying and violence against children and teen pregnancy as issues they wanted to research further (Figure 5.1).

Following initial drawings, the youth council then developed questions that they would use to ask other children about their chosen topics. (See Chapter 6.) Finally, each of the team leaders re-

Figure 5.1. Children can draw pictures to help identify issues in their community. In this drawing, children identified kidnapping (top), fighting (middle). The bottom drawing, showing nature and children playing can be translated as: "This is the Pachuca that children want: a world without discrimination, bullying, or delinquency."
Image credit: Yolanda Corona Caraveo

flected on their experiences. As in the beginning, they drew pictures and wrote reflections about what they had learned or how they were changed by the process of participating (Figure 5.2).[1]

Figure 5.2. Drawing as a reflection tool for what young people learned through the participatory process. In this drawing the child writes that before the participatory process, she was very shy and did not have very many friends nor feel confident interacting with adults. After the process, she feels more comfortable interacting with people of different ages and from different places.
Image credit: Yolanda Corona Caraveo

---

1. Yolanda Corona Caraveo and María Morfín-Stoopen, *Nuestra Voz También Cuenta: Haz Que Se Escuche. Una Experiencia de Participación de Niñas, Niños y Adolescentes en el Municipio de Pachuca (Our voice also counts: make it heard. An experience of participation of children and adolescents in the Municipality of Pachuca).* Chapultepec, Cuernavaca, Morelos, Mexico: Grafimor S.A. de C.V., 2017.

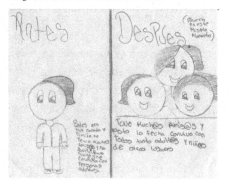

Antes era muy callada y tímida, no tenía muchos amigos y no convivía con personas adultas. Ahora tengo muchos amigos y amigas y hasta la fecha convivo con todos, tanto adultos y niños de otros lugares.

Jazmín (PAMAR Parque de Poblamiento)

Box 5.2. **Drawings to Understand Resilience:** Assets and Vulnerabilities

In 2013, Boulder, Colorado and Mexico City, Mexico became part of the Rockefeller Foundation's 100 Resilient Cities initiative to help communities around the world become more resilient to the physical, social and economic challenges cities face today. The 100 RC approach framed resilience in terms of understanding "acute shocks," such as floods or fires, and "chronic stresses," such as poverty and endemic violence. Growing Up Boulder and researchers in Mexico City partnered to explore children's perceptions of resilience in the two cities using a paired participatory research approach.

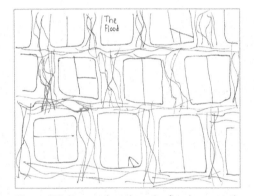

Figure 5.3. One student drew the flood, a natural disaster which had affected the city of Boulder two years prior, as a vulnerability. This drawing depicts aerial views of homes surrounded by water, as the child experienced during the storm. Image credit: Growing Up Boulder

As an initial way to understand children's understanding of their city, we asked children (ages eight to ten) to draw assets and vulnerabilities at their home, school, street, neighborhood, and city scales. We defined an asset as a "valuable person, place or thing that helps you feel safe and supported" and vulnerabilities as "people, places, or things that make you feel afraid, unsafe, unsure, that make you feel exposed, open to being hurt, or that you don't belong."

Students generated asset and vulnerability drawings on two separate visits. At the end of each drawing session, students shared and discussed their drawings as a group. These drawings became the basis for mural collages (Figure 5.6) and a video exchange between children in the two cities. While some children focused on a single asset or vulnerability (such as in Figure 5.3), others compiled many ideas into a single drawing (Figure 5.4).[1]

---

1. Victoria Derr, Yolanda Corona, and Tuline Gülgönen, "Children's perceptions of and engagement in urban resilience in the United States and Mexico." *Journal of Planning Education and Research* (2017): doi: 0739456X 17723436.

Figure 5.4. This student drew many types of vulnerabilities, including car fumes, loud parties, dark places, and stinging bees. Image credit: Yolanda Corona Caraveo

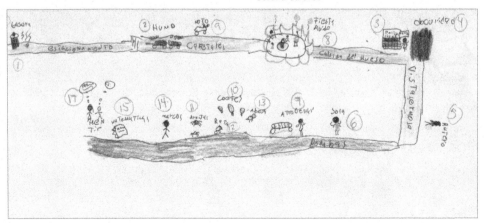

Box 5.3. **Childhood in Kentucky, 1900 to Now**

As part of a project for the Kentucky Oral History Commission, a class of 8-year-olds spent a term studying Portland, their working-class district that borders the Ohio River in the west end of Louisville. Their activities included drawing, painting and writing about their favorite local places and what they did there. At the same time, local residents from their parents', grandparents' and great-grandparents' generations were interviewed about their childhood memories of Portland, and photographs were gathered that showed children in the community from the early 1900s to the present. An artist made colored illustrations of children in places that were repeatedly described in the oral histories. These illustrations were arranged in a border around a large map of the district, with the location of each place marked on the map. All of these materials were hung in a special exhibit in the Portland Museum, a local history museum, including excerpts from the oral histories and the 8-year-olds' drawings, paintings, writings, and other products from their community study. On the opening night, the students served as exhibit guides for their families and other visitors.

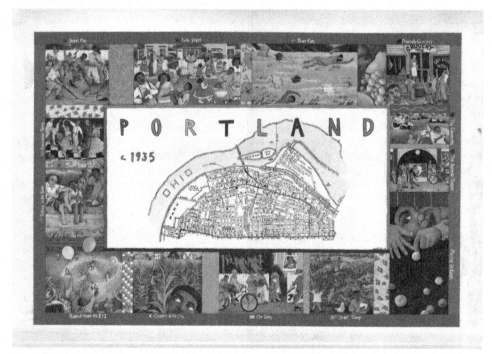

Figure 5.5. Favorite childhood places in the past. Given the importance of quilting in Kentucky culture, Annette Cable, the artist who rendered older residents' memories, assembled her illustrations like bright-colored quilt squares bordering a Portland map. Image credit: Portland Museum, Louisville, Kentucky

Today we are going to make a drawing of the area around where you live and the places where you spend most of your time, where you work, play, or go to school.[6] I want you to include your house and your school, but everything else you draw is up to you.

- If a child is having trouble getting started:

What about if you draw a picture of your house and the places around your house where you like to play, alone or with friends, or places where you ride a bicycle or go with friends or family?

Depending on specific project objectives, you could start with one of these prompts and then add additional details. For example, if you are interested in safe routes to school, you could add:

Now I would like you to draw [you can ask them to use a specific color—like a red pen] how you get to school [or downtown, or wherever is significant for your project]. Draw a line showing the route that you take, and write down if you walk, bike, use a scooter or skate board, drive, or take the bus. If you go more than one way, pick the route and type of travel you use most often. You may add additional details to your drawing as you think about your route to school.

Variation: Intergenerational Drawings

One way to understand how children's use of local environments changes from generation to generation is to compare children's drawings and

---

6. This seemingly simple request is the result of pilot testing at sites around the world during the revival of the Growing Up in Cities program. Some children will spontaneously begin to make free-hand maps, and that is fine, but this neutral request allows children who are not comfortable with mapping to draw their ground-level view of places. We avoid asking them to draw "their neighborhood" unless they have already studied their neighborhood and know its boundaries. Otherwise they may try to comply without understanding what "neighborhood" means (and even geographers debate this word's meaning). See Driskell, *Creating Better Cities with Children and Youth*, 115–117

explanations about the places that they currently use with older generation's drawings of their childhood environmental memories. If older residents are comfortable drawing, this activity can be integrated into an oral history about their childhood engagement in their community. If people hesitate to draw, an artist can illustrate the environmental stories that they tell (Box 5.3).

Murals

Mural making serves a double purpose. It is a medium for young people to share their views and visions about their city, but creating a mural also requires deliberation and collective decision-making about what to communicate, why, and how. Mural making can serve as a contribution to the community, making young people's creativity apparent and bringing life and color to public buildings and streets.

Murals can be a collaborative method for developing ideas early in a project, or for synthesizing ideas toward the end of a project. Either way, the mural represents a summation of ideas that can be shared with others.

Ages. 4 and up.
Young people ages 12 and up may be self-conscious of their drawing abilities, which can inhibit their free participation. When working with youth, it may be helpful to enlist a professional artist who can support artistic development, which can result in a more professional product with less angst from participants.

Materials. Paper for drawing initial ideas; pencils and colored pencils; larger paper, canvas, or reclaimed materials (an old door, board, or bedsheet) for the mural base; paints, paint brushes, and small containers to hold paints; smocks or shirts to protect clothing during painting (optional); dropcloth to protect surfaces

Time to Complete. At least three sessions of approximately 45–60 minutes

Method—Generating ideas

- Introduce the activity—tell participants what you plan to have them do and why

- Provide the materials for the activity—paper and drawing implements

- When everyone is settled with their materials and actively listening, give participants more details about what you want them to do—to make a mural that represents their ideas about why the city is (or is not) a good place for young people (or substitute a different prompt here, such as what they want to see in a new park)

- Ask each participant to draw a picture that represents their response to your question prompt

- Ask participants to share their ideas with each other. This is a collaborative process, so it is important to share ideas early so that young people who are interested in similar ideas can work synergistically

- Have a facilitator write down the key words and ideas each participant shares. If many participants respond to a particular idea, make note of this with a check mark or other notation that reflects how common an idea is.

Method—Planning the mural

- Provide the materials for this activity—the mural base (paper, canvas or other material), paints, and the drawings to be used

- Review the themes generated in the first session

- Ask participants to arrange the drawings they have made onto the mural. Ask them to reflect on the major themes that emerged from their drawings and generate groupings of pictures that reflect all participants' ideas.

- To transfer the images to the canvas, students can cut them out, glue them to the canvas, and paint over them, or they can draw them onto the canvas. If participants desire this alternative, you can bring in an artist or design student who organizes and transfers drawings to create a cohesive and artistic representation.

Method—Painting the mural

- Depending on the amount of time you take to organize and transfer images, you can begin painting the mural on the same day or in another session.

- Lay out a dropcloth on the surface where young people will be painting

- Place the canvas on top of the dropcloth with enough room around the edges for paints

- Review the canvas to be painted—ask participants to discuss and plan out colors and a strategy for completing the mural as a group. Since not everyone may be able to paint at a single time, identify roles for everyone.

- Provide small quantities of paint at a time in small containers. When working with younger children, provide only a few colors at a time, each in its own container to avoid a mixing of all colors, which can result in a brown mural.

- When the mural is about halfway painted, have participants stand up and view the mural for a moment. Ask them to reflect on the colors, balance, and overall progress of the mural. Is there a color that is too dominant? Are all the ideas being expressed with colors and images that feel consistent with the group's original drawings and intentions? Make any revisions or adaptations needed to keep the mural moving in a cohesive way toward completion.

- Allow time for the mural to dry in a level spot

Box 5.4. **Whittier International Elementary School, City Values Mural**

As part of a project to understand children's perceptions of resilience, Growing Up Boulder engaged primary students, aged 8 to 9, in developing a mural. Before beginning the mural, school children discussed their city and identified assets and values that they felt represented their city. These values included open space and parks, care for animals, shelter for people, healthy lifestyles, education, and the arts. Once these values were identified, each student ranked the values from those that they thought were "well done" in the city to those that "need more work."

From their individual assessments, children chose one of the values that was most important to them and drew a picture that reflected their thinking about this value and how it was, or could be, represented in the city. Project facilitators sorted the drawings and created a framework for a mural that would have four quadrants with drawings that reflected: the arts and care for animals; safe neighborhoods; healthy lifestyles, including food for the homeless; and parks and nature. The mural was ringed by Boulder's mountains, as drawn by one student who particularly loved the mountains. After images were transferred to the canvas, students collaboratively painted the mural, with much negotiation over colors and embellishments that gave the mural character.

The completed mural (Figure 5.6) was part of a public presentation to the school board, city plan-

Figure 5.6. Children painting group mural that reflects what they care about in the city. This mural was generated as a part of a resilience project with primary school students. Photo credit: Victoria Derr

ning staff, and community about how to support resilience in the city. It was hung in the school for the remainder of the year. After mural completion, students conducted research and developed recommendations for how to improve those areas of the city that needed "more work."[1]

---

1. Derr, Corona, Gülgönen, "Children's perceptions of and engagement in urban resilience"

Host a venue to share the mural with others. This can be through a focus group with school or city leaders, a video which records young people sharing what they contributed to the mural, or a hanging at a library or gallery space in the city and presentations by the artists during an opening reception.

Variation: Intergenerational Mural Making

When elder artists come together with young people to paint murals, their creations can bridge windows into a community's past with visions of its present and future. When the University of Colorado established a Children, Youth and

Figure 5.7. When young artists painted elements of a child-friendly community, they wanted nature and free movement through city settings, but above all they valued friendly places: friendly people and sharing love with their friends and families. Here they begin by placing the word "amor," love, at the center of a mural. Photo credit: Casey Cass/University of Colorado

Environments Center on its Boulder campus, the center director invited the Society for Creative Aging, a nonprofit organization formed by senior artists and volunteers, to work with children to make murals to decorate the center walls. Elder artists worked with students in two elementary schools to depict a "child friendly community"—inspired by the principle that a community that is friendly to children is also friendly to elders, and a more livable place for all ages.

The elder artists began with two sessions of activities to spark ideas:

- **Word associations/concept mapping:** To brainstorm words that describe a child-friendly community, the artists hung a large sheet of adhesive fabric on the wall and stuck headings at the top that represented different facets of community life, such as Education, Recreation, Government and Nature. Students were given strips of paper and asked to write one word for each of these themes that described what it would be like if it were child friendly, and then stick their words under each heading.

- **Tree of life:** Children painted leaves, cut them out, and wrote a word on each leaf to

tell what they would like to see in a child-friendly community. The leaves were later hung in the Center.

- **Haiku writing:** After the artists gave examples of haikus, each student wrote a haiku about an element of a child-friendly community that he or she found especially important.

- **Definitions:** Each child wrote a paragraph that defined a child-friendly community.

- **Ecological footprints:** Because the children highly valued nature, the artists introduced the concept of ecological footprints. Each child was given an old sneaker and students decorated their sneakers to signify the creative steps they could take to build a more child-friendly and nature-friendly community.

After these activities, the children and artists were ready to work together to transfer their ideas into paintings. They began with individual paintings that were each fixed behind a panel of old wooden window frames to signify Windows on the World of a child-friendly community. Then they worked together to paint long strip murals and large circle murals. The circle form signified Building Bridges in communities where everything connects in the circle of life and cycle of generations. Elder artists painted their memories of favorite features of their own childhood communities, including a woman who remembered what Boulder was like for children 90 years before. Students worked in small groups to illustrate their ideas (Figure 5.7).

Variation: Banners

Banners can serve as portable murals that can be rolled up and taken to a variety of places. Through art stores, you can order durable canvas with grommets, which makes mounting banners and taking them down easy. Places that can be enlivened by children's banners are only limited by the imagination.

Box 5.5. Lily Yeh's Participatory Mural Making at the Dandelion School

In her book *Awakening Creativity: Dandelion School Blossoms*, Lily Yeh describes her evolution as an artist, and how she came to integrate children into participatory mural making, from inner-city transformations of vacant lots in north Philadelphia to her work with the Dandelion School in the outskirts of Beijing, China. This school primarily served the children of a "floating" population of migrant workers. Her initial workshops focused on drawing and writing in which students told stories about themselves, and the emotional burdens they bear from economic inequities and the family stresses that result.

During her first two years of working with the school, Yeh conceived of the Transformation Project which sought to beautify the campus but also "to raise issues such as identity, self-empowerment, democracy, and equality" (p. 51). The Transformation Project engaged the whole school community, including students, teachers, staff, and volunteers, over five years. Her process began slowly, providing a space for freedom of expression, sharing of ideas, and cultivating a sense of hope. In her first year, she held a series of workshops:

1. **Listening.** Through a school-wide meeting, Lily Yeh introduced the project and asked students what they would like to see on their campus, what they thought would add beauty. Their resounding response was for nature in its many forms.

2. **Workshop for teachers.** Teachers in Beijing, like many parts of the world, work long hours and are under pressure to meet performance standards. Yeh's aim for the teacher workshop was to create a relaxing, participatory, and fun environment. In these workshops, teachers created murals with paper-cuts, drawing from the Chinese folk art tradition.

3. **Workshop for students.** Yeh conducted a series of workshops with students as well. She asked students to discuss their thoughts and feelings of the moment and then to transfer these feelings onto paper, using paper-cuts, ink, and watercolors.

4. **Painting big and painting together.** In this phase, students made large paintings on reclaimed bed sheets. They painted their own silhouettes and added details of stars, plants, and abstract patterns.

Subsequent years built on these workshops and generated exhibitions of student's drawings, personal stories, and a "moving assignment" to connect students with their parents. Only then did she move into site design workshops. Through a series of additional workshops, students and teachers designed mosaic murals and a large scale Dandelion Tree of Life. Over time, the entire school campus was transformed by the school community's artwork, a whimsical mixing of mosaic tile and painted murals.[1]

---

1. Lily Yeh, *Awakening Creativity: Dandelion School Blossoms.* (Oakland, CA: New Village Press, 2011).

When Growing Up Boulder began, participants were asked to identify city issues that they wanted to work on and they divided into action teams. Middle school students wanted to make young people's presence in the city more visible through public art that children and youth created. As a beginning, they created a series of banners that depicted their visions for a child-friendly city. Over the years, the banners hung at a large festival in a city park, the city art museum, schools, and a meeting for the city's comprehensive planning process.

Children's banners can also be printed on public service signs in public transport. A third grade class of English language learners in Boulder spent a fall term evaluating the "Hop," a bus line that winds its way through downtown streets and shopping areas, stopping close to their school. One of their recommendations was to add art that would make the bus ride more engaging for children. During the spring term, they worked with an artist to create a linear banner of iconic city places along the Hop line, with bunnies half hidden throughout the picture. Printed as a public service sign, the banner adds whimsy and color to Hop buses and gives young children the challenge of finding all the bunnies. (See Chapter 8 for more information on this project.)

Collage

Collage is an assemblage of objects to create an image. It can be made of anything that catches an artist's eye that can be adhered to a surface, often combined with drawing, painting, and words.

Box 5.6. **Collage and Cutouts to Engage Children in Participatory Budgeting**

with Omayra Rivera Crespo
and Yazmín M. Crespo Claudio

In 2014, participatory budgeting was introduced in San Juan, Puerto Rico. In this process, citizens directly decide how to spend part of a public budget. The San Juan process included an assembly, several meetings of a Committee of Delegates who represented residents of the community, a presentation of projects that citizens wanted to see the city finance, and voting on priorities. The meetings could last for several hours as people discussed their points of view, made comparative tables, and debated the pros and cons of potential projects. As the process unfolded, the architectural collective taller Creando Sin Encargos (tCSE) recognized that a more dynamic and visual process was needed.

To engage children and understand their point of view, taller Creando Sin Encargos helped children and other members of the community create large collages composed of text and images taken from magazines and the internet to represent their visions for each project under consideration for participatory budgeting (Figure 5.8). For example, if a group wanted a community center for different activities, they made a collage

Figure 5.8. Participatory budgeting in San Juan: Collage of images of magazines and prints, prepared with residents of the community. Photo credit: Omayra Rivera Crespo

of people of all ages performing, participating in art workshops, doing exercises, or having a celebration. If they wanted a garden, they glued together images of people planting tropical vegetables and fruits. With this approach, children could also explain the benefits of each project that they envisioned.

In 2015, participatory budgeting was implemented again, in a large community of San Juan named Río Piedras. This time the organizers used collage as a tool from the beginning in order to

When all the objects are gathered from one place, it can represent a locale, or children's journey through a space as they pick up objects along the way: for example, a tracing of a leaf from a tree, a feather, a candy wrapper from a purchase at a snack stand, a word from a sign, shiny paper from street litter, and a selfie snapped with friends along the way. Collages can also be made with cutouts from magazines or children's own drawings. They can also be assembled digitally.

Collages can be made with many purposes. The *nicho* boxes featured in Figures 5.11-5.12 later in this chapter are a form of 3-D collage, created in this case for children to express their identity and culture that they would like to see represented in their city's Civic Area. In the Phila Impilo project featured in Chapter 11, children in a hospital created collages to express their sources of strength and resilience. In Box 5.6, young people created collages as part of a larger process of participatory budgeting to express their priorities for budget spending. (For more information about participatory budgeting, see Chapter 8).

include more children. A few university graduates from architecture and engineering were hired as a Technical Committee to develop participatory methods using images. They prepared boards with maps of existing areas or basic architectural plans, along with cutouts of urban furniture and play areas. Children created collages of what they wanted to see in each area. For example, if they wanted swings in a future park, trees, a sitting area, and a gazebo for informal meetings, then they glued these illustrations where they thought they should be located on the board.

Figure 5.9. Participatory budgeting in San Juan: Board prepared with a basic architectural plan, along with cutouts of urban furniture and play areas. Children glued the cutouts on the board and added drawing and writing. Photo credit: Omayra Rivera Crespo

Presupuesto Participativo 2015
Mejoras al parquecito de niños y niñas de Capetillo

Figure 5.10. One of several renderings that architectural students made, based on children's collage boards for an area. Image credit: Ricardo Curet

They also wrote and drew directly on the boards. Members of the tCSE collective found that asking the children to focus on well-defined areas helped them pay attention to physical characteristics of the environment and issues like density, and generate specific ideas.

Based on the collage boards, the Technical Committee made several 3D drawings so that the children could see different possible results of their proposals and choose the best one. On the day when citizens voted, the boards for different projects were presented together with the 3D drawings. In this way, children felt that the project proposals represented their intentions and not ideas imposed by the city administration.

Nicho Boxes

Nicho boxes are multimedia art boxes inspired by wall niches common to Southwestern architecture, termed *nichos*, and Latin American folk art. Like a personal shadow box, each *nicho* contains small objects like pictures, symbols, figurines, writing, and anything else that expresses a person's identity and culture. Children can create nicho boxes to express their relationship to a place, or what is important to them in their environment.

Ages. six and up

Materials. shoe boxes or cigar boxes; spray paint; multipurpose glue; glue gun for hot glue; magazines and other sources of images to cut out; construction paper; markers; small objects that children bring from home because they find them personally significant but that they are willing to leave in the box. You can save time and mess by spray-painting the boxes in advance. If you don't want to use spray paint, children can glue a covering of colored paper all over their box. Shoe stores and cigar vendors will often donate boxes.

Time to Complete. One to two sessions of approximately 30–45 minutes

---

Box 5.7. Nicho Boxes to Express What is Important to Children

This particular adaptation of nicho boxes was developed by Growing Up Boulder as a culturally-responsive way for children to express what was important to them about their city, as a first point of engagement for a much larger public space planning process.[1] Children, ages 8–9, were asked to consider, "Who am I? What do I love? What would I like in the city that reflects my

Figure 5.11. The nicho box at left reads: "I am a 'red lion' because of my red hair. My favorite places to spend time are Valmont Bike Park and the skatepark." The "Me and Nature" box at right with mirror and animal figurines represents the child amidst the natural world. Photo credit: Growing Up Boulder. The "Me and Nature" nicho box was originally featured in Derr and Tarantini, "Because we are all people."

identity, family and culture?" Parent volunteers collected enough shoeboxes for every child and spray-painted them in solid colors in advance. Children were provided a range of materials including fabric flowers and small animal figurines and children were encouraged to bring their own items from home.

1. Victoria Derr and Emily Tarantini, ""Because we are all people:" Outcomes and reflections from young people's participation in the planning and design of child-friendly public spaces." *Local Environment: International Journal of Justice and Sustainability* 21, no. 12 (2016): 1534–1556.

Method: Generating ideas and assembling objects

- Introduce the activity—explain what nicho boxes are and how participants can use them to express their identity and what is meaningful to them in their environment.

- Provide a prompt question. Give participants time to think about how they want to represent themselves and what matters to them, relative to the prompt. Give them time to write down ideas, or make a list with assistance if they are still learning to write.

- Provide objects that participants can select to begin to construct their boxes, such as construction paper in different colors, magazines or other sources of images that they can cut out. Participants store this material with their box until they are ready to assemble everything.

- Encourage participants to look for other objects at home or in their environment that they want to add. These can include natural objects, little figurines of people or animals, photographs—anything that they find meaningful to express themselves and their relationship to their environment.

Constructing and explaining the boxes

- Participants arrange the images and objects in their boxes and glue them down. Multi-purpose glue will work for light pieces like paper and photographs. Young children may need adult help with a glue gun to secure heavier pieces like figurines, branches or stones.

- Each child writes a few sentences describing their box and why its objects are significant for them. They print out their descriptions and mount them on their boxes. Some participants glue the description on the top or side of their box. Some hang them on the box like a sign.

Box 5.8. Nicho Box to Support Children's Long-Term Health Care

As part of the Phila Impilo! program for children in long-term hospital care in Durban, South Africa, children created simple nicho boxes by pasting a pocket mirror inside a cardboard box and drawing valued people and objects in their lives around it. (For more information about this program, see Chapter 11).

Figure 5.12. Identity drawing with mirror: This boy said that his box showed "that children are important here on earth. You can place important things in your life around you. This reminds you of who you are despite your illness." Photo credit: Monde Magida

Sharing with community members and decision-makers

- Participants share their boxes and their meaning. They can do this just among themselves, or it can be at a public event with parents, city staff and other city leaders invited. When there are many participants, the boxes can be displayed around the room with the creators beside their boxes, ready to explain their work and answer questions as visitors rotate around the room.

Nicho boxes make colorful, intriguing displays for a public place like a library, local art museum, recreation center, school lobby, or hospital (Figure 5.11).

Photographic Methods

Expressing, observing, dreaming—photography is an effective tool for facilitating a range of purposes.[7] This section describes methods and examples of two photographic applications: photovoice and photo-drawing. Other uses of photography that emphasize information gathering, evaluation and discussion are photo-elicitation in Chapter 6, and photo-framing and photogrids in Chapter 7. There is no firm line, however, between photography as an artistic medium and as a tool for documentation and evaluation. Encourage young people to explore how they can bring their artistic vision into all of these approaches.

While each method varies in its applications and potential, participatory photography provides some consistent benefits:

- Many people are familiar with cameras, or can learn to use simple ones fairly quickly. Cameras do not require the ability to read, write, or speak a certain language fluently—they can thus equalize participation for some who would otherwise be marginalized, such as English language learners in the United States context

- It is a useful tool early on in participatory processes, to develop young people's thinking about a particular place

- It helps practitioners understand young people's perspectives

- It provides a visual record that communicates to a variety of audiences at multiple points of a project (from idea generation to project presentations or sharing beyond the life of a project)

- The portability of cameras (and ubiquity of cell phones in many parts of the world) expands the possibilities for this method to include multiple times of day, individual experiences, or otherwise private aspects of experience

- Photography can help people "see" familiar places in a new way, and through images, to develop an expanded sense of a place and its meaning or function

Photovoice

Photovoice is a method for visually describing places and experiences. Photovoice has a rich history in both public health and urban planning, as it supports participation among community members who may not have previous experience expressing their views. With its roots in participatory methods in documentary photography, photovoice emerged in the 1990s from public health assessments with women in China[8] and from Growing Up in Cities' participatory planning with young people.[9] As Caroline Wang and Mary Ann Burris describe it, photovoice seeks to enable people to record their community's strengths and express concerns, promote critical dialogue through small and large group discussion of the photographs, and reach policy- and decision-makers.[10]

Taking pictures is a relatively safe means of beginning to communicate ideas. It helps establish trust and validate ideas, which can lead to enriched discussions and more open sharing than might otherwise happen. It can be used

---

7. The text by Claudia Mitchell, *Doing Visual Research*, is a helpful introductory guide to the ethics and practicalities of community-based photography, including photovoice. (Thousand Oaks, CA: Sage Publications, 2011).

8. Caroline Wang and Mary Ann Burris, "Photovoice: Concept, methodology, and use for participatory assessment needs." *Health Education & Behavior* 24, no. 3 (1997): 369–387.

9. Driskell, *Creating Better Cities with Children and Youth*, 130–133.

10. Wang and Burris, "Photovoice"

as a relatively quick assessment of an area, as a first entry into a proposed project space or public place, and to capture first impressions and ideas. The method has been particularly effective with youth as it provides a mode of creative expression and helps facilitate dialogue. Photovoice can help expand the conversation from youth peer groups to the entire community, through exhibits that invite a larger community of participants.[11]

This method may be used when young people are together as a group—for example, taking pictures on a walking tour outside their school, visiting a public space, or walking in their neighborhood. It can also be varied so that young people take pictures independently at their homes, neighborhoods, or city spaces. The method described here is for facilitating photovoice within a group setting. Variations are given for independent photography.

Ages. six and up

Materials. Hand held cameras (digital, 35 mm, phones or tablets); data sheet, clipboard and pencils (optional); some way to view and share images (projector, computer, printed images); a white board, chalk board, or paper to record ideas during the photograph discussions.

Time to Complete. At least 45 minutes (if digital images). Ideally completed in a minimum of two sessions—one or more for taking photographs, and at least one for discussion

Method—Getting set up and taking pictures

- Introduce the activity—what you plan to do and why
- Make sure that everyone knows how to use the cameras. At a minimum you should cover how to turn on the camera, zoom in and out, use a flash, and snap the picture.

Given time and desire, the photographic process can be one or more lessons in itself, helping students understand basic photographic composition, perspective, and lighting. (See Box 5.9.)

- Optional: Provide data sheets, clipboards, and pencils
- Provide instructions for how and where young people should take pictures. Provide other details such as the number of pictures or specific criteria for pictures. These criteria may be provided on optional data sheets.
- If they will be taking pictures as part of this introductory session, have them begin.
- If they will be taking pictures independently, discuss expectations (number of pictures, goals for taking pictures) and review procedures for taking project cameras or using their own.

Processing pictures and facilitating discussion

- After photographs have been taken, you can upload them for discussion immediately or you can take them to an office or photo lab to upload and organize for a discussion in a separate session.
- Project or print the images so that all participants can view them
- To facilitate discussion, you can choose whether to have students write short descriptions about each photograph (or refer to a data sheet if they used one), ask students to respond to written prompts, or ask each photographer to explain their photographs verbally (Box 5.9).
- Potential prompts, whether oral or written, include: Why did you take this picture? What do you like or dislike in this picture? Why is this important to you? (See Box 5.9 for additional prompts.)

---

11. Driskell, *Creating Better Cities with Children and Youth.*

Box 5.9. **Youth Services Initiative Photovoice Project—Facilitating Photography with Hesitant Youth**

Youth Services Initiative (YSI) is an after-school program run by the City of Boulder's Parks and Recreation Department for children and youth who live in public housing. The majority (95 percent or more) are Latino and many are immigrants. At a planning meeting for a participatory project to redevelop a public space, the leader of YSI expressed concern that youth in her program might not connect with a redesign project when they were concerned about issues such as food and housing scarcity or deportation of family members. YSI youth had said that they were interested in learning photography, and so a new project was developed to understand these youths' experience of the city more broadly.

In this project, young people worked with a professional photographer and undergraduate design student over a ten-week period. The first few lessons were focused on principles and practices of photography, in which youth learned about composition and perspective. They took photographs outside their meeting center from both "worm's eye" and "bird's eye" views. As the project progressed, young people went to public spaces and photographed nature and their friends. In the last weeks of the project, youth took cameras home and photographed their families, friends, houses, and neighborhoods.

To add "voice" to the project, youth responded to a number of written prompts, including:

"From _____ to _____, I come from _____."

"If I could change one thing about the world, it would be _____."

Or simply: "I wish _____."

One participant took a picture of her sister wrapped in a Libyan flag and wrote "From riding horses to hiking mountains, visiting Africa and smelling spices, I come from Libya." Another took pictures of her open refrigerator and food cooking on her stove and wrote "We need to

Figure 5.13. Photovoice exhibit opening.
Photo credit: Lynn M. Lickteig

make sure our refrigerator is always full, so we can feel normal." Another took a picture of his friend, Jesus, and wrote, "If I could change one thing about the world, it would be the way that people in the U.S. treat immigrants—they should be nicer and more accepting of us. They kick us out, tell us mean stuff, and all we are trying to do is have a better life here."

Photographs and words were printed and then mounted on foam boards. The main exhibition was at a recreation center that hosted approximately 1,500 visitors per day. Many visitors stated that they "had no idea" how some of Boulder's youth lived, and some called the recreation department after the exhibit to express their interest and pleasure in learning more through this venue. While many of the photographs caught visitors' attention, it was often the words that conveyed the most. Youth exhibited a sense of pride in their accomplishments as well as at truly being seen and heard.

Two years after project completion, the photographs were again exhibited and presented at a county-wide immigration summit, whose aim was to deepen community understanding of the immigrant experience in Boulder County.[1]

---

1. Victoria Derr, Louise Chawla, Mara Mintzer, Willem van Vliet, and Debra Flanders Cushing. "A city for all citizens: Integrating children and youth from marginalized populations into city planning." *Special Issue on Designing Spaces for City Living. Buildings* 3, no. 3 (2013): 482–505.

Box 5.10. **Photovoice as a Tool to Promote Environmental Health and Leadership among Farmworker Families in Salinas, California**

The City of Salinas, California is home to many migrant farmworkers who contribute to the extensive agricultural production of the Salinas Valley. Farmworker families live in substandard housing with poor access to healthy foods or safe places to play. Researchers and health workers partnered with the Youth Community Council (YCC) in Salinas to employ photovoice as a means to explore environmental health issues that many farmworker families experience in the field and in their home environments. Sixteen Latino youth, aged 14–18, participated in twelve photovoice sessions held on Saturdays at the public library. The youth took pictures independently, with the instruction to take pictures of environmental health issues, including what they perceived as "problems" and "assets" in their community.

In full group sessions, youth identified common themes and issues from all the photographs. Then, each youth selected one picture that they wanted to highlight. Adult researchers facilitated discussion using the "SHOWeD" technique that asks: "What do you **S**ee in this picture?" "What's really **H**appening here?" "How does this relate to

Our lives?" "**W**hy is this happening?" and "What can we **D**o about it?" Each participant wrote narratives for his or her chosen photograph in response to the SHOWeD questions.

The YCC members shared their pictures and narratives with community leaders and at public venues and events, including a local library and a regional health event. They also developed an action plan for two projects to address environmental health issues they had identified. One of these plans resulted in a 5K Run/Walk to address the lack of safe walking and biking spaces, as well as further recommendations for bike lanes and routes. A second plan developed a recycling program at their local high school, with the intent of eventually scaling it up to the school district.[1]

_____

1. Daniel Madrigal, Alicia Salvater, Gardenia Casillas, Crystal Casillas, Irene Vera, Brenda Eskenazi, and Meredith Minkler. "Health in my community: Conducting and evaluating photovoice as a tool to promote environmental health and leadership among Latino/a youth." *Progress in Community Health Partnerships: Research, Education, and Action* 8, no. 3 (2014): 317–329.

- As participants share their ideas, write them on a white board, chalkboard, or large paper so that everyone can see them. When ideas are repeated, place a check next to that idea to indicate the number of participants who share that idea.

- Like the drawing method, if there is time, you might also want to ask participants to respond to what they heard their peers say—ways that they connected with other people's thinking. This helps build connections among the group and also helps facilitators understand how salient, or significant, certain ideas are among the group.

- These themes and ideas can be translated into an action plan (Box 5.9) or to recommendations made directly to city leaders and community members (Box 5.9 and 5.10).

Sharing with community members and decision-makers

Depending on the context of your project, you may invite community members and decision makers to the discussion described above, or you may wish to display images in a public venue. This could be a gallery-like exhibit (Box 5.9) or at a community event (Box 5.10). The photographic displays can help catalyze communication between young people and other community members. As adults look at pictures, they naturally ask questions that the young people can respond to. This helps ease any communication barriers that may exist between age groups (Figure 5.13).

Photovoice implementation with young children

It may be challenging for younger children to juggle the camera, data sheets, and frames (if used, see below). It can be helpful to have adult or youth assistants who can carry materials and facilitate the picture taking. Older assistants can be responsible for recording ideas on data sheets. If taking pictures in an urban environment, they should also be responsible for watching traffic. Children are enthusiastic photographers and can forget that streets and intersections can be risky.

Photo-Drawing

This method allows children to express their ideas and visions for a place through images. It can be used with all ages, but the variation described here is designed to give young children freedom to play and physically experience a place, while adults make observations and take photographs of the places where they are playing. Then, using print images of the photographs, children can draw on top of the image to develop and share ideas for how to improve a space. This method is effective with young children because it lets them explore a site firsthand, without having to step out from the play realm to take photographs. It can be useful for facilitating young children's participation in parks planning or safe routes to school.[12]

---

12. This method was developed by Lauren Shaffer Weatherly at the Boulder Journey School for the Growing Up Boulder Civic Area planning project in 2012. "Boulder Civic Area Project with Prekindergarteners and their Families." Growing Up Boulder.org. http://www.growingupboulder.org/boulder -journey-school-research-process.html. (Retrieved April 2, 2017). It is presented in a modified format here.

Ages. four to six

Materials. Hand-held cameras (digital, phones, or tablets); access to computer and printer; colored markers; clipboards or phone for taking notes. For this method, it is helpful to have a minimum of two adult facilitators—one responsible for taking photographs and another who records children's ideas, activities, and responses to the sites they explore.

If using a 35 mm camera, you will need: 35 mm camera; film; access to photography lab; tracing paper; colored pencils or markers, as well as note taking materials.

Time to Complete. At least two 45-minute sessions—one (or more) for taking photographs, and one for drawing and discussion. Ideally, the two sessions should be close together in time, with no more than a week between the site play and the discussion.

Method—Taking pictures

- Introduce the activity—what you plan to do and why

- Collect the cameras, any film, and note-taking materials

- Take children to the site you want them to explore—this could be a neighborhood street, a park, or a vacant lot. Give children time and permission to explore the space. If you have a small group of four or five, you can give each child a turn to be the "play leader" who chooses a spot where everyone plays for ten minutes . . . and then it is another child's turn to move the group to a new space. This is a good way to cover a territory based on children's curiosities and attractions.

- As adult facilitators, observe children's play. Simply watch—providing for children's safety but otherwise with no interventions. Take photographs of the spaces children interact with. Make notes about what children say and do in the different spaces.

- At the end of the allotted playtime, ask children to share what they enjoyed about the space and if there is anything they would change or add to make the space more enjoyable. Make notes.

Method—Photo Processing

- Between sessions, upload digital photographs to a computer.
- Process the images so that they are at about 40–50 percent saturation. You can make these adjustments in a wide range of photo image processing software, from Microsoft Office[13] to Adobe Creative Suites. You want to lighten the image so children can draw on top of the image while maintaining the elements of the original image as background (Figure 5.14).
- Print each image on paper approximately 8.5 x 11 inches.
- If you are using 35 mm film, print each photograph as 8 x 10 inch prints; tape tracing paper to the top of each picture so that children can look underneath but draw on the tracing paper for their modifications.

Method—Photo Drawing

- When images are ready, compile your materials—this should include the printed images, colored markers, and notes
- First review the pictures with children. Ask children what they remember about playing in this space. Use your notes for prompts to help them remember.

Figure 5.14. Example of a photodrawing by Cyrena at Boulder Journey School. This photo annotation read, "Cyrena called the Boulder Museum of Contemporary Art "Painting Land" and added beautiful colors and paintings to the outside." Image credit: Boulder Journey School

- Ask children to generate ideas about how they want to change or improve the space. Use your notes to prompt them.
- Give children print images to draw on. As they draw, record their ideas.
- Have each child share his/her drawings and ideas.
- Ask children to make connections to ideas they liked from other drawings.
- As a final step, you can scan these images and annotate them with the children's words.

Storytelling and Writing

Storytelling has a rich tradition in cultures around the world. For many cultures, storytelling remains an important means of understanding who we are in relation to the larger world. Stories can also provide a context for discussing complex social issues, including those related to social justice, environmental degradation, or resilience.[14]

---

13. In Microsoft Office, select the image you are modifying, click on Picture Tools, click on Color and select a Recolor option that is sufficiently light for children to draw on top.

14. Sarah Fletcher, Robin S. Cox, Leila Scannell, Cheryl Heykoop, Jennifer Tobin-Gurley and Lori Peek, "Youth creating disaster recovery and resilience: A multi-site arts based youth

Box 5.11. **River of Words—International Art and Poetry Contest**

Founded in 1995 by writer and activist Pamela Michael and then-U.S. Poet Laureate Robert Hass, River of Words was conceived as a way to provide tools and training for educators and after-school programs to support ecoliteracy through poetry and the arts. The program hosts an international art and poetry contest for young people ages 5–19.

There are many ways that communities have adapted River of Words to a local context. In one example, River of Words joined with the San Francisco Estuary Partnership to create the One Square Block Contest for students from twelve counties in the Bay Area to explore their immediate surroundings and to develop art and poetry that reflects their natural, built, and cultural environments.

River of Words is housed in the Center for Ecoliteracy at Saint Mary's College in California. Submission to the contest is free, and the website archives many of the resources that might inspire others to explore poetry and art as an entry point for young people to explore their surroundings.

https://www.stmarys-ca.edu/center-for-environmental-literacy/river-of-words

Box 5.12. **Collaborative Book Writing**

Figure 5.15. This collaborative book shared stories about Mexican children's adventures to parks, nature, and other places (left). Each child wrote an individual story, such as about a picnic to a park (right). Image credit: Yolanda Corona Caraveo

Collaborative book writing has been used as a method in many parts of Latin America to engage children in storytelling about the places where they live and to share their experiences with other children. In the example below, each child wrote a story about their travels to parks, the countryside, and other special places. The stories were compiled into a book with cardboard binding. These books contribute children's voices to local libraries and are used as a means for children to share their experiences with each other and with adults in communities with few resources. Termed *Libros Cartoneros* (roughly translated as cardboard book makers, in reference to the children who construct the books with reclaimed materials), this method is used widely in Mexico and other parts of Latin America to promote indigenous cultures and education.[1]

_____

1. The text *Libros Cartoneros: Una Alternativa para la Integración a la Cultura Escrita* by Eleuterio Olarte Tiburcio and Juana Zacarías Candelario provides additional examples of these books and discussion about how this approach has been used. Dirección General de Educación Indígena de la SEP. http://www.educacionyculturaaz.com/articulos-az/libros-cartoneros-una-alternativa-para-la-integracion-a-la-cultura-escrita. (Retrieved September 25, 2017).

Box 5.13. **I Know the River Loves Me, I Know Salinas Loves Me**

In the picture book, *I Know the River Loves Me,* by Maya Christina Gonzalez, the river is a place of comfort, of a young girl finding her own identity in relationship to nature.[1]

This story was used to facilitate lessons in East Salinas with second grade children, ages 6–7, who are primarily of Mexican descent. While East Salinas is often characterized by its problems and challenges rather than its culture and assets, the ethos of this project was to help children think about their community as a place where they are supported and connected.

Constructed in three phases, the project was developed between university faculty, university students, and an elementary school teacher. In the first phase, children were introduced to isolated images from the book *I Know the River Loves Me* through a gallery walk. The picture book shows a young girl traveling to the river with her backpack. Children were asked to observe the drawings and to describe the feelings evoked through the drawings. Then children read the book as a class and discussed how the river represented a place of potential calm, health, and trust for the girl in the story.

Children were then asked to move from thinking about the book *I Know the River Loves Me* to constructing their own stories for how *I Know Salinas Loves Me.* Mirroring the image of the girl in the backpack, each child took a picture of him or herself in Salinas in response to the prompt: "I know Salinas loves me because . . ." Children used these neighborhood photographs—of themselves at the library, a park, a church—to discuss how Salinas can also be a place of support and comfort.

In the final phase of this project, children moved from the city to the family, developing Mothers' Day cards that expressed how "I know my mother loves me. . ." The project represents a means of integrating storytelling and art in order to support children's emerging identity with their family and community. In this way, children begin to understand that love represents taking care of somebody, or some place.[2]

---

1. Maya Christina Gonzalez, *I Know the River Loves Me / Yo Se Que el Rio Me Ama.* (New York City: Lee & Low Books, Inc., 2012).

2. This project was developed by Dr. Miguel Lopez at California State University Monterey Bay, in partnership with service learning students and teacher Evelyn Mesa. Personal communication between Miguel Lopez and Victoria Derr.

Many approaches support storytelling in participatory practice. These include the reading of published stories, oral history or storytelling from adults, and the making of personal stories. This section focuses on methods that enhance young people's creation of personal stories and help others understand young people's perspectives and experiences. Stories can be powerful as tools for imagining desired futures and narrating heroic journeys through fears or challenges that young people face.[15]

---

engagement research project." *Children, Youth and Environments* 26, no. 1 (2016): 148–163; Louise Phillips. "Social justice storytelling and young children's active citizenship." *Discourse: Studies in the Cultural Politics of Education* 31, no. 3 (2010): 363–376.

15. Marilyn Mehlmann with Esböjrn Jorsäter, Alexander Mehlmann, and Olena Pometun, "Looking the monster in the eye: Drawing comics for sustainability." *EarthEd: Rethinking Education on a Changing Planet* (Washington, D.C.: Island Press, 2017), 117–127; Chris J. Cunningham, Margaret A. Jones, and Rosemary Dillon. "Children and urban regional planning: Participation in the public consultation process through story writing." *Children's Geographies* 1, no. 2 (2003): 201–221.

Stories can be used to understand a wide range of topics, such as understanding how young people experience their city (Boxes 5.11–5.16), how they think about social justice (Boxes 5.16–5.17), what transportation is like in a city (Box 5.14), or how they respond to a natural disaster (Box 5.19). Means of storytelling range from poetry (Box 5.11) to storybooks (Box 5.12) and comics (Box 5.14), to letter exchanges between children in different cities (Box 5.15), and music videos (Box 5.16).

Box 5.14. **Youth Voices for Change**

Figure 5.16. Youth generated comics to express their experiences of the city. In this featured annotation, youth describe their fears for biking in the city. Image credit: Patsy Eubanks Owens

Youth Voices for Change is a long-term engagement program out of the University of California, Davis, that provides skills and training to a multi-racial coalition of youth in West Sacramento, California, so that they can develop and articulate their community vision. The youth group "Sactown Heroes" participated in Youth Voices for Change by identifying likes and dislikes in their community and sharing their thoughts and ideas through a comic book format. As a collaborative project between youth and adults, the comic book portrays "favorite" and "challenging" places with pictures and call-out boxes. In the layout, the comic book style thought bubbles represented youth ideas, and square text boxes represented summary captions written by adults with youth input.[1]

_____

1. Owens, Patsy Eubanks, ed. *Youth Voices for Change: Opinions and Ideas for the Future of West Sacramento.* Center for Regional Change. University of California, 2010. http://artofregionalchange.ucdavis.edu/files/2010/Comicbook_size.pdf. (Retrieved on September 25, 2017).

Box 5.15. **Letter Writing as a Means of Sharing Young People's Experiences of the City**

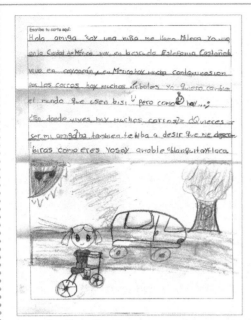

Figure 5.18. Letter exchange from Tepoztlán child to Mexico City children. In this letter the child from Tepoztlán says she likes to play with her dolls, she has many friends, and she likes to sing a lot. Image credit: Yolanda Corona Caraveo

Figure 5.17. Children in Mexico City wrote to children in Tepoztlán, sharing their experiences of the city. In this letter, the child says that in her neighborhood, Coyocán, there is much air pollution because of cars but there are also trees. The child says she would like to change the world, "but how?" She asks if there are many cars where her pen-friend lives. Image credit: Yolanda Corona Caraveo

Article 13 of the Convention on the Rights of the Child provides for freedom of expression, including the right to share information in ways children choose, such as through drawing or writing. Many participatory projects provide a means to both reflect on existing conditions of the city and to imagine a desired future city. Letter writing is a way to engage children with others, in a dialogue that bridges places, and to authentically consider the place where they live. It is also a way for young people to reflect on their city—how they experience it currently, and what they would like it to be.

Letter writing emerged as a method in Mexico as a means for indigenous children to share their ex-

periences with other indigenous children. Rooted in anthropological and linguistic methods, the process seeks to achieve educational as well as participatory goals. Yolanda Corona and her colleagues extended this work to children in different towns and cities, as a way for them to share their experiences of living in the city with others. The method integrates both letter writing and drawing, typically with children between the ages of eight and eleven. Children exchange a series of letters so that they can develop a relationship with each other.

Through children's exchanges between Tepoztlán and Cuernavaca, Mexico as well as between Tepoztlán and Mexico City, Dr. Corona and her colleagues have found that children more readily share their experience of the city when they are writing to other children. They show a sense of intimacy, immediacy, and enjoyment with the exchanges.

In Dr. Corona's most recent project, children from schools in two places—Tepoztlán, Mexico and the megacity Mexico City—wrote letters to each

(Box 5.15 continued on the next page)

(Box 5.15 continued)

other to share experiences that children have had with nature. Children's experiences primarily showed great differences between the two places, with children in Mexico City describing tall buildings, high volumes of traffic and pollution (Figures 5.17 and 5.18). The Mexico City children wrote that the children of Tepoztlán are lucky because they get to live with nature as a part of their homes. Many Mexico City children described only being able to experience nature when they leave the city, to vacation destinations such as Acapulco.

Letter writing is an inviting and simple means to achieve child-to-child exchanges and provide a forum for young people to share their experiences and learn from others, as they consider the place where they live.[1]

_____

1. Yolanda Corona Caraveo, G. Quinteros-Sciurano, and M. Padilla Flores, "Relación epistolar entre niños de dos pueblos: Estructuras y estrategias del conocimiento," *Anuario de Investigación* (Mexico City, UAM-X, 2005), 614–635.; Rossana Podestá Siri. *Nuestros Pueblos de Hoy y de Siempre: El Mundo de las Niñas y Niños Nahuas de México a través de sus Propias Letras y Dibujos* (Universidad de Puebla, 2002).

Box 5.16. **Using Music Video to Spread the Word:** Youth Becoming Flood Resilient Citizen Scientists with Dr. Merrie Koester, University of South Carolina Center for Science Education

Figure 5.19. The Gadsden Creek context for a music video about development and environmental racism. Photo credit: Jared Bramblett

Gadsden Creek was historically a place of swimming and recreation and a vital habitat for many marine plants and animals. Over time, much of the creek was filled in with trash and debris, and then paved over for development.

As a result, vital ecosystem services were lost, and the housing project area has been experiencing severe flooding, especially during high tides (Figure 5.19). Sea level rise is making matters even worse. The most common sign near the school is a ROAD CLOSED sign.

In many cultures and traditions, music is a form of storytelling used to transmit knowledge and experience. In the urban hip hop culture, rap music often conveys stories of profoundly unbalanced systems in the world. Working with Dr. Merrie Koester of the University of South Carolina Center for Science Education and a team of community mentors in Charleston, South Carolina, a class of eighth-grade African American students, ages 13–14, from Charleston Development Academy explored the causes of flooding in their neighborhood, a public housing site built adjacent to what was once a thriving tidal creek.

Dr. Merrie Koester, a science and arts integration specialist, employed principles of place-based learning to position students as resources of knowledge about flooding and development impacts on their community. With significant support from community artists, stormwater engineers, climate scientists, environmental justice specialists, and city officials, students learned about the marsh ecosystem, its history and development, moon phase and tide relationships and then developed artistic digital media competencies to share their knowledge and perspectives at a community event.

The short music video shows the students moving out of their school into the marsh. They rap about the degradation of Gadsden Creek and the ecological and social consequences that come from ignoring nature. They describe the natural cycles of the tides:

> "Hi-Lo, Do Re Neap
> All these tides are flooding our streets.
> Spring, King, not the same thing.
> It all depends on the moon's swing . . ."

And their goals for their neighborhood:

> ". . . We're on a mission—
> Not asking for permission.
> Find a solution for our city's evolution
> Gadsden Creek is filled with trash.
> Now the flooding is a pain in the
>   AS-phalt . . ."

Through their music, they express their concerns for wildlife and their hopes for a better solution than continuing to develop the tidal creek and wetlands. Youth shared this video at a large community gathering and called for the developers

Figure 5.20. Making a music video requires practice and preparation. In this image, youth stand next to receding floodwaters in their neighborhood as they rehearse the video. Photo credit: Merrie Koester

to consider green infrastructure and a reduction in impervious surfacing in their current plans, garnering support from the city's stormwater engineer along the way.[1]

---

1. M. Koester. "On a mission: Creating a climate for rising 'C' levels in science education." Work in Progress. Kids Teaching Flood Resilience: https://www.kidsteaching floodresilience.com/

Digital Stories

Some youth express preferences for sharing their ideas in digital media.[16] Digital stories move storytelling into a digital process that can be used in face-to-face groups or shared across time and space. A wide range of programs support digital stories, including the Center for Digital Storytelling.[17] Its director, Joe Lambert, has developed an excellent resource on digital storytelling methods.[18] He describes approaches to facilitate

a wide range of stories including reflection, intergenerational connection, identity, and activism. Here we provide simple methods that can be helpful in engaging young people in urban planning processes.

There are three basic steps to the digital storytelling process: create a narrative, take or compile pictures that reflect this narrative, discuss and collate into a digital story. Digital stories can be developed from a series of photographs (still images) or from video or film. The images are compiled in a sequence with the narrator telling his or her story. The end product is a personal story that is told digitally.

Ages. 10 and up

Materials. Existing photographs; cameras or video recording technology; computers with

---

16. Joe Lambert, *Digital Storytelling: Capturing Lives, Creating Community*, 2nd Edition. (Berkeley, CA: Digital Diner Press, 2006).

17. The Center for Digital Storytelling provides support for participatory media and storytelling to communities around the world. StoryCenter. "Listen Deeply, Tell Stories." StoryCenter.org. www.storycenter.org. (Retrieved September 24, 2017).

18. Lambert, *Digital Storytelling*.

Box 5.17. Youth FACE IT, Digital Stories

The Youth FACE IT (Youth Fostering Active Community Engagement for Integration and Transformation) was a program of Boulder County, Colorado. The program was designed to engage Latino youth in critical dialogue and paired university mentors with Latino high school students to create multimedia narratives. The primary methods for this work were photovoice and digital storytelling. The combination of photovoice with digital storytelling allowed youth to reflect both on their lived experiences (through photovoice) and then to reflect on their photographs (through digital storytelling).

These methods were important for Latino youth who live in a predominately non-Latino community, to express their identities and struggles within their community. Like the photovoice project with Salinas youth (Box 5.10), youth used the SHOWeD method to discuss their pictures. After discussing the photos, youth wrote captions for their pictures and chose those that conveyed important meanings. These then made their way into the digital storytelling process, and were shared with city leaders.

While many Latino youth generally want the same types of things for their communities—places to hang out with friends, youth-oriented activities, and safe public spaces—they also want places where they feel included and welcome, not discriminated against because of their ethnicity. The photovoice and digital storytelling processes allowed the expression of all these ideas.[1]

---

1. Debra Flanders Cushing, Emily Wexler Love, and Willem van Vliet, "Through the viewfinder: Using multimedia techniques to engage Latino youth in community planning." *Diálogos: Placemaking in Latino Communities,* ed., Michael Rios and Leonardo Vazquez (London: Routledge, 2012), 172–185.

---

movie-making software; a microphone to record the narratives; internet access for royalty-free music (optional); a media storage device such as blank DVDs (and a DVD burner) or USB drive to provide a copy to each participant; sufficiently trained facilitators to assist digital storytelling

Time to Complete. A minimum of one week

Method—Creating a narrative

- Introduce the method and what participants will be doing
- Provide prompts for youth. Prompts that ask participants to reflect on their city, neighborhood, or other parts of the physical environment can include: What do you like about your city? What about your city is friendly and supportive to you? What can the city do so that it is a better place for young people?
- Provide materials and instructions for youth to take photographs (see Photovoice instructions, this Chapter). Or, ask students to compile existing photographs that represent these ideas. Or compile a collection of both.

- Taking photographs and identifying images that will reflect a personal response to the prompts are part of the process for constructing a narrative.

- Youth can share with facilitators and each other the photographs that they take, with prompts such as: What does this picture show? How does this picture reflect [what you like about your city]?[19] Is there anything you could change to make this place better? Is there anything the city could do?

Prompts can ask young people to reflect on both the positive and negative aspects of their community, as they think about what they would like to celebrate and maintain, or change.

---

19. Change the text in brackets to reflect the prompts that you are using.

Figure 5.21.
Storyboard template

Storyboard Worksheet

Title of Digital Story: _____ Sheet # ____ of ____

Shot #1

Description/Dialogue (Insert what you will say about Shot #1 here):

Shot #2

Description/Dialogue (Insert what you will say about Shot #2 here):

Shot #3

Description/Dialogue (Insert what you will say about Shot #3 here):

Shot #4

Description/Dialogue (Insert what you will say about Shot #4 here):

Method—Compile Images and Narrative

- Once youth share their stories, ask each student to create a storyboard. A storyboard is a sequence of images and words that show the progression of the story planned for a film or video. Participants can hand sketch these ideas onto frames or notecards that represent the sequence of ideas they will share in their digital story.

- It may be that participants think of additional pictures they will need or want to include to complete their digital story.

For example, one digital story showed a candle burning as a way to represent a change or transformation in the young girl's life. The participant and facilitator should make a plan for compiling these extra images.

- When the storyboard is complete, it should reflect a basic outline of the images and ideas that will be conveyed.

Method—Create the Digital Story

- Once the storyboard is completed, participants can begin to create their own digital stories using movie-maker software. While the specifics will vary by software program, the process should include the following steps:

- Upload and process all images
- Generate the text that will become subtitles for the story
- Record the storyline
- Find and download any royalty free music that will be used as background
- Assemble and edit the digital story

Sharing with community members and decision makers

When all participants have developed their stories, host a venue to share the stories with others. This can be through a gathering with school or city leaders, a film shorts festival open to the community, and/or a virtual sharing of stories on the internet. Growing Up Boulder, for example, scheduled a special evening with city council members that began with a screening of young teens' digital stories. Most of the storytellers and some of their family members were present. The stories prompted councilors to ask questions, and opened up conversations with the young people about their experiences. Facilitators needed to mediate the evening to ensure that young people felt appreciated and that they understood the councilors' questions as invitations to a discussion—not a cross-examination. (See Chapter 8 for other examples for sharing projects.)

Participatory Video

Participatory Video began in the 1960s as a means of facilitating dialogue between community members and government officials. Participatory video enables collaboration as many participants can shape a story, contribute with different skills, and share in knowledge genera-

tion.[20] Like many of the participatory methods described in this chapter, the *process* of generating the film contributes to social change more than the physical product.[21] Participatory video has been used in a wide range of contexts including environmental and public health, social action, safe schools, parks planning and youth identity. It has also been employed widely in the context of international development.[22, 23] Because filmmaking requires a certain degree of training, participatory video can empower youth by giving them skills in documentary methods as well as developing their capacity to speak up as active citizens.[24]

The steps to creating participatory videos are similar to digital stories. Because of the additional filmmaking skills required, the process is typically implemented over the course of a week-long intensive workshop or over a full year. No matter the time allotted, participatory video requires identification of facilitators with the skills and resources to teach filmmaking. Lunch and Lunch have written an accessible guide to participatory video,[25] and an increasing number of websites share these processes for working with youth.[26]

---

20. Aline Gubrium and Krista Harper, *Participatory Visual and Digital Methods* (Walnut Creek, CA: Left Coast Press, 2013).
21. Katharine Haynes and Thomas M. Tanner, "Empowering young people and strengthening resilience: Youth-centred participatory video as a tool for climate change adaptation and disaster risk reduction." *Children's Geographies* 13, no. 3 (2015): 357–371.
22. Nick Lunch and Chris Lunch, *Insights into Participatory Video: A Handbook for the Field.* InsightShare, 2006. http://insightshare.org/resources/insights-into-participatory-video-a-handbook-for-the-field/. (Retrieved March 10, 2017).
23. Gubrium and Harper, *Participatory Visual and Digital Methods.*
24. Arjun Appadurai, "The right to research." *Globalisation, Societies and Education* 4, no. 2 (2006):167–177.
25. Lunch and Lunch, *Insights into Participatory Video.*
26. For example, see Pukar. "Youth and Urban Knowledge Production." Pukar.org. http://www.pukar.org.in/youth-and-urban-knowledge-production/ (Retrieved September 24, 2017).

Box 5.18. **Lens on Climate Change**

The Lens on Climate Change (LOCC) project, developed by the Cooperative Institute for Research in Environmental Sciences (CIRES) at the University of Colorado, Boulder, engaged youth in developing short films that explore the effects of climate change on young people's lives and communities. Film topics varied—from "Eco-Warriors" who demonstrate the pitfalls of poor environmental behaviors in the home, to "Coyote and the Drought," which builds on Navajo stories to tell the tale of area lakes drying up in the Southwest U.S. All shared common ground in using humor to address a dire issue, valuing collaborative decision-making, demonstrating young people's interest in sharing their lived experiences and culture, and stressing ways to make an impact now.

Youth in the project reflected that they enjoyed using art as a form of expression, learning more about their communities, working collaboratively with peers and mentors, and using film as a means to educate others. One student reflected, "The best experience of LOCC is they let me use my talent in art . . . This is a rare experience for me, and it helps me in so many ways to learn other skills such as leadership, teamwork, and how to cooperate with others." Another student said, "I understand now that the world isn't doomed, but we can fix it and make it better." Similarly, another student said that "the best thing about the LOCC experience is making a film about how people could make a change for the better. . . These films . . . will hopefully make others do their best to help the earth."[1]

1. Adapted from: Victoria Derr, "Young people focus their lens on climate change." *European Network of Child Friendly Cities*, January 12, 2017. http://www.childinthecity.eu/2017/01/12/young-people-focus-their-lens-on-climate-change/. (Retrieved September 24, 2017).

Figure 5.22. Youth selected topics to research related to climate change. In this case, youth interviewed farmers and climate scientists as they investigated the links between ranching, water, and climate change in "Snow to Steak." Photo credit: Lens on Climate Change

Figure 5.23. Youth can engage in all aspects of video production, from interviews and film footage to editing. Photo credit: Lens on Climate Change

Ages. 13 and up

Materials. Video equipment; capacity to upload to YouTube or other storage and sharing space

Time to Complete:. The amount of time varies widely, from a one-week intensive workshop to a year with multiple workshops and phases

Participatory video often involves four stages: an early knowledge and skill building series of exercises; identification of priority issues and storyboarding of messages; an iterative process of learning, filming, and editing; and a final stage that involves a screening, dialogue, and identification of action.

Method—Identifying issues and developing the storyline

* Introduce the method and what participants will be doing.

* The process can begin with open-ended prompts as in the digital story process, such as

  What do you like about your city? What about your city is friendly and supportive to you? What can the city do so that it is a better place for young people?

  Or it can be focused on a more specific set of questions or issues, such as flooding (Box 5.16) or climate change adaptation (Boxes 5.18 and 5.19).

* For open-ended questions, it may be helpful to introduce a series of exercises, such as other arts-based methods in this chapter, to help youth identify an issue for focus with participatory video.[27]

* For a focused topic, such as climate change adaptation, this stage also involves bringing experts and youth together to explore a subject.

* In this stage of participatory video, facilitators will lead a series of exercises that build

knowledge and skills about film-making as well as any subject matter needed.

Method—Identifying priority issues and storyboards

* After an initial phase in which youth explore a topic more broadly, each youth or group will determine an area of focus for their film.

* Youth create a storyboard. A storyboard is a sequence of images and words that show the progression of the story planned for a film or video. Participants can hand sketch these ideas onto frames (Figure 5.21) that represent the sequence of ideas they will share in their film.

* This phase is usually iterative, meaning that youth develop a storyline, get feedback from peers, community members, or experts, and refine their thinking before producing the film.

* When the story board is complete, it should reflect a basic outline of the images and ideas that will be conveyed in the film.

Method—Create the film

* Once the storyboard is created, participants can begin to create their own films. While the specifics will vary by software program, the process should include the following steps:
  * Generate footage
  * Edit the footage
  * Add any subtitles
  * Publish and/or share the film through a screening or workshop

As with digital stories, host a screening or other venue for participants to share and discuss their videos. Establish ground rules for sharing films so that youth retain the feelings of empowerment they developed in the process of production (Box 5.19).

27. Lunch and Lunch, *Insights into Participatory Video* provides many exercises that help build a storyline and film content.

Box 5.19. **Participatory Video for Climate Change Adaptation and Disaster Risk-Reduction**

Like the Lens on Climate Change project (Box 5.18), researchers in Eastern Samar, the Philippines have also used participatory video as a means for children and youth to express their ideas about how to respond to climate change.

This extensive research project provided in-depth training for young people in climate change adaptation and disaster risk reduction as well as documentary filmmaking. When the films were ready for screening, young people and adult researchers and facilitators worked together to develop a process for screening workshops. The process involved screenings in three locations, with government officials, community members, and project participants in attendance. In this process, discussion focused on which problems could be solved by the community and which needed governmental involvement or intervention.

Adult participants and facilitators held briefings with youth both before and after these workshops to discuss likely outcomes of their screenings, identify positive outcomes, identify social and political constraints, and reinforce that, while decision-making is often long-term, actions could happen.

The participatory video project had a significant impact on its participants, with one youth stating, "Our inspiration in making the film is our fellow youth . . . We believe and claim that children hold the future, so let us lessen the risks." Another reflected that "I don't want this to end only after the film. We want [the government] to adopt those practices which could benefit our community."[1]

_____
1. Haynes and Tanner, "Empowering young people and strengthening resilience"

Three-Dimensional Models

Model-making to construct cities, neighborhoods, parks, plazas, and buildings in miniature is an essential practice in architecture and planning because it enables people to see at a glance how all the pieces of a place fit together: as they exist currently, or as they could be transformed under a designer's shaping vision. Given children's pleasure in constructing small worlds, model-making has a long history in progressive education and urban environmental education as a way for children to investigate and represent their local environment and suggest possibilities for its future.[28] As a method of research, asking a child to build a model of their town or the area around their school or home is a way to understand places that are salient and significant.[29] During construction or after its completion, the model serves as a prompt for discussing the child's place knowledge and experiences. Although there are software programs that even children can be trained to use to draw three-dimensional representations of the environment, there is still a great value in the tactile process of making models that people can walk around and manipulate together, using inexpensive materials that can often be scavenged from the waste stream or the natural environment. Ephemeral models may be made outside, scratching map features into the dirt or drawing them in sand, and constructing three-dimensional additions to the map with found objects from nature or the surrounding environment (Figure 5.24).

_____
28. Victoria Derr, Louise Chawla, Ilene Pevec, "Early Childhood," *Urban Environmental Education Review*, ed., Alex Russ and Marianne Krasny (Ithaca, New York: Cornell University Press, 2017), 155–164; Hart, Roger. "Mapping and modelling," *Children's Participation*, (London: Earthscan Publications, 1997).

_____
29. Hart, Roger, *Children's Experience of Place* (New York: Irvington Publishers, 1979).

Figure 5.24. This "found object" model was made from natural materials scavenged from a school playground and represents an enclosure, native plantings, wildlife-friendly pathways, and a creek with boulders for rock-hopping. Photo credit: Growing Up Boulder

Ages. 8 and up, as model making requires the ability to organize ideas in 3-D space

Time to Complete. Two to four 45-minute sessions. Depending on the age of the participants and the level of detail desired, it will take two to four sessions to make and paint the model pieces, locate them on the base, secure them with glue or other means, label them, and share them with others.

Materials. a base that can be as simple as a piece of paper or as sturdy as cardboard or chipboard; multi-purpose glue; glue gun; glue sticks; paint; an assortment of purchased and scavenged materials of all kinds for model building (e.g. blocks, clay, cardboard, construction paper, felt, fabric, ribbons, jar lids, popsicle sticks, tooth picks, straws, pipe cleaners, spools, paper towel and toilet paper rolls, craft store pom-poms, figurines of people and animals, branches, small stones, plastic trees, fabric flowers, or any other materials that are available that invite creative expression).

Method—Preparing a Base

- Base materials and details can be determined in advance, or as part of the participatory process with teachers, adult facilitators, or young people themselves. For example, children can learn about scale as they construct a base map, or older youth can learn about design processes (See Chapters 4 and 7.) The extent that young people are engaged at this stage may depend on the goals of the project as well as the time and materials available.

- The base of a three-dimensional model can be constructed of many materials—paper, recycled cardboard, reclaimed wood slabs, or design materials such as foam board. Materials selection depends on the purposes of the model and ages of participants.

- At its simplest, the base may be a solid form simply for holding a model (Figure 5.24), or may be a simple drawing of key features on a large sheet of paper, on which children can place model pieces (Figure 5.25).

- A printed base map also can be mounted on top of flat cardboard or foam board so that there are reference points (Figures 5.26 and 5.27), or young people can add these details to a blank slate and paint or draw features they think are important. Accurate scale may not be important, but do indicate key features so that participants can orient themselves for their designs.

- Bases can also be constructed so that they show the landforms of a particular place—hills, creek drainages, or gentle slopes. These features are important to think about in the design and imagined use of spaces, and can be represented through model-making itself (with clay, florist foam or other materials to represent changes in topography), or through the construction of a base map that represents topographic features. Base maps can be made with layers of cardboard, foam, or

Figure 5.25. This model was constructed by 8- to 9-year-olds. They generated a hand-drawn base map and then used recycled and repurposed materials to build the model of a child-friendly, sustainable neighborhood. The model also shows use of repurposed and creative materials, including toilet paper tubes, recycled cardboard, recycled juice cartons, and lids. (For more details about this project, see Chapter 11). Photo credit: Lynn M. Lickteig

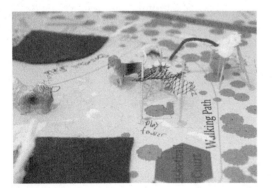

Figure 5.26. This model for a teen-friendly park, designed by youth aged 11–13, began with a pre-printed base map, rendered for simplicity. Photo credit: Growing Up Boulder

Figure 5.27. This model for a public space design used a pre-printed base map showing streets and building outlines. Photo credit: Growing Up Boulder

chipboard to represent these topographic features (Chapter 4).

- For most projects, the scale of the base is not important for model making. Young people will be using a wide variety of materials that will not conform to this scale, and designing to scale may require significant

additional instruction. However, it may be appropriate for detailed topographic models (Chapter 4). In these cases, partnership with a university design program or design firm will be helpful in facilitating the construction of such a base map.

Method—Planning the Model

- Whenever possible, begin with a field trip to walk around the site and discuss existing plans for redevelopment or renovations. If this is not possible, take pictures of the site and post them on a wall. Identify where photos were taken on the base map. (See Chapter 7.)

- Invite city staff or local planners or architects who are responsible for site changes to come talk to participants about design goals and answer questions. If different groups have competing goals for the site, share this information so that young people will be aware of these points of tension. They can consider opposing viewpoints and can think about how competing interests might be reconciled, or take a position of their own that they base on research, reflection, and discussion.

- Provide question prompts to get participants thinking about how the designed space will function. What is the space for? Who will use it? What ages will use it? How many people will use it at a time? What will they do here? How will it function at different times of day, different days of the week, and different seasons of the year? Are the uses by different groups similar or do they conflict in some ways? How can you design a space for multiple types of users?

Method—Building the Model

- Introduce the goals for model-making. This method works best after a project has been introduced and explored through other methods. You should remind everyone what the goals of the project are and how the model will help communicate young people's visions for a place.

- Provide instructions and guidance for model-making. Guidelines can be provided for materials gathering or sharing,

depending on the type of model to be made. Establish a time frame and any ground rules for making models. Guidelines can also include working within constraints of topography (Chapter 4) or budget (Box 5.20).

- Unless each participant is making his or her own model, group decision-making is a central aspect of model-making. Provide simple ground rules for respectful communication and decision-making. Emphasize that group members should listen respectfully to each other's ideas and reach agreement about the model before items are fixed on the base.

- To fix model pieces, use multi-purpose glue, hot glue, or clay. Alternatively, details of models can be attached using toothpicks or small sticks.

- Have participants clearly label their model elements and write a paragraph that describes their piece. They can use the original prompt questions as a guide as they think about what they want to explain. Fix this explanation on the model or display it beside the model (Figure 5.29).

- Take photographs to document the finished models.

Group sizes and scale

If the model base represents an extensive area and it is scaled to be large, young people may work together as a group to develop an overall plan. Once the plan is made, divide it into sections with small groups responsible for building the model pieces for their section. When the base is small, one child or a small group of two or three may plan and construct individual models. It is important for the adult facilitator to initiate the process by helping team members develop guidelines for how they will work together. This sets the tone for collaboration and includes suggestions for how to address disagree-

Box 5.20. **Learning to Design within a Budget:** Picto-Play

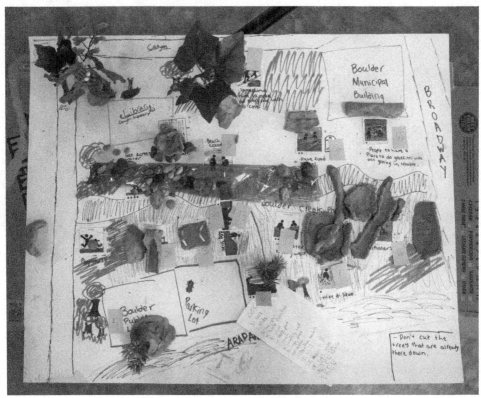

Figure 5.28. When youth, aged 11–13, designed a public space, they worked within a budget of 30 dots. Each icon had a scaled number of dots to represent the relative expense. Photo credit: Growing Up Boulder

A Belgian design firm developed a series of "picto-play" icons with dots that represent the relative costs of different design options. A climbing tree might be one dot, but a full-scale tree house might be two. The icons also show a variety of natural and topographic features—tall grass or a grove of trees, steep hills or small rolling hills—as well as play equipment. Growing Up Boulder used these picto-play icons when youth designed a large public space. Each group was given a set budget of 30 dots. The benefit of using icons with model-making was that it forced young people to identify and clarify their values and interests in the public space. One group chose to focus their dots on activating play at the creek side. Another group used all their dots to provide services for the homeless, whom they had observed at the park.[1]

_____

1. Kind & Samenleving, "Picto-Play 1.0." Kind & Samenleving.org. http://k-s.be/inspraak-participatie /picto-play-10-knip-en-plak-het-speelweefsel-bij -mekaar/picto-play-10-catalogus-en-handleiding/. (Retrieved September 24, 2017).

Figure 5.29. This model, developed by 11- to 12-year-old girls, created a "sanitation station" and homeless services in a prominent public space. The youth chose to label their model with numbers and a key. Photo credit: Growing Up Boulder

ments when they arise. When the models are finished, take time for everyone to step back and share their observations about important elements of their creation.

Sharing with community members and decision-makers

Invite the city staff, architects, or planners who initially briefed participants on design goals to come back to see the finished models, hear young people's ideas, and ask questions or display the models at a public event that is also open to design professionals from around the city, city leaders, parents, other children, and community members. If the models can be displayed at a public place like a library, local museum, or recreation center, add a brief text that gives an overview of the project.

Community events can be a good occasion to gather more citizen input. Hand out cards or have sheets on the wall where everyone attending can contribute their own ideas for the site. Provide prompt questions: What model elements appear particularly creative or useful? Why? Are

there additional elements that they would suggest, and if so why?

Variation: City as Play

City as Play is an approach to model-making developed by the Los Angeles urban planner James Rojas as a way to take planning out of offices and into communities.[30] Given its inherent playfulness, it can be used even with very young children such as preschoolers, but it also taps into the creative "inner child" in adults. Because it requires no special expertise, it levels the playing field for participants from all backgrounds, including immigrants from different cultures and those with low literacy levels.

---

30. See a video and publications by James Rojas at: Growing Up Boulder. "City as Play." www.growingupboulder.org /city-as-play.html. (Retrieved September 24, 2017). See also Bartosh, Sarah, and Victoria Derr. "The power of play in planning with immigrants." European Network of Child Friendly Cities. http://www.childinthecity.org/2016/02/18 /the-power-of-play-in-planning-with-refugees/. (Retrieved September 24, 2017).

Box 5.21. **Using City as Play to Invite Intergenerational Ideas for a Mobile Home Park**

When the City of Boulder, Colorado, was exploring options to upgrade mobile home parks into secure, safe, affordable, and energy-efficient housing options without displacing residents, they asked the Trestle Strategy Group, a community-building consulting firm, to lead an extended community engagement process with residents at Ponderosa Mobile Home Park in north Boulder. After gaining the trust of this community, where older Anglo residents and young Latino families live side-by-side in 68 trailers, Trestle introduced City as Play to gather ideas for redevelopment.

About 60 people of all ages, men and women, girls and boys, gathered around tables full of colorful materials in an outdoor space on the site (Figure 5.30). Several city councilors joined in—evidence of the long road that the city had traveled with Trestle to convince this community that it was a valued partner in redevelopment planning. Instructions that everyone could easily follow were written on a poster, and people spontaneously broke into table groups, with some children forming a table of their own and others making additions and suggestions as the adults worked (Figure 5.31). There was a high level of engagement as people at each table explained their ideas and answered questions, and many good ideas were generated that were integrated into the city plan for the site. The process was recorded with film and photography.

People put careful thought into where to lay new infrastructure and pathways. All ages wanted connection to nature through trees and gardens. They also agreed on a shared laundry facility and play spaces for the children. As they worked together, they realized that the outdoor space that they were sharing could be turned into a common area for community activities. In addition to

these general recommendations, people made many specific design suggestions. The activity formed a significant step forward in the evolving partnership between the residents and the city and helped build resident leadership.

Figure 5.30. Residents of Ponderosa Mobile Home Park engaged in City as Play in an open space among their homes. Photo credit: Danica Powell, Trestle Strategy Group

Figure 5.31. Residents shared ideas across generations for their vision of the redeveloped site. Photo credit: Danica Powell, Trestle Strategy Group

City as Play can be part of public meetings, using trained facilitators. It can also be taken where people are to gather ideas from people who are unlikely to ever attend a public meeting. Rojas, for example, has conducted impromptu workshops on a portable table outside convenience stores in immigrant neighborhoods, engaging people as they come and go.

Age. 3 and up

Time to Complete. 45–60 minutes

Materials. As suggested in the model making directions above, have many objects available, but focus now on found objects in a variety of shapes and bright colors. Although you may include some blocks and cubes, Rojas contends that colorful round objects—such as hair curlers, Mardi Gras beads, and plastic Easter eggs—encourage people to "think outside the box" and design more creatively.

Method—Making the Model

- Briefly introduce the activity and emphasize that all ideas are welcome, no matter how inventive they may seem. Let participants know that the purpose of City as Play is to quickly generate design ideas, and there is no right or wrong idea. Their models will be preserved in photographs, but after their model is completed, all materials will go back in the box for re-use on other occasions.[31]

- Give a prompt question: e.g., "What is a favorite place?" "What would a fun and adventurous playground look like? How would you use it?"

- To streamline the time required for synthesizing ideas and reporting out at the end, you may want to divide participants into groups of four or five.

- Pass out a sheet of construction paper to each person to use as a model base. Each person should design her own model, or if you want to create one large shared model, give people a section to work on.

- Spread all the model materials on the table, or if you are working outdoors or on the floor, on a canvas or fabric sheet.

- Give people 15–20 minutes to select objects and incorporate them into their model.

Method—Recording the models

- While people work, have note-takers from the facilitation team write down the ideas expressed. We suggest two people recording: one taking notes in a notebook, and another writing ideas and recurring themes and design elements on a large sheet of paper on the wall. The process is fast-moving, so recording enables more ideas to be preserved.

- Have a photographer take a picture of each completed model.

Sharing with community members and decision-makers

Participants may share in small groups or with the group as a whole. Ask each child to first consider the most important idea that he or she wants to contribute and then take 30–60 seconds to share it verbally and identify this model element. If the audience has one or two quick questions, allow time for this too. At the same time, recorders can check their lists against the children's public descriptions to make sure they have captured all the main ideas.

Synthesis

- If there is time, ask each small group to create a "best of the table" model together that combines particularly original or attractive ideas from each person. Give

---

31. This method is intended to be ephemeral, and so children should not glue or affix any items.

each group one minute to share it with everyone else.

The note-takers share back the main ideas that they have recorded and check whether their lists appear accurate. Have the main ideas been included in the "best of" model? Are there other important ideas to add? Do participants have any concluding thoughts or observations?

Role Plays, Drama, and Puppet Shows

Role plays, drama, and puppet shows can serve many aims. They can enable young people to try out the perspective and voices of other people and even elements of the environment. They can create open contexts for the free generation of ideas. They can provide a safe medium in which characters explore sensitive topics and express feelings that a child might be too shy to claim as his or her own. Without necessarily naming specific people, they can expose problems in a community and challenge authority, often with doses of humor and fun that make it easier for the message to be communicated. They can build collective identity and strengthen community bonds through the process of creating shows, enacting them with an audience, and the ensuing discussions and community problem-solving that performances invite.[32]

Whereas role plays can be impromptu, with participants assuming the position of real people or imaginary characters and improvising scenarios together, with little need for costumes or props, drama usually involves more polished productions. But the line between these art forms is not rigid. Actors often try out new perspectives through improvisational role playing in preparation for a dramatic production. Role playing also can involve background research, a scripted scenario, and props and costumes when young people take the positions of different stakeholders in

an environmental dilemma. Puppetry, as well, can range from improvised stories with simple cutouts or sock puppets to elaborate staged performances. Depending on how ambitious an outcome you envision, you may be comfortable facilitating these approaches without any training in theater, or you may want to bring in outside artists who know how to work in participatory ways.

Many cultures have traditions of puppetry and street theater that children can draw upon, such as shadow puppets across Asia, the Punch and Judy shows of England, and street plays enacted during carnivals and festivals. The contemporary world of mass media films, television shows, online entertainment, and comic books is full of plots and characters that young people can adapt to their own purposes. Online games enable young people to create characters and adopt avatars, offering new opportunities to play out roles and create collective stories. In contemporary theater, various approaches have developed to bring performances into public places like schools, streets, plazas, and prisons, with professional actors and directors working with local people to research, write, and perform plays that increase awareness about issues of local concern and encourage collective problem-solving.[33] All of these approaches can be applied to dramatize environmental issues, explore community responses, and suggest steps forward.

Given the varying levels of formality and different amounts of time that can be invested in any of these methods, there is no single prescription for how any one of these methods should be applied. Instead, this section offers a few examples of the variety that is possible. What is most important is to follow principles of authentic participatory practice:[34]

---

32. Driskell, *Creating Better Cities with Children and Youth*, 124-126.

33. Jan Cohen-Cruz, *Engaging Performances* (London: Routledge, 2010); Julie McCarthy with Karla Galvão, *Enacting Participatory Development: Theatre-Based Techniques* (London: Earthscan Publications, 2004).

34. This list builds upon David Driskell's suggestions for maximizing young people's participation in dramatic methods in *Creating Better Cities with Children and Youth*, 125.

- Explore environmental topics that are important to the young people involved and their community.

- Take time to listen and learn along with participants. Why is this topic important? What do young people know about it? What are their feelings about it? Does it affect different groups in the community in different ways?

- Discuss the purpose of the role play, drama, or puppet show, whether they want to enact it just among themselves, of if they want to share it with an audience, and in this case, who this audience should be.

- Does time need to be invested in background research? Are there local experts who should be consulted to understand the history of this topic or why different stakeholders in the community respond in different ways?

- Let young people propose the roles they want to play and how they want to present themselves. Let it be an occasion for lots of fun and free-wheeling suggestions.

- Respect young people's boundaries. Don't force anyone to perform in public who does not want to—but value everyone's contributions and create conditions where even shy children can feel comfortable and build self-confidence. Children who are initially hesitant may discover that they can act, sing, and dance as well as their peers. If a child wants to remain private, there are many other ways to get involved such as script-writing, costuming, set design and construction, and advertising.

- Provide time for feedback and discussion at each stage in the process. How do young people feel about what they have created so far? Does anyone have suggestions for adjustments or new additions?

- When participants perform, take time to engage with the audience. The young people have just presented an environmental story, and perhaps they have presented a future they fear, or a future they hope to create with others, and their suggestions for how to get there. How do members of the audience respond? Do they have suggestions of their own? Can they help the young actors realize their ideas? Ideally, the performance will lead to commitments for follow-up actions by the community.

- Evaluate the experience with participants. What was most successful? If they have additional performances planned, is there anything they would change?

Be mindful of the ethical mandate of protecting young people from harm (Chapter 3). If young people are dramatizing environmental events that expose negligence by local officials or a practice that serves powerful elite in the community at the expense of other groups and local ecosystems, discuss how much they can safely reveal in public. It might be useful at this point to bring in trusted members of the community who can provide advice about how to share this information without putting participants at risk.

Role Plays

Personscape.© When Nilda Cosco and Robin Moore wanted to understand how the district of Boca-Barracas in Buenos Aires functioned for its children, one of many methods that they used was the role play, "Personscape."©[35] Children divided into small groups, with each group assuming the role of a different place in their neighborhood. Since then this method has been used in workshops for all ages (Box 5.22).

---

35. Nilda Cosco and Robin Moore, "Our neighbourhood is like that! Cultural richness and childhood identity in Boca-Barracas, Buenos Aires." *Growing Up in an Urbanising World*, ed. Louise Chawla (London: Earthscan Publications, 2002), 35–56. This work is copyrighted by Nilda Cosco and Robin Moore. It is printed here with their express permission.

Box 5.22. A Personscape Workshop©[1]

Nilda Cosco and Robin Moore

Personscape workshops, which conceive of a place as a person, can be done with children ten years old and above, teens, and adults. Participants are invited to think of a city as a live organism, with each individual place within it conditioned by the feelings, values, attitudes, and activities of the people who live there or use the site. A workshop takes two to three hours, depending on the size of the group and age of participants, as they complete the following steps.

1. **Introduction and Organization into Small Groups** (10 minutes)
   Facilitators explain the idea of a personscape, review the agenda, and ask participants to divide into small groups of four or five.

2. **Imaginary Trip to the Past** (30 minutes)
   As a warm-up exercise, participants in each group recall their favorite childhood places, including questions such as: location, size, type, used by, at what age, how often, what for, special names, special qualities? With eyes closed, participants let memories flow (5 minutes), then share with each other (20–25 minutes).

3. **Select a Personscape** (10 minutes)
   Each group chooses a familiar place to interpret as a personscape and chooses a group member to record their ideas. Prompts are listed below but groups are welcome to generate their own ideas.

abandoned site	old railway line
plaza	street market
busy street	park
riverfront	urban farm

dead-end street	playground
schoolyard	vacant lot
garden	playpark
shopping district	wild place

4. **Develop the Personscape's Character** (30 minutes)
   Once a place is selected, each group member imagines that he or she is this place and impersonates it, speaking through its voice. Participants may ask themselves the following questions, and together build up the place history and personality.

   How were you born?

   Who do you consider your parents?

   How old are you?

   What is your name?

   Do you have any nicknames?

   Do you like children?

   Do you like to be alone?

   Do you like visitors?

   Are you polite to people?

   Have you been mistreated?

   Who are your friends?

   Who are your enemies?

   What is your favorite time of day, time of year?

   What is your favorite activity?

5. **Personscape Analysis** (20 minutes)
   Once a personscape is created, it is important for group members to consider the following questions about how well this place functions for children, youth, and their families and what could be done to make it better. This step should result in the identification of particular resources, specific people, and possible action methods.

---

1. This work is copyrighted by Nilda Cosco and Robin Moore. It is printed here with their express permission.

(Box 5.22 continued on the next page)

What do you live for? (your primary purpose)

What kind of shelter are you for children, youth, and families?

What happens to children because of your way of life? What kind of adults do they become?

Can landscape architects, planners, educators, and others help you? How?

6. **Poster** (20 minutes)

Each group creates a poster that communicates the most significant features of their personscape's character and answers the preceding analysis questions.

7. **Poster Presentations and Discussion**
(5 minutes each group—
up to 50 minutes total)
Groups present their posters to the whole who discuss priority actions that would improve how places in their community function for children, youth, and their families.

8. **Wrap-Up Discussion** (10 minutes)
Workshop facilitators lead a closing discussion to highlight main conclusions, identify unresolved issues, and solicit feedback about the session.

9. **Closing** (5 minutes)
Everyone is thanked for their contributions and informed about how they may be used. Participants are encouraged to stay in touch, follow progress, and continue to participate in the future. All are asked to complete the workshop evaluation (then and there on paper—children, or later online—adolescents or adults).

6. **Post-workshop**
Online evaluation transmitted (adolescents or adults).

A Typical Day. Children's experience of their local environment is defined by time as well as movement through space. Therefore it is useful to understand the places they travel through during a typical weekday and weekend schedule. In this exercise, children role play themselves, from the time they get up in the morning, to traveling to school, working and playing in school, traveling home, working or playing after school, to evening activities until they go to bed at night. They can make simple signs that identify each place they move through and hold them up to signify each new setting. When they travel, attend school, play or work together, they can act out these parts of the day together. Do the same for a day on the weekend. (This activity can follow interviews to create daily activity schedules as described in Chapter 6).

Drama

Dramatic productions can be entirely planned, scripted, and enacted by youth, with youth composing or selecting the music, making the costumes, and building the sets.[36] In this case, adults just play a facilitating role and enjoy and celebrate the results. These dramas can be contained within workshops that enable youth to explore material theatrically without the goal of a public performance, or they can be planned and performed to increase others' awareness and action in response

36. Beth Osnes, *Performance for Resilience: Engaging Youth on Energy and Climate through Music, Movement, and Theatre.* (Cham, Switzerland: Springer, 2017); Bethany Nelson. "'I made myself': Playmaking as a pedagogy of change with urban youth." *RiDE: The Journal of Applied Theatre and Performance* 16, no. 2 (2011): 157–172; Kathleen Gallagher, Rebecca Starkman, and Rachel Rhoades. "Performing counter-narratives and mining creative resilience: using applied theatre to theorize notions of youth resilience." *Journal of Youth Studies* 20, no. 2 (2017): 216–233.

to environmental issues that affect young people's lives.[37] In either case, adults can contribute by helping young people learn the many skills that a theater production requires.

Twentieth and twenty-first century traditions like applied theater, community-based theater, and theater of the oppressed bring actors, musicians, dancers and directors together with communities in more collaborative roles

to co-create performances, although the goal of enabling a community to explore and articulate its own social and environmental issues remains primary.[38] While the purpose is often to inspire collective problem-solving, it can be as simple as increasing understanding and appreciation of different groups in the community and valuing local cultures and traditions. The musical *Shine* features such a collaboration between professional artists, young people, and in this case climate scientists, around the theme of climate change and community resilience (Box 5.23).

---

37. For examples of theater workshops with young people in post-Katrina New Orleans and a brief guide to workshop processes, see Jan Cohen-Cruz's chapter on "Gathering assets" in her book *Engaging Performance: Theatre as Call and Response* (Abingdon: Routledge, 2010), 111–133.

38. Cohen-Cruz, *Engaging Performance*.

Box 5.23. *Shine*: Young People Perform for Urban Resilience

Shine is a play co-created by Beth Osnes, a theater professor at the University of Colorado Boulder, performing artists in music and dance, climate scientists, and local youth in seven cities where it toured. It presents young people as resources who can contribute to their community's resilience: its capacity to survive and even thrive despite social stresses and environmental shocks such as climate change and extreme weather events. It combines information from climate-change experts with community-based solutions proposed by youth.

Act One and the play's concluding scene consist of dialogue, song, and dance scripted by Beth Osnes in collaboration with a professional song writer, musician, and choreographer, with climate scientists serving as advisors. About a dozen older children and adolescents enacted the performance in each city where the play has toured. Two teens play the leading roles of Sol (the sun) and Foss (fossil fuel) while other actors are costumed as plants and animals who portray 300 million years of geological history as the sun's energy is captured by plants and stored in the earth's reserves of coal, oil, and natural gas. They weave a fabric that represents their

Figure 5.32. Youth as ancient plants and animals and the Sun in a performance of *Shine* for scientists and the general public at the National Center for Atmospheric Research in Boulder, Colorado in June of 2015. Photo credit: Conner James Callahan

interdependent community. In the end, as the industrial revolution begins humanity's accelerating consumption of fossil fuels, Foss and his team tear through this fabric. As young people rehearse this act, they learn climate science and how human history has brought us to our current dependence on fossil fuels that is impacting the global climate. The act ends with the questions, "What story do we want to tell for our city? How

(Box 5.23 continued on the next page)

(Box 5.23 continued)

do we want to get from this point in history to a resilient future?"

Act Two is authored by local youth, who develop ideas to address climate change and their city's resilience challenges. In small groups, they present a series of skits that show people taking a variety of actions. In the end, the whole cast sings and dances the play's theme song, "Shine," that celebrates what has been accomplished. The play as a whole takes about 30 minutes.

Shine is an example of applied theater that brings professional artists together with community members to generate ideas to address local problems—solutions infused with imagination and humor as well as serious intent. Young people "shine" at doing this. The process is as valuable as the finished product, from initial steps to identify local advocates for resilience planning who agree to host the performance, through action plans to implement the young people's ideas.

The play's director, Beth Osnes, and university theater students begin a few days in advance of the performance by rehearsing with the teen actors who will speak the roles of Sol and Foss.

The songs and music are prerecorded for the cast to sing along and dance. In one intense day, the whole cast gathers in the morning to learn about the play's purpose, do ice-breaking exercises, make simple props, and rehearse Act One. They share lunch with local climate scientists or activists, which gives them an opportunity to discuss their ideas for strengthening their city's resilience in the face of climate change. After lunch, the cast breaks into groups to create several two-minute skits for Act Two that show people taking action, facilitated by adults who ask questions to help them develop their thinking. Each group also writes down its suggestions and they seal them together in an envelope. As the play ends, the cast presents the envelope to city leaders in the audience, asking them to make plans to carry the ideas forward. The performance ends with a community discussion about the ideas generated and other possibilities.[1]

---

1. Osnes, *Performance for Resilience*; for free lyrics, curriculum guides, costume directions, and videos that show the choreography of each scene of *Shine*, see http://www.insidethegreenhouse.org/shine/.

Box 5.24. Performance Art and Co-Design to Facilitate Expressions of the City

with Susan J. Wake

This co-design example was developed following the inspiring performance art project called "Lookout" that was part of the Auckland Fringe Arts Festival in March, 2017. Lookout engaged 16 inner-city schoolchildren, ages 9–10, in an example of "pedagogical theater" that was developed by London artist Andy Fields.[1] The performance has since toured a number of cities globally. Each show is a unique one-on-one con-

versation between one adult theater-goer and one child who joins them to share their views and memories of the city. The title "Lookout" refers to the location of the conversations: somewhere high up in the city, from which participants each look out and reflect on the past, present, and future of the city. Through preparatory workshops the children explored themes intended to provide the adults with a future-focused vision of their city, including natural-disaster conditions that might occur due to climate change. In preparation for Lookout, children workshopped material for two weeks prior to the start of the performances. Performances were partly scripted

---

1. Andy Field, "Lookout Interactive." Andy Field.com. http://andytfield.co.uk/project/lookout/ (Retrieved December 19, 2017).

and delivered via recording to the adult, while standing and "looking out" at Auckland city. Then the adult was joined by a child who gave his or her views and posed questions to the adult, such as "what have you done to improve your city?"

This catalyst performance project also led to an interest in investigating, via design, the ideas of the children about how to improve their city. This occurred as a result of the children's teacher wishing to continue to investigate these ideas with the children after the performances ended. Focus groups that build on the co-design approach (Chapter 8) asked children to recap their experiences of the performance process and suggest urban design ideas that came from this, that they felt would make their city more child-friendly. Their comments and drawings were analyzed and provided strong direction for the design. For example, they wanted their city to be safer, more fun, provide more play opportunities and green space, plus encourage people to be more environmentally friendly. This led to a variety of design drawings, focusing on the streets around the school that the children regularly walked, and the children reviewed these for popularity and suggested design changes. As one example, the children loved the funky rubbish bins that were a part of the design suggestions (Figure 5.33). These bins encouraged recycling and composting in a fun way, but the children wanted teeth added to the landfill bin to make it look more disapproving (Figure 5.34).

Figure 5.33. A rendering of rubbish bins designed in collaboration with children to make the street more fun and cared for. Image credit: Yi Luo

Figure 5.34. Children asked for the landfill bin to have more "teeth" since it is less environmentally friendly than the other disposal bins. Image credit: Yi Luo

Box 5.25. **Exploring an Issue through Puppetry**

In the Phila Impilo program in South Africa, children in long-term hospital care created puppet "friends" that they imagined to be caring companions during their health care experiences. (See Chapter 6 for details about how the puppets were constructed and their role during interviews and conversations.) One aspect of hospital life that evoked strong feelings was clean-up work. What chores should reasonably be done by the children, and what was more appropriately done by nurses? The children came from families where they were used to helping their mothers and other family members, and therefore most of them agreed to taking responsibility for themselves when they were able to, such as picking up after themselves and washing their own dishes and clothes, but some resisted heavier tasks like emptying trash bins. To explore this topic, a few children constructed a cardboard scenery backdrop and enacted a puppet play about chores, with the help of a facilitator. This gave them a way to act out what they could do to help the nurses that they all considered fair (Figure 5.35).

For a profile of the Phila Impilo project, see Chapter 11.

Figure 5.35. Puppetry can help children speak about awkward subjects.
Photo credit: Monde Magida

Puppet Shows

The use of puppets ranges from the unscripted play of young children to some of the most sophisticated forms of art in traditional cultures. Because life-size and larger-than-life puppets capture attention in crowded events, they lend themselves to festivals, carnivals, and political protests. For young children, puppets provide an easy means to explore the roles of animals in their surroundings as well as different people, with a great deal of fun in the process. Because shy children may find it easier to voice their experiences through an alias, such as a puppet friend, it can also be useful to use puppets in interviewing young children about personal topics, enabling children to speak through the puppet rather than directly for themselves. (See Chapter 6, Interview Methods.) Puppets have also been an important means for self-expression, and are used extensively in art therapy and by health workers who use participatory research practices.

6

Interviews, Focus Groups, and Surveys

rticle 13 of the Convention on the Rights of the Child includes the "freedom to seek, receive and impart information and ideas of all kinds . . . either orally, in writing or in print, in the form of art, or through any other media of the child's choice."[2] Interviews, focus groups and surveys are all methods that adults can use to gather information from children and youth, and they are equally methods for young people to gather information from others. We hope that you will apply the methods in this chapter to understand how children use and value their communities as a foundation for participatory design and planning that is sensitive to young people needs. We also offer these tools as a way for young people to carry out their own investigations of the places where they live.

Some of the methods in this chapter are used by professional researchers to gather information from a community for the use of distant decision-makers, such as interviews and surveys to understand what community residents think about an issue or how they act. Conducted with children, research of this kind can enable them to impart important information, for example, their level of mobility or their access to parks. If children simply answer adult questions, however, it is not likely to do much to develop their skills as citizens. Enabling young people to understand how their city works and contribute their ideas and agency is the purpose of this book. Therefore if you use methods in this chapter primarily as a form of consultation, it is important that you report back to your young respondents about

how you shared their information and how it was received and applied.

This chapter focuses on methods that involve asking people direct questions, one-on-one or in group settings:

- Interviews
- Focus groups and other group discussions
- Photo elicitation
- Activity diaries
- Surveys and questionnaires
- Visual preference surveys

Each section describes the method's purpose, gives directions for how to apply it, and offers examples in practice.

These methods range from loosely structured discussions and informal conversations, on one side, to highly structured interviews, surveys and questionnaires on the other. An extended formal community study often proceeds from informal conversations and unstructured interviews, as a way to begin to understand a

1. Jane Goodall, *With Love*, (Vienna, VA: Jane Goodall Institute, 1994), back matter.
2. UNICEF, "Convention on the Rights of the Child." UNICEF.org. http://www.unicef.org/crc. (Retrieved June 30, 2017).

community's history and issues, to semi-structured interviews that focus on selected topics, to structured interviews to find out how many members of the community think or act in certain ways. Whereas it takes considerable time up front to design highly structured tools, the results of less-structured, open-ended approaches may take more time to analyze. Although some of the methods in this chapter may require extensive time and expertise, they can provide essential information for policies, programs, and plans that seek to advance the goal of child-friendly cities. Other methods in this chapter can be applied with little preparation and still yield useful insights.

If you decide to import any of the interview questions or survey measures in this chapter into another language, make sure the translation is culturally appropriate. In her action research with South African children from different tribal groups, Jill Kruger looks for translators who work with children and who know how to find words that will be familiar and comfortable for adults and children alike. She then has this first translation back-translated into the original language, as a way to identify words and phrases that should be re-examined. A third translator reviews these places in the text to determine where changes should be made.[3]

Interviews

Interviews with children to understand how they use and value their environment have a long history. In pioneering work in the city of Hamburg, Germany in the 1920s and early 1930s, the child psychologist Martha Muchow and her students interviewed children as they traced their pathways through their city on maps.[4] Interviews

were also a core method of the urban planners and designers Kevin Lynch and Robin Moore and the geographer Roger Hart as they studied how children used and valued environments in the 1970s and 1980s;[5] and they remain a staple part of ethnographic research with children.[6] They are central to the Mosaic Approach that Alison Clark and Peter Moss developed to hear the views of children under five.[7] Although interviews began as a way for adults to understand children's worlds, children themselves can successfully learn to use interviews to gather information from their families, other children, community members, and experts on the environment.[8] Therefore this section includes both methods for adults to use with children and for children to use with others.

Interviews are generally categorized according to the amount of structure given to the questions:[9]

3. Jill Kruger, personal communication with Louise Chawla, 16 July 2017.

4. Günter Mey and Hartmut Günther, eds., *The Life Space of the Urban Child: Perspectives on Martha Muchow's Classic Study* (New Brunswick, NJ: Transaction Publishers, 2015).

5. Roger Hart, *Children's Experience of Place* (New York: Irvington Publishers, 1979); Kevin Lynch, ed. *Growing Up in Cities.* (Cambridge, MA: MIT Press, 1979); Robin Moore, *Childhood's Domain* (London: Croom Helm, 1986).

6. See, for example: Louise Chawla, ed. *Growing Up in an Urbanising World* (London: Earthscan Publications, 2002); Victoria Derr, "Children's sense of place in northern New Mexico." *Journal of Environmental Psychology* 22, no. 1 (2002): 125–137; Angela Kreutz, *Children and the Environment in an Australian Indigenous Community* (London: Routledge, 2015).

7. Alison Clark, "The mosaic approach and research with young children," in *The Reality of Research with Children and Young People*, ed. V. Lewis, M. Kellett, C. Robinson, S. Fraser and S. Ding. (London: Sage Publications, 2004), 142–161; Alison Clark, "The mosaic approach," in *Steps for Engaging Young Children in Research, Volume 2: The Researcher's Toolkit*, ed. Vicky Johnson, Roger Hart and Jennifer Colwell. (Brighton, UK: Education Research Centre, University of Brighton, 2014), 143–146. Available at https://bernard vanleer.org/publications-reports/steps-engaging-young -children-research-volume-2-researcher-toolkit/. (Retrieved December 5, 2017).

8. Mary Kellett, *How to Develop Children as Researchers* (London: Paul Chapman Publishing, 2005).

9. Robert Wood Johnson Foundation, *Qualitative Research Guidelines Project*, available at www.qualres.org/Home Info-3631.html. (Retrieved December 5, 2017).

- **Structured interviews** consist of precisely worded questions arranged in a fixed order, which are always asked in the same way. They are typically composed of closed questions that require respondents to choose among predetermined answers (such as "yes"or "no"), though they may include open questions (such as "Do you have anything else you want to say about this subject?"). They work well when the goal is to generate quantitative data, such as the percentage of people who believe or act in certain ways. This was the approach teens in Boulder, Colorado, adopted when they interviewed local business owners and managers about their views of teens as customers and employees (Box 6.7).

- **Semi-structured interviews** follow an interview guide that groups similar questions together, but the interviewer can use the guide in different ways with different respondents. It provides for flexibility in the order of the questions and allows follow-up questions, and it gives respondents freedom to introduce unexpected ideas. Semi-structured interviews may include closed questions, but open questions typically form its core. "Expert interviews" often follow this approach, when either a child or adult interviews someone with special expertise, such as a community leader or urban planner. In the Monterey service-learning project featured in Chapter 7 (Box 7.6), students used a semi-structured format for their expert interviews (Box 6.8).

- **Unstructured interviews** have a predetermined focus and goal, but questions can be asked in any order. Questions are typically open-ended, and respondents are free to take a topic into areas that the interviewer may not have anticipated. Given its conversational style, an unstructured interview may extend across multiple sessions. Oral histories fall into this category.

There is also a place for informal conversations when a researcher or community development professional observes a social setting and talks with people there. The interviewer participates, but lets the respondent take the lead. In the Growing Up in Cities project initiated by the urban planner Kevin Lynch, conversations like this were part of the initial phase of "hanging out" at a site, when program leaders were trying to understand how a locality functioned and find partners who shared their goals for creating supportive spaces for children.[10]

Regardless of the type of interview you use, you are likely to move through the following steps.[11] Work through these steps in a team, such as staff from your organization or an advisory group. For advisors, you may want to include project partners, members of the community, young people similar to those you seek to reach, and someone who has experience in designing and conducting interviews.

- Identify the goals and purpose of the interview. What do you want to know? Who has this information? How will you use this information once you have it?

- Determine the means of collecting information. Possibilities include face-to-face interviews, video conferencing, chat rooms, email, recorded videos, and telephone. The means of collecting information that you choose will influence the type of questions you can ask.

- Determine the type of interviews. Will structured, semi-structured, or unstructured interviews best serve your purpose?

- Develop questions. See the description of this process in the following section.

---

10. David Driskell, *Creating Better Cities with Children and Youth: A Practical Manual* (London: Earthscan Publications, 2002), 99–101.
11. A useful guide through key steps is William Gibson and Andrew Brown, *Working with Qualitative Data.* (Thousand Oaks, CA: Sage Publications, 2009).

Box 6.1. **Tips for Successful Interviews**

- Find a setting that is free from distractions, with comfortable places to sit.

- Explain why the information that the participant provides is valuable and how it will be used.

- Get the participant's consent to proceed.

- If you want to use an audio recorder or video camera, get the person's permission for the recording.

- Show that you are listening carefully and that you care about what the person is saying.

- Ask questions slowly and clearly and give the respondent unhurried time to answer.

- Avoid leading questions that imply that you expect a particular answer.

- Ask follow-up questions when someone's answer is unclear or it opens an important line of inquiry.

- If anyone says they would rather not answer a question, accept this choice politely.

- How something is said can be as important as what is said. Note when someone's body language, facial expressions, and mood convey messages.

- Be respectful. Other people's views may be different from yours, but you are there to learn from them, not judge them.

- Put the person at ease by appearing friendly and accepting.

- Avoid interrupting.

- If you need to clarify a point, wait until there is a natural pause.

- Thank your respondents in the end. Ask if they have anything they want to add.

- If you are interviewing adults or older youth, determine how you will introduce yourself and gain consent. If you are interviewing children under 18, have processes in place to gain a parent's consent and the child's informed assent. (See Chapter 3.)

- Pilot the interview. Test the interview with others similar to your target group. Revise it and pilot it again if necessary.

- Conduct the interviews.

- Analyze and present the results. Whereas structured interviews and closed questions lend themselves to quantitative analysis, less-structured interviews and open-ended questions yield general themes about a subject, as well as factual information such as the history of a place. For more detail about generating themes and analyzing information, see Chapter 9.

- Determine recommendations for action.

- Disseminate the results. See Chapter 9 for suggestions for this step.

Some general rules for conducting successful interviews that hold across all categories and ages are listed in Box 6.1.[12]

The following section describes interviews with children conducted by adults. Subsequent sections feature interviews with adults about children's lives, followed by interviews that children and youth design and lead.

---

12. These recommendations are adapted from Driskell, *Creating Better Cities with Children and Youth*; Matthew Kaplan, *Side by Side* (Berkeley, CA: MIG Communications, 1994); Kellett, *How to Develop Children as Researchers*; Perpetua Kirby, *Involving Young Researchers: How to Enable Young People to Design and Conduct Research* (Layerthorpe, UK: York Publishing Services, 1999).

Adults Interviewing Children

In his guide to interviewing children about their community, David Driskell observed that un-structured, semi-structured, and structured interviews have their place at different points in a participatory process.[13] Unstructured interviews and informal conversations are a good way to get to know children, establish rapport early in a project, and begin to learn about local issues. Semi-structured interviews enable you to investigate children's experience in their locality with more depth and detail. Because semi-structured interviews contain open-ended questions and follow-up questions, they take considerable time to conduct and analyze. Therefore they usually involve a small pool of children, who should be carefully chosen to represent the community groups whose lives you want to understand. When Kevin Lynch initiated Growing Up in Cities, he recommended working with 20 children, divided between boys and girls.[14] When his program was revived in the 1990s, interview numbers at most sites ranged from about 20 to 40 children.[15] When people need larger numbers in order to talk about community issues with more authority, they turn to structured interviews and surveys.

Driskell notes that late in a participatory process, it can be useful to return to unstructured interviews or informal conversations to explore issues more deeply.[16] One way to do this, he suggests, is through "walking interviews" or guided tours led by young people (described in Chapter 7). In her research with 89 children aged 10–11 in northern New Mexico, Victoria Derr used this approach.[17] Children began by making maps that they then talked about in interviews. In this process children built rapport and established trust with the interviewer, and general themes in children's experience of their communities became apparent. With a subset of 16 children, Derr went on walking interviews, when the children showed her special places and described their use and importance. By the time the children led walks, they were comfortable with the adult researcher and had developed a sense of ownership over the project in their desire to highlight many diverse places.

Some children may be hesitant to speak freely during interviews, for many reasons. In collectivist cultures that emphasize values of group harmony and conformity rather than individual ideas and achievement, being asked about personal experiences and ideas may put a child in an uncomfortable position.[18] In cultures where children are expected to always show respect and obedience to adults, asking them to critically evaluate environments that adults created and suggest alternatives may violate internalized norms. Some children have little practice articulating their own ideas, and some feel shy speaking with strangers. Some have trouble sitting still for long. For these reasons, many of the variations described in this section represent ways to put children at ease.

The list of "Tips for Successful Interviews" in Box 6.1 applies to interviews with all ages. Additional considerations become important when you work with children (Box 6.2).[19] These points are developed further in the following description of the interview process.

Drafting and piloting the interview instrument

Once you have decided what you need to know, with whom you need to talk, and the type of

13. Driskell, *Creating Better Cities with Children and Youth*, 103–114.

14. Lynch, *Growing Up in Cities*, 85.

15. Chawla, *Growing Up in an Urbanising World*.

16. Driskell, *Creating Better Cities with Children and Youth*, 108.

17. Derr, "Children's sense of place in northern New Mexico."

18. Harry C. Triandis, *New Directions in Social Psychology: Individualism and Collectivism* (Boulder, CO: Westview Press, 1995).

19. These recommendations are adapted from Jo Boyden and Judith Ennew, *Youth in Focus* (Stockholm: Save the Children Sweden, 1997), 83–96; Driskell, *Creating Better Cities with Children and Youth*, 112–113; Kirby, *Involving Young Researchers*.

Box 6.2. Tips for Interviewing Children

- Have young people review questions to ensure that they are written in words that others their age use and understand.

- Consider the value of visual prompts.

- Children often have limited mobility. Schedule the interviews in a place that they can easily reach, where they feel at ease.

- Always sit at the same level as the child.

- Take time to develop trust before beginning interviews.

- The interviewer needs to be fluent in the child's language and sensitive to the child's culture.

- Pair children with interviewers with whom they feel comfortable.

- More than one adult interviewer can be intimidating, so avoid this.

- If a child often uses the environment in the company of a sibling or close friend, consider interviewing them together.

- A shy child may feel more comfortable sharing an interview with a friend.

- Explain confidentiality in simple words that children at each age can understand.

- Make sure children know they are free to decline a question or withdraw from the interview at any time without negative consequences.

- Let children know how the information will be used.

interview that will best serve your purpose, work with others in developing questions. Bring your staff or advisory group together to identify interview topics and brainstorm an initial range of questions. Select questions that are most likely to provide the information you need. Assemble them in a logical order, beginning with straightforward questions such as where young people live and go to school. Group similar ideas. Revise or drop any questions that people find confusing or unclear. For suggested topics and questions to explore young people's relationship with their community, see Boxes 6.3, 6.4, and 6.15.

Have some young people review the draft instrument and check how questions are worded to make sure they reflect the way people their age talk and that they appear relevant to young people's lives. Pilot the draft with young people similar to those you seek to reach, and ask them about their experience and whether any questions could have been asked differently. Video-record the pilot or have someone take notes, and critique it with your project team. Make adjustments.

Make sure the length of the interview is appropriate for the time available and young people's ability to sit still and pay attention. If it is too long, drop questions, divide it into two sessions, or see if you can gather some of the information through other methods.

Format the final instrument so that it is easy to read and follow. Leave enough space for notes after each question. Add instructions as needed. When you need to be able to guarantee confidentiality, use a reference number rather than a child's name on the interview form. See a sample interview in Form 6.1.

Using prompts

In all of the early approaches to interviewing children about their community, the interview focused on some visual prompt that the interviewer and child discussed together, rather than making the person interviewed the center of attention. This made it more like a conversation about something of shared interest and less like a "test" of the child's information. In Martha

Community Places Interview

Name of Person Conducting Interview _____

Reference # for Child Interviewed _____ Date _____

Child's Gender _____ Child's Age _____

A. Introduction: Introduce yourself and explain that you want to learn about places that young people know and use in their community and how they feel about these places. Explain that the interview will take about 30-40 minutes. Review all assent procedures.

B. Interview: Begin by presenting a map of the community. Identify landmarks with the child to make sure he or she can read and understand the map. Then work through the series of prompts below. Use this form to record the basic coordinates and any supporting comments or information to help understand the map notations.

    1. Find your home on this map. Write "my home" on the spot where your home is located.

    2. Find your school on the map. Write "my school" on this location.

    3. In each direction of the map, mark the farthest places where you go on your own or with friends, brothers or sisters. If the place is off the map, draw an arrow toward this location, and write the name of the place.

    4. Which places do you go to most often? How often do you go to each of these places in a week?

Form 6.1. A Sample Community Interview Template.

Muchow's research in Hamburg in the 1920s, the prompt was a map of the child's district and surrounding part of the city, as she asked each child to mark her home, her school, places where she frequently went, and then to "color all streets and public places blue that you know very well, where you play often, that you pass often, and that you can visualize when you close your eyes." When this was done, she asked each child to color the streets red that "you have passed, but you don't know as well."[20] When Roger Hart interviewed children in a Vermont town in the 1970s, he showed them aerial photos of different parts of town and asked each child to tell him "as much as you can about the places on this photograph, and name any places you can."[21] In the Growing Up in Cities program that Kevin Lynch introduced in the 1970s and that was revived in the 1990s, children were interviewed about a drawing or map that they made of "the area where you live."[22] In all cases, the map, drawing, or aerial photographs were the interview focus.

20. Mey and Günther, *The Life Space of the Urban Child*, 66.

21. Hart, *Children's Experience of Place*, 108.
22. Lynch, *Growing Up in Cities*, 89.

Jo Boyden and Judith Ennew also recommend using drawings, cartoons, photographs of community activities or events, or segments of films or videos as prompts for interviews about community issues.[23] They note that pictures of difficult issues, such as a small boy confronted by a bully, can encourage children to talk about topics they might not bring up on their own. It enables them to talk about a problem in a general way rather than exposing their own pain or embarrassment.

Photographs and videos of places can be especially useful for engaging children with disabilities in discussing how places function for them, as the images can show physical details of the environment that affect mobility. In a project in Ontario, Canada, children with physical disabilities took photographs and used GPS devices (Global Positioning System technologies) to generate maps of the places where they traveled. The photographs and maps were then used as prompts for them to discuss mobility issues in interviews. (See Box 6.18 in this chapter and Box 7.17 in Chapter 7.)

Finding the right interviewers

Because successful interviews depend on a comfortable relationship of trust, members of a local organization who already know the children and their families may form the most appropriate interviewers. Or children may learn to interview each other, and after discussing what constitutes a successful interview, decide who has the skills, interest and good rapport with others to do this well. In some cultures, it may only be appropriate for children to be interviewed by someone of the same sex. When there are several interviewers on a team, see whom children gravitate to and with whom they already appear comfortable.

As the following section of this chapter shows, young people as well as adults can master the skill of interviewing. If children or youth are members of your interview team, then you can ask the young people you interview whether they prefer to talk with adults or others their age.[24] No one else is likely to know their peer culture and language as well, or be as well prepared to understand how participants feel in local settings or difficult situations. On the other hand, respondents may be more reluctant to disclose their feelings when the peer interviewer is someone they know and will continue to see, or when the interviewer belongs to a different social group from their own. Young people may also be reluctant to share information that they assume the peer interviewer already knows. In this case, they may explain themselves more fully to outsiders who don't have the same local knowledge.

Practicing interview skills

Moving through questions in a balanced way in the time available, while making respondents feel at ease and unrushed, takes practice. Rehearse an interview with people similar to your intended respondents. Video-record or audio-record it and play it back, making your own observations and inviting others you trust to critique the session, identify its strengths, and recommend how it could be improved. Have novice interviewers accompany a more experienced person a few times, and then have the more experienced person join them for the first few sessions that they lead.

Finding the right setting and schedule

Find a neighborhood setting where children feel comfortable and you can have a quiet, undisturbed place. This could be inside, like an after-school program or youth center, or outside in a corner of a public place. Have comfortable seating that is appropriate to the child's culture, whether it be chairs, benches, cushions, the floor or the ground, where you can be on the same level. If you are at a table, sit side by side—do not have the table between you.

Children in low-income communities may work long hours, doing chores or work for pay,

---

23. Boyden and Ennew, *Children in Focus.*

24. Kirby, *Involving Young Researchers*, 20-22.

with little time for recreation. When you interview working children, they may be taking time away from work to talk with you—which raises the question of compensation. [25] People who know the local culture well may be able to advise you in this case. You may want to pay the equivalent of their lost earnings, but if it gives the children pride to feel that they are helping you, then a small but useful gift may be more appreciated.

Conducting interviews with children

Ages. 3 and up

Materials. interview schedule, printed on paper or on an iPad; if you are recording on paper, a pen or pencil and clipboard or other writing surface; audio recorder or video camera (optional); prompts (optional but recommended).

Time to Complete. Typically 30 minutes to an hour.

In her work with young children under age 5, Clark found that even 3-year-olds could sit through an interview of 14 open-ended questions, if it was about their daily activities, but it was most productive to use a "mosaic" of different methods including "walking interviews" or child-led tours and child-taken photographs.[26] By age 7 or 8, most children can remain engaged in an interview for 45 minutes, and older children and youth even longer. Beyond 45 minutes, if you have more material to cover, schedule breaks for movement, games, and snacks, or schedule more than one session.

As you work through the interview, keep the following points in mind:

- Make sure children are not too hungry or too tired to engage with you. All children may appreciate beginning with juice or a snack.

- Sit at the child's level, whether the child is comfortable in a chair or on the floor.

- Begin by explaining who you are and the purpose of the interview, using simple language.

- Using simple language that the child can understand, ask for the child's consent to be interviewed and explain that anything shared will be kept confidential.

- If you plan to audio-record or video-record the interview, get the child's consent.

- Starting with a drawing, song, or game can help a child feel relaxed and happy to participate.

- Don't rush. Give children time to formulate their thoughts.

- If any question makes a child appear uncomfortable or distressed, never pressure the child to continue. If the child appears able to manage painful emotions and wants to go on, be sympathetic.

- If you suspect children are not telling the truth, don't get angry. Try to understand their reasons.

- Break up a session if you notice signs of restlessness. After taking time for a song, dance, or playful stretching, children may be ready to resume. If not, pick up the rest of the interview on another day.

- Thank children for their participation, and ask them how they experienced the interview. Tell them how the information that they shared will be used.

Even if you recorded an interview, it is a good idea to keep basic notes, using the child's own words as much as possible. This also shows the participant that you find their ideas important. Expand your notes as soon as the interview is over. If you recorded the interview, note where there were points when the child said something that appeared particularly significant, where you might want to play the audio recording or video back to get the child's exact words. Identify when

---

25. Boyden and Ennew, *Children in Focus*, 88-89.
26. Clark, "The mosaic approach and research with young children."

Box 6.3. **Growing Up in Cities Interviews**

When the Growing Up in Cities program that was initially conceived by the urban designer Kevin Lynch in the 1970s was revived in the 1990s, it involved children aged 10–15 in low-income urban areas around the world. Interviews provided a window into young people's lives and how they used and evaluated their environments. An initial one-on-one interview with each child, lasting about an hour, began with basic information about where they lived and went to school. Each child was then asked, "Would you please make a drawing or map of the area around where you live, and show me whatever you know in it." (For more information on eliciting sketch maps, see Chapter 7.) Using the map or drawing as a prompt, children were then asked about places that they knew and used in their area, special places, problem places, and whether they felt a sense of ownership or control over any places. (See Figure 6.1.)

Figure 6.1. In the Growing Up in Cities program, interviewers asked children to talk about maps, drawings, and activity diaries that they created. At a program site in India, a staff member from a local organization interviews a boy about how he uses and experiences his local environment. Photo credit: David Driskell.

For each place that a child used, questions included:

What do you do there?

Do you go there alone or with others?

What do you like or not like there?

What would you change in this place if you could?

Other key questions included:

Of all these places, which are the most special to you or your favorite?

Are there places in your area where you don't like to go? Why don't you like it?

Are there places where you aren't allowed to go? Who forbids you? What are their reasons?

Are there dangerous places in your area? What makes them dangerous?

Are there any places where you feel as if you own them? Which places? Why do you feel as if they are yours?

Are there places where you feel uncomfortable, like an outsider? Which places? Why do you feel like an outsider there?

Because the program was introduced in different countries with diverse cultures, a second interview explored children's daily schedules and family networks—aspects of their lives that affected their use of their locality. It concluded with questions about their perceptions of change and aspirations for the future:

Has this area where you lived changed in your memory?

Has it gotten better or worse? Why?

If you could travel into the future, what do you think this place would be like in ten years?

If you could make changes in your place, what would they be?

Ten years from now, where would you like to live?

When Growing Up in Cities was initiated in the 1970s, and again in the 1990s, interviews provided essential information about children's experiences.[1]

---

1. For a complete guide to the interviews, see Chawla, *Growing Up in an Urbanising World*, 245–247. These questions and others are also shared by Driskell, *Creating Better Cities with Children and Youth*, 110–111.

a question appeared especially meaningful for a child, or when a child appeared uncertain about a question or uncomfortable. Add your reflections.

Box 6.4. Children's Views about Friendly Places

When Samira Ramezani and Ismail Said wanted to understand children's feelings for public places in a rapidly modernizing district of Shiraz, Iran, they walked through the district during summer holidays and asked children they met if they would be willing to participate in an interview.[1] In this way they conducted 106 interviews with boys and girls ages 6 to 12. Using the six dimensions of child-friendly places that Sudeshna Chatterjee derived from her research with children,[2] they asked each child to nominate one place in the district under each category:

- a place that you respect and care for
- a place with which you have meaningful exchanges
- a place that you learn from
- a place that you consider your own territory, that you can create and control
- a secret place
- a place where you can freely express yourself

Many places that children nominated fell into more than one category. The interviews showed the value of small places in children's home precincts as well as public parks with nature and diverse activity settings.

---

1. Samira Ramezani and Ismail Said, "Children's nominations of friendly places in an urban neighbourhood in Shiraz, Iran." *Children's Geographies* 11, no. 1 (2013): 7–27.
2. Sudeshna Chatterjee, "Children's friendship with place." *Children, Youth and Environments* 15, no.1 (2005): 1–26.

Variation: Interviews with Puppets

Puppets can make an engaging medium for children to speak through. Young children are likely to be familiar with expressing themselves this way, which can be playful and serious at the same time. It shifts attention from the child to the puppet, which can be liberating for a shy child or in cultures where children are expected to be seen but not heard. The puppets can be as simple as a cut-out glued to a Popsicle stick, or a set of plastic "eyes" sewn on a sock. Given time and resources, identifying and constructing the puppet characters can be an extended activity.

Puppets can invite children to project themselves into someone different from themselves to imagine how the environment appears from this perspective, for example, how a child who works on the street experiences the street, or how a child in a wheelchair navigates a public plaza. In this case, puppets lend themselves to drama and role play (Chapter 5). When the goal is to gather information about a child's personal experience of the environment, puppets should be similar to the child, or children should be invited to create their own alias. (See Box 6.5: Puppet Friends.)

Adults Interviewing Other Adults about Children

When Kevin Lynch initiated the Growing Up in Cities program, core methods included interviews with city officials whose decisions directly affected the quality of children's environments, such as urban planners and designers, engineers, park managers, and political leaders.[27] The interviews served two functions: gathering information about how decisions were made, and discussing connections between children's needs and urban policies. Ever since Growing Up Boulder was created as a variation of the Growing Up in Cities program, conversations with city staff have been an essential starting point for each

---

27. Lynch, *Growing Up in Cities*, 55-56, 77-78, 85, 104.

Box 6.5. **Puppet Friends**

The Phila Impilo! project in South Africa works with children in long-term care in hospitals and other care settings. It seeks to understand children's hopes and fears in these settings and sources of distress and resilience, sensitive subjects that children may not feel comfortable revealing. Rather than asking these children to talk about themselves directly, each child was given an opportunity to create a puppet "friend" to talk through. Colorful socks, buttons, and plastic eyes were spread on a table to choose from, and facilitators helped the children sew on the buttons and glue the adhesive eyes on top. The children were asked to name their puppets, and the discussions that followed showed how strongly the children felt about their new friends. As they acted out conversations with their puppets, they were able to confide their thoughts and feelings about hospital experiences, and the puppets

Figure 6.2. By speaking through their puppets, children in the Phila Impilo! project were able to express their experiences in hospitals and other settings for long-term care. Photo credit: Julie Manegold

were able to talk about their owners in caring ways. The children kept their puppets among their personal belongings, and sometimes went to bed with them for comfort.

For a profile of the Phila Impilo program, see Chapter 11.

project. As a rule, if you want your project to result in changes to city programs and places, it is important to talk with key decision-makers during the planning stage and revisit them later to discuss potential responses as young people express their experiences and ideas.[28] (See also the section on "Key Informant Interviews" in Chapter 4.)

If you are working with young children who may not know the names and locations of places in their lives, interviews with parents may also be important. They also provide an opportunity for you to present your project and gain parents' support. Parents can explain reasons for their rules that govern children's use of the environment, and suggest changes in the environment

that would encourage them to give their children more freedom. Because children may tell you about places that they keep secret from their parents, be careful not to share information without a child's permission.

Interviews with parents, other community members, and city leaders about their childhood memories of city life and changes for children since that time can have the effect of rallying support for changes to improve the quality of contemporary children's lives. This has been the result of the play maps collected for four generations in Tokyo, Japan (Box 7.16). Oral histories in Louisville, Kentucky, (Box 5.3) also vividly showed the loss of former community places that once offered children play quality, adventure, and social and environmental learning, as well as the continued significance of other places. Children themselves may become expert collectors of oral histories, as the following section shows.

28. Louise Chawla, Natasha Blanchet-Cohen, Nilda Cosco, David Driskell, Jill Kruger, Karen Malone, Robin Moore and Barry Percy-Smith, "Don't just listen—Do something!" *Children, Youth and Environments* 15, no. 2 (2005): 53–88.

Children and Youth Interviewing Adults and Other Young People

Over and over again, we have seen that when young people are asked to think about the design of public spaces, they consider the needs of other groups in addition to themselves. By interviewing community adults, they can open dialogues about shared values, potential conflicts, and how different generations can respect each other's needs and contributions to city life. This can be a powerful way for young people to understand that different people can have very different ideas about the same place. Through interviews with city leaders and decision makers, they can gather information about current policies, how their own ideas are viewed, how decisions are made, and potential partners to help them advance their ideas. When they interview other young people their age, they bring an insider's understanding of their peer culture and local environment.

All of the considerations for adults interviewing young people, reviewed in the preceding section, also apply to young people interviewing others their age. Young people too should work in a team to determine the information that they need to collect and with whom they need to talk, brainstorm questions, create a draft instrument, plan how they will introduce themselves and record sessions, pilot the draft instrument and make revisions, and find a comfortable setting that will put their respondents at ease.

Like adults, young people need training and practice to develop their interview skills. They may need help developing initial questions. What do they know about this topic? What are their own views? What do they need to learn? Who can best provide this information? What type of interview will serve them best? Mary Kellett recommends passing out transcripts of structured, semi-structured, and unstructured interviews for young people to read and discuss, where they can see how different types of questions are used.[29]

They may also watch films of different types of interviews and practice different ways of wording questions on each other. Practice sessions should be video-recorded or audio-recorded and played back so that young people can hear what worked well and what they would do differently in the future.

Young people may begin by accompanying seasoned interviewers (adults or skilled youth) to observe, listen, and begin to co-interview.[30] Roger Hart noted that carrying equipment like a clipboard and audio recorder is not just practical, it conveys young researchers' credentials and gives them confidence in their role.[31]

Before young people set out, they need to practice courteous ways of introducing themselves, addressing an older person, and showing appreciation in the end. In some cultures, conventions for greeting, parting and asking questions vary depending on a person's age, sex, and social position. Although some young people may be well schooled in these courtesies, it cannot be assumed, especially in this age when many interactions with other people occur through social media rather than face-to-face.

Young people often feel more at ease interviewing adults in pairs or small groups. In this way one person can serve as the recorder while another asks questions or thinks about follow-up questions. Sometimes an adult may also feel more comfortable if they have a companion with them, because being interviewed by a child or adolescent may be a new experience for them and they may not be sure what to expect.

Sometimes one good question is enough for an interview. This was the case in the Great Public Places interview that high school students shared with family members, described in Box 6.6. An interview with family members is a good way for

---

29. Mary Kellett, *How to Develop Children as Researchers.* (London: Paul Chapman Publishers, 2005), 72–73.

30. For more suggestions and activities for training young people as interviewers, see Lea Esterhuizen, *Child Led Data Collection.* (Stockholm: Save the Children Sweden), https://resourcecentre.savethechildren.net/node/5901/pdf/5901.pdf. (Retrieved January 3, 2018).

31. Roger Hart, *Children's Participation.* (London: Earthscan Publications, 1997), 173.

Box 6.6. **Great Public Places Interview**

When Growing Up Boulder initiated youth engagement in a visioning process for the redevelopment of the city's Civic Area, a class of 15- to 16-year-olds in one of the local high schools wanted to focus on the area's cultural history. Students visited the local history museum and learned about the Native Americans and early settlers to the region. In order to understand what gives public spaces vitality and meaning in different cultures, the youth in this socioeconomically and ethnically diverse class were asked to interview a family member about "What made a great public space where you grew up?" Stu-

dents asked this question either by phone or in person, and when possible, they also gathered a picture of this space. Responses varied from Central Park in New York to Mexican plazas, but common themes that emerged were that these places felt safe, many people congregated there, and there were food vendors and natural settings for relaxation. These themes helped young people think about what makes a "great" public space and identify their own vision for a public space that could integrate these themes in the context of Boulder.

young people to begin building their confidence as researchers.

Although young people may initiate, design, and carry out interviews on their own, adult support is still vital. When teens in Boulder, Colorado, for example, wanted to investigate teen-friendly business practices by interviewing local business owners and managers, a doctoral student and a professor from the local university met with them for a series of Saturdays to help them define their goals and develop their interview skills.[32] These advisors also accompanied them on their first few interviews, staying nearby in case they had questions. Another vital piece of support was a letter of introduction from the university professor that the teens carried with them, which explained their project and listed adult sponsors and partners. This helped establish their legitimacy. (See Box 6.7 and Figure 6.4.)

Through expert interviews with urban designers, planners and other professionals, young people can learn about different possibilities for

creating socially and environmentally sustainable cities. Expert interviews can help young people ground their ideas within the frameworks of existing city structures. For example, in Monterey, California, youth interviewed experts to help shape service projects in their community (Box 6.8).

Sometimes face-to-face interviews are not feasible or efficient, and phone interviews, online interviews, or video interviews are required. When Growing Up Boulder involved young people in visioning new uses for a large plot of land that the city acquired, young people wanted to know how their ideas were received and how they affected the city's plans. Given students' schedules and the busy schedules of city staff, it was impractical to get everyone together physically. Instead, young people were video-recorded asking their questions, and the video link was emailed to staff in the city's Department of Community Planning and Sustainability. Staff watched the video when they had time and shared their answers, and then their answers were combined in a department letter that was mailed back to the young participants.

When children interview other children, they may have creative ideas to make it playful,

32. Victoria Derr, Louise Chawla, Mara Mintzer, Debra Flanders Cushing, and Willem van Vliet, "A city for all citizens: Integrating children and youth from marginalized populations into city planning." *Special Issue on Designing Spaces for City Living. Buildings* 3, no. 3(2013): 482–505.

Box 6.7. **Interviews to Assess Teen-Friendly Businesses**

When Growing Up Boulder was just beginning, a youth steering committee identified teen-friendly businesses, public art, and nightlife as issues they wanted to explore. Action groups were formed for each of the three topics (See also Box 6.17). For the Business Action Group, teens were trained in research practices and collaboratively developed an interview protocol to use in the downtown area. They decided on a short, structured interview that included several open-ended questions, such as "How do you feel about high school students coming into your business?" and either "If you do not employ youth under 18, why not?" or "What is your best experience employing a minor?" It also included a sheet for their observations when they entered a store, such as how long they had to wait to be helped and how they were treated. Teens conducted the interviews in small teams of two to three students and developed a video to summarize the findings. The video was shown in a range of settings, including school assemblies and city council. The project resulted in the establishment of a database of teen-friendly businesses and local jobs for teens.

Figure 6.3. Two teens review their notes after interviewing a business owner about teen-friendly practices.
Photo credit: Debra Flanders Cushing.
This image initially appeared in Derr et al., "A city for all citizens."

Figure 6.4. Three teens work as a team to interview the owner of a local business and video-record the session for a short documentary.
Photo credit: Debra Flanders Cushing

Growing Up Boulder A Child- and Youth-Friendly City Initiative

Initiative Partners
University of Colorado -
Children, Youth & Environments:
Willem van Vliet-
Louise Chawla
Debra Flanders Cushing
Mara Mintzer

Boulder Valley School District
Deirdre Pilch
Andre Lanier

City of Boulder
David Driskell
Darcy Johnson

Community Members
Dorothy Rupert
Bodh Saraswat
Supriya Saraswat

Youth
Middle-School and High-School Students of Boulder

Sponsors
CU Outreach Committee
Cynda Collins Arsenault
Moe's Bagels
Breadworks Bakery

Contact
Coordinators
Mara Mintzer and
Debra Flanders Cushing

University of Colorado, CB 314
Boulder, CO 80309-0314 USA
bouldercyfc@gmail.edu
Phone: 303-735-5199
Fax: 303-492-6163
www.cudenver.edu/cye

September 11, 2009

To whom it may concern:

This letter introduces a team of local high-school students, interested in learning more about opportunities and experiences for local youth in downtown Boulder businesses. Through their survey, they intend to highlight practices that can serve as models. We hope that you will take a moment to answer their questions.

The students will present their findings at the Growing Up Boulder kick-off event on Oct. 10. Some background is attached. The website has more information on this new initiative, which is a partnership between the City of Boulder, the University of Colorado, and the Boulder Valley School District, in collaboration with local organizations, aimed at making Boulder a better place to grow up.

We would appreciate it if you could post a flyer for the kick off in your business. If you'd like to know more or want to support Growing Up Boulder, please contact us by email or phone.

Thank you,

Willem van Vliet—
Director
Children, Youth and Environments Center
University of Colorado

Figure 6.5. A letter from an established adult can help provide legitimacy and facilitate positive youth research. Image credit: Growing Up Boulder

---

Box 6.8. **Providing Support for Expert Interviews**

As part of a place-based service learning project, 10 to 11-year-old students in Monterey, California, identified individual projects that they planned and implemented to improve the conditions of their city (Box 7.6). As part of this process, a number of students decided to interview an expert to learn more about their project topic. (Topics included ocean pollution, wildlife protection, and support for the local animal shelter). The teacher helped students develop their interview questions by working with them in the following ways:

- Identifying goals of the project overall

- Brainstorming types of questions that students wanted answered

- Collaboratively generating questions on a one-on-one basis

If the students had more time, they could have generated their own questions first, discussed them with each other, received teacher feedback, and then revised them to arrive at a final set of questions. However, given a short time frame, the collaborative question generation worked well.

The semi-structured interview format meant that students knew the questions they needed to ask in order to develop their projects, while still allowing flexibility so that they could be responsive to the ideas that the expert provided.

Box 6.9. Easy Targets: *Participatory Interviews with Undocumented Youth*

In order to understand the challenges that undocumented youth face in going to college, a team of researchers that included academics, community members, and youth aged 14–18 developed interviews for a neighborhood in western Salt Lake City, Utah where many immigrant and working class families reside. Over two years, the Easy Targets research team conducted interviews with undocumented students and family members to identify barriers to considering college, applying to, or attending college. Interviews were also used to identify a means of addressing these issues. One of the biggest barriers young people faced was their immigration status, along with the feelings of discrimination they experienced and a lack of supportive services. The research team decided to create a documentary so that students would have a "safer space" to speak out (in contrast to speaking in public,

which would have revealed their immigration status in vulnerable settings). While the project sought to influence public policy, it also provided a forum for young people to speak out against the racism and discrimination they experienced in their city and to "speak back" to stereotypes of undocumented immigrants. For young people who experience a marginalized status in their cities, the issue of immigration transcends most aspects of their life. Collectively, the Easy Targets research team chose how to frame their research, and by moving interviews into a documentary film, also to raise awareness about the experiences of undocumented youth in their new home.[1]

---

1. Caitlyn Cahill, "The road less traveled: Transcultural community building." *Transcultural Cities: Border-Crossing and Place-Making*, ed. Jeffrey Hou, (New York: Routledge, 2013), 195-206.

---

such as pretending that they are doing interviews on a radio program (if the local radio likes this idea, this may be an option). When youth in the Growing Up Boulder program worked on drafting a Child and Youth Bill of Rights, they wanted to know what other young people thought these rights should be. They put a chair in front of a blackboard where this question was written, and then each respondent took turns sitting in the chair and giving an answer. This was a way of "playing school" that rapidly collected many suggestions.

Given the ease of filming on mobile phones now, this way of recording interviews is easier than before, and it lends itself to sharing results with community groups. When youth in Harlem, New York, explored the impact of gentrification on their community, they asked a number of residents about this topic, video-recorded them, and turned responses into a short documentary that evoked animated discussions when it was

shared.[33] In Salt Lake City, Utah, a research team that included youth created a documentary that enabled undocumented youth to speak without jeopardizing their vulnerable status (Box 6.9). (For more information on participatory videos, see Chapter 5.)

When young people create interviews together, they should review results together. To make analysis easier, they may want to divide it into parts, working on different tasks in small groups based on their interests.[34] Armed with results, they will be ready to discuss explanations and recommendations, and at this point in the process, it is a good idea to bring in other people. What do the interview respondents think about the results and preliminary interpretations and recommendations? Is there further information

---

33. David Driskell, "Growing Up in NYC: Reflections on Two Summers of Action Research." *Children, Youth and Environments* 17, no. 2 (2007): 472-783.

34. Kirby, *Involving Young Researchers*, 101-103

that could help explain results? Does a draft report reflect the views of everyone consulted? Who needs to hear the interview results? Which recommendations appear most achievable? Who could help carry recommendations forward? These are questions that invite discussions with larger circles of young people, project partners, and community members.

Reminiscence Interviews

Older residents are history carriers whereas young people will inhabit a distant future. To create livable and sustainable cities, the wisdom and vision of the full age spectrum is required. In his guide to intergenerational design and planning, Matt Kaplan suggests that young people work in small groups to interview senior residents in their community.[35] He recommends that they begin by developing a timeline that goes back 100 years, broken into five-year increments, on which they mark major events like wars, economic booms and busts, political milestones in their nation's history, and social movements. Senior adults and young interviewers begin by placing their birth dates on the timeline, and then the seniors may add additional events. If people want to take this activity further, both young and old participants can bring in photos of themselves and their families and memorabilia from different periods to place on the timeline or display in an exhibit.

With this historical context, young people are ready to ask the seniors about their lives: where they were born, their childhood families, childhood chores, school life, out-of-school work and recreation, city institutions that they found important, their professions, their families as adults, and their concerns and aspirations for their community. Details about daily life like clothes, food, music, and media are also fun to explore. Small groups of seniors can ask the young people similar questions, including,

"How do you think life will be for you when you get to be my age?"

Focus Groups and Other Group Discussions

Group discussions are a core tool for participatory planning and design. Participatory projects need to reflect the experiences and aspirations of young people and other community groups, and one of the best ways to understand a group's perspective is to engage in discussions with representative members. It is also a way to understand how much agreement there is within a group and how the views of one group compare with those of another.

This section presents a variety of ways of structuring group discussions. Discussions can be used to guide decision-making, assess a policy or service[36] (Figure 6.6), or generate design ideas for a new space (as in the co-design facilitation described in Chapter 8 in Box 8.1). They can be helpful at the start of a project, to generate ideas or interests that young people have (Figure 6.7), comment on design concepts or other proposals midway through a project (Box 6.10), plan a course of action (Figure 6.6), or evaluate a project as it draws to a close (Chapter 10). They can also be used to interpret data such as results from interviews or questionnaires. In some projects, they can be used as a primary method of engagement, as in the example of the Junior Rangers who participated in photo-framing and a focus group to generate and share ideas for open space planning in the City of Boulder (Chapters 5 and 11). Group discussions enable young people to share and build on each other's ideas.

---

35. Kaplan, *Side by Side.*

36. Anne-Emmanuel Ambresin, Kristina Bennett, George C. Patton, Lena A. Sanci, and Susan M. Sawyer, "Assessment of youth-friendly health care: a systematic review of indicators drawn from young people's perspectives". *Journal of Adolescent Health*, 52, no. 6 (2013): 670–681.

Figure 6.6. A middle school focus group discusses ways to change policy so that they can have more free time during lunch. The image illustrates some focus group principles: a group of five students, with a facilitator and recorder, in a comfortable setting within the school. Photo credit: Lynn M. Lickteig

Focus Groups

As the name implies, focus groups are a method for discussion *focused* on a particular topic among a *group* of similar people.[37] They are a form of interviewing that brings together groups of people with some similarity, such as similar ages, gender, neighborhood of residence, or interests, and asks them to share their perspectives as a group. Boyden and Ennew define a focus group as "a purposeful, facilitated discussion between a group of respondents with similar characteristics, within a fixed time frame, focus-ing on a limited number of questions."[38] Focus group members usually meet once, though they can come together a few times.

The role of the moderator is critical. She sets up a framework for discussion, establishes ground rules, creates an environment in which young people feel comfortable talking freely, and moves the discussion along so that all questions get covered in the allotted time. Instead of asking questions of each person in turn, she introduces a question and then encourages people to talk to each other, exchange views, comment on each other's experiences and perspectives, and ask related questions that engage more deeply with the topic. Participants are generating as well as sharing group knowledge about a topic. In the process, their interactions may be as revealing as their words. Focus groups may develop consensus around a theme or clarify divergent viewpoints.

37. Hennink, Monique, Inge Hutter, and Ajay Bailey, *Qualitative Research Methods*. (Thousand Oaks, CA: Sage Publications, 2011). This section also draws on Anna Bagnoli and Andrew Clark, "Focus groups with young people," *Journal of Youth Studies* 13, no. 1 (2010): 101–119; Driskell, *Creating Better Cities with Children and Youth*, 147–152; Boyden and Ennew, *Focus on Youth*, 128–133; Marilyn Hoppe, Elizabeth Wells, Diane Morrison, Mary Gillmore and Anthony Wilsdon, "Using focus groups to discuss sensitive topics with children," *Evaluation Review* 19, no. 1 (1995), 102–114.

38. Boyden and Ennew, *Focus on Youth*, 129.

The role of a recorder is also important. Even if a session is audio-recorded or video-recorded, it is helpful to have someone making a "group memory" by recording main ideas on a flip chart or a large sheet of paper on the wall.[39] (Make sure the paper is two sheets thick so that marker ink won't stain the wall.) If you video-record, you can more easily connect contributions to individual respondents when you go back to make notes on the session.

In order for focus groups to be effective, the setting needs to feel safe and relaxed for the participants to express their views and opinions. Focus groups are usually comprised of five to ten people (Figure 6.6). For younger ages, have four to six participants so that they all have time to express their views without losing interest or getting wiggly.

Ages. 10 and up. It is possible to conduct a short focus group with children aged 8–9. However, this method is more effective with youth, who can stay actively engaged in discussing and listening for longer periods of time.

Materials. Name tags or folded name cards for each participant, markers, flipchart sheets, or large sheets of paper on the wall for recording, a video camera or audio recorder if you want to save the session for later analysis. Children can be asked to choose the name they want to be called, or if confidentiality is important, a nickname. Asking children to decorate and personalize their name card can put them at ease in the beginning.

If the session begins with a prompt, then materials for this purpose also need to be supplied.[40]

Time to Complete. Approximately one-half to one hour to facilitate. Older youth may remain engaged for two hours. Expect to spend at least as much time preparing beforehand and reviewing notes afterwards.

Method

Richard Krueger and Mary Ann Casey offer several suggestions specific to conducting focus groups with young people that we use to frame our discussion of this method:[41]

- Select the right moderator
- Ask age-appropriate questions
- Keep the age range of participants within two years
- Avoid close friends
- Facilitate young people talking to each other rather than to the adult facilitator
- Provide food, a friendly location, and a relaxed and flexible atmosphere
- Ask youth for their assent to participate (See Chapter 3)

Selecting the Right Moderator. Moderators should have a natural interest in eliciting young people's views. They need to relate well to children and youth, listen actively, and enjoy playful conversation. They may be able to build more immediate connections if they share characteristics with participants such as the same ethnicity or community of residence. When issues in a community are contentious, however, there may be an advantage in having an outside moderator who is perceived to be neutral.

Training Moderators. Like interviewers, moderators need training. They should begin by observing skilled moderators in action and then practice by leading a group of volunteers who are the same age as their target group, or practice with staff from their own organization or partner organizations who can role-play challenging participants whom they are likely to encounter—such as the dominating speaker, rude interrupter, shy silent child, or bored bystander. Members

---

39. Driskell, *Creating Better Cities with Children and Youth*, 152.

40. Erminia Colucci, "'Focus groups can be fun.'" *Qualitative Health Research* 17, no. 10 (2007): 1422–1433.

41. Richard A. Krueger and Mary Anne Casey, *Focus Groups: A Practical Guide for Applied Research*. (Thousand Oaks, CA: Sage Publications, 2014).

of the practice group should share their experience and suggestions. Practice sessions should be video-recorded so that the moderator-in-training can play them back and discuss what went well and what could be done better with someone who is already a skilled facilitator.

Finding a Comfortable Location. Places such as schools represent adult-driven decision-making for students. Locations such as an after-school club, youth center, or library room may feel more comfortable for young people. Have comfortable seating and a quiet, well-lit place, free from interruptions. The seating should all be at the same level to express the equality among participants and reflect what children are accustomed to, whether participants sit in chairs, on cushions on the floor, or on the ground.[42] Arrange the seating in a circle so that everyone can make eye contact. If you are in a sterile room, make it inviting by hanging colorful cloth or posters appropriate to the age group you are working with.[43]

Food is a natural icebreaker for any age. Young advisors can suggest what young people their age would like to eat when they gather at the beginning of a group.

Identifying the Purpose and Questions. Topics and questions for the focus group need to be established in advance. Begin by asking the purpose of the focus group: What kinds of information are important? Who will use the information? With others in your organization or an advisory group, brainstorm an initial list of questions. If you want to go into one topic deeply, four or five key questions are enough. If your purpose is to collect information about several topics more superficially, you can have twice this number.

Make sure they are questions that interest young people. This is more likely to be the case

Figure 6.7. In this focus group, youth (ages ten to eleven) brainstormed various impacts on ocean health and discussed them as a group. Then each student used sticky dots to identify the issue they were interested in learning most about as a way to shape future engagement in a school coastal stewardship program. Photo credit: Victoria Derr

if young people have a role in developing the questions or have a voice in reviewing and selecting them. Activity-oriented questions, such as brainstorming, rating, ranking, sorting, and storytelling, can encourage reflection.[44] (See, for example, Figure 6.7 and Box 6.10.) Test questions in advance and ask young people to provide feedback on their relevance, clarity, and age-appropriate wording.

Organize questions in the following order:[45]

- Introduce the *purpose and topic*
- Begin with an "*icebreaker*" game if participants don't already know each other, followed by one or two questions that ask children to share something about themselves and establish rapport. You might ask, for example, "What is your favorite animal?" or "Where is your favorite place to play?" (These questions are rarely analyzed).
- Generate questions that *introduce the topic*. (For example, "What types of places

---

42. Boyden and Ennew, *Youth in Focus*, 130.

43. Hoppe et al., "Using focus groups to discuss sensitive topics with children."

44. Colucci, "Focus groups can be fun."

45. Hennink et al., *Qualitative Research Methods*.

Box 6.10. **Discussion Groups that Respond to Conceptual Designs**

An important stage in the design process is the development of Conceptual Drawings, in which professional designers begin to render ideas about what a space might look like. This is a prime opportunity for feedback in the design process. In Boulder, Colorado, 22 youth (ages 11–14) participated in a Growing Up Boulder discussion group to review concepts for a prominent public space that was part of a larger planning process for the city's Civic Area. Prior to the discussion, youth had visited the site multiple times (see Chapter 7, Box 7.8), and had suggested design ideas of their own through City as Play model-building (see Chapter 5). An independent design firm who was consulting on the project received young people's initial ideas for the site (as well as suggestions from adults in community workshops), and developed a series of four digital drawings, or renderings. The drawings included:

- a nature play area along the creek that ran through the site

- a multi-use space with play areas and open lawn, with a child flying a kite

- an outdoor open-air café primarily with adults sitting

- a farmer's market with a long farm-to-table gathering

The renderings were shared at several public meetings to solicit feedback about both aesthetics and programming. They were highly finished and polished, or of "high fidelity," to show what might appear on the site.

Youth viewed the drawings in class and participated in a focus group to share their perspectives. To facilitate discussion, youth were each given an engagement form, which contained the four images and a series of words for the young people to choose from to describe their feelings about each image. Response options included "happy," "inspired," "excited," "underwhelmed," "unhappy," "confused," and "other" (Figure 6.8). Youth were asked to complete the forms individually and then discuss them in small groups of three to four students. Then each table shared their responses with the whole class. The renderings led to a lively discussion about what youth wanted for the site. They motivated some of the students, who did not think the renderings reflected their ideas well, to work harder so they could communicate their alternative design ideas clearly.

do young people use to socialize in this community?"[46])

- Move into *key questions* that provide in-depth information, that ask young people to explain themselves and examine the topic more deeply.

- Near the end of the session, if parts of the discussion were contradictory or confusing, leave a place for *questions of clarification.*

- Use *closing questions* to wrap up a topic, such as ranking the ideas generated in their order of importance, or summarizing themes that people heard.

Aim for open-ended questions, not binary yes/no questions. Marilyn Hoppe and her colleagues found that concrete questions that children could associate with their experience were catalytic.[47] Rather than asking a theoretical question, such as, "What does it mean to feel safe?"

46. Ibid., 144.

47. Hoppe et al., "Using focus groups to discuss sensitive topics with children."

Responses on the engagement form were compiled by categories to provide city partners and the design firm with quantitative feedback for each image, but it was the discussion that best revealed students' responses to each image. Students spoke to three themes: the aesthetics and style of the digital images themselves (more than the design itself), the programmatic goals that the images suggested, and their own desire to have more inclusive spaces rather than age-segregated functions. Youth also commented on the practicality of some of the designs, asking if it was appropriate to have tables so close to the creek, or who would maintain the elaborate nature play area.

Our reflection as facilitators of the process was that rather than soliciting emotional responses to the images, it was more instructive to ask youth to reflect on details of the proposed design. The group discussion provided this opportunity more than the response sheet.

Figure 6.8. Sample worksheet for focus group feedback, which included renderings, emotions for circling, and written feedback. Image credit: Growing Up Boulder

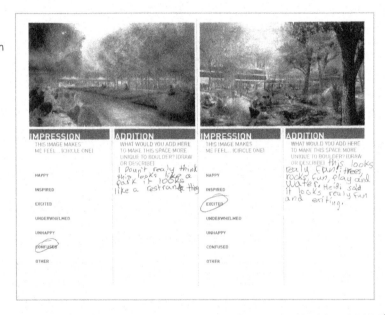

ask instead, "What are some things you do to keep yourself safe?"

During the discussion, have probing questions ready, such as:

Tell me about that.

Does anyone else have an opinion about that?

What do you mean by that?

Give me an example of that.

Anything else?

Could you explain that?

Don't forget the value of nonverbal communication, such as a pause with a look of expectation or a gesture to say more.

Grouping Participants. Because children and youth move through different developmental stages and associated perspectives, focus groups work best with young people of a similar age. Krueger and Casey suggest that participants be no more than two years apart in age.[48] Our experience also supports this. Furthermore, we

---

48. Krueger and Casey, *Focus Groups.*

have found that grades matter, such that mixing middle and high school students (even within two years) has not been effective. Young people who have more in common will find it easier to share ideas and trust each other. Kreuger and Casey also recommend that focus groups should not be comprised of close friends.[49] If friends group together it can not only limit their own thinking, but it can sometimes lead to a feeling of "cliques" within the group that prohibits sharing ideas among the entire group.

By early adolescence (ages 11–14), it may be desirable to conduct focus groups with boys and girls separately.[50] Girls and boys often have different views at this age, and they can feel awkward together. In some cultures, if boys have a tendency to dominate conversations that include girls, separating groups by gender may be helpful even in childhood, and some have found separating groups by gender helpful into early adulthood.[51] At other stages in a participatory project, groups can come together to share the ideas they generated in separate focus groups.

Obtaining Informed Consent. Make it clear to everyone that their participation is voluntary and they may withdraw from the discussion at any time.

Conducting the Focus Group

- If you have an agenda, post it where everyone can see it.[52]

- Begin by introducing yourself and the recorder. Then have participants introduce themselves, using their given names, or nicknames for confidentiality.

- Explain the purpose of the discussion and how the information will be used. Give participants time to ask questions.

- Establish ground rules. You can present a set of rules for the group to review, confirm, or modify, or ask participants to define rules. The final list should be posted in the room. It should include the following basics:

  - Respect each person's input.

  - Keep individual input confidential— what individuals say does not leave the room.

  - There are no right or wrong answers.

  - Let everyone have a chance to speak.

  - Avoid interruptions and put-downs.

You can also let people know that if someone is not participating, you will call on them.

- Consider if you will begin with writing. If a discussion takes off in one direction, some participants may feel afraid to express a divergent view. You can begin by passing out cards and giving everyone one to two minutes to write down their answer to the first key question. This gives you a written record of everyone's thinking before the open discussion begins. You can also collect these cards and bring in new perspectives if some people have not shared their views.

- Avoid positive reinforcement, because people are likely to interpret it as reinforcement for that particular answer.

- If someone brings up a topic early (for example, they begin to talk about question #4 during question #2), let them. Then when #4 comes along, pick up their contribution. "You have already talked about … and people said …. Is there anything else people want to say about this?"

- Monitor the group's rhythm. If participants appear to get tired during a long

---

49. Ibid.

50. Ibid.

51. Uracha Chatrakul Na Ayudhya, Janet Smithson, land Susan Lewis. "Focus group methodology in a life course approach–individual accounts within a peer cohort group." *International Journal of Social Research Methodology*, 17, no. 2 (2014): 157–171.

52. This list of recommendations draws on Krueger and Casey, *Focus Groups*.

session, give them a chance to take a break and move around.

- At the end, briefly summarize results and thank everyone for their participation.

Reviewing the Session. As soon as the session is over, review notes with the recorder and fill in gaps. Discuss how the session went and whether new questions arose that should be followed up with another group or through other methods. If you prepare a written summary, consider sharing it with participants as well as others in your partnership.

Focus groups began in the United States, and they represent a Western tradition of free and open discussion without turn-taking. In some cultures this is not the norm. Instead, it may be customary for each person to take their turn in voicing an opinion. In this case, adjust these directions to fit the cultural context.[53]

Other Group Discussions

In addition to focus groups, there are many other interactive ways to elicit young people's ideas in small groups. Many take less time and skill than a formal focus group, and they can serve different stages of a project's progress. At the most informal end are the many conversations that take place as young people plan and carry out methods described in this book, such as planning what to include in a mural or a child-led tour, what to exhibit out of many pictures taken during photo-framing, what to place on a community base map, or what actions to take to improve their environment. Research on the development of young people's civic values and behaviors shows that democratic values are promoted by frequent discussions about local, national, and international issues in a climate of acceptance for diverse views.[54] For this reason,

one of the operating axioms for the Growing Up in Cities program became, "Don't just do something. Talk about it."[55]

Discussions become more formal when they have to be planned and scheduled in advance, but, even then, all that may be required is a topic to discuss and informed and engaged participants. For example, after 9- to 10-year-olds evaluated a commercial street near their school that was targeted for revitalization, they decided on a set of suggestions to make the street more inviting for pedestrians and worked in small groups to develop practical but playful suggestions. On an "expert day," people came from the community and city government. One or two experts met with each small group, such as a landscape architect with the group that was recommending more trees and gardens, and a public artist with the group that wanted murals. After the young people briefly presented their ideas, open discussions followed, with participants asking questions back and forth, students explaining the reasons for their choices, and experts sharing their knowledge. (See Figure 6.9. For more details about this project, see Chapter 8.) Many successful discussions primarily require making time to put the right people together.

A variety of activities can be used to prepare a fertile base for discussions, such as brainstorming, sentence completion, storytelling and free listings (for example, "What is the first word that comes to your mind when I say 'Central Park'?").[56] The "Problem Tree" provides a systematic process for groups to analyze root causes of problems in their community, as a way to identify where they might most successfully concentrate their efforts to leverage change.[57]

53. Boyden and Ennew, *Children in Focus*, 131.

54. Constance A. Flanagan, "Volunteerism, leadership, political socialization, and civic engagement," in *Handbook of*

Adolescent Psychology, ed. R. M. Lerner and L. Steinberg (New York: John Wiley, 2004).

55. Louise Chawla, "Participation as capacity-building for active citizenship," *Les Ateliers de L'Ethique*, 4, no. 1 (2009), 69–76.

56. Colucci, "Focus groups can be fun."

57. Sheila Evans, *PAR Guide: Promoting the Participation, Learning and Action of Young People*. Kingston, Jamaica: United Nations Children's Fund, 2004), 36–38.

Figure 6.9. On "expert day," experts in landscape architecture, public art, public works, and the mobility needs of the elderly visited a classroom to hear students' initial proposals to revitalize a commercial corridor near their school and to discuss how their ideas could be realized. Photo credit: Erika Chavarria

For suggestions for small group discussions that focus on project assessment, see Chapter 10.

Two methods that involve drawing can be used to explore many community themes. "Four Pictures" puts young people in groups of four, and each group begins by dividing a large sheet of paper into four quadrants.[58] Each child takes a quadrant, draws a picture in response to a prompt, and then tells the picture's story. Prompts can be general ("what is good about our neighborhood") or personal ("where I go when I feel sad and want to feel better"). In either case, the activity requires that young people share and compare concrete places and situations. Body Mapping invites young people to draw connections between resources in their community and aspects of their internal world.[59] Each individual lies down on a large sheet of paper and another person draws around their body shape. If young people are studying children's rights, for example, they begin by listing inside their body the rights that they think children should have. On the outside, they write resources in their community that help them realize their rights. When youth in Nairobi, Kenya, embarked on participatory mapping of their settlement, they began with a variation of Body Mapping called personal asset mapping, which asked them to write down all their personal strengths inside the outline of their body, and then, around it, all the local institutions, places, and people that helped them develop their strengths. (For more about this project, see Box 7.18.) What all these activities have in common is that they are productively done in small groups, and they harvest ideas that a group can evaluate and develop in more detail later.

58. Ibid., 22–23.

59. Claire O'Kane and Rita Panicker, "Body mapping," in *Steps for Engaging Young Children in Research, Volume 2: The Researcher's Toolkit*, ed. Vicky Johnson, Roger Hart and Jennifer Colwell (Brighton, UK: Education Research Centre, University of Brighton, 2014), 115–118. Available at https://bernardvanleer.org/publications-reports/steps -engaging-young-children-research-volume-2-researcher -toolkit/. (Retrieved December 8, 2017).

Box 6.11. Youth Creating Disaster Recovery and Resilience Project

The Youth Creating Disaster Recovery and Resilience project is a Canadian-U.S. partnership between the ResiliencebyDesign Research Lab and Colorado State University. The project has used arts-based methods to engage youth in participatory workshops in communities affected by natural disasters. Through a series of workshops, project leaders engaged youth, ages 13–22, in a series of trust- and team-building activities. They employed art as a storytelling method for youth to share their recovery experiences from disasters and to identify ways youth had contributed, or would like to contribute, to recovery. Methods included the Magic Carpet Ride, Visual Explorer, Photostory, Graphic Recording, and Digital Stories. (For instructions for creating Digital Stories, see Chapter 5.)

For the "Magic Carpet Ride," participants stood on a tarp, imagined themselves flying over their community, and attempted to turn the tarp over without anyone falling off. By successfully managing the challenge of flipping the tarp carpet, the youth experienced the ride as a metaphor for the collaborative aspects of disaster recovery.

Facilitators also adapted the photo-elicitation method developed by the Center for Creative Leadership called Visual Explorer. The Visual Explorer method provided participants with a set of 200 photographs designed to elicit discussion about "what it means to be a youth in your community?" Participants were given the question, then they walked around a gallery of photos, choosing those that reflected their perspectives. They then shared their picture selections and reflections, in pairs and then as a larger group.

The Photostory method was employed in a similar fashion to photovoice, in which participants took their own photographs and wrote narratives in response to prompts. The facilitators added Graphic Recording by combining graphic images with phrases and colors that resulted in wall-sized projected murals.

In Canada, facilitators also used stop-motion animation as a kind of digital story. Working with a professional spoken-word artist, youth crafted their personal stories of experiencing disaster and recovery. They used mixed media to develop their stories, for a final product in stop-motion digital animation.[1]

---

1. Sarah Fletcher, Robin S. Cox, Leila Scannell, Cheryl Heykoop, Jennifer Tobin-Gurley, and Lori Peek. "Youth creating disaster recovery and resilience: A multi-site arts based youth engagement research project." *Children, Youth and Environments* 26, no. 1 (2016): 148–163.

Photo-Elicitation

Photo-elicitation uses visual imagery to elicit discussion about a particular topic. It has emerged from a growing field of visual research in the social sciences.[60] The use of photographs can help trigger memory and help build trust and rapport with children. Like photovoice (Chapter 5), it can be a useful tool to facilitate discussion, particularly about topics that may be hard for young people to talk about, such as cultural exclusion or resilience (Boxes 6.9 and 6.11). Topics for photo-elicitation can be determined by a project, such as park planning, but they can also come from young people themselves. In a study to explore youth resilience, researchers asked young people to identify images that could be used for discussion. In this way, the topics to be discussed emerged from the photographs youth selected.[61] More often, topics are selected by adults. While

---

60. Iris Epstein, Bonnie Stevens, Patricia McKeever, and Sylvain Baruchel. "Photo elicitation interview (PEI): Using photos to elicit children's perspectives." *International Journal of Qualitative Methods* 5, no. 3 (2006): 1–11.

61. Linda Liebenberg, Michael Ungar, and Linda Theron. "Using video observation and photo elicitation interviews

photo-elicitation can be used as an interview tool, here we discuss its use to facilitate group discussions, which is its most common application in participatory work with young people. Similar processes can be applied to film-elicitation, when video is used as the prompt.[62]

Ages. 4 and up

Materials. Photographs (or drawings, cartoons, graffiti, or any public image) and display space (a table, a cloth on the ground, a wall)

Time to Complete. Approximately one hour to facilitate, plus time for setting up

Method

- Prior to the start of the activity, set up a space with a variety of images. The pictures may depict a wide range of subjects (such as people, nature, cities, animals) that represent different experiences and that might evoke different types of feelings. Display the images in the space where the discussion will be held. They can all be arranged on a table, or a cloth on the ground, or hung on a wall. Arrange the space so that participants can sit in a circle for discussion, in chairs or on the ground.

- Introduce the activity and its purpose. State your goals for the session.

- Ask the young people to take about five minutes to walk around the room and look for images that reflect their feelings or experience on the topic you are exploring, using a specific prompt that reflects your goals. For example, if you are interested in learning about young people's experience of the city, you might ask, "Think about

what your experience as a young person is like in your city. Walk around and look at the images in the room. Select one that best represents your experience." (If there is time, participants may select two or three, but keep to a small number that allows for discussion.)

- Have participants return to the discussion circle.

- Have young people divide into small groups of three to five people. Ask participant to take turns sharing the photos they chose, explain why they chose each one, and tell what it represents in relation to your question.

- Ask all participants to rejoin the full circle and share with each other what they heard. Sometimes it is easier for people to share what they heard from other youth than to share about themselves. Depending on your purposes, youth can identify common themes that they hear and generate "what next" ideas.

Activity Diaries

Young people's lives unfold in time as well as space. The places where young people go typically depend on the day of the week and the time of the day. Activity diaries are a tool to understand how time and space function together. They can document not only where young people go but when, for how long, with whom, and what they do there. They have been used to understand patterns of place use by children who move independently through their community; but they can equally show when a child's life is constrained to a few places or always under the supervision of adults.

Activity diaries are most useful as the focus of a brief interview about the places that a child moves through on a typical weekday and a day out of school. In the Growing Up in Cit-

to understand obscured processes in the lives of youth resilience." *Childhood* 21, no. 4 (2014): 532–547.
62. Lesley Murray, "Mobile video," in *Steps for Engaging Young Children in Research*, Volume 2, 75–77.

Form 6.2.
A Sample Activity
Diary Template.

Activity Diary

Name of Child Completing Diary _____ Child's Gender _____

Nickname (Pseudonym) for Child _____ Child's Age _____

Reference # for Child _____ Name of Adult Who Helps Complete this Diary _____

Date that this Schedule Records _____ Day of the Week _____

Was there anything special about this day? _____ Yes _____ No

If yes, please briefly write down what made this day special? (For example: "it was my friend's birthday" or "my grandparents visited from out of town.")

To the best of your ability, carefully remember and record below what you did from the time you got up in the morning to the time you went to sleep at night.

Time	What I Did	Where I Did It	With Whom I Did It
6:00 am			
6:30 am			
7:00 am			
7:30 am			
8:00 am			
8:30 am			
9:00 am			
9:30 am			
10:00 am			
10:30 am			

Continue these time blocks on subsequent pages until a typical bedtime for the age of the child.

---

ies program, activity diaries formed one of the main parts of a second interview that focused on understanding how children's use of their community was structured by time and family networks, as children in some sites lived in extended families, so that they moved among the homes of aunts, uncles, and grandparents.[63] Activity diaries show how much time children have outside of school, work, and home routines, when they can freely choose places for recrea-

tion, adventure, or hanging out. They can also illuminate differences in the ways children use time and space depending on whether they are girls or boys, or belong to different social classes.

In societies where children's lives are run by the clock, diaries often take the form shown in Form 6.2, in which a typical day is recorded in half-hour intervals. Depending on how much detail you want, the time intervals can be longer (6:00 a.m., 7:00 a.m. …) or shorter (6:00 a.m., 6:15 a.m., 6:30 a.m. …). If you are collecting schedules for just one weekday or weekend day, make sure it was a typical day. Children should

---

63. Chawla, *Growing Up in an Urbanising World*, 247; Lynch, *Growing Up in Cities*, 20, 90–91.

record their schedules on the evening of the assigned day or one day after.

Tailor the form to your participants' lives. When Angela Kreutz wanted to understand typical days in the lives of the Aboriginal children she worked with in Cherbourg, Australia, she found that it was enough to break the day into three parts: "in the morning," "during the day," and "at night time." She added a fourth column to ask not only where they went, with whom, and what they did, but also how the child was feeling during each activity.[64]

An alternative format is to draw a large clock face with space around it. Children work their way around the clock, labeling their activities beside each hour's interval. They record an inner circle for morning hours and an outer circle for afternoon and evening hours. Another alternative is to draw a linear timeline from morning to evening.

Ages. 8 and up, when children have basic literacy to fill in the forms and a structured sense of time. Younger children can fill in activity diaries with the help of family members.

Time to Complete. 15 to 30 minutes for a child to complete, depending on whether they fill in one form for a typical weekday or two forms for a weekday and a Saturday or Sunday. Approximately the same amount of time for you to review and discuss their diary with them.

Materials. Diary schedules, pencils, writing surface.

Method

Explain the activity and its purpose. Ask young people to recall what they did the day before, or on the recent weekend, if it was a typical day. They should select a day that represents a fairly typical routine.

The diary schedules can be filled out on their own time—but in practice, few children have the discipline to do this. This activity works better if you pass out the schedules for children to fill in as a small group activity, when you are available to help with spelling, prod their memory, or answer questions. Or you can fill out the schedules one-on-one, as an opportunity to talk through a typical day with each child.

If you sense any resistance or embarrassment from a child about disclosing what they did during any part of the day, don't probe. Leave this part of the day vague and move on to the next part of the schedule.

Variation: Aerial Geographic Diaries

When Roger Hart was studying the place experiences of children in a Vermont town, he gave children seven identical aerial photographs of the town as well as seven diary schedules in order to record a week of their summer activities. For each day, from morning to night, each child listed "where I went," "who I went with," and "what I did." Hart met each child each day to help complete the diaries, and then to mark on the map the places that each child visited each day, and to trace the routes that he traveled, using a red pen when he traveled by bike or by foot and a green pen when he traveled by car.[65]

Variation: Sunrise to Sunset

When Sheridan Bartlett and other representatives of Save the Children developed a participatory process for the rebuilding of villages destroyed by the 2004 tsunami in South Asia, they needed to understand local routines in order to plan accommodating physical spaces, and how new spaces might encourage new, more de-

64. Kreutz, *Children and the Environment in an Australian Indigenous Community*, 32–34.

65. Hart, *Children's Experience of Place*, 42.

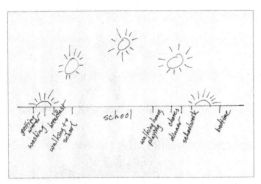

Figure 6.10. A sunrise to sunset timeline that can illustrate the activities of different groups in a village or urban neighborhood. Image credit: Louise Chawla

sirable routines.[66] For this purpose they worked with separate small groups who represented men, women, teenage boys, teenage girls, school-aged boys, school-aged girls, and caregivers for young children. With each group they filled in a timeline of routine activities that followed the path of the sun from sunrise to sunset. (See Figure 6.10.)

As the facilitators worked across each timeline sketching and writing activities, they asked: "Where do you do this?" "Who do you do it with?" "What kind of spaces would make it possible for you to do any of these activities more easily?"

This process led to adjustments in the village plan. Women shared, for example, that after they finished their morning chores they had time to socialize with each other before older children came home from school and it was time to begin preparations for dinner. They said that it would be nice to have a place to relax together where small children could play in their sight. This led the planners to locate several shaded sitting areas beside play spaces for small children.

Surveys and Questionnaires

Surveys are a process for collecting and analyzing information from a group of people.[67] The process includes designing a study, writing questions, selecting a sample of respondents, and collecting and analyzing the data. Surveys are often used to gather information from large, randomized samples in order to draw inferences about a population's attitudes, opinions, knowledge or behaviors. In participatory research, survey results are often purely descriptive because samples are not large enough and not randomly selected, and often not appropriate for statistical analysis. Instead, community surveys commonly rely on convenience samples, such as people in a park or other public space or people attending a public meeting. In some cases, it may be possible to survey everyone in a population of interest, such as all the children in an after-school program or all the residents of a mobile home park. Surveys are used extensively by government agencies and non-governmental organizations to understand communities across the world.

A questionnaire is a set of printed or written questions in a fixed order. It commonly includes instructions for the interviewer, when questions are asked face-to-face, or for respondents who fill out the form independently. It is usually composed of closed questions, such as multiple-choice questions, rating scales, and questions that ask how much people agree or disagree with given statements. Questionnaires can be designed to collect individual data, such as when you ask a child to fill out a sheet of questions about all the places where she has lived and all the schools she has attended, to learn about her environmental history. But frequently, they are used to collect group data. Surveys often use questionnaires, though they can also collect information from observations and interviews.

66. Sheridan Bartlett, *Making Space for Children: Planning for Post-Disaster Reconstruction with Children and Their Families.* (Chennai, India: Save the Children, 2007). Available from cergnyc.org/files/2011/09/Making-space-full-version-11.pdf. (Retrieved December 8, 2017).

67. Johnny Blair, Ronald Czaja and Edward Blair, *Designing Surveys* (Thousand Oaks, CA: Sage Publications, 2013).

These are major distinctions between the words "survey" and "questionnaire" in social research,[68] but in everyday speech the terms are often used interchangeably.

Questionnaires have traditionally been distributed by mail or filled out during phone interviews. Increasingly, they are distributed online or via mobile phones. These new technologies have the advantage that results are compiled instantly. Even if you are working with youth who all have their own computers or mobile phones, you will face the challenge of getting their attention to fill out a questionnaire. You are more likely to get responses if you ask children and youth to fill out questionnaires when they are together with you, or ask partner organizations to collect them during scheduled programs with young people.

If you wish to conduct a systematic survey that can be generalized to a large population, we recommend that you consult with an expert in survey design at a university or research firm. Most of the examples provided here involve local surveys with small samples—which are often most useful for local planning and design. When survey data exist for a city, the data are usually so general that they do not capture variations and details in a specific community. Very commonly, the data are not broken down by sex or age, with data specific to early childhood, school-aged children, and adolescence.[69] Frequently, marginalized communities are not well represented in city survey data—if they are represented at all.

If you want to speak with authority about conditions for children in your project area, consider conducting your own door-to-door survey. This was necessary in the Growing Up in Cities program, for example, to understand family conditions in an informal settlement on the periph- ery of Bangalore, India, and a squatter camp in Johannesburg, South Africa.[70] Household surveys were also an important part of the Safe Community Program in slums in Mumbai and Bhopal, India, featured in Chapter 11; and surveys of children, youth, parents, local authorities, and other service providers form the core part of UNICEF's Child Friendly Cities toolkit to assess the quality of children's living conditions.[71]

Surveys can be useful at successive stages in a project. Early in a participatory process, they can gather data about children's lives and show how young people and adult community members rank the importance of local issues. Mid-way, they can help you gather data for more focused design and planning. Near the end of a project, they are a way to get feedback on proposals for action. Surveys can be used, for example, to:

- Assess the child-friendliness of a community (Box 6.15, Table 6.1)

- Understand how children travel to school and the places they use (Chapter 11: mobility surveys for children and parents in the Designing a Child-Friendly Neighborhood profile)

- Understand young people's perspectives on a particular topic (Boxes 6.14–6.17)

- Understand the accessibility of the city for children of different ages or abilities (Box 6.18)

- Identify safety concerns in the city

- Assess the physical environment itself (Boxes 6.15 and 6.18). (See also Chapter 11 for a site inventory checklist in the Participatory Schoolyard Design profile from Ontario, Canada.)

- Understand whether young people feel heard by city leaders (See Chapter 11:

68. Research Connections. *Child Care and Early Education Research Connections.* The Regents of the University of Michigan. https://www.researchconnections.org. (Retrieved December 27, 2017).

69. Sheridan Bartlett, Roger Hart, David Satterthwaite, Ximena de la Barra and Alfredo Missair, *Cities for Children* (London: Earthscan Publications, 1999).

70. Chawla, *Growing Up in an Urbanising World.*

71. UNICEF, "Child Friendly Cities." UNICEF.org. http://www.childfriendlycities.org. (Retrieved June 28, 2016).

Table 6.1. UNICEF's Child Friendly Cities Initiative and UNESCO's Growing Up in Cities program have both developed frameworks for young people to evaluate their cities, from their own perspectives. This table combines frameworks for evaluation used in both contexts.[1]

Evaluate your City	What Works Well	What Needs More Work
Social Inclusion *We feel welcome in our community*		
Gathering Places *There are places we can meet friends, play sports or games, or "hang out"*		
Freedom to Move About *We can move around our city on our own, and without concerns about safety*		
Access to Nature *There are places where we can see or play with nature*		
Cultural Identity *We can see and learn about the culture and history of people in our community through arts or in public spaces*		
Basic Amenities *We can access basic things like food, water, and go to shops that carry items we need*		*Education*
Health *We can freely exercise and play, we have access to healthy foods and water, we feel supported in our community*		*Digital Equity*

1. Driskell, *Creating Better Cities with Children and Youth*; UNICEF, *Child-Friendly Cities Assessment Toolkit*. UNICEF.org. http://childfriendlycities.org/research/final-toolkit-2011/. (Retrieved June 30, 2017).

the Child Friendly City Assessment in the Great Neighborhoods profile.)

Given the great variability in survey designs, this section focuses on instructions for developing questionnaires, as a key part of most surveys.[72]

72. This section draws on Driskell, *Creating Better Cities with Children and Youth*, 139–146; and Craig A. Mertler, *Action Research: Teachers as Researchers in the Classroom* (Thousand Oaks, CA: Sage Publications, 2008).

Developing a Questionnaire

Ages. 6 and up. While it is not essential, it is helpful if children can read and write in order for fill out a questionnaire. For younger children, questions can be generated using visual icons, or an adult or older child can read out the questions orally.

Materials. Paper or computer for generating the questionnaire, access to a copier or printer to reproduce questionnaires, clipboards or other hard surface if you will be collecting information from the community on foot, pen or pencil.

Time to Complete. Filling out a questionnaire may take only a few minutes, or 20–30 minutes for longer forms. It can take weeks or even longer to develop questions, pre-test and revise them, collect responses, and analyze results, depending on the number of responses you seek.

Method—Questionnaire Purpose

As a group, discuss the reasons for the questionnaire, answering the following questions: What do you want to know about? Who do you want to know this from? What groups of people will you collect information from (what ages, ethnic groups, schools, neighborhoods)? What languages will the questionnaire be in? Will you use words and/or icons? How many people should you collect this information from? Once the questionnaire is written, how will you gather the information? Will you issue it in person (Box 6.15) or through a digital platform or designated station (see Box 6.16)? How will you use this information once you have it?

Method—Question Development

- To begin, brainstorm a range of questions. This can be done in small groups or with one larger group.
- Place similar questions together and select the words and ideas that are most important. You can do this by underlining key words in a color or marking them with a star.
- Write a list of all the questions that the group has agreed upon.
- Clarify the question wording. Good questions follow at least two rules: they are simply worded, and they ask about only one thing at a time (Box 6.12)
- If you are using icons, have young people draw them, or find copyright-free images from the internet.

- Pre-test the questions on representative groups of young people. Orally, or in writing, ask for their feedback and suggestions. Revise.

Some general tips for question development are given in Box 6.13.

Method—Determine How People will Respond

You will need to determine the appropriate types of responses for each question. Questionnaires can use a variety of response formats. These are generally either fixed, in which people choose among a predetermined set of responses, or open-ended, in which people provide responses in their own words.

- **Fixed Response:** You can use words and numbers to represent a range of experiences (e.g., using a scale from "strongly disagree" to "strongly agree" that corresponds to numbers 1 to 5).
- **Fixed Response:** If asking about young people's attitudes or feelings, you can use icons to represent a range of feelings (Form 10.3).
- **Fixed Response:** You can also use Venn diagrams to show relationships between two or more ideas (Box 6.14).
- **Open-ended Response:** You can also ask open-ended questions for which there are no set responses (Box 6.15 and Box 6.16). Open-ended questions are useful when you do not know the types of answers. However, if you choose this method, you should also be prepared to spend more time grouping and analyzing results (see Box 6.16 and Chapter 9).
- **Fixed Response with Open-Ended Comments:** Some questionnaires ask questions with set responses but then provide a comment box. This allows you to both quantify the range of responses to structured questions but also to provide some of the

Box 6.12. **Only one question!**

A common mistake when writing questions is to ask multiple questions at one time. These "double-barreled" questions make it hard for the person answering the question to respond, and it makes it hard for you to know what your results mean. For example:

This question asks more than one thing:

> My community is a great place to play and make friends.

It should be re-phrased as two questions:

> My community is a great place to play.
>
> I am able to make friends in my community.

In the first question, a person who has friends but few good places to play (or vice versa) would find it hard to respond. It will also be hard for you to know if they agree or disagree with only one part or both parts of the statement. The re-phrased questions enable you to learn about one thing at a time.

Box 6.13. **Tips for Question Development**

- Collect needed information only. Keep the questionnaire as short as possible.
- Keep questions as clear and specific as possible. Define terms where this will be helpful.
- Start with easy-to-answer questions that give respondents a chance to feel comfortable.
- Have the questions follow a logical flow, going from general to more specific.
- Group questions on a similar topic together.
- When it is possible, use questions that have already been tested and used in similar contexts.
- In multiple-choice questions, include all possible options, including "don't know," "no opinion" or "not relevant to me."
- Make the questions easy to code for the purposes of analysis
- In general, if you include a few open-ended questions, put them after structured questions.[1]
- If you ask any demographic questions (such as age or gender), do this last.

1. Adapted from Melvin Delgado, *Designs and Methods for Youth-Led Research* (Thousand Oaks, CA: Sage Publications, 2006), 164.

thinking that people have in response to the question.

Method—Assemble the Questionnaire

Once the questions are determined, group them by topic, from the more general to more specific. As a rule, begin with straightforward factual questions and then move on to questions that elicit opinions. Leave open-ended questions to the end. Add an introductory paragraph that explains the survey purpose, and any instructions that respondents will need to know how to complete different sections.

Method—Conduct Training

If the questionnaires are filled out during face-to-face interviews, you may need a team of in-terviewers who can survey different parts of a community at different times of day. Have the team practice so that everyone introduces the survey and fills out questions in the same way, and knows how to put respondents at ease. Anticipate and share questions that respondents ask so that all interviewers can provide similar answers.

Box 6.14. **Using Venn Diagrams to Describe a Sense of Connection**

Child friendly surveys provide a range of information about the qualities and experiences of children's environments. Sometimes it may also be helpful to understand children's sense of connectedness, to a park, to nature, or to a community.

Wes Schultz developed a visual research measure using simple Venn diagrams for individuals to describe their sense of connection with nature. The method provides a scale of connectedness between "nature" and "self," with participants choosing among a range of options, from completely disconnected from nature (with circles completely separated, A) to completely connected (with circles completely overlapping, G). The survey is designed for participants to choose the Venn diagram that most closely aligns with their individual feeling of connection with nature. With younger children, you might offer a simple

explanation that when the circles are completely overlapping this means you feel very close to nature, such that "me and nature are one," whereas when the circles are completely disconnected, you do not feel connected to nature in any way. Or you might adapt the circles to contain simple icons of a person and a tree to represent the same ideas without the need for words. This method has since been applied in a range of contexts, including "me" and "community."

Such a survey instrument could serve as a starting point for dialogue to understand the range of feelings young people associate with a particular place, with nature within their community, or with their community as a whole.[1]

---

1. Wesley P. Schultz, "Inclusion with nature: The psychology of human-nature relations." *Psychology of Sustainable Development*, ed. P. Schmunck and P. Schultz (Springer U.S, 2002), 61–78.

Figure 6.11. "Me and Nature" Venn diagram.
Image credit: Emily Tarantini

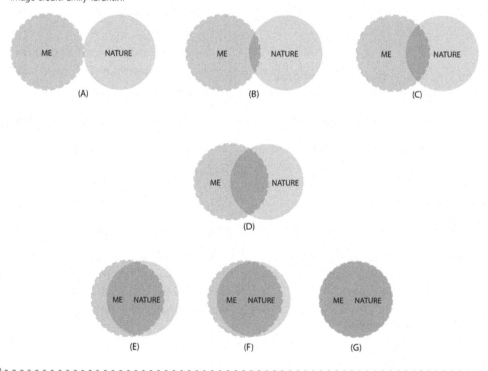

Box 6.15. **Child Friendly Cities Questionnaire for Kindergarten and Fifth Grade**

Approximately 150 children in grades kindergarten and fifth grade (ages 5–6 and 9–10) participated in a neighborhood development project in Dapto, New South Wales, Australia. The process was implemented in two phases: a participatory research phase in which

Figure 6.12. Two versions of this two-page survey were used to interview children in kindergarten and fifth grade. An adult asked children individually about each question and wrote responses on the forms. This survey was used with the fifth graders. Image credit: Karen Malone

University of Wollongong

child friendly asia pacific

Child Survey Number _____

Dapto Public School: How Child-Friendly is My Community
Grade 5 Survey

Name _____ Alias _____ Age _____

Gender _____ Suburb _____

Where were you born? (tick) ____ Australia ____ Other, please specify _____

What are your five favourite places? **Circle** your most favourite.	Are there any places you don't like to go? **Circle** the one you dislike the most.	What are your favorite activites? **Circle** your most favourite.	What are your five **least** favourite actvities? **Circle** your least favourite.
What do you like most about your neighbourhood?	Can you name any places that are especially for children?	Do you play any adult organized activities? (sport, art, music). Make a list and note how often you do these.	Are you allowed to play outside of your garden without an adult? Yes _____ No _____
			If yes, where do you go? Who do you go with? If no, why not?
What do you dislike most about your neighbourhood? (anything unsafe, dangerous)	How do you mostly travel to school? (Circle). With who? Car Walk Ride bike Transport	Do you go to any playgrounds or parks close to your home? Which ones? Who with? What can you do there?	Make a list of any issues for children in your neighbourhood? **Circle** the most significant.

Describe your house and garden, the streets around your house, and the town you live in.

Finish this sentence: I am lucky because . . .

(Box 6.15 continued on the following page)

(Box 6.15 continued)

children contributed their design ideas, and a second phase focused specifically on design. (See Chapter 11 for a detailed case description.) In the first phase, Karen Malone and her team of adult researchers asked survey questions orally during interviews with children. The survey asked children about favorite places, places they liked or disliked in their neighborhood, places especially for children, and places with adult-organized activities (Figure 6.12).[1]

1. Karen Malone, *Designing and Dreaming a Child Friendly Neighborhood for Brooks Reach, Dapto* (University of Western Sydney, Bankstown, NSW, Australia, 2011).

University of Wollongong | child friendly asia pacific

Child Survey Number _____

If you could wish for anything to improve the life of other children, what would it be?

Draw me a picture of your neighbourhood.

Draw me a picure of your dream town.

Box 6.16. **Youth Council Action Groups in Pachuca, Mexico**

Through a participatory action research project, children and adolescents in the city of Pachuca de Soto, in the state of Hidalgo, Mexico, identified priority issues and conducted research with their peers. The research was conducted through five youth councils comprised of four to eight children and adolescents on each council and was facilitated by adult advisors to each group.

The project began with young people identifying issues of concern through drawings (see Chapter 5). These issues included bullying, safety from street violence, and teen pregnancy. After priority issues were selected, youth councils were developed to investigate these issues in more detail. These councils developed a set of survey questions that they could ask other children and youth in their schools and community. Youth councils then solicited input from their peers over a month-long period in which they asked questions in person and also left questionnaires in public spaces and schools for students to respond. For example:

The youth council *Consejo Pamar la Raza* was interested in bullying. They developed a series of questions that they asked 60 adolescents, ages 13 years and older, specifically from the La Raza neighborhood. To conduct their survey, they used the idea of a "gossip column" by placing a notebook in public places with questions for adolescents to answer.

The youth council *Consejo Pamar Villas de Pachuca* was also interested in bullying. They installed a mailbox in their school in order to collect proposals from students about how to reduce bullying in their community. They also made the mailbox available to adults, "because adults also have good ideas." When the mailbox did not result in many proposals, they decided to make a handprint wall in which each student made a painted handprint, along with a suggestion for how to end bullying. This team also made a short video for adolescents about how to prevent bullying and about the links between bullying and addiction.

The youth council *Consejo Pamar Revolución* was interested in teen pregnancy prevention, so they developed ten questions that they asked other young people, aged 9 and up. They also recorded interviews on video. The youth summarized responses in a table that presented gender, age, and responses to each of their questions.

Just as each youth council developed its own questions and research approach, the councils used diverse means to develop recommendations. For example, the youth council that focused on bullying wanted to understand the motives of bullies. By asking, "What causes you to bully others?" and "What do you feel when you bully?" they were able to identify clear proposals for addressing the problem. The youth councils developed a variety of recommendations, including awareness building and a *seguridad entre cuates* (safety between guys) team to provide security on walks to school.

Youth councils analyzed the results from their questions and generated recommendations that they presented and shared with government and other community institutions. Some of the results were presented in pie charts, some as lists, and some as posters. *Consejo Pamar la Raza* asked open-ended questions through their gossip column, which made it challenging to analyze, and so they had to summarize the most common answers. In the end, this council developed a rap song to prevent school harassment.

During the process of facilitating this research, children also internalized the idea that they were agents of change. While it was not part of their initial goals, children noticed that the park where they played needed improvement. They decided to make recommendations for changes to this

(Box 6.16 continued on the following page)

(Box 6.16 continued)

park in addition to the research they were carrying out, and worked with local officials to transform the park into a better place to play. Initially the park officials said they would have adults do some of the hard work, such as planting trees, but the children said, "No, we want to do that." Through their increased sense of agency, they were able to transform the park. This outcome highlighted the importance of flexibility in adapting to young people's interests and desires for community change.

Another outcome of this project was that the children and adolescents felt so successful and engaged in their work that they proposed a longer-term strategy for participation. As a result, the city created seven school councils, which young people attend once a week to discuss their rights and develop projects to promote their interests and concerns.[1]

_____

1. Yolanda Corona Caraveo and María Morfín-Stoopen, *Nuestra Voz También Cuenta: Haz Que Se Escuche: Una Experiencia de Participación de Niñas, Niños y Adolescentes en el Municipio de Pachuca (Our voice also counts: make it heard: An experience of participation of children and adolescents in the Municipality of Pachuca).* Chapultepec, Cuernavaca, Morelos, Mexico: Grafimor S.A. de C.V., 2017.

Box 6.17. **Nightlife Action Group**

In the early stages of Growing Up Boulder, a Nightlife Action Group formed to identify safe, healthy, and affordable evening activities for young people. The group was comprised of youth from area schools and an existing YMCA Teen Advisory Board. The teens met several times to design, administer and analyze the results of a survey that they issued to approximately 500 youth. Survey questions asked about existing and desired nightlife activities, how much money teens could spend on events, mechanisms for communicating about events, and modes of transportation to events. Because the students collected such a large sample, the survey garnered the attention of city council members and led to a number of outcomes, including the development of monthly teen nightlife activities at the local YMCA and a computer programming class that developed a website portal for teen activities. Teen's development of this survey involved extensive oversight from university faculty, primarily to guide teens in developing a reliable survey tool.[1]

_____

1. Victoria Derr, Louise Chawla, Mara Mintzer, Debra Flanders Cushing, and Willem van Vliet, "A city for all citizens: Integrating children and youth from marginalized populations into city planning." *Special Issue on Designing Spaces for City Living. Buildings 3*, no. 3(2013): 482–505.

Method—Collect the Information

The most common means of collecting questionnaire information is by distributing them in person and either asking the questions orally, by distributing paper surveys in public spaces or through school classrooms or after-school programs. Increasingly, questionnaires are distributed digitally. A wide range of open-access survey instruments exist, many of which also tally responses.

Method—Analyze and Present the Results

Chapter 9 reviews a range of methods for coding, analyzing, and presenting data. As questions provide for a range of responses, you generally count the number of individuals who responded to each choice and then present this data in either a bar graph or pie chart (Box 6.19). If you have collected both fixed responses and open-ended comments, then you can provide a chart that quantifies the fixed responses, followed by sample comments that share representative comments.

Box 6.18. **Surveys to Assess Elementary School Accessibility**

The ScHaN (School, Home and Neighborhood Accessibility) Project was a participatory research study supported by the Canadian Institute of Health from 2008–2011 to evaluate the accessibility of the environment for children with disabilities in Ontario, Canada. Using multiple methods that are child- and disability-friendly, children aged 8–14 with physical disabilities engaged in an evaluation of their school, home, and neighborhoods. They identified barriers to mobility and accessibility, as well as creative strategies to improve these environments. The project involved a range of methods including case studies that were developed with thirteen children who had a range of mobility impairments. Paired with a research assistant for three 90-minute sessions, children discussed accessibility and environmental quality by reviewing and discussing photographs, sketching spaces using computer software (Camtasia Studio), and interviews. These case studies then informed the development of a survey that was issued to 624 children by mail. Three youth who had mobility impairments worked with the research team to develop a colorful, child- and disability-friendly survey. The survey itself asked questions about the mobility methods children use, features to enter and move about the school, accessing washrooms, navigating playgrounds, and overall challenges in navigating the school. Children were asked if they went outside for recess, and the reasons why they remained inside during this time. This information was used to inform school policy to improve accessibility.

While the focus here was on schools, such a process could also be used to assess other physical environments, such as a neighborhood, park, or public space. One of the important findings from this research was that while many practices and policies ensure children's physical safety, these interventions sometimes further exclude children with disabilities from important social and educational opportunities. Children's involvement was central to understanding this context for decision-making.[1]

---

1. Lindsay Stephens, Helen Scott, Henna Aslam, Nicole Yantzi, Nancy L. Young, Sue Ruddick, and Patricia McKeever, "The accessibility of elementary schools in Ontario, Canada: Not making the grade." *Children, Youth and Environments* 25, no. 2 (2015): 153–175.

Visual Preference Surveys

Visual preference surveys are used to understand people's aesthetic preferences for an area to be re-designed, such as streetscapes, parks, or public spaces.[73] They are a visual adaptation of the survey method. In the landscape design field, visual preference research has helped us understand not only people's preferences for natural landscapes but also how people process visual information.[74] These studies show that people do not solely rely on an image alone, but also information they associate with the image. For example, an image of a creek may not only indicate water, but also opportunities for kayaking and skipping stones. This means that people do not only respond to the aesthetics of an image, but also potential activities they can imagine taking place there.

As a tool for participation, visual preference surveys help young people express their feelings, associations, and preferences for different kinds of spaces. They can also help young people see a range of possibilities, by showing examples of

---

73. Henry Sanoff, *Community Participation Methods in Design and Planning* (New York: John Wiley, 2000), 88–96.

74. Stephen Kaplan and Rachel Kaplan, *The Experience of Nature: a Psychological Perspective* (Cambridge University Press, 1989); Stephen Kaplan and Rachel Kaplan, "The visual environment: public participation in design and planning." *Journal of Social Issues* 45, no. 1 (1989): 59–86.

Box 6.19. **Presenting Questionnaire Results**

In the Great Neighborhoods project (Chapter 11), Growing Up Boulder modified a child-friendly cities survey instrument to ask young people their attitudes about participation, and if these attitudes changed over the course of the project. Young people who participated in the project answered the same three questions both at the beginning and end of the project. Thus, the questionnaire was used as a way to evaluate changes in children's perspectives on participation as an aspect of a child-friendly city. These results were then graphed using a bar graph. One of the most dramatic changes occurred with secondary students in response to the statement,

"The government asks me my opinion about my life or community." Prior to the project, 5% of students responded that this was "sometimes true" or "mostly true" for them. After the project, 55% responded "sometimes true" or "mostly true." The bar graph gives a clear visual representation of this change.[1]

_____

1. Victoria Derr, and Ildiko G. Kovács, "How participatory processes impact children and contribute to planning: A case study of neighborhood design from Boulder, Colorado, USA." *Journal of Urbanism: International Research on Placemaking and Urban Sustainability* 10, no. 1 (2017): 29-48.

Figure 6.13. Pre- and post- project responses to the statement: "The government asks me my opinion about my life or community." Image credit: Growing Up Boulder

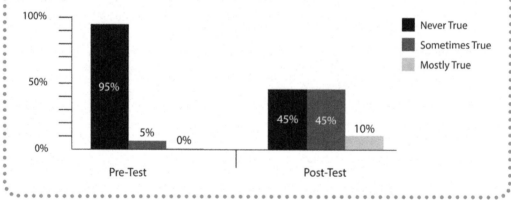

model parks, public spaces, or transportation projects from around the world. There are many ways to construct a visual preference survey.

- **Community-specific surveys** use images from the community to draw on familiar experiences with a place (Figure 6.14);
- **Conceptual surveys** provide design drawings or renderings about a conceived space that has not yet been built (Box 6.10); and
- **Generic surveys** assemble images from a wide range of places that have characteristics similar to the project for which you

are seeking preferences (Figure 6.15, Boxes 6.20 and 6.21).

In participatory processes in which young people will be developing their own designs or design recommendations, you may want to expose young people to a range of ideas that are appropriate to that setting. For example, if you are asking young people to design a city park, you may want to present a range of examples of city parks that have won design awards, that are similar in ecological context, and that fit the same budgetary constraints.

Figure 6.14. Community-specific visual surveys. These images were taken from different parks in the City of Boulder to represent parks that children would know, where they could respond to the play value in each. Photo credits: Victoria Derr

Figure 6.15. Generic visual surveys. These images were assembled from parks in Denmark and Sweden and were used as examples to stimulate discussion about play preferences and design. Photo credits: Victoria Derr

Ages. 10 and up. While younger children can also participate in visual preference surveys, it can be hard to understand what motivates their preferences. Pictures of places are more effective with children under ten than conceptual renderings. For this younger age group, three-dimensional models, drawings, and field trips are usually more engaging.

Materials. Preprinted or digitally projected photographs of the examples you will use for the survey, posters or projector, survey instruments

Time to Complete. Approximately one hour to facilitate; approximately two to five hours to prepare the survey

Box 6.20. **Visual Preference Survey for Park Design**

When the City of Boulder's Parks and Recreation Department began to develop a Valmont City Park concept plan, they partnered with Growing Up Boulder in a range of participatory methods that included a field trip to the park and a visual preference survey with youth aged 11–16. The visual preference survey was presented using Power Point slides. A total of 22 slides presented images related to the categories of: *transport*, both to and within the park; *social*

spaces, including seating and picnic options; *playground* structures and settings; and *food vendors*. Slides presented two, three, or four images for each category. Most also included a short verbal description to clarify which aspect of the image youth should respond to. In this survey, youth were asked to distribute their responses along a spectrum of most-preferred to least-preferred image. Some of the most-preferred results were compiled into collages for a final report.

Box 6.21. **The Use of Precedents:** Parks that Flood

When the City of Boulder began planning a redevelopment of its downtown Civic Area, Growing Up Boulder engaged young people in primary, middle, and secondary school in a process of co-design for the "Park at the Core" of this public space. (See Chapter 8.) After a series of initial activities, including *nicho* boxes with primary-school students (Chapter 5) and field trips (Chapter 7), students reviewed precedents for "Parks that Flood" as a visual preference survey. Because the city park was located in the immediate flood zone of Boulder Creek, whose waters rise and fall with seasonal snowmelt from the mountains, students could learn from other parks that were located in the flood zones of rivers and use these examples to creatively think about their own park designs.

For the survey, examples were drawn from parks all over the world, including Mill Race Park in Columbus, Indiana, and the Bishan-Ang Mo Kio Park's ecological restoration in Singapore. In this

context, the visual preference survey was used to deepen young people's thinking by showing them design examples and enabling them to discuss with each other what they liked and did not like in these images, within the context of flood zones. The images inspired children to think about the creek and its banks not only as a place where they liked to play but also as an integrated part of flood plain management. Children's ideas included underwater viewing areas, a series of "monkey bars" that spanned the bottom of a creek bridge, and treehouses above the creek where people could read books, learn about nature, and hear the sounds of the creek and the birds.[1]

---

1. Victoria Derr and Emily Tarantini, " "Because we are all people": Outcomes and reflections from young people's participation in the planning and design of child-friendly public spaces." *Local Environment* 21, no. 12 (2016): 534–1556.

Method—Preparation

- **Determine the purpose of conducting a visual preference survey.** What do you hope to learn by conducting a visual preference survey with young people? What kinds of information are you seeking? Do you hope to learn about their aesthetic preferences or their activity preferences? Are you trying to expose them to a range of places so that they can make their own design recommendations? You will need to determine if you will be conducting a community-specific, conceptual, or generic survey, or some combination.

- **Choose categories.** Select a range of five to six categories that you would like to gather information about. As an example, for an urban park you might want to include play equipment, seating, nature spaces, public art, and food vendors. These categories will help you collect images and sort them. You will want to have approximately four to six images per category.

- **Collect images.** You may take or find photos for existing places within the city, assemble designer images proposed for a site, or collect copyright-free images from the internet.[75] Images for each category should present a diversity of materials, colors, and design features. It may be helpful to have more than one person collecting images so that the collection will represent a range of aesthetic preferences.

---

75. A few sources for images include the Project for Public Spaces website; American Society of Landscape Architects design awards; Landezine, a landscape architecture website with a wide range projects, from streets to large scale parks; and the Child in the City, European Network's website. Picasa also has albums of urban features. Make sure to give proper attribution and respect copyrighted or protected images for all images that are downloadable from the internet.

Method—Develop and Implement the Survey

- **Develop the format of your survey.** Survey responses can be collected through a wide range of formats: on-line surveys, paper questionnaires, posters with sticky-dot voting, voting by hand-raising, automated response systems (commonly called clickers), focus groups, or facilitated discussions. It is generally best to present images one at a time for voting or discussion. However, if time does not allow this, people can be given a certain number of votes to distribute among their preferred images.

- **Surveys with structured voting.** If you want numeric voting, where participants rate a response, you will need to use an on-line or paper format. Numeric voting should provide a scale, with categories that range from strongly like (or strongly appealing) to strongly dislike (or strongly unappealing). These categories should be rated as follows:

	Strongly Like (+2)	Like (+1)	Neutral (0)	Dislike (-1)	Strongly Dislike (-2)
Image A					
Image B					
Image C					

Another adaption of this method can be to prepare a poster with a series of images, and give each person a set of sticky dots, so that they can select the image they prefer from each category. The sticky dots can then be totaled as a numeric score. The benefit of a "fixed" response (such as through on-line surveys or voting) is that you can quantify the number of people who like a particular design or feature.

- **Surveys as focus groups or facilitated discussions.** In focus groups or facilitated discussions, the same survey process can be used, with young people voting by a show of hands, and then discussing aspects of each image that they like or do not like. Compared with structured votes, these settings allow more time for discussion about why different people respond the way they do. These discussions can help you understand young people's aesthetics, as well as the activities and types of experiences they desire. This feedback can be helpful not only for professionals, but also for young people themselves.

By listening to others, young people begin to shift their perspectives from "what *I* want" to "what *we* want."

To complete the visual preference survey, you can assemble a collage of the images that people preferred most. This enables young people to identify common themes that guide preferences. Groups can make posters of the images that inspire them to carry their own design thinking further, or they can use images as precedents for their own design recommendations.

Into the City

*"You call us the future,
but we are also the present."* [1]

I n participatory methods that send children and youth into the city, two traditions converge. According to one, the best way for adults to understand young people's urban conditions and experiences is to venture out into the city with them. This research tradition began in the 1970s when urban designers Kevin Lynch and Robin Moore and geographer Roger Hart shared the methods they were developing to document young people's environmental knowledge, values, and behaviors.[2] When they asked individual children and small groups of playmates to lead them through important places in their lives, they found themselves on spontaneous and often unexpected journeys of discovery. They learned that places that are meaningful to children are often invisible during formal processes of urban planning, development, and design. These pioneers in fieldwork with children believed that this direct grounding in children's experience is a necessary foundation for child-friendly planning and design.

According to a second, educational tradition, the best way for children to understand their city is to explore it systematically. In this case, forays into the city are usually led by adults so that young people can have vivid experiences that they investigate further when they return to the classroom. Since the beginning of the 20th century, the tradition of progressive education that descends from John Dewey has promoted project-based learning, including the study of local places. Inspired by Dewey's philosophy that children have an innate drive to explore and shape their world, education that helps children develop habits of discovery, deliberation, and action when they venture into their community is essential for a strong democracy.[3] These ideas emerged again in *Streetwork: The Exploding School* by Colin Ward and Anthony Fyson, who described innovations in built-environment education in Great Britain in the 1960s and 1970s,[4] and they continue in the practice of place-based education.[5] (See Box 7.1 for a contemporary example of a school

1. Gabriela Azurday Arrieta (age 13) and Audrey Cheynut (age 17): 2002 representatives of the Children's Forum, addressing the U.N. Special Session on Children.

2. Roger Hart, *Children's Experience of Place* (New York, Irvington Publishers, 1979); Kevin Lynch, *Growing Up in Cities* (Cambridge, MA, MIT Press, 1977); Robin C. Moore, "Collaborating with young people to assess their landscape values." *Ekistics* 47, no. 281 (1980): 128–135.

3. John Dewey, *The School and Society: The Child and the Curriculum* (Chicago: University of Chicago Press, 1991) (originally published in 1900 and 1902).

4. Colin Ward and Anthony Fyson, *Streetwork: the Exploding School* (London: Routledge and Kegan Paul, 1973).

5. Greg Smith and David Sobel, *Place- and Community-Based Education in Schools* (New York: Routledge, 2010); David Sobel, *Place-Based Education* (Great Barrington, MA: The Orion Society, 2004).

Box 7.1. **Education for Civic Life**

The Cottonwood School of Civics and Science, a public charter School in Portland, Oregon, practices place-based education that uses the community as a classroom. It is based on John Dewey's principle that in a democratic society, students need to learn habits of active citizenship in addition to practical skills and knowledge of the arts and sciences. This means that students engage in free exchanges around common interests with their classmates and other communities beyond the school. Serving kindergarten through 8th grade (ages 5 through 14), teachers aim for children to learn about the place where they live, invest in caring for it, and understand how their locality is connected to the larger world.

Democratic practices begin in the classroom. At the beginning of each school year, teachers and students work together to create class agreements that state the rights and responsibilities of the teacher and students. In weekly class meetings, anyone can voice issues for the group to deliberate and address through collective problem solving. Each school term, each class adopts a place-based project. In the early years, it might be to study important institutions in the neighborhood, such as a nearby bank, hospital, and firehouse. Later, classes might learn about local

Figure 7.1. Kindergarten students in the Cottonwood School of Civics and Science are taking their first trip to Oaks Bottom to tour the refuge. They will come back in early winter to plant native shrubs with 7th/8th graders, in the spring to maintain the plantings, and in later spring to learn about pond ecology and life cycles.
Photo credit: Jessica Montigue

with a place-based mission.) These ideas are also central to education for sustainability.[6]

The methods in this chapter are a legacy of both traditions. They provide a means of getting young people into the city to learn about and analyze places, as well as a way for planners, de-

signers, and other urban professionals to see and understand the city through young people's perspectives. Each method needs to be approached with an open mind because the heart of urban exploration is surprise and spontaneity. Be prepared that you may need to deviate from a predetermined pathway or lesson plan in response to unexpected encounters and young people's emergent ideas.

Article 29 of the United Nations Convention on the Rights of the Child requires "that the education of the child shall be directed to . . . the preparation of the child for responsible life in

6. Ken Winograd, ed., *Education in Times of Environmental Crises: Teaching Children to be Agents of Change* (New York: Routledge, 2016); Rebecca A. Martusewicz, Jeff Edmundson, and John Lupinacci, *Ecojustice Education: Toward Diverse, Democratic, and Sustainable Communities*, 2nd Edition (New York: Routledge, 2015); John Huckle Stephen Sterling, eds., *Education for Sustainability* (London: Earthscan Publications, 1996).

geology or immigrant groups who came from all over the world to make Portland their home. Each project involves field trips, guest speakers, and a service component. In the examples given, young children created a welcome guide to their neighborhood for other children, for the neighborhood association to distribute to new families, and older students designed a geology scavenger hunt for other classes and planned a reception at their school to welcome newly naturalized citizens. In middle school, students choose a public issue that they want to research and they make presentations and recommendations to a public agency based on their findings.

Each grade adopts a nearby public land, such as a park or wildlife refuge, and visits this place at least six times during the school year, studying it, doing service in it, and learning how green spaces and wild places in the city are created and protected. One place, Oaks Bottom Wildlife Refuge, is adopted each year by the school's youngest and oldest students, from kindergarten and a combined 7th/8th grade. This provides many opportunities for mentoring and relationship building between the ages; and students who stay in the school all nine years get to come back as 7th/8th graders and see the impact of the restoration work that they did when they were small.

This type of education builds long-term partnerships between the school and other city organizations and residents. It communicates that "it takes a city to raise a citizen," as people from all walks of life visit classrooms and welcome students to their workplaces. It shows that children are citizens who can already make valuable contributions to their communities. Research finds that place-based education is associated with increased student engagement in learning, better problem-solving and critical thinking skills, increased civic and stewardship behaviors, and reduced disciplinary problems. When achievement-test scores of students in classes that practice place-based education have been compared with the scores of students in conventional classes, they are at least equal and often significantly higher.[1]

---

1. Sarah Anderson, "Taking hands on civics to the street." *Community Works Journal*. Available online at https://communityworksinstitute.org/cwjonline/articles/articles-text/Anderson_civics.html. (Retrieved August 13, 2017); Sarah Anderson and Anne Gurnee, "Our students as home-grown citizens." *Community Works Journal*, 2016. Available online at https://medium.com/communityworksjournal/our-students-as-home-grown-citizens-democracy-is-not-so-fast-and-easy-362c09964c41#.b0j11ge0b. (Retrieved August 13, 2017); Sarah Anderson, *Bringing School to Life* (Lanham, MD: Rowman & Littlefield, 2017).

---

a free society, in the spirit of understanding, peace, tolerance, equality of sexes, and friendship among all peoples" and to "the development of respect for the natural environment."[7] In cities, a diversity of peoples, their cultures and constructions, and the natural environment coexist—though not always in peace and friendship. Exploring the city involves learning about its history, cultures, and ecology as well as its built structures. With this knowledge, young people can deliberate about how different peoples and diverse species can share the city in harmony. The methods that follow support interdisciplinary learning and civic engagement. They enable young people to experience the city, analyze what they encounter, articulate what they like and what they would like to change, and communicate their values, ideas, and visions to their communities and city leaders. These methods include:

- Child-led tours
- Learning expeditions

---

7. UNICEF, "Convention on the Rights of the Child." UNICEF.org. www.unicef.org/crc. (Retrieved June 30, 2017).

- Photo-framing
- Photogrid
- Bioblitz inventories
- Mapping application software
- Map-making

This chapter provides a brief history and context for each method, gives directions for how to apply it, and provides examples of its use. Some methods provide a means for exploring and experiencing a site, such as field trips, guided tours and photo-framing. Others show how to analyze a site in detail, such as photogrids and participatory map-making. These methods allow young people to share their experiences and ideas about a place while generating knowledge, as they respond to the social and physical environments around them.

Child-led Tours

Child-led tours allow young people to take an adult, small group of adults, or other children around their local territory to share their experiences—places where they hang out, places they avoid, places they find scary, dirty, friendly, or fun. In essence, the tour is a "walking interview" with young people, showing how they use and experience the stops that they choose along the route (Figure 7.2[8], Box 7.3, Figure 7.26). The method emerged from geography and urban planning in recognition of young people's expertise about the places where they live.[9]

Figure 7.2. Child-led tours can be by bike if young people prefer. In this case, youth in Frankston, Australia, led adult researchers to a special cycle track they had constructed, and they lobbied the city council to safeguard it. Photo credit: Karen Malone

A tour can be led by a single child, but because children commonly explore their local area with siblings or friends, it can also be led by a self-selected group. Avoid putting children together who don't have close and comfortable relationships; the point is for the leaders to show places they use alone or with their group. Because the number in a tour is small, you will need to schedule a series of tours to cover all the children in a class or an after-school group, or divide them among a number of adult note-takers if they all set off at the same time. Or you may choose to work with a subsample of children who represent the larger group's diversity.

Use this method after young people have gotten to know you and developed trust (Box 7.3). Young people take their role as guides seriously, so introduce this activity at least two days in advance so that they can plan what they want to share. Tours work well with drawing (see

---

8. Barry Percy-Smith and Karen Malone, "Making children's participation in neighbourhood settings relevant to the everyday lives of young people." *PLA Notes* 42 (2001): 18–22.
9. For classic examples of child-led tours, see: Lynch, *Growing Up in Cities*; Robin C. Moore, *Childhood's Domain* (London: Croom Helm, 1986) (republished by MIG Communications in 1990); David Sobel, *Children's Special Places* (Tucson, AZ: Zephyr Press, 1993) (republished by Wayne State University Press in 2002); David Driskell, *Creating Better Cities with Children and Youth: A Manual for Participation* (London: Earthscan Publications, 2002).

For reflections on child-led tours in urban poor settlements in India, see: Anupama Nallari, "In-situ and child-led tours." *Steps to Engaging Young Children in Research, Volume 2: The Researcher Toolkit*, ed. Vicky Johnson, Roger Hart, and Jennifer Colwell (Brighton, UK: Education Research Centre, University of Brighton, 2014), 78–82, available at https://bernardvanleer.org/publications-reports/steps-engaging-young-children-research-volume-2-researcher-toolkit.

For a more recent example, see: Angela Kreutz, *Children and the Environment in an Australian Indigenous Community.* (New York: Routledge, 2015).

Box 7.2. **Envisioning a New Barrio**

In a workshop in Bogotá, Colombia, to re-envision city streets in low-income neighborhoods, Osa Menor and Lunárquicos, two arts education firms, began with guided tours of the neighborhood, taking pictures of the environment as they walked through the streets. They then printed these photographs, and children drew their ideas for how to make the streets more child-friendly. They created these drawings by laying transparent paper (acetate or trace can work) and drawing their vision of what they wanted to see over the existing images. The workshop was commissioned by Bernard Van Leer Foundation.

Figure 7.3. Images of streets on the walking tour, and children's drawings overlain. Each composition is titled, "the streets in my neighborhood." Photo credit: Osa Menor and Lunárquicos

Chapter 5) and mapping (this chapter). You can ask the leaders to draw the territory they want to cover and label the landmarks they want to show, or plot and annotate the route on a map. Or you can let the route unroll spontaneously. Once underway, tours work well with photovoice (Chapter 5) and photo-framing (this chapter). Some young people talk more easily about their locality when they "speak" through the perspective of a camera. Even if young people are recording the trip visually, you may want to take pictures of your own. After the tour, the leaders can reflect about what they shared by writing about their photos, or drawing and writing about especially significant places. They can also draw how they envision improving some of the tour sites (Box 7.2, Figure 7.3). Children often bring playful interactions as they observe the city (Figures 2.1–2.2, Figure 7.2, Figures 12.2 and 12.3).

Materials. A map and notebook for marking stops and taking notes and a camera for visually recording important places. You may want to bring a short set of interview questions to guide conversations at important stops.

Time to Complete. If you are asking young people to stay within a limited area that is the focus of a design intervention, 30 to 45 minutes may be enough time. If you are asking them to show you every place in their home range that they consider significant, a tour can take a few hours, or unfold over more than one day.

Method—Introduction and Taking Pictures

- Introduce the activity—what you plan to do and why. Lynch,[10] Driskell,[11] and Hart[12] asked children to share a range of places: favorite places, disliked places, dangerous places, frightening places, and other places they found significant or visited regularly. Hart also asked his guides to show their ten most favorite places (with the understanding that the number might multiply on the way). Tailor your instructions according to the information you seek.

- Introduce ground rules for safety that are specific to the age of participants and area where the tour will occur.

- If you are working with a large group that needs to be subdivided, break into small groups with one to four tour leaders. Each group needs its own adult participant and note-taker.

- Each group may begin by plotting simple landmarks and destination points on a map, or group members may make a schematic drawing of where they intend to lead you—unless they already prepared this in advance. Review the map as a team before setting out. Keep in mind that destination points may change, and that spontaneity along the way is a welcome part of the process!

- Conduct the tour. As you walk, let young people lead. Observe their behaviors. If they are playing with the leaves under a tree, make a note of this. If they stop to stare through a shop window, allow time

for them to experience the place and share it with you. Make notes about what they do along the way as well as what they tell you.

- At each stop, ask the young people when they visit this place, why they come, who they come with, what they do there, and their feelings and observations about it.

- If several small groups go out at the same time and then reconvene, ask both the young people and their adult companions to share some of the highlights of their trips. If you are working with one group, give members time to reflect on what they experienced.

- At the end of the session, make sure that your notes and annotations are complete so that you will be able to recall the details later. Share your notes, or a summary of your main points, with the young people and ask them to make modifications or additions.

It can be useful to combine child-led tours with adult-led tours through the same place as a way to hear different views about the environment. Begin with the tour led by children. Then ask adults who plan, design, or manage this place to lead you along the same route and explain how each stopping point is intended to function for children. As you go, share what children said, based on your notes from the child-led tour. Or alternatively, have the children return to lead these same people through these spaces. At each stopping point, ask the adults to respond to issues the children raise and consider how they could make these spaces more responsive to children's needs. Fiona De Vos and Selim Iltus found this method useful in a hospital where child patients, doctors, nurses, and other staff led separate tours through wards and treatment rooms, talking about how these spaces served children.[13] De Vos and Iltus recommend video-

10. Lynch, *Growing Up in Cities.*
11. Driskell, *Creating Better Cities with Children and Youth.*
12. Hart, *Children's Experience of Place.*

13. Vicky Johnson, Roger Hart, and Jennifer Colwell, eds. "Child-led group tours with children and adults." In *Steps*

Box 7.3. **Child-led Tours to Special Places in Nature**

After you have completed initial activities with young people and they have come to know and trust you, they may lead you to personal places beyond public view. These are often wild edges of cities and towns: overgrown lots, weed coves on the margins of developed land, dense shrubbery, wooded areas, wild corners of parks, creek sides, riverbanks, steep hillsides and ravines. Children's greatest fear in wild urban places is usually dangerous people, but by banding together with friends, they can colonize their own special places.

Figure 7.4. Aboriginal children in Cherbourg, Australia led researchers to favorite places in their community. Photo credit: Angela Kreutz

When Angela Kreutz asked children in Cherbourg, an Aboriginal settlement in Queensland, Australia, to lead her on place expeditions to their favorite places, many brought her to sanctuaries in nature (Figure 7.4). In town, children faced the stresses of a low-income community with high rates of poverty, unemployment, alcoholism, drug use and violence. In the surrounding bush, they could find quiet places, make cubbies or dens, play adventurously on the slopes and up in trees, mold materials like dirt and sand, and enjoy the sounds of wind and water. They could find "prospect refuges" (a term coined by the geographer Jay Appleton)—places where they felt sheltered while they surveyed the town below. A large body of research documents the importance of opportunities for children to connect with nature. The challenge for planners and designers is to legitimate places of this kind. This requires going beyond managed parks and gardens to allow children to create special places of their own in nature.[1]

_____

1. Jay Appleton, *The Experience of Place* (London: John Wiley, 1975); Louise Chawla. "Benefits of nature contact for children." *Journal of Planning Literature*, 30, no. 4 (2015): 433–452.; Kreutz, *Children and the Environment in an Australian Indigenous Community*; Robin C. Moore, with Allen Cooper, *Nature Play and Learning Places* (Raleigh, NC/Reston, VA: Natural Learning Initiative/National Wildlife Federation, 2014).

taping these dialogues or making notes on a map or plan.

Variation: Child-led Tours through Simulated Environments

In some urban areas, it may be more practical for children to lead adults through a simulated

_____
to *Engaging Young Children in Research, Volume 2: The Researcher Toolkit* (Brighton, UK: Education Research Centre, University of Brighton), 23–24, available at https://bernardvanleer.org/publications-reports/steps-engaging-young-children-research-volume-2-researcher-toolkit.

environment rather than crowded or hazardous streets. This variation also has the advantage that children can show how they use private and hidden spaces as well as public places. The urban planner Sidney Brower developed this method in the 1970s when he made models of parts of a Baltimore neighborhood, such as a typical rowhouse block, and asked individual children to arrange the model pieces so it would look like their home territory. Then he gave each child small dolls to represent themselves and their friends. He asked questions such as, "You have just come home from school and your mother says you can go out to play—where do you go?" Then the children acted out the answer.[14]

When Sudeshna Chatterjee and project partners investigated where children found places to play in areas of crisis and disaster in six countries, they used models when places were too crowded at all times and children would have felt uncomfortable leading an adult around while others were watching.[15] Simulations were also valuable for places children used without adults' permission. Project leaders created a model of the landscape, and working with children in pairs, asked one child to pick out a small doll to be herself, and the second child to pick out another small doll to be an imaginary visitor. The first doll showed the second where it found places to play, alone and with playmates, and how it felt about these places. Then they changed roles. Some elements of the model could be moved around and added to from a pile of materials so that the children could show how they manipulated spaces during play.

Project partners found that children in different cultures wanted different levels of realism. In some settings, children were happy using stones and pieces of wood whereas in others they wanted recognizable cardboard streetscapes and furnishings. Children were encouraged to pretend that this was their familiar environment, they were going on an imaginative walking tour through it, and they could talk about features of the environment that might not be represented in the model.

Variation: Town Trails

Town trails are child-made tours for people to follow, guided by signposts, sidewalk painting,

brochures or maps.[16] For permanent installations like signposts, young people need to negotiate with planning departments or other agencies, and similarly with libraries or tourism offices for the distribution of maps and brochures. Local artists and graphic designers may serve as mentors. Only young people's interests limit the themes for town trails. They can guide people through urban nature—like the signposts about trees, birds, and insects that young children wrote and illustrated for a nature trail in Kristiansand, Norway.[17] They can tell local history, like the Piccolo Guides (little guidebooks) that students in Cremona, Italy, wrote to tell other children and their families about city history from unique perspectives, with games to play along the way.[18] They can ask people to think critically about stopping points, drawing attention to degraded and uninviting landscapes as well as attractions, and encouraging people to experience places through their ears, nose, touch, and hearing as well as sight.

Learning Expeditions

Young people plan the routes of child-led tours to show places that they already know and use. Learning expeditions are more likely to be planned by adults, as everyone heads out into the city together on a journey of discovery focused around a particular theme. The goal can be to evaluate a public space (Boxes 7.4, 7.9 –7.10) or a transportation corridor (Box 7.5), uncover local

14. Sidney Brower, La Verne Gray, and Roger Stough, *Doll-Play as a Tool for Urban Designers* (Baltimore: Department of Planning, 1977).

15. Sudeshna Chatterjee, *Access to Play in Crisis: Synthesis of the Research in Six Countries.* (IPA World (International Play Association), 2017).

16. Roger Hart, *Children's Participation* (London: Earthscan Publications, 1997), 180–181; Colin Ward and Anthony Fyson, *Streetworks* (London: Routledge & Kegan Paul, 1973), 40–47.

17. Kirsti Vindal Halvorsen, "Steps in the Plantain Project: the ideas, activities, and experiences of the Plantain Project, a scheme to safeguard children and their environment." *Children's Environments* (1995): 444–456.

18. Judith Wilks, "Child-friendly cities: A place for active citizenship in geographical and environmental education." *International Research in Geographical and Environmental Education* 19, no. 1 (2010): 25–38.

Figure 7.5. Young people from Nairobi's informal settlement, Kibera, visited other communities as a way to gain inspiration for their own. The grassy field in a neighboring community inspired a playing field in their own settlement. Photo credit: David Driskell

history (Box 7.6 and 7.7), study the ecology of a creek (Box 7.8), discuss teen-friendliness of a place (Box 7.9), find inspiring examples, or precedents, in other areas of the city (Figure 7.5), or explore any other aspect of the city that will prepare participants to engage in local planning and design in an informed way.

Because learning expeditions take a variety of forms that involve different ages and group sizes, it is impossible to provide one set of instructions that cover all possibilities. Basic rules for child-led tours apply here too:

- Give clear directions about the purpose of the activity and how it is structured.

Box 7.4. **Documenting Children's Movements about the City**

with Tuline Gülgönen

In an effort to understand and improve children's access to public spaces in Mexico City, Tuline Gülgönen, Associate Researcher of the Center of Mexican and Central American Studies (CEMCA), with the collaboration of the *Laboratorio para la Ciudad* and the funding of the French Embassy in Mexico, published *Jugar la Ciudad* (Play the City), a document that explores the quality of public spaces for children in Mexico City. Following this publication, CEMCA invited five young people (ages 3–13) to lead adults around the city, on their daily routes to and from school and to other spaces in the city. The young people came from different parts of the city and from different economic backgrounds including a wealthy neighborhood and semirural areas within the city limits. Children and their families were invited to participate together. Adults filmed the city from the viewpoint of the child, so that the documentary would show the city through the eyes

and voices of children. The film follows children on city buses and private transports to schools, through streets and plazas, and to playgrounds. It documents some of the ways that they play in the city. The purposes of the film are to show the diverse ways children experience the city, obstacles they face in navigating and accessing public space, and inequities in access to public spaces.[1] For the initial screening, children and their families were invited to a showing of the film with popcorn and icy fruit drinks, special food treats for children in Mexico.

---

1. The documentary was coordinated by Tuline Gülgönen and Ana Álvarez Velasco. Tuline Gülgönen, Associate Researcher of the Center of Mexican and Central American Studies (CEMCA) coordinates te Project "Urban play spaces for children in Mexico City." With the collaoration of the Laboratorio para la Ciudad and the funding of the French Embassy in Mexico, Dr. Gülgönen published *La Jugar Ciudad: Reimaginar lo espacios públicos urbanos de juego para la infancia en la Ciudad de México* in 2016.

Box 7.5. The Walking Laboratory Tour with Young Children

Because of their small size, young children experience the street differently. They notice details that adults often overlook; but conversely, they are too short to see many things in adults' view. When the Department of Transportation in Boulder, Colorado, began its 19th Street corridor improvement planning, staff wanted to consider all types of transportation users—and all ages. They highlighted children as an important demographic for public engagement, and developed Walking Laboratories with community partners to integrate children's voices into multimodal transportation planning. A Walking Laboratory is a way for participants to evaluate the walkability of a transportation corridor and register their likes and dislikes.

Children ages 2–4 and teachers from Boulder Journey School, a pre-kindergarten school in the 19th Street study area, participated in the Walking Laboratories project with an emphasis on what they enjoyed and what made them feel unsafe on the street. They shared cameras, and the teachers and tour organizer recorded the children's reactions and discussions. The children walked (and ran and jumped) down the street, identifying colors, textures, and places to play and explore (Figure 7.6). They also noticed signs of neglect, including trash, graffiti, dog waste, and cracked sidewalks, and identified intimidating street crossings. They suggested several ways to enhance the street for greater explora-

tion and play, including art at a child's eye level, natural play spots, places to observe nature and wildlife, and a variety of sensory experiences. To visually connect their preschool with a nearby elementary school and middle school, they suggested that students from each school create sidewalk paintings.

The tour organizer prepared a report of their recommendations for the Department of Transportation. The children showed that it is not only important to improve streets for walkability, but also to enhance the quality of interactions with stopping places along the way.[1]

Figure 7.6. A boy exploring a ditch on the Walking Laboratory tour of a city street.
Photo credit: Boulder Journey School

1. Adapted from: Morgan Huber and Victora Derr. "Walking laboratories: Young people's experience of the street." European Network of Child Friendly Cities, April 28, 2016. http://www.childinthecity.org/2016/04/28/walking-laboratories-young-childrens-experience-of-the-street/. (Retrieved August 21, 2017).

- Introduce ground rules for safety.
- Bring a map and a notebook to record how the young people respond and what the group learns.
- A camera is an optional but useful tool for you and young participants.
- At the end, take time to share highlights and reflections about the expedition

(on the spot, or the next time the group convenes).

If you are the one planning the route, walk it in advance. Make sure you have more than one adult on the day of the expedition (several if it is a large group). In the event that a child gets hurt or acts recklessly, someone needs to be free to focus on this child's needs. You may

---

Box 7.6. **Guided History Walk in Monterey, California**

Self-guided or docent-led history walks are ways to introduce young people and project facilitators to the special character of a site. In Monterey, California, 5th and 6th grade students (ages 10–11) who were engaged in a coastal stewardship planning project took a self-guided historic tour of Cannery Row as a way to familiarize themselves with local cultural and environmental history. They visited original corrugated tin cannery buildings, houses of cannery workers formerly inhabited by Chinese, Japanese, and Sicilian fishermen, and the restoration and redevelopment of ocean habitat by the Monterey Bay Aquarium. Because the route is a historic site within the city, they followed interpretive signage. This was the first of a series of walks and expeditions in the vicinity of the school. Other walks to a local beach, the aquarium, and local businesses were part of the curriculum. Regular walks led to the generation of a set of community values that were used to inform service-learning projects in their community. In this case, expeditions were planned by the teacher; however, community values and service learning projects were developed by the students.

As a start to the service-learning unit, students made observations about the values they had observed within the neighborhood. Students had observed "flows to the bay" markers near storm drains and had played a game of counting cigarette butts to talk about trash on one of their walks. They observed that the bike path adjacent to their school reflected the city's value for physical activity. Collectively, students identified nine values, including ocean health, views of nature, caring for wildlife, and tourism. Each student then selected a personally meaningful value to explore more deeply.

Over four weeks, students developed individual service projects that would benefit the community and that reflected the community value they had chosen. Project identification began with background research, and in some cases students conducted interviews with local experts or community representatives to identify a project or develop it more fully. This work challenged students to think about how their project improved their community. Projects included collecting materials for the local animal shelter, constructing a wildlife crossing sign at a place of frequent roadkills, and raising awareness about the need to reduce plastic pollution in the ocean. Results were shared at a school open house with parents, school administrators, and members of the greater school community.[1]

---

1. Victoria Derr and Jeffery Morton, "Empowering young people through action on community environments." *European Network of Child Friendly Cities*, May 4, 2017. https://www.childinthecity.org/2017/05/04/empowering-young-people-through-action-on-community-environment/. (Retrieved August 21, 2017).

want to invite local experts to the site you are visiting, but make sure you leave ample time for young people's hands-on exploration. Lectures by experts should be brief and as interactive as possible, with time for young people's questions.

This section offers a few examples of the many forms that learning expeditions can take, involving different ages and children with different physical abilities.

Box 7.7. **Local Culture Embodied in Urban Design in the Mission District of San Francisco, California**

James Rojas, a pioneer in Latino Urbanism and community engagement, took 12 Latinx students, ages 8–15, on a Latino Urbanism tour of San Francisco's Mission District. He asked the students to observe what made this place different from other parts of the city and what made it similar to the communities they came from. They examined the people on the street, the types of stores, the hand-painted street signs, the murals (Figure 7.7), merchandise on the sidewalks (Figure 7.8), and sounds, smells, colors, textures, and symbols. According to Rojas, "The urban design of 24th Street represents how Latino residents with few resources use their creativity to imagine, investigate, and construct their place using their bodies, objects, and the landscape at hand to create a community. Every intervention represents struggle, survival, and identity. And because they use their own body to create this place, it is one of the most intimate in scale and personal nature."[1]

––––––––––––––––––––

1. Personal communication with James Rojas and the DaVinci Camp Summer Institute. July 21, 2017.

Figure 7.7. A guided walk to explore San Francisco's Mission District with Latinx youth. Photo credit: Gabriela Gonzalez and DaVinci Camp Summer Institute

Figure 7.8. Youth explored storefronts, fruit markets, restaurants, murals, and signs. Photo credit: Gabriela Gonzalez and DaVinci Camp Summer Institute

Box 7.8. **Place-based Learning at Boulder Creek**

In preparation for making design recommendations for the redevelopment of the Civic Area in Boulder, Colorado, the Applied Science class at a nearby middle school took weekly field trips for five weeks to Boulder Creek, which runs through a greenway and park in this area. This group of 11- to 13-year-olds participated in the following series of activities:

- A Five Senses observation and sketching trip
- Playing at the creek's edge, throwing rocks, and looking at ducks
- Playing a food web game
- Measuring streamflow in the creek
- Taking pictures using the photogrid method

The primary purpose for these repeated visits was to provide the young people with a variety of means to experience the creek and understand its ecology before formulating any design recommendations of their own. While specific activities were planned for each day, time was also given for exploring the site through free play (Figure 7.9).

While the structured activities generated some ideas, most of the young people's design concepts came from their free exploration at the site. One group, for example, designed a series of play spaces along the creek based on their observations that it was currently hard to access the water. As a result of talking with a fisherman who explained that he came to the creek for solitude, another group designed fishing stations at suitable distances from the play areas so that the two types of activities would not conflict. A third group, who had observed homeless visitors at the site, designed a Sanitation Station and Resource Center for the homeless in the park.

Figure 7.9. Youth playing a food web game, which identifies plants and animals who live at the creek and depend on each other for food, shelter, or space. Photo credit: Growing Up Boulder

Box 7.9. An Exhibit of Teenagers' Spatial Stories in Dublin

with Jackie Bourke and Dorothy Smith

Figure 7.10. Teenagers placing temporary signs around their neighborhood as commentary about how they feel in public space. This sign reads "Smell that fresh air," jokingly referring to the bad smell from inner city horse stables used to support carriage rides throughout Dublin. Photo credit: Jackie Bourke and Dorothy Smith

Figure 7.11. Teenagers often do not feel welcome in public space. Teenagers in Dublin hung "please loiter" and other signs to challenge a tendency by police to move them along when they gather in groups to socialize. Photo credit: Jackie Bourke and Dorothy Smith

Teenagers in Dublin, Ireland worked with an artist and a children's rights researcher to investigate their experience of everyday walks through public space. Using a combination of walking fieldwork, photography, drawing, and creative mapping, the group asked questions such as:

- Is this space welcoming or hostile?
- What is public space?
- What do we mean by 'public'?

- What rules govern public space?
- Who makes the rules?

Although public space is important for teenagers, discussions revealed that while they carve out a sense of belonging, they don't always feel welcome. As one participant said, "Alone you feel vulnerable, but in a group you are seen as suspicious." The project culminated in an exhibit of drawings, photography and text capturing the teenagers' experiences of their walks to school and hanging out with family or friends. The exhibit was held at Bí Urban, a community space and shop in Stoneybatter in the heart of Dublin City. (Bí is an Irish word meaning "to be.")

The exhibit extended into the urban public realm, with temporary posters mounted on lampposts stating "Teenagers Welcome," or "Please Loiter" as a playful response to some of the negative encounters the teenagers have in their neighborhoods (Figure 7.10). These posters were designed collaboratively by the teenagers and a graphic artist.

Through their work, they conveyed a sense of playfulness, an acute awareness of architectural detail and the built environment, nature in the city, environmental neglect (Figure 7.11), and the important role of friends and family in their everyday lives. Visitors to the exhibition described the work as poignant and thought-provoking.[1]

1. Spatial Stories was developed and facilitated by Jackie Bourke (Children's Environments Researcher) and Dorothy Smith (Artist). They are indebted to the group of teenagers who shared profound insights into how the city works, to Megan Ní Raghallaigh and Stephen Averill for their support of the project. The project was funded by The Arts Council of Ireland, Engaging with Architecture Scheme. Jackie Bourke and Dorothy Smith. A summary of this project is reported in "Spatial stories of Dublin's youth." Child in the City European Network, May 24, 2017. https://www.childinthecity .org/2017/05/24/spatial-stories-of-dublins-youth/ (Retrieved September 15, 2017).

Box 7.10. **A Scavenger Hunt Walking Tour**

When the Department of Parks and Recreation in the City of Boulder, Colorado, began planning improvements to the park that borders the city reservoir, Growing Up Boulder (GUB) teamed up with EXPAND, the city's therapeutic recreation program for adults and youth with disabilities. GUB and EXPAND staff worked together to adapt the idea of a guided walking tour by creating a scavenger hunt for a group of young people who had a range of disabilities (physical, cognitive, and/or social-emotional). All participants could walk on their own or with assistance. To establish a positive experience for all young people and gain meaningful information, Growing Up Boulder and EXPAND staff met to discuss possible methods, and to develop an approach that the EXPAND staff thought would work well with their populations. Scavenger hunt questions and locations were written and revised based on this feedback. Scavenger hunt questions included:

- A favorite place
- A least favorite place
- A place that is hard to get to
- A place that is easy to get to
- Something wet
- Something dirty or yucky
- Something fun
- Something green
- A place with people
- A place with more than two animals
- A place you would like to change

While some of the questions were intended to engage participants in a playful sensory exploration of the park, others sought to understand how participants experienced the park from a mobility perspective. Additional trained staff attended the field trip for those participants who needed extra assistance to navigate participation.

Through this exercise, Parks and Recreation staff learned that some of the young people's favorite places (such as sand and the water's edge) were the hardest to get to, whereas some of the most accessible places, such as the park's pavilion, were the least interesting. This information informed changes in the park's design. Participants in the scavenger hunt received a colorful certificate to acknowledge their contribution to the design process. EXPAND staff emphasized the importance of recognizing their participation in this way, and the certificates made many young people very happy.

Photo-Framing

Photo-framing began as a method to spread information about a participatory program in a community and encourage conversations about the smells, sights, sounds, tastes, and local practices that give a community vitality and identity. It was originated by the landscape architect Isami Kinoshita as part of a multi-method initiative to

Figure 7.12. Photo-framing, showing a boy photographing public-space elements that he likes through a green frame. Photo credit: Brendan Hurley. This image initially appeared in Derr et al., "A city for all citizens."

animate public life in Tokyo and to bring people together to consciously create the kind of community future that they wanted (Box 7.11).

A variation on this method is to use frames that have been painted red and green to indicate what participants like (green frames) or do not like (red frames). With these colors the framing serves as a tool for young people to "code" their pictures, and also as a visual record of their positive and negative feelings.

Photo-framing uses steps similar to Photovoice (Chapter 5), with the following additions.

Materials. Prepare enough frames in advance for every set of young people in your group. They can consist of recycled picture frames or be fabricated from heavy cardboard, picture frame matte board, or other sturdy materials. You may leave them in their original colors, if using recycled frames, or paint them orange for purposes like a street gallery (Box 7.11), or red and green as a tool for evaluation (Figure 7.12). (They can be red on one side and green on the other so that only one frame per group is needed). You will also need a camera for each small group and a data sheet to record why each photograph was taken (Table 7.1).

Time to Complete. You should allow at least 1-2 hours to prepare the materials, and additional time for paint to dry. For the photography, the time required is the same as for photovoice: at least 45 minutes for a photo shoot, and another session for discussion.

Method—Additions to the Photovoice Method (from Chapter 5):

- When you pass out the frames, also provide cameras and data sheets
- Demonstrate how to hold the frames while taking pictures. It can be helpful for young people to work in pairs for this activity, with one person holding the frame and the other taking the picture (Figure 7.13)

Box 7.11. Photo-Framing During the Street Art Workshop

When Isami Kinoshita introduced photo-framing as part of a three-day festival in the Setagaya Ward of Tokyo in 1992, one of his primary motives was to encourage discussion about how to protect children's freedom to explore community spaces and participate in local culture. To draw attention to the initiative, he painted the frames bright orange. To inspire people to see local streets as a "museum" of collective life, participants—including a group of children—set their frames on easels in front of intriguing spots. This, of course, prompted conversations with nearby people about what they were doing, why, and the view that was suddenly brought into focus. It also brought people out of their homes, shops, and workplaces to explain the history behind selected spots. Who set the bathtub-turned-goldfish-pond outside a house and why? What was the story behind the dolls in the pharmacy window? Whose cat is that who sleeps on top of the wall? Participants usually worked in small groups and recorded why they chose the scenes they framed and the ensuing conversations and stories.

They also took photos of the "street museum" frames, and these images were projected on an outdoor screen on the final night of the festival. The festival included "gallery talks" in front of the frames, drawings of children's changing culture of street play across generations, street theater, and a street studio for making traditional toys and handicrafts such as carp streamers.[1]

---

1. Isami Kinoshita and other program animators, *The Street Art Workshop*. (Tokyo: Unpublished program report, 1992); Driskell, *Creating Better Cities with Children and Youth*, 157.

Table 7.1. Sample Data Sheet for Photo-Framing.
This example from open-space planning shows image numbers and notes that Junior Rangers recorded during a photo-framing activity. (See Chapter 11 for a profile of this project.)

Junior Ranger Open Space Planning: Photo-Framing Data Sheet	
Please record the <u>image number</u> and <u>notes about why</u> you are taking each photograph.	
What I <u>Like</u> About Open Space (Green Frames)	**What I <u>Don't Like</u> Within Open Space (Red Frames)**
71 Rolly pollies are cool	72 Construction causes pollution and destroys nature and wildlife homes
73 Birds are natural and cool to look at	75 Social trails are bad because they disrupt natural wildlife and vegetation
74 Colorado views are cool and should not be blocked by development	76 Littering is bad
75 Diverse habitat on trail is good and makes the hike more interesting	79 There should be paths down to the lake so hikers don't make their own trails
77 Wildlife is cool to see	80 Road noise detracts from the overall experience
78 Wildlife diversity is fun	

Figure 7.13. Working in pairs helps participants manage frames, camera and data sheets. It is often easier to frame the desired image if one participant holds the frame while the other takes the picture. Photo credit: Victoria Derr. This image initially appeared in Derr, Ruppi, and Wagner, "Honoring Voices, Inspiring Futures."

Figure 7.14. Sample data sheet for photo-framing. This example was used in transportation planning and asked students to identify aspects of transportation according to the six categories. The pictures could be framed red or green, depending on each person's experience with that element. The data sheet contained a check mark as well as a space where young people could write why they took each picture. Image credit: Growing Up Boulder

- Give an example of how to fill out a data sheet (Table 7.1, Figure 7.14). During the photo shoot, it is important for child and youth participants or adult facilitators to record *why* pictures are taken (i.e., the ideas they represent). Data sheets help preserve the immediate thinking that can otherwise be lost when participants take many pictures before returning to discuss them. They link image numbers to the photographer's ideas.

- If using red/green frames, explain that red frames are to be used for parts of the physical environment that young people do not like and would like to remove or change. Green frames indicate places or elements of the environment that they like.

- To further capture young people's ideas, you can prepare yellow-framed paper with

Figure 7.15. When planning a city park, youth were given green and red frames to evaluate the existing physical space. Then they were given yellow-framed papers to draw what they wanted to add to the space. This drawing reflects one youth's desire for a culturally relevant food truck. Image credit: Growing Up Boulder

a blank space for young people to draw what they *wish* existed in the environment (Figure 7.15).

- To assemble the ideas, group photographs in a collage or digital presentation format (Figure 7.16).

- To facilitate discussion, ask young people to write a short description and to share and compile images with the entire group of participants They may want to refer to their data sheets for this purpose. (See the photovoice section in Chapter 5 for prompts and discussion ideas).

- Compile themes into an action plan or recommendations, depending on your project goals. (See Chapter 5.)

Junior Rangers' Photoframe: Elements they like in open space

From left: Positive messaging of signs; Bike racks at trail heads; Biking and fishing

Figure 7.16. A photo-framing collage of open-space images. Image credit: Growing Up Boulder

From left: Ability to see wildlife (also birds, wildlflowers); diverse vegetation and wildlflowers (although too many invasives and non-natives); Attractive, positive, educational signs

From left: Winding trails with shade; Responsible dog owners and happy dogs; Recreational use of trails

From left: Wide-open unobstructed views; Ducks and wildlife make hiking experiences more interesting; Nature inspires creativity

Photogrids

A photogrid is a method for assessing the physical characteristics of a site and recording what is present. It involves superimposing a grid on an aerial map of the site and taking one or more photographs at each grid point.[19] Set the scale of the grid according to the size of the area you are covering and the level of detail that you want to record. Photogrids are a good method for gaining familiarity with a project site before you begin to work with a community (Chapter 4); but alternatively—and this is the focus of this section—young people can create a photogrid with you to study a site systematically and record what is important to them personally. Photographs can then be arranged to display interesting or problematic aspects of a site and facilitate discussions about what to preserve and what to change.

Ages. 10 and up

Materials. Aerial map with grids overlain (can be hand or digitally drawn—see preparation below); hand held cameras (digital, phones or tablets); access to computer and printer (optional); clipboards; pencils

Time to Complete. At least two 45-minute sessions—one for taking photographs, and one for annotating the grids and discussion. Ideally, the two sessions should be close together in time, with no more than a week between activities.

Method–Preparation of Materials:

In preparing materials, you need to determine how to arrange the grid on your project site. Your goal is to arrange the grid lines so that you capture the overall quality and character of the site.

- Determine the general direction, orientation, and length of transect lines in the project area

Figure 7.17. Photogrid. The base map was made by printing a large-scale map and mounting it on foam. String and push pins were used to mark the grid intervals. The large map was used to introduce youth to the method and for them to identify familiar landmarks on the map. When students had taken all their pictures, it was also used to systematically compile their images (Figure 7.20). Photo credit: Lynn M. Lickteig

- Determine the intervals at which people will pause to take pictures. Factors to consider in establishing these intervals include the overall distance to be covered, changes in slope or terrain, and the total number of photographs required.

- Mark the grid lines on the map. You can do this by hand, by drawing lines or using string (Figure 7.17) or use a computer program (Figure 7.18). You can also draw the grid on tracing paper so that notes and markings can be removed while maintaining a clean map.

Figure 7.18. Example of a photogrid that is marked digitally and then printed. This map was printed on the reverse side of the instruction sheet and given to each student group. Each group carried the map and instructions and made notes directly on the grid as they walked and took pictures. Image credit: Lynn M. Lickteig

19. Driskell, *Creating Better Cities with Children and Youth.*

Figure 7.19. Photogrid note-taking. Having a designated note-taker allows young people to focus on site evaluation and photography. If you do not have enough adults to serve in this role, young people can take turns so that each person has the opportunity to take pictures that reflect their own assessment of the site.
Photo credit: Lynn M. Lickteig

Method–Introduction and Taking Pictures

- Introduce the activity—what you plan to do and why

- Introduce the entire group to the map and grids. If you have a large map, help all participants orient landmarks and features together (Figure 7.17).

- Break the participants into pairs (or groups of three to four, depending on your entire group size), and assign each group to a line of the photogrid. (If you are working with a small group, all participants can assess the entire site).

- Provide each group with the materials they will need: a clipboard with a printed map, a pencil or permanent ink pen for making notations on the map, and a camera.

- Explain that each group will walk along the line of the grid. They should take at least one photograph at the intersection of each grid square. As they take the photograph, another group member should make notes of the direction of the photograph as well as why they are taking the photograph (Figure 7.19).

- Participants will continue in this way, taking photographs at each grid section and recording notes, until they have covered each area.

Method–Annotating the Grid and Discussion

- Prior to the start of the second session, facilitators will need to print photographs (if using print pictures to annotate), or upload all photographs to computers.

- Review the map with the group. Ask each group of participants to recall where they walked and some of the observations they made.

- Direct participants to annotate their photographs. Participants can annotate print pictures by hand (Figure 7.20), or they can annotate the pictures digitally (Figures 7.21 and 22). Digital annotation can be completed in a software program such as PowerPoint or Publisher, or in a program such as Adobe Illustrator.

- Ask participants to annotate any observations they made as they took photographs. This can be as simple as what they found there, what they liked or did not like, or what their experiences have been at that place over time.

- When all the pictures are annotated, have each group share their annotations with each other. Look for themes, trends, and ideas that can help identify important places or ideas for change.

Figure 7.20. Photogrid assemblage. This large-scale base map was used both to introduce the method (Figure 7.17) as well as to compile all student images in a single location. Students annotated their photographs to explain what each picture reflected from their evaluation of the site. The assembled photogrid was then shared at a community event (Figure 8.14).
Photo credit: Lynn M. Lickteig

Figure 7.21. Photogrid annotations made digitally using PowerPoint software. Image credit: Growing Up Boulder

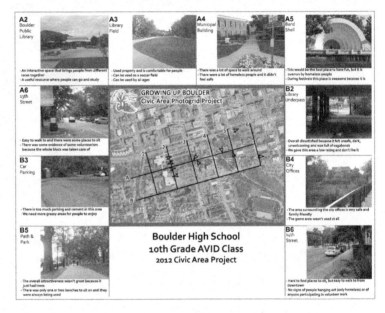

Figure 7.22. This treasure map (see Chapter 4) was annotated with student ideas after a photogrid exercise.
Image credit: Emily Tarantini

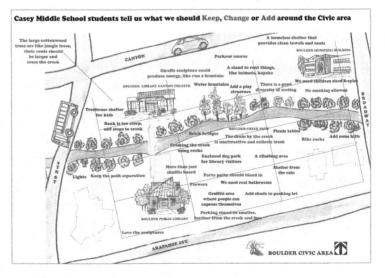

Box 7.12. **Bioblitz at Burke Park**

The bioblitz at Burke Park was part of a four-week class that culminated in design recommendations for the park adjacent to the school. The project provided an intensive process to build knowledge about the ecology, culture, and history of the site. In the second week of this class, students explored the park, with an emphasis on its soil, water, plants, and wildlife. A series of experts introduced them to the site's geology and ecological zones and taught them how to test water, smell soil and identify its texture, identify plants by leaves and stems, and identify wildlife using a variety of signs (from scat to tracks and nests). The bioblitz was enriched by diverse methods for exploring nature on any given day, including soil painting, sun prints made with leaves and photographic paper, and botanical sketching. In the third and fourth weeks, students imagined new designs for the park. Their recommendations included seating and points for viewing nature for the elderly, places for diverse sensory and aesthetic experiences, restoration of native species and ecosystems, and quiet reading spaces where visitors could be enclosed in nature.[1]

1. Victoria Derr, "Urban greenspaces as participatory learning laboratories." *Urban Design and Planning*, special issue titled Built Environment Education and Participation of Children and Youth, edited by Angela Million, Rosie Parnell, and Thomas Coelen, (2017):

Figure 7.23. Young students summarized their findings from a bioblitz by labeling what they found on a base map. Annotations included: "we saw scat," "we found a lot of bulrush," "wildlife tunnel," "we want more willow trees," "we like how wildlife lives here," "we don't like that the fish were dumped here," "wasp nest the size of a soccer ball!!" and "a web that was covering the tree." Image credit: Growing Up Boulder

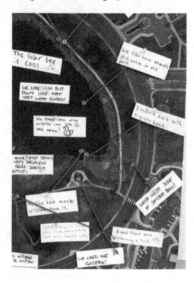

http://www.icevirtuallibrary.com/doi/abs/10.1680 /jurdp.17.00009.

The bioblitz process was documented on the project's website. Growing Up Boulder. "Explorations in Burke Park." www.explorationsinburkepark.weebly .com. (Retrieved July 23, 2017).

Bioblitz Inventories

Like learning expeditions, a bioblitz is intended to bring people together in a physical space. A bioblitz is an intensive survey of a physical area in which participants try to identify all the species they find within the area. As a means to inventory biological diversity, it can serve both biological assessment and educational purposes. A bioblitz is usually conducted over an intensive day or two, as a means of engaging local people with experts to identify, categorize, and learn

about a site's ecology.[20] The first recorded bioblitz was in 1997, when the Carnegie Museum of Natural History held a bioblitz in Riverview Park in Pittsburgh, Pennsylvania. This was the first event that invited community members to collaborate with scientists to conduct a biological inventory.[21] As a participatory method, a bioblitz can help young people learn about an urban green-

20. National Geographic, "Bioblitz." National Geographic. org. http://www.nationalgeographic.org/encyclopedia /bioblitz/. (Retrieved September 16, 2017).
21. Ibid.

space or park, and it can potentially inspire design recommendations for a project (Box 7.12) or changes to habitat (Box 7.13).

Ages. 8 and up

Materials. There are many reference materials and ecological identification tools available, but basic resources should be provided to aid in the identification of species: field guides (paper references of common species or local natural history books), hand lenses for magnifying insects or seeds, specimen containers for collecting water samples, butterfly nets, and binoculars. Also provide a map of the area to be inventoried, colored flags or cloths to mark boundaries, and clipboards and data sheets or a white board or paper for recording a species list.

In order to identify and categorize species on site, it is important to involve a local expert. This could be an environmental educator from a local nonprofit or a local ecologist from a university or government agency.

Time to Complete. Ideally, a bioblitz is conducted over a 24-hour period so that all times of day are included, which allows identification of species that are active in the day and night. A bioblitz might also be conducted over several days or even seasons to fit a project's timing and goals.

Method

- Introduce the activity—what you plan to do and why.
- Introduce the area that will be inventoried. If you have a map of the site, include it and show the boundaries for collection. If not, provide these instructions verbally or demarcate these areas with colored flags or cloth.
- Break the participants into small groups based on the methods of inventory. If the site is particularly diverse, you can create

Box 7.13. Habitat Mapping

Young people can link bioblitz or other wildlife inventories in their cities or schools with an on-line mapping tool through the Habitat Network. This application, managed by the Nature Conservancy and the Cornell Lab of Ornithology, invites young people to generate local maps—a schoolyard, backyard, or city space, identify habitat requirements for that area, and design recommendations for change. The mapping application allows uploading of local habitats to the Habitat Network website and sharing, with an on-line community, ways to improve local wildlife habitats. Young people often express interest in improving their cities for wildlife. The application provides a resource for learning how to do this.[1]

1. The Nature Conservancy and The Cornell Lab, "Habitat Network," Powered by Yardmap. www.habitat.network. (Retrieved October 7, 2017).

teams that focus on different ecological zones, such as a creek, a woodland, or an upland. Have the ecologist(s) explain methods for collection to each group. Introduce the ethic that all specimens should be collected with care and returned to their home after identification.

- As participants find new species, they should work with the expert(s) to identify each species, record the names of species found, and contribute to a running list.
- When all specimens are identified, the ecologists can help sort species by taxonomic category and review the diversity of species on the site.

The results can be displayed as a list, in a series of drawings, or as an annotated map (Figure 7.23).

Box 7.14. A Tool for Young People's Participation in Park Evaluation

Concerned that many children and teens in the United States fail to get enough regular physical exercise, and knowing that they are more likely to be active if they live near parks that they find attractive, Gina Besenyi and her university colleagues developed a software app that young people can download on a mobile phone or tablet to evaluate their city parks. The researchers had already created a paper-and-pencil Community Park Audit Tool for adult citizens and community groups, but they believed that young people would find an electronic version that they could carry with them into parks more appealing. For this purpose they created eCPAT (the electronic Community Park Audit Tool) and modified it for young people's needs.

Working with the Parks and Recreation Department in the City of Greenville, South Carolina, Greenville County Parks, Recreation, and Tourism, and LiveWell Greenville, Besenyi and her team recruited 52 youth, aged 11 to 18 and offered them a small stipend to participate in the audit. Participants attended a one-hour training to understand the project and learn how to use the app. eCPAT consists of questions under four headings: park information, access and neighborhood, activity areas, and quality and safety. The tool asks young people to share both objective information and subjective assessments. For example, it asks:

- Are there signs that state the park name? Park hours?

- Is there a public transit stop within sight of the park?

Software Applications for Site Information and Evaluation

Specialized software applications, or apps, for computer and mobile devices like iPhones and iPads have created a new universe of rapidly changing possibilities for information and communication as well as recreation and business. Many apps enable users to access and share information about their place, such as apps for maps and natural history identification. They can amplify young people's learning during an expedition down city streets, a photogrid, or a bioblitz, as well as help them synthesize and share the information they gather. Box 7.13, for example, describes an app for wildlife habitat mapping that can increase possibilities for learning and action during and after a bioblitz. As with any electronic device, it is important to balance the potential of apps with time for embodied experiences of a site through all of the senses. Apps should be used to help young people understand where they are and what they find there, not to draw their attention to a two-dimensional screen at the expense of the multidimensional real world.

Apps are being developed that young people can carry into parks and other places for on-site evaluations. Box 7.14 describes the Community Park Audit Tool that was designed for this purpose. Because app tools are continuously being created and updated, and because apps go in and out of popularity, it is important to work with young people as reviewers and advisors for any tools that you consider using. Do young people find the app you suggest appealing? Do they have ideas for how to improve it? Can they suggest other tools that might better represent their own culture and engage them in participatory site evaluation, planning, and design? Young people are the experts in the media most likely to attract the attention of their own age group and enable them to speak with their own voice.

- What are the primary land uses around the park?

- Are there playgrounds? Are they in good condition?

- Are there sports fields? A swimming pool? A skate park? Drinking fountains? Trash cans? Restrooms? Trees throughout the park? A water feature? Are they in good condition?

- Are park quality or safety concerns present in the park?

Young people were sent out in pairs to evaluate 47 parks that were representative of the total of 103 parks in Greenville County and their surrounding neighborhoods. Each pair assessed two parks. Project staff were present during each park visit to ensure safety and clarify instructions if the young people had any questions.

When young people's ratings were compared with those of a trained researcher, they proved valid and reliable. In follow-up focus groups, most participants said that the audit was easy, fun, and different from anything they had done before; however, some felt uncomfortable and unsafe in their assigned park. Most participants said that it introduced them to new parks and made them more aware of park qualities. It also made some more conscious of disparities in park quality in different neighborhoods.[1]

1. Gina M. Besenyi, Paul Diehl, Benjamin Schooley, Brie M. Turner-McGrievy, Sara Wilcox, Sara, Sonja A. Wilhelm Stanis, and Andrew T. Kaczynski. "Development and testing of mobile technology for community park improvements." *Translational Behavioral Medicine*, 6, no. 4 (2016): 519–532.; David Gallerani, Gina M. Besenyi, Sonja A. Wilhelm Stanis, and Andrew T. Kaczynski. "We actually care and we want to make the parks better." *Preventive Medicine*, 95, (2017): S109–S114.

Map Making

The educator David Sobel said that, "Maps are the clothespins that hitch our lives to our places."[22] Like other images young children make, he noted, their hand-drawn maps represent things they find emotionally important. Maps are a means for children to locate significant elements of their known world in relation to each other, surrounded by peripheries that are still *terra incognita*, where their curiosity extends. Later, older children can learn how to use scale, direction, and other formal rules of map-making, but at their best, maps at every age combine knowledge and feeling and express a developing sense of place. Chapter 4 discussed the value of maps and map-making for the adults who initiate participatory planning and design with young people, as a way to understand a project site. This section explores the value of maps in young people's hands.

22. David Sobel, *Mapmaking with Children* (Portsmouth, NH: Heinemann, 1998), 3.

There are many geography books for teaching children how to read and make maps, but the aim of this section is not learning about maps as a general skill. It is about using maps as a medium of expression: a medium for individual children to organize and share information about places they use in their locality, and for young people in groups to compile information about their community. On maps, children can also draw their visions for improvements. This section begins with hand-made maps, where young people have the most creative freedom, and then moves to computer generated maps. Ephemeral maps can be made outside by drawing and mounding lines in the dirt, laying out lines with sticks, and using found objects to designate landmarks. More often, maps are made inside, but experientially rich maps require a continuous back-and-forth movement between the drawing table and the surrounding city, as children record their experiences of their environment on their maps, and the maps show empty margins and blank spaces that need to be filled in with further exploration.

Area Sketch Maps

When children younger than 7 or 8 are asked to draw a map of places where they go around their home or their favorite places, they typically draw pictures of their surroundings at eye level. This is fine, but their limited map skills may mask how much they actually know. The geographer Roger Hart found that children ages 4 through 7 share their knowledge of local places more accurately through model making.[23] He gave each child blocks and landscape model pieces to place on a large sheet of paper. (See directions for model making in Chapter 5.) When a child was done with her arrangement, Hart showed her how to trace around the model elements, and he labeled each element as she explained it. When the child removed the model pieces, she had made a map!

With a little help, young children can quickly learn to read a close-up aerial photo that covers their everyday range of movement, and pick out familiar objects such as their home, street, friends' houses, the neighborhood playground, and their school. If a child marks these elements on the photograph and an adult labels them and transfers them to tracing paper, this forms an alternative way for young children to produce a map of their nearby world with assistance.[24]

The instructions that follow are for children ages 7 or 8 and up. By age 8, many children begin to use elevation, beginning with oblique views that combine pictures of elements like buildings and trees with layouts of streets and pathways (also described as a panoramic view). Later, they move to aerial perspectives that reduce objects to symbols, such as a square for a house (Figure 7.25). As they transition, it is common for them to combine perspectives (Figure 7.24).[25] Their

map-making skills reflect their experience with maps as much as their age. Maps form a good jumping-off place for interviews about the places that children know and use in their environment. (See Chapter 6 for suggested interview questions). This section focuses on map-making itself.

Materials. A large sheet of paper, about 20 inches or half a meter square; pencils with erasers; crayons or marking pens. Have extra paper available in case some children need to extend their paper's boundaries.

Time to Complete. Children of age 7 or 8 can usually draw and explain their map in 30 minutes or less. Older children can use 45 minutes or an hour. Great explorers of their environment may want to go longer and extend this activity to more than one day. When a child reaches the edge of his paper and has more to share, be ready to tape on additional sheets.

Method

- Explain to an individual child, or a group of children, that you would like them to draw a map of the places where they go around their home. Suggest that they start by drawing the location of their home and then work out from there. If you work with a group, give each child his own space so that he will not be tempted to copy another person's ideas.

- David Sobel suggests that if children are puzzled by the notion of a map, you can explain that a map is a picture of where things are or how things in their environment are arranged.[26] If a child still appears hesitant, encourage her to draw pictures of places she uses.

23. Hart, *Children's Experience of Place.*

24. Hart, *Children's Participation,* 168.

25. For typical trajectories in map skills, see Hart, *Children's Participation,* 165–168 and Sobel, *Mapmaking with Children,* 13–22.

26. Sobel, *Mapmaking with Children,* 13.

Figure 7.24. Map of an 8-year-old girl's home area in Cherbourg, Australia. This map combines partially elevated oblique views of important buildings with an aerial view of the roadway. Map courtesy: Angela Kreutz

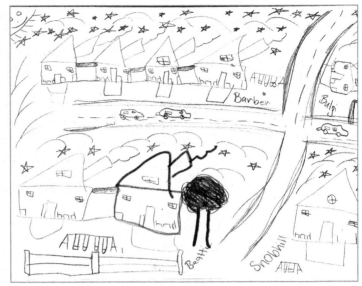

Figure 7.25. Map of Cherbourg in Queensland, Australia by an 11-year-old girl. Using an aerial view, this map covers the central streets, buildings and other town elements around the girl's home. Map courtesy: Angela Kreutz

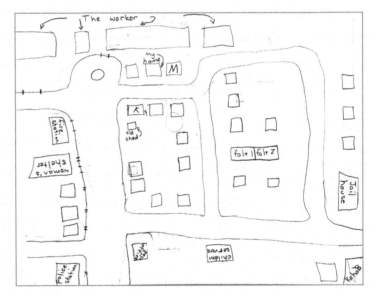

- Your exact instructions depend on your aim. You might ask children to make a map of:

  - Places where you go around your home
  - Places that you know in your area
  - Places where you go to meet friends
  - Your favorite places
  - Dangerous and scary places
  - Your neighborhood (after children have discussed the idea of a neighborhood)
  - Your most special place

- Have the children do the basic drawing by pencil. When they are satisfied with the general placement of things, suggest that they go over their pencil lines with crayons or markers and add more details if they wish.

- Label the maps as children are drawing, or when they talk about their map one-on-one at the end.

In her research on children's place use and mobility in Cherbourg, an Aboriginal settlement in Queensland, Australia, the architect and ethnographer Angela Kreutz found that children could productively do their mapping in pairs.[27] While one child was drawing a map, the other videotaped with a handheld camera and asked questions, such as, "Is that your house there?" or "You go further than the dump, don't you?" Then they exchanged roles. In this way they prompted each other to represent their local knowledge accurately.

Children can use their completed maps as a basis for discussion or writing activities by describing the places they have drawn, or as guides for child-led tours.[28] They can go out with cameras to take pictures of places they represented and then glue these pictures on their maps, or arrange the pictures in a band around their map, with labels or symbols on the map to show the location that each photo represents.

Route Maps

Route maps show the sequence of things that a child encounters, laid out along the pathway traveled (Figure 7.26). The materials and time required are the same as for a freehand area map. Route maps are useful for understanding children's independent mobility, alone and with friends, and the quality of routes. For example, children can be asked to draw:

- The route that you travel from your home to school, and then using a different color, your route from school back home (is it the same?)

Figure 7.26. A route map by a 9-year-old girl that shows her favorite places to go in her town of Dixon, New Mexico. Map courtesy: Victoria Derr

- Routes you travel around your area with friends and landmarks that are important to you along the way
- Your favorite route for exploring (Figure 7.26)

Different routes can be kept distinct by using different colored pencils, crayons or pens. Like area maps, route maps form a basis for elaboration and discussion. Children can be asked about their favorite part of a route and what makes it appealing, or parts that feel dangerous. The discussions that accompany these maps often reveal not only important place features but also the social or psychological benefits children derive from a place.[29] They can be asked to draw in traffic lights, stop signs, medians and crossing lines where they think it would make a route safer.

Route maps can combine expeditions outdoors with synthesizing drawings indoors. As a take-home activity, children can be asked to follow a chosen route, alone or with friends, and take notes along the way about points of interest. They can later lay out these places on a drawing of their route. Or they can take photos of these places and glue the printed photos in sequence along their route.

27. Kreutz, *Children and the Environment in an Australian Indigenous Community*.
28. For the use of mapmaking and complementary methods to understand how the quality of housing and the nearby environment impacts children's lives, see Johanna Hill, "Household mapping exercise in Nepal," In *Steps to engaging young children in research, Volume 2: The researcher toolkit*, ed. Vicky Johnson, Roger Hart, and Jennifer Colwell (Brighton, UK: Education Research Centre, University of Brighton, 2014), 78–82 available at https://bernardvanleer.org/publications -reports/steps-engaging-young-children-research-volume-2 -researcher-toolkit.

29. Victoria Derr, "Children's sense of place in northern New Mexico." *Journal of Environmental Psychology* 22, no.1 (2002): 125–137.

Figure 7.27. In a variation of sound mapping, children in Boulder, Colorado, visited a parcel of land slated for development as a city park. Children led each other on blindfolded sensory walks within the site, in order to use their senses of hearing and touch. Many children heard prairie dogs, and in their imagined playgrounds, drew tunnels that could mimic the prairie dogs' underground networks. Photo credit: Stephen Cardinale

Variation: Sound Maps

Materials. Notebooks and pencils to bring on the walk; long sheets of paper to record the route and descriptive words.

Time to Complete. Do this activity in one day if possible, when the memory of the experience is still fresh. There are lots of sounds in cities, so the route can be short. Plan at least 30 minutes for the walk and another 30 minutes to create the maps.

Method

To encourage children to experience and describe their environment through all their senses, they can be led along a path and asked to focus on other senses besides sight. Doing this forms a good preparation for a multisensory evaluation of places. A soundscape is an important dimension of a place.[30] Sounds along a street or in a public park or plaza can be stressful, soothing, mysterious, or pleasantly animated. It is useful to prepare for sound mapping by first asking a group to identify a few sources of sounds in their environment and generating a poetic and

playful list of descriptive words for each sound. For example, if someone says "motor scooter," give every child a minute to write down words that describe this sound, and then share the possibilities. This gets creative descriptions flowing.

Sound mapping can be done with eyes open or blindfolded. When participants keep their eyes open, the guide—who could be a child guide—slowly leads a small group along a route. Everyone walks silently and makes notes about what they hear. Rather than just writing nouns like "bus," "bicycle bell," or "bird," participants should be encouraged to find words that creatively describe each sound.

To encourage attention to sounds and turn off the dominant sense of vision, children can work in pairs, one blindfolded and the other leading slowly and safely (Figure 7.27). After proceeding on the route for some distance, they change places. The blindfolded child gives words for the sounds she hears, and her partner writes them down.

When the walk is completed and the group returns inside, each child individually, or the group as a whole, compiles their words in sequence. The result is a sound map poem that invites other people to re-experience the route in their imagination. Hear the example in Box 7.15.

---

30. David Sobel describes sound mapping led by an artist in his book *Mapmaking with Children*, 50–52.

Box 7.15. **Sound Map along Monterey Coast Trail**

Figure 7.28. The coast trail includes views of the wharf (top left), commercial buildings (top right), and the bay itself (above). Photo credits: Victoria Derr

Figure 7.29. A sound map constructed by an 11-year-old. Image credit: Eli Morton

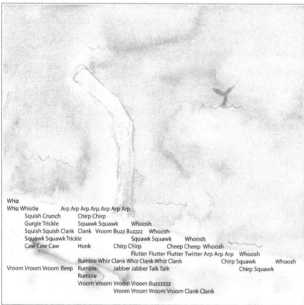

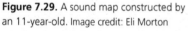

The vicinity near the Monterey Wharf and coastline in central California provides rich opportunities for discovery. (See Boxes 6.8 and 7.6 for examples of place-based learning using interviews and guided tours in this same context.) The Monterey Coast Trail is a pedestrian and bike trail that follows the coastline, moving through semi-industrial boat yards, piers, commercial centers, and parks along the Monterey Bay (Figure 7.28). It is buffered by some trees a short distance from a major road artery.

This sound map was constructed by walking about one quarter mile along the Monterey Coast Trail and wharf (Figure 7.29). Sounds were recorded on a sheet of paper. These sounds were arranged on a watercolor base map to represent their relative locations. Primary sources of sounds were California sea lions, seagulls and shorebirds, bikes, boats in the harbor, and bikes and pedestrians along the trail. These were accompanied by a steady source of cars, trucks, and waves on opposing sides of the trail walk. Map construction took approximately 20 minutes for the walk and another 20 to generate the illustration.

Variation: Collage Maps

Materials. Drawing tablets, pencils, crayons, a bag for storing found objects.

Time to Complete. 30–60 minutes for the walk, depending on the length of the route and whether children do drawings along the way; 45–60 minutes to create and label the map.

Method

As well as collecting sounds, smells or other sensory experiences as they walk, children can collect objects that they later glue or sew in sequence along the line of their route map. Encourage them to be observant and think creatively. What do they find that they associate with stopping places along the route? They could, for example, make rubbings of bricks, tree trunks, leaves, or inscribed words or dates on walls or monuments, draw pictures of things that catch their eye along the way, collect a fallen feather, ask a storekeeper for a fast-food bag with the store logo, or bring earth, grass, or flowers indoors to rub into the map for local color. Back inside, the children paint the route on a long strip of heavy paper or fabric and attach the cut-out rubbings, drawings and objects in sequence. They label the place that each collage element represents, and they can add sensory words that describe each place. Like soundscapes, this can be an individual or group activity.

Variation: Stream or River Maps

Materials. Drawing tablets, pencils with erasers, colored pencils, crayons, marking pens or paint, crayons, cameras (optional).

Time to Complete. The time required depends on your goals for this activity. If you focus on a short portion of a nearby stream or river, the walk and note taking could only require 45–60 minutes and the indoor map-making about the same amount of time. If you explore a local stream from the point where it surfaces to the point where it goes underground or joins a larger branch of the watershed, you may need a few hours for your walk. If you are ambitious and want to show a section of a watershed, with different water sources that empty into a large creek or river, this activity can be spread across several days.

Method

David Sobel recommends stream mapping as a way to bring local watersheds to life and satisfy children's explorer spirit.[31] Do advance exploration to know how far a local stream can be followed above ground or where a local river can be followed without running into barriers. The group gathers at a starting place, which could be where a stream surfaces. They follow it as far as they can, or until it disappears underground or flows into another body of water. Or they walk the borders of a river for a designated length. As they walk, they make notes and draw or take photos for individual maps or a collective map that they later assemble indoors. For the map, they draw or paint the waterway, and then make notes and attach drawings or photos of land uses that border it.

Children can create individual or group maps. This activity also forms a good foundation for a group mural. (See the section on mural making in Chapter 5.) Children can also record the expedition in writing. Once the group has explored visible sections of the waterway, they can trace the rest of its length on local maps or Google Earth.

Mobility Maps

Materials. pencils with erasers, rulers (optional), large sheets of paper about 20 inches or half a meter square.

Time to Complete. About 30 minutes

---

31. Sobel, *Mapmaking with Children*, 70–72.

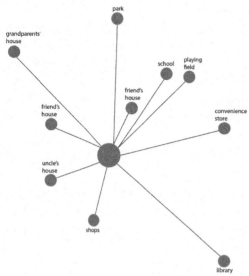

Figure 7.30. An example of a mobility map.
Image credit: Emily Tarantini

Method

Sometimes it is important to know local resources that a child uses frequently and how far they are from the child's home. A useful tool for this purpose is a mobility map (Figure 7.30).[32] You can generate a list of important resources through a group discussion, or leave the list up to each child. For example, a list might include the child's school, a park, a playing field, shops, friend's houses, and relative's houses. Some of these categories may include more than one place.

- Explain that the purpose of this map is for children to show places that they often use, how far they are from their house, and in what direction.

- A child begins by drawing a circle in the middle of the paper to represent home.

- Each child adds and labels circles around their home to represent places where they go, showing relative distance and direction.

- Using a ruler or freehand, they draw lines connecting each destination to their home in the middle.

As a variation, children can replace the circles with small drawings of each destination.

Community Mapping— Creating and Using a Base Map

In a broad sense, community mapping is any process that community groups use to visually record local knowledge and experience.[33] Given this book's emphasis on physical spaces for children and youth in cities, community mapping focuses on maps of shared territories. (For examples of intergenerational community maps, see the method of Gulliver's Footprints in Chapter 8 that involves residents of all ages in annotating and illustrating a large map of a public place, as well as the play maps featured in Box 7.16.) This section describes how young people can create a large base map as a tool for group study and reflection. A base map contains enough geographical information to give "the lay of the land," such as major streets, parks, plazas, and rivers. Around these reference points, children can fill in more data, depending on the focus of their project.

By making a large map of a project area, children create spaces where they can add details and annotations. For group work, the map should be large enough to hang on a wall or roll out on a large table or the floor. There are different processes for enlarging or "gridding up" a map for this purpose.[34] A simple method is described here.[35]

---

32. Mobility maps were introduced by Victoria Johnson, Joanna Hill and Edda Ivan-Smith in *Listening to Smaller Voices* (Chard Somerset, UK: ActionAid, 1995).

33. Jackie Amsden and Rob VanWynsberghe, "Community mapping as a research tool with youth." *Action Research* 3, no. 4 (2005): 357–381.

34. See Hart, *Children's Participation*, 169 and Sobel, *Mapmaking with Children*, 53–55.

35. This description is adapted from Hart, *Children's Participation*, 169.

Materials. a scale map of the selected area, obtained from the local planning office, library, geography department in a local university, or printed out from Google Maps™ or OpenStreetMap; a large sheet of paper or canvas, several feet or meters in length and width; a long ruler; scissors; pencils; marking pens, crayons or paint

Time to Complete. At least 60 minutes to create the enlargement, depending on its size. Adding details, map symbols, and a map key can be done later.

Method

Begin with the existing scale map of the chosen area, which may be a small hand-held map. Decide which features the group wants to transfer to the large map, and have someone trace over them with marking pens.

1. Using a ruler, divide the small map into as many grid squares as there are children in the group, or pairs of children.

2. Divide the large sheet of paper or canvas into the same number of grid squares.

3. Number each square on the small and large map with corresponding numbers.

4. Cut out the squares in the small map and assign one to each child or pair of children.

5. Each child, or each pair, takes their small grid square and enlarges it on the corresponding square on the large map. Begin by drawing features in pencil. It is helpful to work in pairs because one child can hold up the small square for the other child to copy, and make suggestions to ensure that all the highlighted features are accurately placed.

6. Once the group is satisfied with the accuracy of the large map, they can color in or paint the map features. If they are using paint, begin by working on the floor and mount the map on the wall after the paint dries.

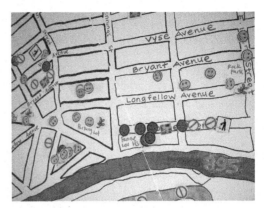

Figure 7.31. Youth annotated a street map with yellow happy faces and red sad faces to represent their experience of the city in the Growing Up in New York City initiative. Photo credit: David Driskell

As an option, children can take copies of their small gridded map into the field to add more features that they can transfer back to the large map. Or they may know their local area well enough to begin adding details immediately with drawing and writing.

Stickers or icons are an effective way to identify places with different types of values for children (Figure 7.31). They can be as simple as smiley faces and sad faces for liked and disliked places, or more varied such as different categories of resources for children or different activities children engage in. Invite children to design their own symbols and create the map key or legend. If young people are interested in the natural ecology of the city, they can emphasize natural features and wild species that make their home in the city.[36]

As in the case of individual sketch maps, only the purpose of your project limits the features children and youth add, and in this case, they are working together to map places of collective importance. They may map, for example:

- parks for all abilities
- friendly businesses

---

36. Sheila Harrington, ed., *Giving the Land a Voice: Mapping our Home Places* (Salt Spring Island, BC, Canada: Land Trust Alliance of British Columbia, 1999).

Box 7.16. **Intergenerational Play Maps**

The method of play maps was pioneered by the landscape architect Isami Kinoshita and the Taishido Study Group in the Setagaya Ward of Tokyo. Kinoshita and his colleagues interviewed children about their most visited and favorite play spaces, what they did there, and with whom. In one-on-one interviews, they spread out a base map of Taishido with a few landmarks for orientation and asked each boy and girl to locate these spaces. Young children drew pictures on separate cards for each favorite place, and then positioned the cards on the map. Older children drew and wrote directly on the map. When children were unsure about locations, their parents were asked to help. After Kinoshita and his colleagues collected ten to twenty individual maps for different age groups from 7 to 12, they integrated this information on separate large base maps for each group, so they could compare where different ages played. To verify information, they gave questionnaires with similar questions to school classes.

Kinoshita and his colleagues also interviewed older generations and asked parents and grandparents to create their own maps of where they played as children and what they did. The study group has been doing this since 1981, so that now it has four generations of childhood memories and experiences. When the composite maps of the generations are compared, they show changing patterns of play as Taishido has become increasingly developed. The maps reveal disappearing places to meet friends spontaneously, enjoy street play, and encounter nature, as well as decreasing opportunities to play outdoors in general and mix with all ages in public spaces. The maps have spurred adults and children to work together to improve Taishido as a place for young people.[1]

1. Isami Kinoshita, "Charting generational differences in conceptions and opportunities for play in a Japanese neighborhood." *Journal of Intergenerational Relationships* 7, no. 1 (2009): 53–77; Isami Kinoshita, "Play maps in Japan." In *Steps to Engaging Young Children in Research, Volume 2*, 78–82; "Three generations of play in Taishido." *Children's Environments Quarterly* 1, no. 4 (1984): 19–28.

Figure 7.32. Detail of first generation play map showing where grandparents played when they were growing up in the Setagaya Ward of Tokyo in the 1930s, when there were still large green fields and safe streets. Image credit: Isami Kinoshita

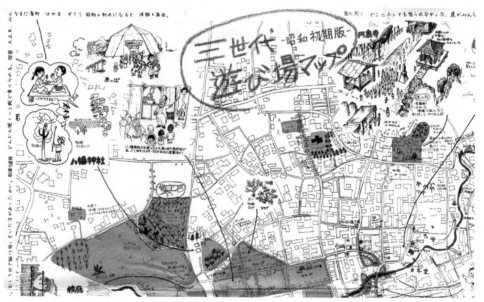

Figure 7.33. An explorer map generated from Google Maps and GIS that gives young people just enough information to find a place that invites further investigation. This map was drawn by an 11-year-old after his exploration along an urban creek. The typed annotations provide the explorer's comments. Image credit: Eli Morton (explorations and drawing), Ben Harden (base map), Victoria Derr (annotations).

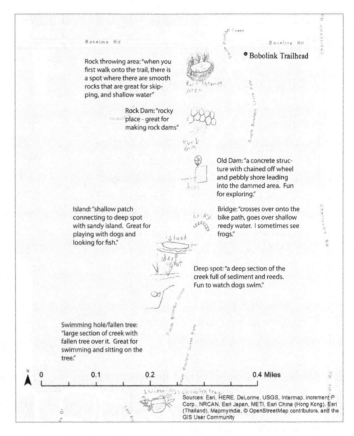

- businesses that discriminate against children and teens
- places to meet and hang out with friends
- peaceful places to be alone or with friends
- dangerous crossing points on the way to school
- fresh water pumps and latrines in a slum area

The completed maps can inform action. For an example of intergenerational community mapping that has led to action to protect places for children's outdoor play in the densely developed city of Tokyo, see Box 7.16.

Variation: Explorer Maps

This is a method developed by David Sobel to encourage children's natural curiosity and expand their knowledge of their locality.[37] Because

37. Sobel, *Mapmaking with Children*, 67–70.

it takes children into largely unknown areas, it is best done in small groups with an adult companion to ensure safety. Sobel calls the groups "explorer clubs." They begin by looking at a large community base map that they created together or a small-scale map of their local environment. Do they find empty spaces on the map? What is in these spaces? Some children may have suggestions, but these become possibilities to be verified by groundtruthing, or checking the realities of a place on foot. By using the "enlarge" function on a photocopy machine, gridding up this section, or tracing this section on a large wall map, create an individual map of each *terra incognita* in a size that children can carry into the field on a clipboard. Include just enough boundary points for orientation. (See the example in Figure 7.33.) Each area of mystery becomes the subject for a separate field trip. Children travel to the site and draw and write on the map what they find there, and later add this information to their large community map.

Variation: Three-Dimensional Relief Maps

Young children, and young people who live in areas with stark changes in elevation such as deep canyons and high hills, may find it easier to orient themselves on 3-D maps of their area. Ephemeral relief maps can be molded on the ground or with wet sand in a sand table. The directions here produce more permanent maps. Follow a process similar to the directions for producing a large community base map on paper, described above. In this case, each child or group of children creates a relief map for their section of the community grid, and then they assemble all of the grid squares on a large table to create the completed map. David Sobel describes this process in his book *Mapmaking with Children*.[38]

Materials. an example of a relief map that you can show; a large quantity of modeling clay, depending on the number of children working and the size of the final map (preferably choose a non-hardening modeling clay that doesn't dry out, so children can go back and make changes, and a kind that comes in different colors, such as blue for water and brown for land forms); two copies of a paper map drawn to scale, at the size you choose for the final assembled map; a heavy cardboard or plywood base for one of the paper maps; pencils; rulers; pointed sticks to draw features on the modeling clay.

Time to Complete. The amount of time required depends on the size of the map and the map skills that children bring to the activity. After you explain the process and children divide up their grid squares, they need to research the geography of their section. Since this book focuses on local areas at a scale where children can influence planning and design, you can apply other methods in this chapter to gather this information, such as walking tours and photogrids that enable

children to observe and document changes in topography. If young people know how to read contour maps, they can draw on this resource.

Method

- Glue one paper map to strong cardboard or plywood for the relief map base, and divide it into grid squares depending on the number of children or small groups that will be working.

- Draw similar grid lines on a second map of the same size on a table where children will assemble the completed relief map. Number the two maps with matching numbers in each grid.

- Cut up the working map and give each child or group their grid square to develop.

- Determine the vertical scale, which is different than the horizontal scale on the flat paper map. You need to accentuate the height of hills and the depth of ravines or channels for rivers and streams, so that they will be clearly visible. This requires a larger vertical scale. You can explain this process and assign a scale for the children to follow, or make this decision through a group discussion. Keep in mind that the more that you accentuate height and depth, the more modeling clay you will need. Sobel recommends marking the vertical scale of the tallest heights and lowest depressions on toothpicks that children can use as their standard.

- Everyone needs to begin by covering their square with modeling clay to the same depth. With pointed sticks, they outline the topographic features that they will represent. For river or stream channels or depressions in the land, they carve down into the surface, while they mound up hills and other heights.

- When the grid squares are finished, children assemble them on the table map and smooth the edges together.

---

38. Sobel, *Mapmaking with Children*, 95–99.

When the relief map is created, children can locate elements on it, such as small blocks or cut-out pieces of a sponge for their homes and school, ribbons of different widths for streets, and patches of green construction paper for parks. With toothpicks, they can add labels.

Participatory GIS

In the 1990s, community mapping projects similar to those described above began to go digital, initially with adult populations. They took advantage of Geographic Information Systems (GIS)—computer software systems to collect, store, manage, and analyze spatial information and related data.[39] Participatory GIS (PGIS) projects with young people can be particularly useful when it is important to communicate exact spatial locations in the planning and design of a public space. They are also helpful for larger scale or land-use planning projects that already draw from GIS data to generate maps of the city. Many PGIS projects are emerging that link stories about places with mapping. These applications enable young people to mark personal landmarks in the city and add their stories and reasons that explain why these places are significant.

By putting this technology in the hands of community groups, Participatory GIS (PGIS) enables people to represent their local knowledge on two- and three-dimensional computer-generated maps. The practice of PGIS brings together a technical expert in GIS with community members who hold local knowledge, and may include city decision-makers. It is occasionally used with children under adult direction, and in the hands of teens and older youth, it can be an important capacity-building tool. As simplified, user-friendly applications of GIS and similar programs become more common, their use is extending to younger groups.

All of the general principles of ethical participation need to be respected in PGIS (see Chapter 3 on the ethics of work with children, youth, and communities). This issue applies to non-digital maps as well, but given the potential for GIS maps to be shared via computers, issues of confidentiality become heightened. Aline Gubrium and Krista Harper share the example of initiatives in New Zealand to record Maori traditions, sacred sites and resource knowledge on maps of native lands, on the condition that some of the GIS data will only be available to Maori communities or elders.[40] Similar discussions about confidentiality are necessary when children share personal information, such as secret spaces and peer-group activities.

A GIS expert may facilitate PGIS processes from the beginning to end of a project. This involves not only working with people to gather information about their locality, but also helping community members interpret the maps produced and present them in public meetings. Alternatively, PGIS may involve "upskilling" when the expert trains local people to take over his or her role.[41] This enables communities to maintain and update information on their own, reducing the need for costly outside support, and it gives the new local experts valuable skills. Given the widespread use of GIS software in mapping and data management today, an "upskilling" approach can open career paths for youth.

PGIS can be linked to methods already presented in this chapter, such as child-led walks, learning expeditions, photogrids, sketch maps, and annotated community base maps, as well as other methods in this book such as photovoice (Chapter 5). Once information is gathered, the expert adds it to the GIS system. Children and youth may also work directly on a large-scaled base map or aerial photo printed out from the GIS program, discussing where they go and sharing their local knowledge, or draw and make

39. Jon Corbett, Giacomo Rambaldi, Peter Kyem, Dan Weiner, Rachel Olson, Julius Muchemi, Mike McCall, and Robert Chambers, "Overview: Mapping for change—the emergence of a new practice." *PLA Notes 54, Special Issue on Mapping for Change*, (2006): 13–19.

40. Aline Gubrium and Krista Harper. *Participatory Visual and Digital Methods* (Walnut Creek, CA: Left Coast Press, 2013), 162–165.

41. Ibid., 155.

notes directly on the map or on clear overlays. The expert transfers this information to two or more digital overlays and attaches links to further data such as sources of the information. (For an example that integrates PGIS and children's mapping, see the profile of the Safe Community Program in India in Chapter 11.)

PGIS is useful for answering the following types of questions:[42]

- Where is something located?
- Where is it concentrated?
- What are the distances between places or services?
- What kinds of things occur together in a place?
- How is a place changing over time?

PGIS could show, for example, where schools or other services are located relative to children's homes; where children's choices of favorite, boring, and dangerous places are concentrated; and whether schools are close to sites that children consider dangerous. If information has been gathered over a period of time, PGIS could show historical changes in community conditions.

A popular use of GIS and similar map-linked multimedia information systems is "story-mapping" which links video, audio, and text files to map locations. Box 4.5 in Chapter 4 presents an example of storymapping, as it links places in the city of Boulder, Colorado, to transcripts from oral history interviews of people who grew up in the city, recalling how they experienced these places as children. Storymapping forms a flexible medium to archive information about the meaning of places for people of all ages. Once the base map is created, anyone with access can add information.

ArcGIS™ has become the standard GIS system used by government, businesses, and academic institutions, but in addition to requiring a high level of technical training, it is expensive. Free open-source GIS software is available, but it also requires a high level of expertise. Other map-linked systems such as Google Maps™ and Google Earth™ offer simplified GIS applications with more limited features, and there are map-linked multimedia systems such as mapbuilder.net, communitywalk.com or ESRI's ArcGIS Story Maps that can be used for storymapping.[43] These simplified mapping applications can be easily learned by young people. Given the regularly updated and changing nature of these technologies, it is important to find an expert advisor who can guide you through options, although many tutorials also exist to help those who are comfortable exploring new software applications on their own.

GIS can be linked to other digital data sources, such as Global Positioning Systems or GPS. Now embedded in mobile phones or small handheld or wearable units, GPS gathers spatial and time coordinates of participants' movements as they travel through landscapes. Participants can record their experiences of places as the GPS unit tracks where they are. Box 7.17 shares a project from Ontario, Canada, that combined GIS with GPS to understand mobility issues of children with physical disabilities.

These linked systems can require considerable expertise, so that some applications are primarily relevant for adult-led research about children rather than research by children. They offer new tools, however, to understand children's movements through space that can be combined with other information about the places children use (supplied by children themselves or derived from other data sources). A study of children's routes to school, for example, could combine GPS tracking of children's pathways, children's evaluations of the safety of crossing points along the way, and data on traffic volumes during the hours before and after school.

In most countries, youth in the 15- to 24-year age group are the peak users of computers, internet, and mobile phones, in terms of time online.[44] Falling prices for mobile phones and

42. Ibid., 154.

43. Ibid., 158.

44. UN-Habitat, *ICT, Urban Governance and Youth*. (Nairobi: author, 2012)

Box 7.17. **Exploring the Mobility and Accessibility of Everyday Environments for Children with Disabilities in Ontario, Canada**

Children with physical disabilities have a right to participate and inform decisions that affect their lives, but they are often not included in participatory planning. Qualities of the physical environment can significantly impact their ability to enjoy their surroundings; and the more severe their disability, the more these effects are heightened. Sean Doherty and colleagues developed a method for using Global Positioning System (GPS) tracking and GIS mapping with children with disabilities to collect and visually present data about neighborhood qualities. Using a combination of automated tracking technologies, on-line interactive activity-travel diaries, GIS maps, and interviews, children were able to discuss issues in the physical environment that affected their mobility and the quality of their experiences in their neighborhoods. Children ages 10 to 14 participated, who relied on a range of mobility devices, including wheelchairs, braces, walkers, crutches, canes, and orthotics. Each participant wore a tracking device and entered on-line travel diaries, which resulted in individual maps that were then used for interviewing. In this way, children were able to describe places where they traveled and the accessibility challenges they experienced. These methods were developed so that children with disabilities could contribute directly to discussions with city officials about their experiences of the city.[1]

---

1. Sean T. Doherty, Patricia McKeever, Henna Aslam, Lindsay Stephens, and Nicole Yantzi. "Use of GPS tracking to interactively explore disabled children's mobility and accessibility patterns." *Children, Youth and Environments* 24, no. 1 (2014): 1–24.

both "narrowband" and broadband access have put new information and communication technologies in the hands of growing populations in all regions of the world. This enables youth to not only receive information, such as news about local events and services, but to also send information to other youth, citizens of all ages, and their governments. Through their facility with digital media and their resourcefulness, youth can open new communication avenues as interns and new hires in government agencies and civil society organizations. By offering training in information and communication technologies, governments and organizations can also promote the inclusion of youth. This can create new opportunities for youth in careers and leadership. As youth and other marginalized populations appropriate these tools, governments and other institutions need to reskill their staff to be responsive to these new forms of citizen engagement.[45]

The influence that youth can have through digital community mapping is illustrated by Map Kibera in Nairobi, Kenya, featured in Box 7.18. By using GPS and PGIS to assemble information about their informal settlement, youth literally and figuratively put Kibera on the map. Links between social media applications, news blogs, videos and radio broadcasting are also enabling youth and other citizens to voice their struggles, achievements and dreams in their communities with new immediacy. The voice platform connected with Map Kibera, for example, provides a local news service, and in South Africa, the Khanyisa Youth Network enables a large network of youth groups to discuss issues in their informal settlements with an audience of hundreds of thousands.[46] Digital media are opening new forums for child and youth civic engagement by increasing access to information, citizen networks, local leadership, and governments.

---

45. Björn-Sören Gigler and Ballur, Savit, eds. *Closing the Feedback Loop: Can Technology Bridge the Accountability Gap?* (Washington, DC: The World Bank, 2014).

46. UN-Habitat, *ICT, Urban Governance and Youth.* (Nairobi: author, 2012), 32.

Box 7.18. **Putting Kibera on the Map**

Map Kibera is one of the earliest large-scale PGIS initiatives, based in the informal settlement of Kibera in Nairobi, Kenya, which is estimated to be one of the largest slums in the world. It remains an active community-mapping project that has spread to similar settlements like Mathare and Mukuru, managed by Map Kibera Trust. Its goals are to serve as an interactive information and media source that can amplify people's voices and improve community conditions. Since the project began in 2009, it has primarily relied on the energies and skills of youth. Before they set to work with expert training and support, this bustling settlement was a blank space on official city maps.

Young mappers collect data about their community with GPS devices, and then work with computers to edit and upload the information, using OpenStreetMap, a free and editable map of the world generated by volunteers, open-source software like QGIS, and on occasion ArcGIS™. After creating a base map with features like building clusters, pathways, drainage ditches, and markets, they overlay a series of thematic maps that focus on assets and problems of particular interest. In this way they have mapped places important for health, education, water, sanitation, and security.

Although a variety of processes can be followed to create a new map, some typical steps are illustrated by the mapping workshops sponsored by UN-Habitat to train youth in Nairobi and two other large African cities in these skills in 2009. The workshops began with a personal asset-mapping exercise that asked youth to identify their strengths such as personal characteristics and skills, as well as community assets such as

key relationships and institutions. (For instructions for personal asset-mapping, see "Other Group Discussions" in Chapter 6.) After youth did this individually, they compared their results. For example, if they listed creativity, then they compiled a list of Kibera institutions that helped them develop their creative skills. They wrote the names of the local assets on sticky notes and then located them on a Google Earth map of Kibera.

Youth then broke into groups to cover different areas of their community. Each group visited each of the points identified in their area, equipped with a GPS unit (which today could be simply a mobile phone). They marked the GPS point, took a photo, and gathered information about each point. For example, if they visited a local video library, they would ask about the materials it carried and its hours of operation. The images and information were then uploaded via GIS.

In this case, a group of young mappers began by pooling their own knowledge of their community. The process can also begin by youth engaging with other groups to interview them about their local knowledge. The themes for new map overlays are only limited by the interests of community members and civil society organizations.[1]

_____

1. For the official project website, see: Map Kibera. "Map Kibera: Making the Invisible Visible." mapkibera. org. (Retrieved October 9, 2017); Doug Ragan, "Using mapping to engage youth in planning and governance." (Unpublished paper, 2011); Jennifer Shkabatur. "Interactive community mapping: Between empowerment and effectiveness." In *Closing the Feedback Loop: Can Technology Bridge the Accountability Gap?,* ed. Björn-Sören Gigler and Savita Ballur (Washington, DC: The World Bank, 2014), 71–106; UN-Habitat. *ICT, Urban Governance and Youth.* (Nairobi: author, 2012), 33–34.

8

"We are united by our struggle to make the world a better place for all."[1]

Workshops and Community Events

Workshops, presentations and other community events are opportunities to bring the generations together, for young people to meet new people and hear diverse perspectives, and for adults to see the creativity, capacity, and concern for the present and future that children and youth bring. When workshops come early in a participatory process, they help young people understand different users of a space and their needs. During presentations at public meetings and other community events, young people have a chance to see that their work matters to others, take their ideas further in response to questions and discussions, and see that they can be a part of larger processes of urban governance. When some of their aims are achieved, they can enjoy the satisfaction of success at celebrations. These multigenerational events not only enable young people to have a voice in local decisions that affect them, consistent with Article 12 of the United Nations Convention on the Rights of the Child, but these events can also integrate them into the cultural life of their community, consistent with Article 31.

At their best, participatory design and planning processes support transformative learning for all participants. If people are willing to hear each other with respect, it can build social and civic capital and open the way for planning and design solutions that no single group could have generated alone. When people come prepared to speak for social equity and ecosystems—to ensure that the interests of marginalized people and silent species will also be heard—essential ingredients of sustainable cities

come together. In our experience, young people often play this role by expressing a concern for nature and a sense of fairness.

As part of Growing Up Boulder, we evaluated a process that involved primary and middle school children and local adults, including elders from a senior center, in redesigning a school ground that would serve as a neighborhood open space after school hours and in suggesting improvements for an adjoining park. We found that a public workshop early in the process and an open house where children later shared their design models and drawings were especially significant (Figure 8.14). In the words of a teacher: "The community piece was the biggest. Working with all the different people. For the kids to have the courage to speak about ideas, the ability to listen to others, to feel empowered. Kids have very few opportunities like that." In the words of a 12-year-old girl, "We learned about considering everyone in the neighborhood and the neighborhood itself."[2] This is local democracy in action.

---

1. Gabriela Azurday Arrieta (age 13) and Audrey Cheynut (age 17): 2002 representatives of the Children's Forum, addressing the U.N. Special Session on Children.

2. Angela Kreutz, Victoria Derr, and Louise Chawla, "Fluid or fixed? Processes that facilitate or constrain a sense of

This chapter describes the following opportunities to bring all ages in a community together, enabling young people to have a voice and hear the voices of others:

- Charrettes + Co-Design
- Child-Participatory Budgeting
- Child and Youth Presentations
- Young People Speaking at Public Events and City Council Sessions
- Celebrations
- Gulliver's Footprints
- Futures Festivals
- Living Laboratories
- Improving Community Commons

Some of these events are methods of engagement to study and evaluate communities, share ideas, and make collaborative decisions. Others are examples of intergenerational activities and celebrations that we hope will inspire you. We present them here because they all provide occasions for different groups in a community to come together to share and learn from each other.

Charrettes + Co-Design

Charrettes bring designers and local users of a space together to collaboratively envision a new design or plan.[3] At these events, designers can directly hear the ideas of participants, while ordinary people, who do not necessarily have a depth of experience with design, can see their ideas translated into design language. The group discussion allows many different ideas to be expressed, and for individuals to listen and adapt their own visions to the needs and interests of a group. While charrettes and other design workshops primarily rely on drawings and other visual media, they can include other creative forms such as role plays (Box 5.22).

While some people see charrettes and co-design as equivalent processes, co-design has emerged as "more than" a charrette in that it engages people throughout the design process and places more balanced value and weight on decision-making by designers and participants.[4] Co-design is especially well suited for participatory workshops with young people because it emphasizes active, hands-on methods for young people to work collaboratively with designers.[5] This differs from some charrettes used in public planning in which design proposals are developed in advance and workshop participants are asked to comment on them.

Method—Introduce the Project

Designers or city representatives begin by introducing the site to be designed, the workshop process, and any other relevant concepts or information.[6] At this stage, precedents, or examples from other places, can be used, as well as a field trip to the site for everyone to become familiar with its features. (For examples of the use of precedents and field trips, see the visual

inclusion in participatory schoolyard and park design." *Landscape Journal* 37, no. 1 (2018); Alessandro Rigolon, Victoria Derr, and Louise Chawla, "Green grounds for play and learning," *Handbook on Green Infrastructure*, ed. Danielle Sinnett, Nick Smith and Sarah Burgess (Cheltenham, UK: Edward Elgar Publishers, 2015), 281–300.

3. Henry Sanoff, *Community Participation Methods in Design and Planning* (New York: John Wiley & Sons, 2000). The importance of aligning all partners and participants behind shared goals before an intergenerational charrette begins is discussed by: Sharon Sutton, and Susan Kemp. "Children as partners in neighborhood placemaking: lessons from intergenerational design charrettes." *Journal of Environmental Psychology* 22, no. 1 (2002): 171–189.

4. Rosie Parnell, "Co-creative adventures in school design." *School Design Together,* ed. Pamela Woolner (London: Routledge, 2015), 123–137.

5. Stanley King, Merinda Conley, Bill Latimer, and Drew Ferrari, *Co-Design: A Process of Design for Participation.* (New York: Van Nostrand Reinhold, 1989).

6. For tips on bringing people together and putting everyone—including yourself—at ease during a workshop, and for conducting some commonly used participatory processes effectively, see: Robert Chambers, *Participatory Workshops: A Sourcebook of 21 Sets of Ideas and Activities* (London: Earthscan Publications, 2002).

Figure 8.1. This concept drawing (at right of photo) integrated many children's ideas for a park and playground redesign. This drawing was brought back to young people and was showcased at a community open house to represent children's design intentions. Photo credit: Growing Up Boulder, with drawing by Kate Armbruster

preference survey for parks that flood in Chapter 6 and learning expeditions in Chapter 7).

Method—Idea Generation

Participants then break into small groups and begin to develop their ideas. Facilitators can use a variety of methods to spark ideas. Possibilities include:

- **Cut out pictures of various design elements:** play equipment, benches, tables, different types of lighting, landscaping elements (such as trees, different kinds of grasses, shrubs, garden beds, hills, water), and so on. Participants select items that they like and often place these elements on a large base map of the space.

- **Interactive mapping**, in which young people place icons or labels onto maps to describe specific place uses or experiences, identify positive or negative spaces, or imagine new places. See the *Move Around and Play* workshops in the Netherlands in Chapter 11.

- **Art-based methods**, including photography, drawing, model-making, and music. For example, young people can draw over pre-printed photographs of an existing area (Figure 5.14, Figure 7.3, and Box 8.1). They can generate drawings of favorite or "dream" places (Box 8.2), or places where they feel safe or vulnerable (Box 5.13). They can build models out of found objects, scrap materials, or clay (Figure 5.24).

Simple pre-printed base maps help facilitate model-making in workshop formats (Box 4.4 and Figure 5.24). Youth can also generate ideas through music (Box 5.16 and Box 8.3). Chapter 5 provides detailed instruction for many arts-based methods that can be integrated into co-design workshops.

- **Social media.** A wide range of social media apps can be used to facilitate group voting and to analyze and organize ideas into themes and then share them with a wider public (Box 8.4).

At the end of this process, people typically share their ideas with each other and select priorities. During this stage designers and participants identify broad themes, such as a space for increasing biodiversity, or a space for interactive art, as well as some specific design details. Idea generation can be achieved in one long workshop or broken into a few shorter ones.

Method—Draft and Review Initial Plans

In the next stage, designers generate concept plans (or simple drawings) that convey participants' essential ideas. If time permits, this can occur during the charrette, with designers drawing the ideas that they hear. (See Variation: Co-Design Youth Manual, p. 207). More typically, designers take all the ideas generated in a workshop and go back to their offices, generate drawings, and come back a week or more later to share them with the group (Figure 8.1).

Box 8.1. **Co-Design in Auckland**

City officials in the Auckland, New Zealand, metropolitan area have made young people's participation a priority. The Auckland Plan of 2012 called for "putting children and youth first" and in 2014, the city drafted a strategic plan to accomplish this. Around the same time, the Waitematā Local Board in the Auckland area determined to become a UNICEF Child Friendly City. Young people's participation has thus become integrated in a variety of projects that illustrate co-design.

One example was a "Child-Friendly Audit" of Freyburg Square in Auckland in 2015. For this process, researchers at Massey University's SHORE and Whariki Research Centre and Auckland Council staff worked with children by first inviting them to explore the square, taking photographs of things they liked and didn't like and discussing their observations (Figure 8.2). Then they participated in a charrette-style co-design workshop. Here they selected and annotated photos to share their responses to current features of the square (Figure 8.3). In a third session, the Council design team presented the draft plan to the children, explaining where the children's ideas were applied, and the children returned to the square to write more specific suggestions on copies of the draft. The children also evaluated the participatory process.

In a second example, a Masters student in landscape architecture at Unitec Institute of Technology worked with her supervisor to facilitate four schoolyard greening co-design workshops at an Auckland elementary school. First, the school students were introduced to the project and basic landscape architecture design principles. Then they conducted a simple site analysis (such as measuring area dimensions and plant identification) before making lists of suggested design ideas. At the second workshop, they chose from these ideas and made models of the space. The

Masters student photographed and analyzed these models and used them to drive her design. For the third workshop, she presented a draft concept plan and invited the students' feedback, which was collated and used to modify the design. Finally, at the last workshop, students were presented with the final design (see final poster, Figure 9.2) and asked to provide an evaluation of the process and what they had learned.[1]

Figure 8.2. Children playing in the public square as part of a Child-Friendly Audit. Photo credit: Karen Witten

Figure 8.3. Children writing responses to design possibilities for the public square in Auckland. Photo credit: Karen Witten

1. Susan J. Wake and Qian Wang, "Developing the greenery: Results from a co-design project with landscape architects and schoolchildren in Auckland, New Zealand." *Fifty Years Later: Revisiting the Role of Architectural Science in Design and Practice: 50th International Conference of the Architectural Science Association*, ed. J. Zuo, L. Daniel, V. Soebarto (University of Adelaide, 2016), 269–278; Penelope Carroll and Karen Witten, "Children as urban design consultants: Children's audit of a central city square in Auckland, Aotearoa/New Zealand." *Designing Cities with Children and Young People*, ed. Kate Bishop and Linda Corkery (New York: Routledge, 2017), 105–118.

Box 8.2. **A Child-Friendly Play Space in a Busy Shopping Precinct**

The Centre for Educational Research at the University of Western Sydney engaged young children ages 3–8 in a series of activities and workshops to contribute to the design of a Food Terrace Musical Play Space in a shopping district of the Rouse Hill Town neighborhood. Workshops with children involved a series of exercises:

- Drawing their favorite play space and their dream play space

- Evaluating a series of photographs of play spaces and play elements from around the world

- Choosing favorite play spaces

In addition to the workshops, children took photographs in their neighborhoods and homes, with subsequent interviews and focus groups.

Adult researchers counted the play elements in children's drawings and evaluations to compile them into six major themes: climbing, sliding, and going fast; encountering nature; feeling safe and good; experiencing different types of play; imagining and creating; and playing with family and friends. Two reports were prepared—a detailed report that the developers could use to integrate these themes into the new play space and a child-friendly report. (See examples of the analysis and reports in Chapter 9).[1]

---

1. Karen Malone, Katina Dimoulias, Son Truong, and Kumara S. Ward, *Researching Children's Designs for a Child Friendly Play Space at Rouse Hill Town Centre* (Sydney: Centre for Educational Research, University of Western Sydney, 2014).

Box 8.3. **Hip-Hop Architecture**

As a means to engage minority youth in Madison, Wisconsin, Madison College professor and architect Michael Ford integrated hip hop into a series of workshops to envision the city, asking youth to consider how they would like to see their city 20 years from now, and what would support or hinder their progress toward this vision. To accomplish this, Ford first had young people listen to the lyrics of hip hop, identifying environmental themes and stories in the songs. Throughout the camp, young people explored themes of contemporary society and learned basic architecture skills. After four weeks, the

workshop participants compiled their ideas into a three-dimensional representation of what they want for their community. Project collaborator Rob Dz also assembled their ideas and words into a rap song. The project is a means to engage youth in architecture but also to help them reflect on their daily experiences in meaningful ways.[1]

---

1. Nicholas Garton, "Community Remix: Hip Hop Architecture Breaks Down Walls to Build Bridges." Madison 365, February 6, 2017. http://madison365.com /community-remix-hip-hop-architecture-breaks-walls -build-bridges/. (Retrieved September 18, 2017).

They may present a single concept plan, or a few possible scenarios. They should be prepared to show how they took the original ideas proposed by young people and incorporated them into the plan. For example, a poster can be created to illustrate how designers applied young peo-

ple's ideas (Figure 9.2). An important aspect of this phase is to allow time for all participants to discuss their responses to the designs, suggest adaptations or changes, and influence decisions. Whenever possible, this stage should be spread out over time so that young people and designers

Box 8.4. Combining Workshops and Social Media: #OurChangingClimate

Participatory planning is especially important as a tool for engaging vulnerable and less heard groups within a community. This pertains to climate change and resilience planning because young people will inherit this challenge and should have a right to influence planning for their futures. A research team from the University of California, Davis, sought to explore engagement strategies with youth using digital communication technologies including social media and the creation of digital narratives. #OurChangingClimate was developed as a participatory design project to engage youth in multiple cities with the goals: 1) learning to visualize local impacts from climate change; 2) creating images and narratives from young people's neighborhoods that reflect vulnerabilities or signs of resilience; 3) encouraging intergenerational conversations about climate-change resilience.

To accomplish this, researchers conducted a series of workshops in six communities. Workshops were one or two half-day events in the cities of Oakland, San Francisco, Davis, and Santa Barbara, California; Milwaukee, Wisconsin; and Plymouth, England. In these workshops, participants learned about projections of climate-change impacts on their own communities through imagery such as regional vulnerability maps, aerial photography, and street-view maps.

After the workshops, youth participants were asked to record evidence of vulnerabilities and resilience in their communities and to share images and narratives about the images through their chosen social media accounts. Youth contributed posts from their community for approximately six weeks.

Youth then returned for a second workshop. Their images and narratives were sorted onto white cards (resilience) and magenta cards (vulnerabilities). Youth generated social media hashtags and selected photographs that they wanted to share as a means of coding the images and narratives, using terms such as #foodwaste, #heat, or #theview. The images were also geotagged to connect the images and text with specific physical locations.

Youth then chose a theme from the initial process and developed a longer narrative. These stories told a personal experience of climate change using Storify or Wordpress digital media. In this process, youth explored a range of topics that relate to climate change including food and waste, health, transportation, green space, flooding, storm vulnerability, and safety features. Some youth also explored alternate futures, from an underwater subway to a transformation of degraded spaces into parks.

This mixing of workshops and technology allowed youth to build their understanding of the science behind climate change while also making personally relevant connections and recommendations for resilience planning.[1]

---

1. N. Claire Napawan, Sheryl-Ann Simpson, and Brett Snyder, "Engaging youth in climate resilience planning with social media: Lessons from #OurChangingClimate. *Urban Planning* 2, no. 4 (2017): 51–63. OurChangingClimate.us

---

can discuss different phases of design development, allowing for repeated iterations and adaptations before reaching a final plan.[7] Many variations exist for how plans are drawn and considered in a co-design process, but a central element is that young people and designers work collaboratively to develop and discuss the design.

7. Kreutz, Derr, and Chawla, "Fluid or Fixed?"; Rigolon, Derr, and Chawla, "Green grounds for play and learning."

Variation: Co-Design Youth Manual

Stanley King and Susan Chung developed a *Youth Manual for Sustainable Design*, which describes in detail a series of methods for engaging young people in a co-design process. They have used this process to facilitate co-design for a wide range of places, including school gardens, a youth space in a public library, a waterfront park, transportation planning, and strategic planning for environmental education.[8]

Stanley King tells the story of his son and his friends in Montreal in the late 1960s. His son ran up breathlessly, exclaiming, "A bulldozer has bulldozed our playground! What are the rules?" For them, the land was full of castles and fighting areas, and all kinds of spaces for their imagination. After King explained that the rules favored the developer's right to bulldoze the site, he showed the children proposals for the design, which they did not like. When he said, "Well, what are your ideas?" his co-design process began.

King and Chung emphasize that while co-design may look like simple rapid renderings of design ideas, it is something much greater. It is a process of citizen participation that includes collaborative drawing, in which people generate ideas that the artist collectively draws, but also other methods. King and Chung's co-design process with young people includes the following exercises:

- **City on the Wall**, in which young people imagine when the land was new, and then draw what the first human settlers built, adding more and more constructions as the population grows. They then consider all the things they could and could not do in the city they have drawn. This sets a framework for thinking about a desired future place.

- **Establishing rules**, which include "say I, not we," "consider all possibilities, not

solutions," and "don't criticize the ideas of others" (instead, state an alternative, or just note that an idea needs more thought).

- **Drawing A Day in the Life** of their current place over a 24-hour period, and of their desired, imagined environment.

- **A Site Walk**, an environmental exploration called Personal Experience and Perception (PEP), in which young people visit the site, explore it using all their senses, and think about how existing or proposed experiences might be supported there.

- **Facilitated Drawing**, when an artist works with small groups and draws what participants imagine doing, seeing, and experiencing in their ideal space (Box 8.5, Figure 8.5).

- **Voting**, when workshop participants vote on specific elements found in each group's drawing. They give each element in the drawing one of three ratings: "I Love It! Go For It," "Needs More Work," or "Belongs Elsewhere."

With teenagers, King and Chung often use a "graffiti wall" (a long piece of butcher paper and a supply of markers) to draw current and future cities. Some self-conscious teens express their ideas more freely if they can do so anonymously on the wall and then consider them as a group. Co-design methods emphasize quality of life as a measure of the quality of a design. This work is based on the Co-Design Group of western Canada, which has facilitated award-winning co-design with young people since 1971. After training university students, faculty, and city staff, Growing Up Boulder employed this method for transportation and open-space planning projects (see Chapter 11), and city staff adopted it for a nature play workshop described in Box 8.5.[9]

---

8. Stanley King and Susan Chung, *Youth Manual for Teachers and Youth Leaders.* http://youthmanual.blogspot.com/p/about-us.html. (Retrieved July 22, 2017).

9. King and Chung, *Youth Manual;* A book that also details the process with both adults and children: Stanley King, Merinda Conley, Bill Latimer, and Drew Ferrari. *Co-Design: A Process of Design for Participation* (New York: Van Nostrand Reinhold, 1989).

Box 8.5. **Co-Design for Nature Play**

When children and other age groups expressed their vision for the redevelopment of Boulder's Civic Area, a clear desire emerged for an area for adventurous nature play beside Boulder Creek. To learn more about specific features that people would like to see, the Department of Parks and Recreation organized a multigenerational workshop that applied the process developed by Stanley King and his Co-Design Group in Canada. The public was invited to work through the following sequence of activities.

Exercise 1: A Favorite Place in Nature (45 minutes)

Everyone sat at a table with paper and marking pens, with children at a table of their own. Adults were asked to think back to their favorite place in nature when they were a child—and the children, to their favorite nature place currently. After people traveled to this place in their imagination, they were asked to sketch it or write a paragraph about it. When they were finished, they came to the front of the room where a large sheet of paper was mounted on the wall, divided in half with a diagonal line, with the top half labeled Urban and the bottom half labeled Wilderness

(Figure 8.4). They placed their drawings and writings along this continuum, from most-urban in the upper left to most-wild in the lower right. Then they spent time viewing the display, asking each other questions, and talking about what they observed.

Exercise 2: Nature Play Sketching (1 hour)

For the next hour, people worked at their tables, with a facilitator and an artist/designer at each table (Figure 8.5). They began with a discussion about the activities they wanted the nature play space to afford, and listed their ideas on an easel (10 minutes). Then they took each key idea and answered questions from the facilitator and artist about how they wanted to experience this activity setting. (What is the feeling of this place? What do you hear? What do you see? Are you in sunlight or shade? . . .) As people envisioned each setting, the artist rapidly sketched it (10–15 minutes). After several ideas were drawn, the artist asked people to envision how these settings fit together—again, with attention to all the senses. As each person made a suggestion, the artist drew it, fitting their ideas into a composite sketch of the play space (30–40 minutes).

Figure 8.4. Multiple generations sketched their favorite nature experiences from childhood and placed them on this continuum on the Urban to Wilderness continuum. Photo credit: Darcy Varney Kitching

Figure 8.5. Graphic facilitators draw what people want to see and experience in a place through the Co-Design Method. Photo credit: Darcy Varney Kitching

Exercise 3: Voting (30 minutes)

While people took a break and enjoyed snacks, the artist and facilitator at each table filled in a score sheet that listed the major design elements in the composite drawing. Beside the list of elements were three columns that said: I Love It! Go For It, Needs More Work, or Belongs Elsewhere. Each table's composite drawing was displayed on an easel, with its score sheet beside it. People circulated around the room and voted on the elements in each drawing, with a check mark beside each item.

This process generated a creative flow of lively ideas and helped communicate the value of a nature play area to the public. While some ideas were far-fetched (e.g. water cannons to shoot back and forth across the creek), many suggested feasible possibilities, from large aims, like water and sand to mix and channel, to details, like plantings for butterflies and other insects. Children shared their ideas as equals, while adults were invited to reconnect with their childhood selves.[1]

1. King et al., *Co-Design: A Process of Design for Participation.*

Box 8.6. **Applying Co-Design in an Applied Science Class**

with Erin Hauer and Maggie Fryke

In a learning exchange between university environmental-design students and middle-school applied-science students, two undergraduate designers engaged their team of middle-school students (ages 11–12) in the co-design process to consider the wildlife habitat on the middle school's campus. The project included a series of six interactive lessons, ranging from field exploration to graphic development and oral presentations. The lessons began with an intro-

duction to Boulder's native habitats, followed by a habitat hunt in which students related campus flora and fauna to the larger Boulder ecosystem. Students then used photographs, drawings, and words to map existing habitat conditions (Figure 8.6). The undergraduate designers initiated the co-design process with middle-school students by completing "existing" and "imagined" ecological pies (Figure 8.7) to develop goals and a concept for the design. The team then began the facilitated graphic illustration process, based on Stanley King and Susan Chung's youth manual. This method of co-design was well suited for gathering each individual's perspective and ideas. When the visioning was completed, the group presented to their classmates for feedback and revisions (Figures 8.8 and 8.9). This dialogue supported further iteration of the design into a common vision. While the implementation of the final vision was not possible in the timeframe of the class, the students began with a small intervention by creating "seed bombs" of clay, soil, and seeds, and scattering them in selected habitat locations across the school's campus.[1]

Figure 8.6. Habitat Inventory sheet that summarizes student findings of campus ecology in relation to local ecology as part of a co-design process. Photo credit: Erin Hauer and Maggie Fryke

1. King and Chung, *Youth Manual.*

(Box 8.6 continued on the next page)

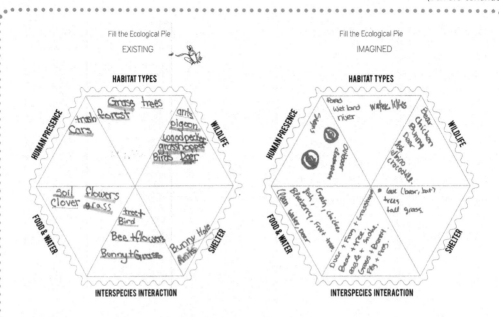

Figure 8.7. "Fill the Ecological Pie" worksheets for existing and imagined future conditions. Image credit: Erin Hauer and Maggie Fryke

Figure 8.8. Sharing the co-design drawing with classmates. Photo credit: Victoria Derr

Figure 8.9. Final result of schoolyard habitat co-design process. Illustration credit: Erin Hauer.

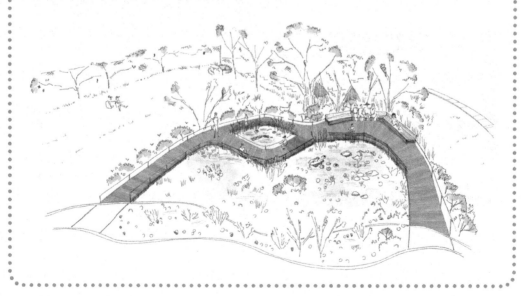

Child-Participatory Budgeting

Whether cities have child-friendly places and programs depends, in large part, on whether they are allocated in municipal budgets. The practice of participatory budgeting arose in Porto Alegre, Brazil, in 1989 during a period of progressive government, when strong organizations of civil society demanded more direct citizen involvement in decision-making.[10] From there it spread across Brazil, Latin America, and then the globe. Participatory budgeting allows non-elected citizens to participate in planning and allocating public finances. Good practices reflect five criteria:[11]

1. The process focuses on how a limited budget should be used.

2. It operates at a city level or district level, as budgets at these levels determine neighborhood expenditures.

3. It is repeated over years.

4. It provides for public deliberation in meetings dedicated to this purpose.

5. There is accountability so that people know whether final decisions reflect the public will.

Most participatory budgeting involves adults, but there are currently initiatives around the world to include children in these processes. Chapter 5 in this book, for example, shows how young people used collages to express their priorities for open-space funding during a participatory budgeting process in San Juan, Puerto Rico (Box 5.6).

In 2016, the Committee on the Rights of the Child issued an official comment on Article 4 of the United Nations Convention on the Rights of the Child, which states that, "States Parties shall undertake all appropriate legislative, administrative, and other measures for the implementation of the rights recognized in the Convention."[12] The committee specified that this obligation includes budgeting for children's needs, including regularly hearing children's views on budget decisions that affect them. To achieve this aim, it noted, governments must allocate resources to educate children and child-rights advocates about budget policies and processes, provide mechanisms for their meaningful and sustained participation, give reasons for spending priorities and decisions, and keep children informed about the outcomes of their recommendations. For an example of efforts to fulfill this obligation on a national scale, see Box 8.7: Scaling-Up Youth Participatory Budgeting in Portugal.

A review of 27 child-participatory budgeting initiatives from around the world illustrates different approaches to the inclusion of children and youth.[13] Some programs worked through existing children's clubs, youth councils, and youth advisory boards, whereas others involved child and youth representatives who were either selected by adults or elected by their peers. Representatives were responsible for consulting with other children to gather their views about spending priorities, and many made a special effort to talk with disabled children, children out of school, and other marginalized groups. In some cases, youth delegates developed proposals for project funding that they submitted to a large number of children for a vote. Some cities gave young people authority to determine how to spend a specified sum allocated for children's use.

The review of international initiatives concluded that child-participatory budgeting is

10. Yves Sintomer, Carsten Herzberg, and Giovanni Allegretti. *Participatory Budgeting Worldwide—Updated Version*, Dialog Global No. 25. (Bonn, Germany: Global Civic Engagement, 2013).

11. Ibid.

12. United Nations Committee on the Rights of the Child, *General Comment No. 19 on Public Budgeting for the Realization of Children's Rights* (art. 4), CRC/C/GC/19, 2016.

13. Marshall, Chelsea, Laura Lundy, and Karen Orr. *Child-Participatory Budgeting*. (Belfast, Ireland: Centre for Children's Rights at Queens University, 2016). Available online at https://plan-international.org/publications/child-participatory-budgeting. (Retrieved December 15, 2017).

Box 8.7. **Scaling-up Youth Participatory Budgeting in Portugal**

Giovanni Allegretti and Marco Meloni

Today Portugal has a network of more than 118 local governments which are experimenting with participatory budgeting, and more than 60 of them engage youth. In 2006, the rural city of São Brás de Alportel became the first municipality to have a participatory budgeting process especially dedicated to school children. It gives young citizens opportunities to discuss public resources, and helps them gradually widen the scope of their vision from their school, to their surrounding living environment, and then to the city as a whole. From this beginning, participatory budgeting for young citizens spread to the cities of Lisbon and Trofa. In Trofa, the city government established two funds that young people can allocate to their priorities: one for school areas, and another for improvements to public spaces. With the collaboration of the Ministry of Education, the Mayor of Trofa also created a certified training course in participatory budgeting for school teachers, and "weighted voting" was established as a mean to reduce competition for resources and foster solidarity, encouraging young citizens to support proposals that benefit socially vulnerable groups. In Condeixa, the municipality used participatory budgeting by young people as leverage to introduce shared-budget decision-making by all citizens. In Cascais, the city government introduced a role-playing game to engage young people in writing the rules for youth participatory budgeting, which youth review and amend each year.

More recently, the European Union funded a project called "Empatia," which includes an internet platform where adults, teenagers, and school children can find age-specific versions of "Empaville"—a role-playing game that prepares them for high-quality experiments in participatory budgeting. In 2017, some schools used this tool to train teachers and students for an experiment

by the Ministry of Education of Portugal, which made participatory budgeting mandatory in all Portuguese schools, giving students control over small amounts of the national budget. In the same year, a national account of 300,000 Euros was created by the Secretary of State of Sports and Youth Affairs to fund proposals by youth ages 14 to 30 in the areas of inclusive sports, science education, social innovation, and environmental sustainability (Figure 8.10).

Figure 8.10. A team of students present their proposal for public funding to improve sports facilities. The proposals that go forward are decided by a youth vote. Photo credit: Alberto Bougleux

These innovations are the result of a bottom-up movement, which convinced institutions at both local and national levels to invest in participatory budgeting as an important tool for civic growth. Organizations which encouraged this development include In Loco Association (a non-profit for environmentally- and socially-just local development), the Center for Social Studies of Coimbra University, and the Training Center for Portuguese Civil Servants, together with several city and borough administrations.[1]

---

1. For more information, see the websites http://www.opescolas.pt and https://opjovem.gov.pt. See also Giovanni Allegretti, Maria Andrea Luz da Silva and Francisco Freitas, "Experiências participativas da juventude em Portugal," *O Público e O Privado*, no. 20 (2012): 153–205. The "Empaville" role-play can be found at: https://empaville.org. (Retrieved December 15, 2017).

most successful when it includes the following features:[14]

- Children are provided with accessible information about the budget process.
- They receive support to develop and express their views freely.
- They have time to process the information and prepare their inputs.
- Adults listen to their views and engage with respect.
- Children receive feedback on what happened to their input.

In the most successful cases, the process was sustained for a number of years, enabling children to develop trusting relationships with city officials and budget directors. Adults, on their side, had time to see that information provided by the children enabled them to make decisions that better served children's needs. The involvement of local media was also important, to educate city residents about the process and to make officials' commitments to children public. Children who participated also spoke about the vital role of the facilitators who helped them understand budget issues and civic processes as well as how to formulate and express their views.

Child and Youth Presentations

This section describes different ways for young people to share their ideas in a familiar space of their own, such as their classroom or an after-school setting. This is a more comfortable arrangement for most young people than formal processes in adult spaces such as a city council chamber or city hall. More young people are also likely to have the important experience of presenting their ideas to others if adults come where they are, rather than expecting young people to travel to adult meeting places. Many young people face practical problems in getting

to an unfamiliar place, as they generally have less independent mobility than adults. Beyond this logistical barrier, many hesitate to venture into adult spaces where they are afraid that they will feel uncomfortable, intimidated, outnumbered, and bored. In spaces of their own, they feel more control, as visitors follow the agenda they have prepared.

To make sharing sessions a positive experience for everyone involved, advance planning is required. The following steps can help these sessions run smoothly:

1. Ask young people how they would like to present their work
2. Tailor presentation formats to project goals, structures, and needs
3. Respect young people's privacy and ownership of their ideas
4. Provide time to review and rehearse
5. Prepare the adult audience to be supportive

Ask young people how they would like to present their work

Begin by discussing different potential formats and invite young people to make suggestions of their own. Do they want to stand at tables with displays of their work, or in front of exhibits of their work on the wall, while adults circulate around the room and ask them to explain what they have done? Do they want to communicate through PowerPoint™ talks, a video, or a performance? Do they feel comfortable standing up alone or prefer to present in small groups? Do they each want to speak, or do they want to elect a few representatives from their group to speak for them?

After listing the possibilities, give each person a voice. Some children may feel pressure to say the same thing that others have already said, so you can pass out cards and ask each person to write down his or her preference. Then everyone can discuss the advantages and disadvantages of different options and come to a

---

14. Ibid., 41.

group decision. It isn't necessary to follow one format alone. The group may decide on a sequence of presentation styles that accommodate different participants' preferences.

Tailor presentation formats to project goals, structures, and needs

In addition to honoring the preferences of young people and their ideas for presentations, it is also important to structure presentations in ways that meet project partners' needs and goals. This may be at a single point in time, toward the end of an engagement period, or may be at specific intervals. In the case of the transit study (Box 8.11), children presented their ideas in a single, culminating session. For the intergenerational evaluation of a commercial district, an interim and final session were organized to share and develop ideas with a broader range of project partners (Box 8.10). Because the goals differed for each of these two sessions, so too did the formats and means of presentation. For a large scale public space planning event, young people shared their ideas with project leaders in multiple formats and venues, some of them small scale and informal as ideas developed, some to make recommendations and share design thinking, and some in community events or city council sessions (See next section, Box 8.12 and 8.13, Figure 8.13). In this way, the methods themselves, as well as the format for presentation, help all partners, including young people, learn from each other in meaningful ways.

Respect young people's privacy and ownership of their ideas

Young people need to decide whether they want their names on the work that they display. Many methods in this book collect self-revealing information, such as photographs or interviews about special places or places where young people feel supported or vulnerable. Young people may

also be critical about existing places or power structures in their community. Make sure that participants know that they don't need to present anything that they prefer to keep private. Discuss whether they want to use their own names on their work or choose a pseudonym. In general, the default choice is anonymity: but for some young people, identifying themselves with their work may be an important experience of healthy pride and self-affirmation (See the opening stories to Chapter 1).

If you have any reason to believe that a public presentation may put participants at risk in any way, protecting them is your top priority. In this case explain your decision. Review rules governing confidentiality, permission, and protection during work with children and youth, introduced in Chapter 3.

Take time to review and rehearse

If time is short or presentation plans are simple, you may just list the presentation agenda that everyone has agreed to and review the roles that each person will play. If you think a presentation is more likely to go smoothly or young people will feel more confident if they have time to practice, group members can serve as an audience for each other, or another class or family and friends can form an audience. When the rehearsal is over, ask everyone to talk about what went well before suggesting what could be done better. If technology is required, make sure participants know how to operate it, or that technical support will be available. If young people will be using microphones, give each person time to practice speaking clearly at the right volume. If they will be using their natural voice, make sure they can all be heard clearly at the back of the room. This is especially important if older adults will be attending! Go over how to dress on the day of the presentation and how to stand and carry themselves to express self-confidence.

In our experience, adolescents tend to feel more self-conscious and nervous in front of an audience than younger children, and therefore they may need more time to practice. Some children, however, are constitutionally shy. Speaking in public despite apprehension can be an empowering experience—but never force anyone to speak against his or her will.

Prepare the adult audience to be supportive

Adults who are invited also need coaching so that they know how to be supportive and encouraging while leaving young people with room for further thought. Some adults see public meetings as occasions to question and challenge the presenters and advance their own views. This may be appropriate at adult hearings on controversial issues; but if young people are confronted in this way, they may feel that they are being attacked and their ideas belittled. For this reason, Growing Up Boulder often provides guests with a letter in advance that tells them what to expect at each event and how they can affirm what the young presenters have done while still feeling free to ask questions, share their own experiences, and suggest other potential possibilities. See Box 8.8 for a sample letter, and Box 8.9 for sample questions. Expectations for everyone's roles should also be announced at the beginning of the presentation.

Events can be scheduled at different stages in a project. They can be held early as a way to let community members know what a project is about and contribute perspectives and suggestions that may benefit the project as it unfolds.

Box 8.8. Guidelines for Experts Working with Children and Youth.

This letter was used mid-way through a project, when adults visited young people in their classrooms to share their expertise:

Guidelines for Experts Working with Students

Students are working individually (at Casey) and in groups (at Boulder High) to come up with their own visions for the Alpine-Balsam Ecodistrict Redevelopment Project. As an expert, you are going to be interacting with students—imparting knowledge, answering questions, and helping them make their ideas better. You do not need to prepare anything. Feel free to bring these guidelines and refer to it during your time with students.

You can assume that the students:

- Will have identified a project and are still in the research phase.
- Will be fairly committed to their ideas and have their own opinions.

- Will have questions for you.
- May not want to show you what they don't know. . . be positive and supportive and teach them. Speak at their level. They will respond in kind.
- May not have thought about their project through an Ecodistrict lens yet.

You can help by:

- Asking them to explain to you what their ideas are so far.
- Listening very carefully to what they say.
- Providing realistic, yet positive feedback.
- Asking questions or restating what you heard them say. Examples:
  - Have you thought about _____?
  - What I heard you say was that you want to _____.
  - Did I get that right?

(Box 8.8 continued on the next page)

(Box 8.8 continued)

- Teaching them something—in manageable parts.
  - What I know about building a structure like that is _____.
  - The other thing you need to consider is _____.
- Giving them direction for their next steps.
  - I've heard about these parts of your idea, but nothing about _____. The next thing you need to do is _____.
  - If they are WAY off base, finding a way to give feedback that puts them back on track. Asking them how they will present their idea to city leaders? Will they create a PowerPoint? Model? Create a video? Use Sketch Up?

- Pointing them to websites that will give them the kind of information that they need.
- Asking them how the Ecodistrict 6 priorities fit into their plan or teaching them about the 6 priorities and how they might fit into their plan.
- Advising them how to make a compelling case to the city leaders. Give them insight into what city leaders are hoping for in regards to ideas from the community.

Again, thank you for sharing your expertise and time with our students. If you are interested in hearing the students present their final project ideas, please let us know and we'd be happy to include you.

Box 8.9. Sample Questions That Adults Might Ask Young People at the End of a Project

- What was your favorite part of this project? What was the hardest?
- How did you and your peers decide on final recommendations? What process did you use to generate ideas and agree on final proposals?

- What will be the next steps for these things to happen? Can you do some of these things on your own? Who do you need support from?
- What sort of projects should our city work on next?

Once young people have begun to study a site and generate ideas, it can be helpful to call in experts who can review what they have done and provide feedback that will help them take their ideas to the next step (Box 8.8). An event at the end of a project is an opportunity to showcase and celebrate what participants have accomplished and discuss how their ideas will be carried forward (Box 8.9). See Box 8.10 for an example of a project that scheduled sharing at different points for different purposes, and Box

8.11 for an example of a thoughtfully structured end-of-term event.

At the end of a presentation, some kind of response from the audience is important so that young people know that they were not only listened to but heard. It is empowering if city officials or other influential decision-makers in the audience can immediately identify some follow-up steps that they will take. If they need time to assimilate what the young people have suggested and consider how their ideas could be

Box 8.10. **Sharing Ideas to Revitalize a City Street**

An eight-week intergenerational project involved a class of fourth graders, ages 9 to 10, and seven elderly mentors in evaluating how to make a commercial street near their school and senior residential facility more environmentally friendly, artistic, fun, safe, and attractive for pedestrians. The class broke into groups that each included approximately four children, a senior citizen who was named a "thought partner," and an undergraduate environmental design student. Each group evaluated a different block of the street in order to propose improvements.

Figure 8.11. Seniors and students in front of a large street map that shows their ideas for an improved pedestrian experience on a local street corridor. Photo credit: Ethan Herrold

The class and senior citizens took a field trip to map and photograph their assigned blocks, and then each group created a poster to express what they saw. Undergraduate students then helped children locate precedents—street features in other places that suggested inspiring possibilities.

Students presented their work at three points in the project. After they formulated their preliminary ideas, they shared them on an Expert Day when visitors from the fields of urban design and planning, public art, creative placemaking, and health and the built environment came to their classroom to answer questions and help the students refine their ideas. A month later, the same experts, Department of Transportation staff, school district officials, and other visitors returned

Figure 8.12. During a final project presentation, a student indicates where his group placed their ideas on a base map of the street they were evaluating. Photo credit: Erika Chavarria

(Box 8.10 continued on the next page)

(Box 8.10 continued)

to hear the students present their final proposals and give feedback. The following week, students shared their work again during an open house for the community.

In preparation for the final events, the undergraduate design students created a four-foot by twelve-foot base map of the street, and the children cut out images of precedents and glued them on each location along the street that needed enhancement, such as street trees and gardens, colorful benches, creative bus stops, whimsical trash cans, and dramatic murals. Each event began with a slideshow that presented the project's background, and then each group presented its work. As members of each group described each idea, they showed its placement on the map. Visitors asked questions and then filled out a half-page feedback form that included suggestions for how ideas could be developed further as they were passed on to city agencies.

Box 8.11. **A Better Bus Ride for Young Children**

When the Department of Transportation in Boulder, Colorado, decided that it was time to upgrade riders' experience of the HOP, a public bus that loops around core nodes in the city center, it wanted input from all age groups. One group that contributed was a second grade class of twelve English Language Learners, ages 7 to 8, at Whittier International Elementary School. Transportation experts visited their class and students learned about public transit, mapped out the HOP route, rode the bus, identified current advantages and disadvantages of the line, and made recommendations to improve the riding experience for young children. In addition to their teachers, a Growing Up Boulder coordinator and two environmental design students mentored them through the process.

At the end of the term, the students made posters to present their conclusions to city staff, university faculty, a local planner, and other community members. Before the event, students identified questions that the visitors were likely to ask, and practiced asking and answering these questions with partners. They also rehearsed their explanations of the posters to their peers until they felt well prepared.

On the day of the event, teachers provided a brief introduction to the project and then guests circulated around the room to stop at the small groups of children who stood beside exhibits of their work. Separate displays contained the following information, which students explained to their guests:

- a large map of the bus route that they had drawn and labeled

- photographs they had taken of features that they liked and disliked during their bus ride, classified into the categories of safe, fun, comfortable and convenient

- a chart that listed advantages and disadvantages of their riding experience

- suggested action steps to improve the HOP experience

When the children finished their presentations, visitors returned to their seats and each adult made a brief observation, pointing out specific positive points about the children's analyses and communication. Staff from the Department of Transportation explained that they would study the students' recommendations and report back about how they would respond. Students were each then called to the front of the class to receive a certificate of appreciation for their contribution to the HOP study. For one of the outcomes of this process, see Figure 8.18.

applied, then it is reasonable to explain this—but this should be done with an assurance that the young people will be kept informed. See Chapter 9 for different ways to report how young people's ideas are incorporated into plans or policies, and see the Great Neighborhoods case in Chapter 11 for a letter that illustrates how a city department communicated directly to youth.

As a general rule, the size of the audience in young people's own spaces should not outnumber the presenters, or it can feel more like a formal public meeting and less like a comfortable exchange on young people's own terms. For some purposes, the audience may be as small as a few experts or a single key person. For example, when four-year-olds at Boulder Journey School were invited to share their suggestions for redeveloping the city's Civic Area, they decided to turn their classroom into a large-scale model of their vision for this site. In this case, the city's Senior Urban Designer visited so that they could show him what they had done, ask questions, learn about his job, and discuss the city's aims with him.

Variation: Young People Speaking at Public Events and City Council Sessions

When young people share their ideas in "adult" spaces like city council chambers or city hall, the settings and format can be intimidating. These formal spaces often are unfamiliar, as many young people may be visiting these city buildings for the first time. The meetings are organized in a bureaucratic manner, with rigid rules for time and tightly structured agendas. Adults may be literally elevated on daises and stages that convey their power and authority.

In his participatory research with three programs for youth action in the Bay Area of San Francisco, Ben Kirshner described how program staff provided facilitation and apprenticeship to guide young people's entry into adult worlds.[15]

To prepare youth for public presentations, they gave higher levels of coaching and feedback while refraining from imposing their own views. Although these opportunities may require high levels of support, they are important for both young people and adults. In Boulder, city council members have continued to refer to the ideas young people shared in council sessions long after the timeframe of a single project, and youth have spoken of feeling empowered when they pushed themselves outside their comfort zone. With the right support, these settings can be places of high impact.[16]

The tensions, and potential, associated with formal public meetings can be illustrated by the case of a high school student who spoke in front of the Boulder City Council. She represented her class of about 20 students who all belonged to a special program for young people who aspired to be the first person in their family to attend college. Most were Latinx and from families with low-incomes. She was the only one who agreed to speak to the city councilors to share her group's ideas for the redevelopment of the Civic Area. The coordinator for Growing Up Boulder sent her several email reminders about the date and picked her up at her home to take her to the municipal building. When the young woman saw the council chambers and the councilors in rows of benches on a stage, she told the program coordinator that she did not want to speak. The coordinator reassured her that she did not have to if she did not want to. As the young woman later explained, she knew that her family was watching the council session on the city's public television channel and that they were excited and proud that she had this opportunity. She had written out her talk—and when her turn came, she stood up and read it.[17] She said afterwards:

---

15. Ben Kirshner, *Youth Activism in an Era of Educational Inequality* (New York University Press, 2015).

16. Victoria Derr, Louise Chawla, Mara Mintzer, Debra Flanders Cushing, and Willem van Vliet. "A city for all citizens: integrating children and youth from marginalized populations into city planning." *Special Issue on Designing Spaces for City Living. Buildings* 3, no. 3 (2013): 482–505.

17. Ibid.

I got over my biggest fear which was talking to a big crowd of people, to the mayor, I was even live on TV! When I'm applying to colleges it will look good on my application. . . I am so excited to do another project like the Civic Area. I'm so glad I did it. Don't get me wrong. At first, I was a little unhappy because I didn't know what to expect. . . I'm glad that in the end everything came out great.[18]

The redesign and redevelopment of Boulder's Civic Area was an extended process that also brought elementary school and preschool children into the council chambers. In 2014, all three third-grade classes in the Whittier International School near the city center participated in a series of activities to study the Civic Area and generate suggestions. Their ideas were shared with city staff immediately through sessions in their classroom and a project report; in addition, a year later, they had a chance to present their ideas to the city council. Five of them volunteered to write letters to the councilors that summarized some of their group's key ideas and read them at the lectern (Figure 8.13). Before the session began, one of the city councilors saw them sitting to wait their turn and came over to speak with them, to make them feel welcome and put them at ease—a good example of how figures of authority can show support.

Young children (ages 4–5) from Boulder Journey School also dictated letters to the city councilors to share their ideas for the Civic Area and deliver them in person (Box 8.12). For them, this was a follow-up after presenting their ideas at a public workshop where other city groups also shared ideas.

There is a value to dedicating special sessions of a city council or a city department meeting to young people's issues so that young people have more time to present their positions and dialogue with city officials and staff. In this case, work with everyone involved to en-

Figure 8.13. Elementary school students present their ideas for the Civic Area to Boulder City Council. Photo credit: Willem van Vliet

sure that the meeting format feels comfortable to the young presenters. The Youth FACE IT initiative described in Chapter 5 (Box 5.17) was able to secure two sessions with city councilors for Latinx high school students to express their experiences as minority youth: one in the City of Boulder and one in the City of Lafayette in Boulder County, Colorado.[19] Rather than speaking to the councilors directly, each presenter created a digital story that described a special place or program in their city that helped them feel competent and centered in their lives. The young people and their families were present as the councilors listened to each student's story composed of photographs of this special place and a recorded narration. In the end, the councilors spoke about what they had learned and asked the young people questions.

The sessions demonstrated that all the rules for successful sharing apply to public meetings too—including preparing councilors to be supportive. In one of the city council sessions, councilors jumped into questions as soon as the digital stories ended. The councilors were accustomed to scrutinizing adult speakers and treated the youth storytellers in the same way. The youth interpreted the councilors' questions as critical

---

18. Ibid., 13

19. FACE IT stands for youth Fostering Active Community Engagement for Integration and Transformation.

Box 8.12. **Preparing Young Children for a Visit with City Council**

with Lauren Weatherly

In order to prepare young children (ages 4–5) to present their ideas to city councilors, staff at Boulder Journey School organized the following steps:

1. Discuss what a city council is, and who the councilors are so that young people understand their role in the city, in language that is relevant to young children, for example: "Councilors make decisions to help make the city better. Part of their job is listening to all of the people who live in the city about their ideas. City council meetings are times when councilors talk to each other, and anyone in the city can go and talk to them about things they think are important."

   This discussion served the goal of children understanding that this was a special opportunity to share their hard work in developing recommendations while also recognizing that everyone in the city can talk to city council.

2. One to two weeks prior to the city council meeting, bring young children to council chambers.

   In this visit children sat in the audience and in council member chairs and spoke with city employees, including those who had already visited the children's classroom. This helped make the space more familiar.

3. Have the children help prepare materials they will share with a city council.

   Children were invited to create a short video explaining their perspectives on the Boulder Civic Area that could be played at the meeting. In this way, they could express their perspectives but not feel the pressure of "performing" during the council session. Children helped select photographs for the video and recorded voice over. The children watched the video several times before the meeting so that they were very familiar with it.

4. Have children make gifts, such as handmade drawings, photographs from project activities, or thank you cards, for each of the council members, to hand deliver at the council meeting.

5. Finally, have teachers envision the steps of what will happen when they visit the council chambers:

   i) children, families, and teachers will meet in the lobby;

   ii) everyone will walk into council chambers together and sit in the front row;

   iii) a designated planner, teacher, and parent will all give a short introduction about the project;

   iv) everyone will watch the video in the council chambers;

   v) children will present gifts to council members; and

   vi) children, families, and teachers will go outside to the playground.

   These steps were reviewed many times with children so that by the time they got to the council chambers, the experience was as predictable as possible. This provided a framework for children to feel comfortable and shine in their experience.

Box 8.13. **The Importance of Comfortable Settings for Young People**

One of Growing Up Boulder's first projects was with a Teen Mothers Action Group. The project included young women (ages 13–19 years) and their children (ages 0–3 years). Working in their high school classroom, GUB worked with the teen mothers to identify positive and challenging aspects of living in Boulder. The teenage mothers raised a range of issues from serious concerns about becoming homeless under the city's existing housing policy (which was only available to people 18 or older), as well as a desire for underage nightlife, safe and inclusive spaces, and affordable services. Participants wrote their ideas in letters to city council and GUB staff arranged a date for the young women to speak to city council members. GUB arranged food and child care for the meeting, but in the end, not a single young woman attended the council session.

Reflecting on this, GUB then arranged for two city councilwomen to visit the teen parenting program at the high school. In this more comfortable setting, 20 young women attended and shared their suggestions for ways to improve the city for teen mothers as well as young children. The councilwomen in turn listened to their ideas and responded by discussing existing low-cost services as well as plans that were already in the works. The timing was such that an affordable housing taskforce had been created, and so the councilwomen also solicited ideas for housing amenities and policy changes during this exchange.[1]

_____

1. Derr et al., "A city for all citizens."

challenges and evidence that the councilors did not value the experiences they revealed. Many young people have to gather their courage before sharing their lives in public, and adults need to be reminded in advance that their role is to listen openly and make suggestions where they can be helpful—not to judge what young people offer. Since this event, facilitators in Boulder have taken similar steps (as in Box 8.8 and 8.9) in preparing councilors to positively receive and affirm child and youth perspectives.

Celebrations

Young people commonly bring energy and enthusiasm to participatory processes. At its best, child and youth participation offers many intrinsic benefits, such as opportunities to experience new activities with friends, acquire new skills, learn more about their city, and feel that their ideas matter. When young people see some of their recommendations implemented, they are also rewarded with tangible outcomes. Take time to celebrate accomplishments, tangible and intangible. This helps young people realize that they have done something significant and it can be a way to communicate their contributions to others in their community and to stakeholders in a project.

Figure 8.14. Open house celebration. This park planning project was celebrated at a school-wide open house, where children and youth shared their ideas for redevelopment of a neighborhood park with park staff, neighborhood residents, families, and the school community. Photo credit: Lynn M. Lickteig

Celebrations can mark milestones at different steps in a project. They can recognize work well done, such as the successful completion of a community map or survey. These can be occasions for simple celebrations like going out to a nearby pizza shop or ice cream parlor. Young people's work can also be showcased with the community at large through public exhibits and open houses (Figure 8.14). It is nice to give participants something they can take away from these events, such as certificates of accomplishment. (For an example, see Figure 8.15.)

Other celebrations may come long after young people finish their work, when their ideas are realized in new city features. Figure 8.16, for example, shows a celebration on the opening day of a playground that young people helped design. Figure 8.17 shows ribbon cutting when a new pedestrian bridge was opened that included features that young people suggested. Figure 8.18 shows the second graders who evaluated

Figure 8.16. Celebration of playground opening. Project funders, city leaders, and project participants were invited to an afternoon celebration for the opening of a playground that had been part of a participatory design process. Project leaders gave short speeches and the local news interviewed the mayor, project leaders, and children. Photo credit: Stephen Cardinale

Figure 8.17. Two years after elementary school students in Boulder, Colorado, made suggestions for the redevelopment of the city's Civic Area—including features for a new pedestrian bridge—students were invited to attend the bridge's opening. The students cut the ribbon and were the first participants to cross the bridge. Photo credit: City of Boulder, Bryan Bullock

Figure 8.15. An example of a certificate to acknowledge young people's contributions. Image credit: Growing Up Boulder

Figure 8.18. During their evaluation of a city bus line, second graders recommended a bench at the bus stop near their school. A few months later, the Department of Transportation invited them to show up at the bus stop at a specified day and time. Within minutes, a city facilities truck pulled up and workmen unloaded and installed the bench. The bench displays a plaque thanking the children for their input. Photo credit: Louise Chawla

a city bus line (featured in Box 8.11), as they witnessed the installation of a bench at the bus stop near their school, which was one of their recommendations. They also recommended public service banners inside the bus to entertain young children and make them feel welcome, and for this purpose, they worked with an artist to paint a banner that challenged children to find all the bunnies hidden in their painting of city landmarks—consistent with the name of the bus line, the HOP, and its icon, a bunny. Within a few minutes after the students sat down on the new bench, a bus pulled up, they got on board, and they discovered that their banner had been printed and installed. The class rode downtown to play and explore before returning to school.

In some cases, children can celebrate the accomplishment of their ideas within a few weeks or a few months after they made their suggestions, while their group is still together. The wheels of government, however, tend to turn slowly. In other cases, it takes long-term relationships with young people or their school or after-school programs in order to maintain contact and bring them together again after a year or more has passed since they initially shared their ideas for city improvements with the departments in charge of implementation.

All of these events create good opportunities to share news about young people's accomplishments through press releases to local media. Participants should also be thanked in project reports and annual program reports that go out to all stakeholders. A celebratory card at the end of the year is a way to thank everyone who contributed to your program in any way.

Gulliver's Footprints

Gulliver's Footprints is a type of shared mapping that forms a special event. It was created by the Urban Study Group in the Setagaya Ward of Tokyo as a way to collect residents' memories and thoughts about a neighborhood or public space.[20] It enables people to record their sense of place, as an activity by itself or as a foundation for redevelopment plans that respect local history. The main material required is a large map of the area printed on canvas or sturdy paper. The map is unrolled on a floor or smooth backing on the ground, with marking pens scattered on it. It can be part of a festival or other public event that brings many people together, or in a public library, community center or other space that has a regular flow of foot traffic. It can be initiated outdoors and then moved indoors for further elaboration. A facilitator invites people of all ages to be Gullivers[21]—giants surveying their territory—and to get down on the map and leave their footprints by writing and sketching beside places they find significant.

Your city planning agency or the planning department at a local university may be able to assist in preparing the map. A scale of 1:250 or 1:500 is usually large enough for people to annotate and embellish neighborhood details, but for small spaces such as a plaza or pocket park, you may want an even larger scale. The map needs to be large enough so that several people can add comments around local landmarks such as a popular café or playground. Extending the work over a week or two gives people time to come back with photographs or other artifacts that illustrate their notations on the map. When the map is done, hang it in a public place for further viewing and discussion. David Driskell suggests that the material that people contribute can be exhibited around the map, or in a series of panels that focus on different sections of the map.[22] The map should be recorded through photographs

20. Driskell, *Creating Better Cities with Children and Youth*, 185.

21. Gulliver is the central character in Jonathan Swift's 1726 classic *Gulliver's Travels*, which chronicles Lemuel Gulliver's voyages and fantastical adventures. Gulliver's first adventure comes after a shipwreck when he finds himself captive of the tiny Lilliputian people, who are less than 6 inches tall, rendering Gulliver a giant in the story.

22. Ibid.

and a digital archive of the material people contribute, and used to make design and planning for this area sensitive to local memories and place meanings.

A facilitator is critical for this process, to explain what the map is for and invite people to participate. The facilitator may need to help children orient themselves to the map, and, with young children, may need to help them record their comments.

Futures Festivals

A Futures Festival is a one-day event that brings community residents of all ages, public officials, and representatives of local institutions and organizations together to share ideas for future community development.[23] Although it is open to all ages, special efforts are made to ensure that children, teens, and older adults are well represented and that activities are inviting and engaging for them. On both ends of the lifespan, young people and elders are particularly reliant on the resources of their immediate neighborhood and safe access by foot or other independent means to local services and attractions. A challenge for cities that seek to be friendly for all ages is to balance public spaces that all ages can share with settings that serve the distinct needs of different ages. Therefore it is important to hear from people in every season of life.

A Futures Festival brings different ages together around the question, "What would you like to see in the future of your community?" The focus of discussion can be a district or neighborhood, or smaller spaces like a park or central square. Matt Kaplan, an environmental psychologist who has helped organize Futures Festivals in diverse communities in the United States, notes that although the festival may last only one day,

its success depends on months of advance planning, followed by plans for action.[24] He recommends beginning two to four months in advance. This gives time for a coalition of community partners to form who can take ideas generated at the festival forward.

A festival unfolds through the following sequence of steps.[25]

- Organize an event coordination team. The team should include people who represent organizations invested in the community, such as city agencies, local schools, the local library, block associations, places of worship, and organizations that serve children, youth, and the elderly. Key individuals such as elected officials should be invited, and kept informed about the planning process if they cannot attend. In the United States, county extension offices have a community development extension agent who may be able to help. You may also find resource people in local colleges and departments of planning, the social sciences, media and communication, or public health. Include groups interested in different dimensions of community life, such as a bird watcher's club or history club, and welcome volunteers such as artists, designers, and photographers.

- Determine the festival location and date. It can be a separate event or integrated into an existing event that draws local crowds, such as an annual fair or holiday celebration. It can be indoors or outdoors, or flow between indoor and outdoor spaces.

- Recruit exhibitors, presenters, and performers and generate awareness and interest. Using all of the coordination

23. Matthew Kaplan, Frank Higdon, Nancy Crago, and Lucinda Robbins. "Futures Festivals: An intergenerational strategy for promoting community participation," *Journal of Intergenerational Relationships* 2, no. 3–4 (2004): 119–146.

24. Matthew Kaplan, *The Futures Festival: A Facilitator's Guide.* (State College, PA: College of Agricultural Sciences—Cooperative Extension, Pennsylvania State University, 2001). 25. Ibid.

team networks and local media, distribute information about the festival and invite local agencies, institutions, and organizations to prepare displays and activities.

- Provide guidelines and assistance so that all contributions reflect the three principles of a successful festival:
  - An atmosphere of discovery. Exhibitors and presenters should share information about the community, their goals for its future development, the planning processes they follow, and how residents can get involved.
  - Opportunities for participation. Every contribution should create an occasion for residents to ask questions and voice their needs, concerns, and suggestions.
  - Intergenerational dialogue. Offer activities for intergenerational groups and provide active roles for children, youth, and older adults.

- On the day of the event, offer an array of festival activities. Provide activities for residents of all ages as well as exhibits and presentations by local agencies, institutions, and organizations. Kaplan's suggestions include:
  - Mural painting to illustrate visions for the community's future
  - Model building so that participants can express their ideas for community development through three-dimensional models
  - Land-use mapping that enables participants to color in and annotate community base maps or aerial photographs
  - Photography exhibits about significant local places and photo-collages of elements that people would like to see in their community
  - Theater skits to dramatize local issues and new ideas

- Documentary films
- Oral history interviews
- Games, where older adults can teach games from their childhood to contemporary children and young people can share games of their own
- Debates about controversial issues
- Community forum discussions

The goal is to offer a day full of opportunities for local learning and exchange. In this process, any of the participatory methods featured in this book could be adopted, including the co-design workshops and Gulliver's Footprints mapping described in this chapter. Hands-on activities through the arts, mapping, and model building appeal to all ages, but the festival also presents an opportunity to collect survey data about residents' aspirations and opinions, and to hold public discussions and debates. It is essential to have facilitators who can explain each activity and encourage participation by all ages, as well as recorders who can capture what people say. Also have members of the coordination team and volunteers circulating through activities to ask participants before they leave, "What did you learn from your experiences today?"

Plan for post-event communications and organizing. Through press releases and perhaps also a festival report, ensure that residents' views and visions get shared with all of the participating organizations, elected officials, and the community at large. A follow-up forum could be organized for local leaders and agency staff to report back to the community about what they learned and how it will affect their planning, and to announce follow-up actions.

In the "Where Is This Place?" activity at a Futures Festival in Fayette County, Pennsylvania, the display generated extensive discussions among family members of different generations, as it was usually the oldest family member who could identify and explain local historic sites. Festival exhibits like this are intended to draw attention to a community's cultural and natural resources and cultivate conversation and a proud sense of place identity.

Although planning and conducting a Futures Festival does take time and energy, it is a strategic investment in the community. Benefits can include strengthened community connections among groups of all ages, more open communication between residents and the organizations that serve them, and the potential for consensus around key features of a community that meets diverse residents' needs. If an initial festival is successful, you may want to consider making it an annual event. In this case, each festival may have a theme focused on a different community issue or public space.

In England and Wales, a related initiative entitled Intergenerational Forums aims to bring community organizations that represent different ages together to generate strategies to address local needs. Key principles for this work are recognizing that all generations should be valued and respected, providing meaningful roles for all participants, fostering relationships and reciprocity between older adults and youth, and being responsive to community needs.[26]

Living Laboratories

The city as a living laboratory is a concept developed by the Danish architect and planner Jan Gehl and his firm Gehl Institute.[27] It grows out of a 50-year tradition of collaboration between design researchers in the School of Architecture at the Royal Danish Academy of Fine Arts in Co-penhagen and city departments of urban design and planning. This approach has primarily relied on observations of how public spaces support—or fail to support—public life; but as methods have evolved, they have come to include small scale interventions that might make cities function better for people, followed by observations of how people respond. The city becomes a laboratory for design and planning experiments.[28]

For example, a busy street might be temporarily closed to traffic and café tables introduced, or a line of temporary bollards might be installed to create physical protection between a bike lane and adjoining lanes of traffic. Design researchers then estimate how many people take advantage of the new opportunities created and record their activities. People participate by showing whether they gravitate to the changed spaces. If these inexpensive experiments appear to be a success, then the changes may be made permanent. These interventions may target children and youth, such as temporarily closing a street adjoining a school to traffic to see whether students take over this space for outdoor classrooms, socializing, and play.[29]

The goal of these incremental changes is to make cities more sustainable.[30] This has primarily involved encouraging social vitality in public spaces, more walking, and more cycling. Box 8.14 shows how this approach can be extended to "landscape laboratories" to introduce more opportunities for connection with nature into cities. In this case children were happy to

26. Matthew Kaplan and Alan Hatton-Yeo, *Intergenerational Forums* (Stoke-on-Trent, UK/University Park, PA: Beth Johnson Foundation/Penn State, 2008). Available at http://aese .psu.edu/extension/intergenerational/program-areas/community-planning-visioning/intergenerational-unity-forums/intergenerational-forums

27. Jan Gehl, *Cities for People.* (Washington, DC: Island Press, 2010); Jan Gehl and Birgitte Svarre, *How to Study Public Life.* (Washington, DC: Island Press, 2013).

28. These kinds of interventions are sometimes referred to as *tactical urbanism*. Street Plan has developed free resource guides including the *Tactical Urbanist's Guide to Getting it Done* and *Tactical Urbanism 2: Short-Term Action, Long-Term Change* by Mike Lydon and colleagues. These resources are available at http://tacticalurbanismguide.com and http:// issuu.com/streetplanscollaborative/docs/tactical_urbanism _vol_2_final.

29. Angela Million, "Preparing children and young people for participation in planning and design." *Designing Cities with Children and Young People*, ed. Kate Bishop and Linda Corkery (New York: Routledge, 2017), 223–236.

30. Gehl, *Cities for People.*

Box 8.14. **The Landscape Laboratory**

with Erin Hauer

Developed by Professor Roland Gustavsson of the Swedish University of Agricultural Sciences, a landscape laboratory is a multidisciplinary meeting place involving children and youth in creative nature management. Here, two important elements for the design and planning of sustainable cities are merged: 1) how future landscape features will appear and provide ecosystem services in urban areas, and 2) who is involved in the design and management of these features. In the forest village of Sletten, Denmark, landscape laboratory experiments encouraged by the municipality include a 'collective zone' where residents are invited to co-manage the edge-zone of a young woodland bordering their private gardens. Children have been the first to approach and engage with the forest by modifying and making spots of their own, leading adults to participate as well (Figure 8.19).

At the Alnarp Landscape Laboratory in Sweden, children and youth play a role in the evolution and character of landscape prototypes. The landscape laboratory facilitates outdoor learning workshops for visiting school children, whose huts and hanging hammocks enrich the area with

Figure 8.19. Children experimenting with loose parts in the Landscape Laboratory. Photo credit: Roland Gustavsson.

a sense of place that comes with the freedom to appropriate their natural surroundings.[1]

---

1. Hanna Fors, and Anders Busse Nielsen. "Landscape laboratories: Sletten (DK) – offering residents spaces for activities between the garden and the woods." *'scape, The International Magazine for Landscape Architecture and Urbanism* 15 (2016): 114–115; Anders Busse Nielsen. "Landscape laboratories: Pocket woods for 21st century urban landscapes." *'scape, The International Magazine for Landscape Architecture and Urbanism*, 15 (2016): 103–109.

accept an invitation from their municipality to "co-manage" a woodland edge. Although this approach is different than formal processes to integrate children's voices into urban design, it is consistent with the goals of many formal initiatives—which are commonly to increase children's opportunities for informal participation in the public life of their city. It can show how children and youth, too, respond to opportunities to experience their city in new ways.

Improving Community Commons

Children and youth can play important roles in constructing and maintaining community commons, or spaces that are open to the public and managed through shared governance. Based on more than 40 years of work supporting the development of community commons, Karl Linn asserted the importance of these spaces for enlivening the senses, expressing community visions, and building relationships.[31]

---

31. Karl Linn, *Building Commons and Community* (New York: New Village Press, 2007).

Figure 8.20. Children and designers co-created a graffiti art wall in the inner-city neighborhood of Segbroek, The Hague, a case featured in Chapter 11. Photo credit: Speelwijk

In his book *Building Commons and Community*, Karl Linn describes the evolution of a North Philadelphia neighborhood vision for the "Melon Block Commons," comprised of a sitting area, playground, sports field, and amphitheater for teenagers.[32] After clearing rubble, community members, including young people, collected, sorted, and cleaned bricks that were used to frame the sandbox in the playground. Neighborhood youth were involved in construction of the steps leading up to the amphitheater. Constructed in the 1960s, the project was an early model of sustainability, using repurposed, found, and salvaged materials as much as possible. Additional examples of commons that combined built structures and nature are the entrance to the community center and the beachside stairs and bench that children helped create during the design-build workshop in San Juan, Puerto Rico, featured in Chapter 11 of this book. Children and designers also worked together to improve community spaces in The Hague, as described in Chapter 11 (Figure 8.20).

Community commons are often green spaces, such as a pocket park that surrounding residents manage, or community gardens. Lindsay Campbell and Anne Wiesen call these spaces "restorative commons" when people introduce nature, with all of its healing effects, into the built structure of cities.[33] Marianne Krasny and Keith Tidball call joint work by community members to protect, create, and enhance these green spaces "civic ecology": practices that simultaneously restore urban ecosystems and renew communities.[34]

Urban nature centers form oases for surrounding schools and families and often provide similar benefits as community commons. They are often built with the assistance of community volunteers, including children. Access is commonly restricted to hours when staff are present, but at many centers staff support a combination of structured environmental learning and free play, as well as arts events and social gatherings proposed by local residents. In Lund, Sweden, for example, Sankt Hansgården offers a place that children from local schools and housing developments regularly visit, where they can engage with nature through free play, gardening, and learning practices of ecological design and building (Box 8.15).

32. Linn, *Building Commons and Community*.

33. Lindsay Campbell and Anne Wiesen, ed., *Restorative Commons*. General Technical Report NRS-P-39. (Newtown Square, PA: USDA Forest Service, 2009). For summaries of studies that document the restorative effects of connecting with nature, see: Florence Williams, *The Nature Fix* (New York: W. W. Norton, 2017); Louise Chawla. "Benefits of nature contact for children," *Journal of Planning Literature*, 30, no. 4 (2015): 433–452; Research Library of the Children and Nature Network, www.childrenandnature.org/learn/research.

34. Marianne Krasny and Keith Tidball, *Civic Ecology* (Cambridge, MA: MIT Press, 2015).

Box 8.15. **Integrating Play, Design, and Building through an After-School Program**

Figure 8.21. At the Sankt Hansgården after-school program, children from Lund play with natural and scrap building materials as well as participate in ecological design. Photo credits: Victoria Derr

Sweden provides public funding for the greening of schools and after-school programs. In the city of Lund, the Sankt Hansgården outdoor play and learning center provides several hours of daily contact with nature. Up to 200 children in grades 3–6 can attend the center on a daily basis. Located in the heart of the city, a short walk from

some of Lund's public housing, students learn gardening, animal husbandry, blacksmithing, and ecological design and building. While there are daily jobs, children also have free time for self-directed imaginative play, including construction of tree houses, dens, and baskets (Figure 8.21). In addition to the after-school program, Sankt Hansgården supports school group visits during the school day. The center provides continuity in care and maintenance through consistent staffing skilled in permaculture and ecological design. Self-directed construction projects also

build skills to prepare students to participate in the design and construction of buildings. Students learn principles of ecological design and assist with the physical construction of buildings, such as the earthen building and sod roofs (Figure 8.21) and a blacksmithing workshop (Figure 8.22). Students leave their handprints on buildings they help construct (Figure 8.22).[1]

---

1. A. Wånge Kjellsson. Personal Communication with Victoria Derr, Lund Nature School. Nordic Light on Children's Outdoors, Malmö and Lund, Sweden. October 2, 2014.

Figure 8.22. Children who help construct buildings leave their handprints, as on the blacksmith workshop (top and bottom left detail) and chicken coop (bottom right). Photo credits: Victoria Derr

Figure 8.23. Children watering herbs in the community garden that they created for their housing development. Photo credit: Corrie Colvin Williams

Box 8.16. **Planting a Forest Garden**

To enrich opportunities for learning for environmental science and agricultural biology classes at Roaring Fork High School in Carbondale, Colorado, community volunteers, university design students, and high school students and their teacher worked together to build a geodesic dome greenhouse and plant a large vegetable garden and orchard on a sagebrush-covered corner of the school ground. A few years later, students in the environmental science class decided to organize a community work day on Earth Day to improve the soil around the fruit trees and create a "forest garden" where other plantings could be introduced. The 17-year-olds recruited volunteers, arranged to feed them, brought in enough cardboard, leaves, and composted manure to cover the quarter acre area in a deep layer of organic matter, and directed the work day. By the time the organic material decomposed, a fertile garden space was prepared that could serve the high school and the broader community. In the words of one of the students: "In school students are not put in a position to make decisions. So this was a very different experience for all of us. This was something real. I was part of the team and I was blown away by how well it went. And how significant it was."

The high school teamed up with a nonprofit that serves Spanish-speaking immigrant families in the region, including families in an affordable housing development near the school. Families were offered plots in the forest garden, where vegetables and flowers now grow too. Parents, grandparents, and children often work there together, reaping the harvest of healthy food, while high school students continue to maintain other parts of the garden and the greenhouse.[1]

---

1. Pevec, *Growing a Life*, 101–111.

Box 8.17. **Transforming a Trash Dump into Community Greenspace**

In Puebla, Mexico, a former trash dump that was turned into a beautiful garden beside a free preschool for working-class families illustrates the different levels of engagement that this kind of community regeneration involves. Because high-school students in this city are required to perform 300 hours of community service before they graduate, they form a reliable labor force for the garden: from the early stages of clearing trash and breaking the hard ground through helping the 2 to 6-year-olds plant and harvest. Because one of the primary purposes of pursuing an education in their society is to escape manual labor, most teenagers have never held a shovel before, and planting a seed and seeing it grow is a source of wonder for them as much as it is for their small apprentices. For ambitious projects like designing and painting a mural for the garden wall, summer work camps bring youth and student volunteers together. On a routine basis, local university students and residents provide sustained maintenance. Volunteers have also written a curriculum for the preschool and trained the teachers to use the garden as a learning center. Spaces like this become nodes that can bring diverse parts of a community together.

Figure 8.24. Volunteer high school students help pre-schoolers plant their school garden in Puebla, Mexico. Photo credit: Illène Pevec

Children often play a role in creating and maintaining community gardens. In some gardens, they have their own plots or help with family plots, while other gardens primarily serve children and teens. Figure 8.23 shows children from an after-school program in the garden that they designed, dug, and planted to grow food for their families and other residents in their low-income housing development. In her book *Growing a Life*, Illène Pevec presents a variety of ways to create and manage community gardens with youth and young people's testimonies about the benefits of participation.[35]

With students' help, school grounds can be turned into sites that serve both students and their communities. Box 8.16 and 8.17 provide examples of such spaces, where compacted soil or trash dumps are converted into a fertile center for community through the collaborative work of teenagers and adults. For a profile of the participatory construction of a green school ground in an elementary school in London, Ontario, in Canada, see Chapter 11. After drafting the school ground design, students planted more than 25 trees and large shrubs, and then volunteered on a Community Build Day to plant small shrubs and flowers.

---

35. Illène Pevec, *Growing a Life* (New York: New Village Press, 2016).

9

Organizing, Analyzing, and Reporting Ideas

The methods described in Chapters 4 through 8 present a variety of ways for people to share and integrate information about their cities. It is often useful to compile results from all the methods used in a project in a report or other summary document. These artifacts can serve different audiences. They can record the process and ideas:

- for young people to share with their friends, families, and communities
- for use by city planners and designers
- to inform future projects
- to help others develop similar projects in other places

This chapter shares a range of methods to organize, analyze, and present the outcomes of participatory processes. These outcomes may be described with qualitative data, such as images and words, with quantitative data that present counts or percentages, or most commonly, a combination of the two. This chapter also reviews potential means for sharing project outcomes, including via posters and flyers, websites, or reports generated by young people or adults.

Ideally, young people play a role in organizing and analyzing the ideas they have constructed. In this way they apply their own ideas and words to final products, with minimal interpretation needed by adults. Some methods, such as an annotated three-dimensional model or a video, need little additional explanation. In many cases, however, additional organization and analysis is important to synthesize and prioritize ideas—especially when a project used multiple methods. In this case, you need to schedule this phase of work into your project plan.

Reviewing Goals and Identifying Outcomes

In the planning stage of your project, you identified specific goals that you hoped to achieve (see Chapter 2). You may have wanted to better understand young people's perspectives on a topic such as transportation or ways to support resilience and present their recommendations to a city agency. Or you may want to integrate children's design ideas into a schoolyard or park. You will want to revisit these goals, as they provide you with a framework for organizing, analyzing, and presenting your data based on your project's initial goals and final outcomes.

Analyzing and Interpreting

There are many approaches to analyzing and interpreting data. Some common analysis methods that are useful in working with data generated from planning and design processes include annotation, simple counts, and coding and sorting. Analyzing and interpreting data are closely related. Just as for drawings in Chapter 5, it is important to work with young people directly to understand how best to interpret data so as not to bring an incorrect interpretation to any ideas or recommendations that young people generate. The following sections identify examples where interpretation with young people is important.

Annotation

Strengths

Annotations highlight how young people's ideas are integrated into physical space. Annotations can use young people's own wording.

Limitations

Simple annotations typically fail to show the frequency or importance of ideas

In some cases, simple annotation is sufficient to convey young people's ideas for a project. A three-dimensional model, for example, could involve children labeling elements and writing short paragraphs that describe details of the place and how they imagine it would be used. In a photo exhibit, the young photographers could label the significance of each picture. In other cases, labels can be overlaid on a map or drawing to show young people's suggestions. These labels can be added by young people themselves or by adults. Labels can be handwritten or typed (Figures 9.1 and 9.2). Annotations of project models or concept drawings have the advantage that they directly connect young people's ideas to

Figure 9.1. This annotated map created for Growing Up Boulder represents ideas that three different groups of young people (ages 8–9, 11–13, and 15–16) generated during a year-long participatory process to ensure that the redevelopment of the city's Civic Area would include child-friendly elements. Each master plan element that young people recommended is labeled, and the number of dots represents whether it was requested by one, two, or three of the different age groups. Image credit: Civic Area Plan courtesy City of Boulder with Annotations by Growing Up Boulder

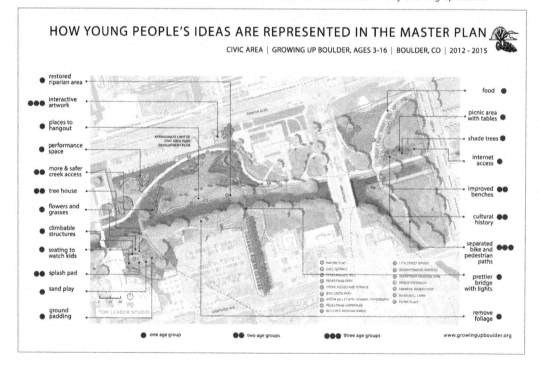

Figure 9.2. Annotation showing how young people's initial images and ideas were integrated into the concept plan for school grounds (See Box 8.1). The pictures of the maze path, children's sculpture, and pizza oven all show children's original models and ideas. Image credit: Qian Wang and Susan J. Wake

physical elements of the environment, but they often have the limitation that they do not show the frequency or importance of ideas. This is not invariably the case, however. Figure 9.1 shows a simple addition of dots to annotations to denote features that more than one age group proposed for a public space redevelopment.

Simple Counts

Strengths

Counts show the frequency of an idea. They can be used to compare the consistency of ideas across ages or other groups.

Limitations

The frequency of elements in young people's words and images does not necessarily equate to their importance.

Simple counts work just as the name implies: counting the number of times a specific idea or type of idea emerges from a collection of young peoples' work. If children draw pictures of their ideal park, these counts could include how often they draw specific items of play equipment such as slides and swings, or categories such as "play equipment," "nature," "seating," or "artwork." By counting, you begin to see trends and priorities among the group (Figure 9.3).

This analysis can also be applied across different project methods. For example, if you used three methods (such as drawings, photovoice, and a three-dimensional model), you could generate simple counts from each method and then compare the results. Using different methods in this way provides a form of *triangulation*:

	J. Frederic Ching Planetarium	Constitution Soccer Complex	Natividad Creek Park
Green Dots (good memories)	3	7	22
Orange Dots (places that need work)	0	7	7
Pink Dots (unfamiliar places)	7	1	0

Figure 9.3. In this *Map of Good Memories*, participants marked places in the city that they associated with happy memories with green stickers, places that needed improvement with orange stickers, and unfamiliar places with pink stickers. Simple counts show how often each category of stickers was associated with each place. Photo credits: Victoria Derr

by comparing outcomes from more than one method, you can see which ideas occur most consistently.

Stickers are a popular and effective means for children to categorize their ideas by placing the stickers directly on elements of a map or drawing. You may choose the stickers based on what you want to know, or involve young people in generating sticker categories. There is no limit to possibilities, such as favorite places, friendly places, eating places, adventure places, boring places, dangerous places, child-made places, hang-out places, and so on. Color-coded sticker dots work well when there are just a few categories (as in Figure 9.3). (In this case, an alternative is to draw the dots with colored magic markers.) For more complicated systems, you may want to use labeled stickers or sticker icons (such as a bolt of lightning for a dangerous place or a heart for a favorite place). Children can have fun generating the icons!

If young people are involved in the process of counting, then they can discuss not only which ideas occur most frequently, but also which ideas they consider most important. Dialogue at this stage is essential. It may be, for example, that all children drew benches for a park but only two drew an art wall; yet during this process of analyzing ideas, many children agree that an art wall would be an important feature for the park, even if they had not originally thought of it them-selves. Thus while counts may represent children's initial ideas, they may not represent their final reflections and desired outcomes. If you do the counting yourself, then present the counts back to young people and record this second level of discussion. Counts can be recorded on a board or flipchart paper to capture key discussion points for inclusion in the final analysis.

Coding and Sorting

Strengths

Coding and sorting helps to organize and consolidate a large number of ideas.

Limitations

Counting and sorting can lose some of the specificity and originality of young people's initial ideas.

In many cases, simple counts yield many different kinds of design elements: so many that it is hard to absorb the variety of ideas. Then it is useful to not only count but also code and sort the ideas into broader categories. Coding and sorting is a simple method that can be done with hand tallies or using a spreadsheet on a computer.

To apply this approach, first gather information from all the methods to be analyzed. Then make a list, on paper or a computer spreadsheet, of each of the elements listed, using young people's words and terms (Table 9.1 and Box 9.1).

Table 9.1: An overview of the three steps involved in coding and sorting sets of qualitative data

Listing	Generating Categories	Sorting the List
List all the elements young people generate	Identify categories (codes) that can be used to group similar elements	Sort and count the initial list by tallying the elements represented in each category
Sample list:	**Sample Codes:**	**Sample Sorting:**
Flower beds, frogs, trees, birds, a creek, fruit trees, a pond, willow tree, dragonflies, tadpoles, water striders, cattails, ducks, wading area	Plants Wild animals Water elements	Plants = 5 (flower beds, trees, fruit trees, willow tree, cattails) Wild animals = 6 (frogs, birds, dragonflies, tadpoles, water striders, ducks) Water elements = 3 (a creek, a pond, a wading area)

To generate codes from the list, look at the words and think about similarities among them, or how they represent different aspects of a design process (such as seating, landscaping, play structures). For an example of how individual ideas or design elements can be transformed into codes, see Table 9.1 and Box 9.2.

Once you have generated codes, begin to sort the initial list of elements into the different coding categories. Tally the number of elements that fall under each code (Table 9.1 and Box 9.3). Your goal at this stage is to maintain the essential ideas that young people generated, while also simplifying them into a manageable number of ideas. As you sort, you may find that categories should be further condensed or expanded to accurately reflect young people's thinking.

Coding and sorting may be accomplished with young people as well. In this case, young people review the list and make their own suggestions for coding categories. By the age of about 10, they can sort and count the data themselves once the process is explained to them.

These data can then be visually compiled into a bar graph (Figure 9.4), a pie chart (Figure 9.5), a word cloud (Figure 9.6), or a drawing with words and numbers (Figure 9.7). When displaying visual information, strive to choose a graphical form that presents the greatest amount of information in an easy-to-digest format. Edward Tufte's *The Visual Display of Quantitative Information* is an excellent and easily understood resource for visually communicating information.[1] Some of Tufte's recommendations for displaying information include:

- Integrate verbal description (or visuals) with numbers
- Present multiple levels of analysis about the data, from overview to specific detail. (See Figure 9.7 for one way to achieve this.)
- Use graphic displays that help the viewer see the *data* rather than think about indi-

1. Edward Tufte, *The Visual Display of Quantitative Information* (Cheshire, CT: Graphics Press, 1983).

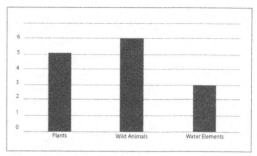

Figure 9.4. A graph visually summarizes data from Table 9.1 and helps people understand the frequency of an idea or recommendation.

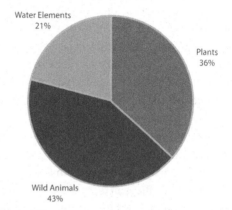

Figure 9.5. A pie chart that summarizes data from Table 9.1. Pie charts make data easily understandable through visual means and help people to understand frequencies and relative proportion of ideas.

vidual aspects of the process (such as the methods themselves or the technology used to produce the graphic).

Project partners should decide how to best represent data in a way that supports understanding project goals.

In many cases, ideas will be more numerous and complex than the simple list shown in Table 9.1. However, the same process of listing, categorizing, sorting, and counting applies. An example of recommendations from a Growing Up Boulder open space planning process with a group of Junior Rangers shows how this method can be employed with more complex information (Boxes 9.1–9.3). In this case, Junior Rangers categorized initial recommendations into groups that were used for voting (Boxes 9.1 and 9.2)

Figure 9.6. This word cloud shows coded elements as well as the original ideas and words generated by young people from Table 9.1. Thus the word cloud visually portrays the frequency of themes through the size of the fonts and also retains the initial words, which helps to maintain the authenticity of young people's ideas. There are a number of free resources to generate word clouds available through the internet.

36%
of children recommended
more trees and plants
in their neighborhood

Figure 9.7. Data can be presented using a combination of visual images, numbers, and words that combine children's images with data from Table 9.1. Image credit: Growing Up Boulder

and then GUB staff tallied official counts for each item after the workshop. Because there were clear priorities in recommendations, the full tallies were not made at the workshop to save time.

Priorities for action can be identified quickly if codes are recorded on large sheets of paper or a board, and then young people place check marks or sticky dots next to their action preferences. In the process, young people may decide that some of the codes overlap and regroup them into new categories. This was the process used for the open space example (Boxes 9.1–9.3). Time can

be a limiting factor in many processes. To save time, it is possible to generate an entire list of recommendations and ask participants to select priorities with sticky dots, check marks, or other means of voting. However, if time permits, it is desirable to condense categories this collaboratively, (rather than an adult doing this later) as the process of condensing leads to interesting discussion.

As with simple counting, remember that frequency does not necessarily equate with importance. Sorting and tallying consolidate the range of ideas that young people generate when they evaluate a place, but these processes are not solely able to predict the actions young people might prioritize. For example, while only two Junior Rangers wrote an initial recommendation about educational materials for the trails (through development of a take-along brochure or a smartphone application), after discussion of the recommendations, Junior Rangers voted for this recommendation as a top priority. If facilitators had only analyzed the listing of recommendations and tallies, it would appear that addressing open space signage was the top priority (Box 9.3). However, only two Junior Rangers voted for this as a priority. Discussion about ideas is thus just as important as counting results in order to understand and develop priorities. In this case, Junior Rangers loved the idea of the educational information but only two people had thought of it initially. Because open space staff were a part of this discussion, they also heard much discussion about signage and took this recommendation to heart also. Thus, both ideas ultimately were addressed through planning and educational departments of the agency.

Only the on-going involvement of youth in planning processes can maintain the integrity of their ideas. In the case of open space planning, Junior Rangers had an opportunity to respond to coding categories and generate priorities for action. Both processes gave useful information. Staff in the Department of Open Space and Mountain Parks used the young people's suggestions about signage to rethink how they

Box 9.1. **Listing**

In this example, Junior Rangers generated a list of recommendations for open space as part of the North Trail Study Area planning process (See Chapter 11). Junior Rangers wrote out their own recommendations on large sheets of white paper. The following represents a simple list of recommendations, prior to any discussion.

- Increase access to scenic mountain views
- Create sustainable trails that are designed to keep water off the trails and people on the trails (not step in adjacent vegetation)
- Allow dogs to be off leash with sight and sound tags
- Provide more signs to educate visitors about the local flora and fauna and natural/cultural history of the area
- More trash cans and compostable dog waste bins
- Condense information into fewer signs
- Standardize sign design
- Plant trees or create barriers between houses and open space
- Build away from developed areas when building future trails
- Increase monitoring of trail damage
- Build close to attractive physical features (lakes, rock formations, etc.) when building new trails
- Keep only necessary signs and structures
- Sleuthing guide
- Avoid scarring lesser populated areas
- Create barriers to social trails in a natural manner (bushes, logs, trees)
- More swimmer-friendly lakes
- Periodic benches/places to sit
- Signs or some other way to tell people about common wildlife and plants
- Place directive signs only where they really need to be and color/design them
- Visual privacy between houses and habitats
- Dog bag dispensers at the start of trails
- Trash cans along trails

Box 9.2. **Codes**

This initial list of categories was generated through discussion with the Junior Rangers by grouping recommendations shown in Box 9.1 prior to voting. This was accomplished by visually summarizing common themes observed and making a list of those categories that best reflected the recommendation content.

- Sustainable trail design
- Dog leash policies
- Education
- Trash disposal
- Signage
- Maintain integrity of nature experiences
- Increase access to nature

Box 9.3. **Sorting**

This table represents the categories (Box 9.2), initial elements (Box 9.1), and tally counts of each code. This table was compiled by GUB staff after the workshop to link initial ideas with categories generated in the workshop.

Code (from Box 9.2)	Recommendations made by Individuals (from Box 9.1)	Tally (counting # of Sample Elements)
Sustainable trail maintenance/ design	Create sustainable trails that are designed to keep water off and people on Increase monitoring of trail damage Create barriers to social trails Plan re-routes of unsustainable trails	IIII
Dog leash policies	Allow dogs to be off leash with sight and sound tags	I
Education	Sleuthing guide Education brochure or smartphone application so that people can learn about common plants or animals	II
Trash disposal	More trash cans and compostable dog-waste bins Dog-waste bag dispensers at the start of trails Trash cans along trails	III
Signage	Provide more signs to educate visitors about the local flora and fauna and natural/cultural history of the area Condense information into fewer signs Standardize sign design Keep only necessary signs and structures Place directive signs only where they really need to be Altitude markings	IIIII I
Maintain integrity of nature experiences	Plant trees or create barriers between houses and open space Built future trails away from development Avoid scarring lesser-populated areas Visual privacy between houses and settlements	IIII
Increase access to nature	Increase access to scenic mountain views Build close to attractive features (lakes, rocks) when building new trails More swimmer-friendly lakes	III

designed, messaged, and located signs. Because the staff regularly interface with youth in the Junior Ranger program, they can continue to explore educational opportunities on the trails together.[2] For projects where groups do not interact as frequently, returning to check in with young people at key points of project development or decision-making is essential.

2. Victoria Derr, Halice Ruppi, and Deryn Wagner. "Honoring voices, inspiring futures: Young people's engagement in open space planning." *Children, Youth and Environments* 26, no. 2 (2016): 128–144.

Figure 9.8. In the open space planning examples (Boxes 9.1–9.3), youth expressed an interest in natural views and wanted to reduce conflicts between housing developments and nature experiences on public lands. This is most readily understood through the combination of images and words, and this pairing of information can be used in any presentation of ideas, from posters to websites or final reports. Photo credit: Growing Up Boulder

"It is important to leave the landscape around trails natural."

"There is a need for better stewardship and better design guidelines in the Wildland-Urban Interface."

Expressing Ideas through Young People's Words and Images

After young people have evaluated a place or topic, and they have identified its major positive and negative characteristics and their priorities for change, their main ideas can be vividly expressed through their own words, photos, and artwork. Their own words and images convey the authenticity of their ideas and the specificity of their visions (Figure 9.8).

One well-chosen photo and accompanying quotation can speak volumes. While youth were conducting photovoice activities for open space planning for the Department of Parks and Recreation in Boulder, they came upon a small park that only had play structures for children ages 5–8. Many teens expressed a desire for parks in which they could also play. The photo and girl's comment shown in Figure 9.9 summarized this sentiment in an unforgettable way. The frustration that the picture and quotation conveyed captured many planners' attention and informed a future "parks for teens" planning process.

Figure 9.9. "We want parks for teens, too. . . I am so tired of moms yelling at me!" When teens were evaluating parks in Boulder, Colorado, some commented on how there were no parks for them. This became a recommendation that resonated with many teens. Photo credit: Victoria Derr

Compiling Project Ideas into Reports and Other Formats

At the end of a project, it is important to report back to everyone involved about the participatory processes you followed and the main ideas that emerged. The format you use will depend on your project partners, but even if you compile a comprehensive written report for a city agency, donor organization, or your program directors, you will want a more condensed and accessible way to report back to young participants and their community. Posters, flyers, annotated pictures, and brief child-friendly versions of reports all work well for this purpose. These different formats can complement each other. In our experience, busy city agency and organization staff also like child-friendly reports, posters and annotated pictures! These products not only summarize main results in visual ways that everyone can quickly grasp, but they can be displayed as evidence of the participatory process that everyone shared.

Summary documents should include the following information:

- The goals of the project
- Who was involved—include numbers of children, youth, and adults and names of any affiliated institutions
- The dates and length of time of work
- The methods used
- A summary of results
- Images and quotes that describe the results in young people's own words
- Next steps for research or action
- Acknowledgements of support—both in-kind and financial

You may not be able to communicate all of this information in a brief format such as a poster, but all information should be recorded and archived somewhere. (See Form 9.2.) Reporting materials should give enough detail so that people can understand the processes involved and results achieved and so that other people can repeat the process in another community.

Plan up front to get as high-quality photo documentation as your resources and situation allow. Pictures of young people and adult allies in action communicate project activities as effectively as many words, and reproductions of young people's drawings or models help communicate their ideas.

When you share information and images in public products, make sure that young people have given you permission to share their ideas, and that you have permission to reproduce photographs, especially when they show children's faces. Generally, young people are excited for their ideas to be taken seriously. However, ethical practice dictates that children's assent, and sometimes parental consent, should be obtained prior to publishing material on websites or in reports (See Chapter 3).

Posters and Flyers

Sometimes you will want to summarize a project in simple terms and images to give a very brief overview of a process, ideas generated during a workshop, or to summarize an entire project. Posters (often in 24- by 36-inch dimensions) are a useful way of conveying information that will be hung at a public space or presented at a community meeting. Flyers or a single paper printed on one or both sides can be helpful to distribute at public meetings, to city council, or at conferences. These summary documents should still convey the partners, participants, and key ideas and themes. These documents should incorporate as much visual imagery as possible to convey details with fewer words and space (Figures 9.10-9.12).

Reports Generated by Young People

Young people can be involved in generating reports. If they participate in analyzing and summarizing project results, this is a natural next

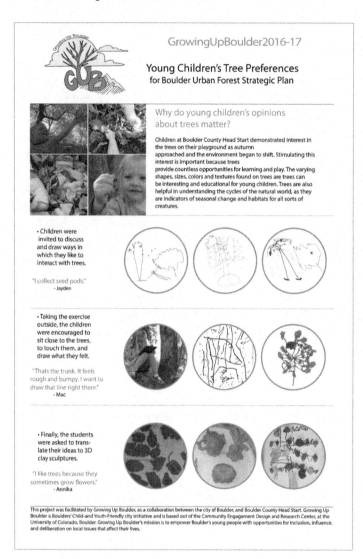

Figure 9.10. A sample poster summarizing young children's ideas about the value of urban trees and forests. Image credit: Growing Up Boulder

step. It ensures that their assessment of their environment will be presented in their words at each step of the way. It also maximizes their opportunity to develop new communication skills across the course of a project.

For example, *The Kids' Hood Book* was a neighborhood guidebook created by primary students in grades four and five in Denver, Colorado. They worked in collaboration with their teachers, a university design professor, and her students to summarize the neighborhood mapping and place use evaluation that they had undertaken. The guidebook was bilingual, in English and Spanish, with images of children actively evaluating their environment, photographs

that the children took during their evaluations, maps they produced, and children's summary assessments of their school, everyday places, play spaces, eating places, and "bad" places. At the opening of the book, a "Who we are/Quién somos" section introduced each of the twelve children and included each individual's photograph, name, and favorite thing to do in the neighborhood.[3]

3. Pamela Wridt, *The Kids' Hood Book: A Neighborhood Guidebook by the Students and Teachers of Stedman Elementary School*, in collaboration with Children, Youth and Environments Center for Research and Design at the University of Colorado (Unpublished report, Denver, Colorado, 2006).

Figure 9.11. A poster that summarizes threats to children's safety and conditions that promote safety in one of the communities in the Promoting Safe Communities Program in Mumbai, India. (For details about this program, see Chapter 11.) Image credit: Sudeshna Chatterjee

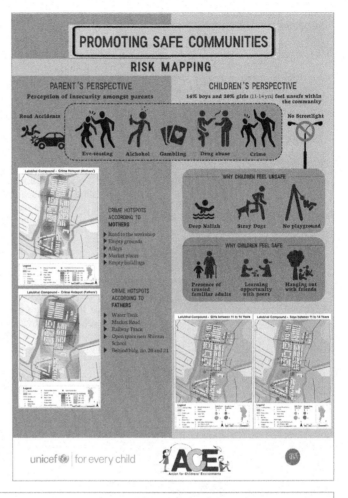

Figure 9.12. This excerpt from Growing Up Boulder's Great Neighborhoods Report shows the integration of a child's statement (top), recommendations by different age groups involved (middle), and representative images associated with the recommendations (bottom). With an explanatory caption, it could also be turned into a poster. (For details about the Great Neighborhoods project, see Chapter 11). Image credit: Growing Up Boulder

Building Typology

"We recommend different colored buildings so we know which house is ours and our friend's."

Recommendations by age

Elementary Students	High School Students	ENVD Students
• Variety of housing types (e.g., apartments, townhomes, single family	• Limit housing to 2-4 stories	• Create unique identities for housing typologies
• Mixed use buildings with coffee and ice cream shops	• Colorful buildings with front and back yards	• Implement a strong use of passive solar design and best managment practices
• Variety of building materials and colors	• Underground parking and alleys	• Balance density and aesthetic desires of the residents along with mixed use design

Rendering by Jungwha Yuh

Photo by 3rd grade student

Sweet Cow

A popular place for students to spend time very close to school, especially great to go on hot days. Very friendly to kids.

Moe's Bagels

Great place for students to get breakfast before school, or lunch. Very popular to go on Wednesday mornings before late start.

Wide Sidewalk

Wide sidewalks are good for kids to walk home with their parents and being able to walk with your friends. It could be even wider.

Figure 9.13. What We Liked—excerpt from the Growing Up Boulder 15-Minute Neighborhood report generated by Casey Middle School youth. Image credit: Growing Up Boulder

Skinny Sidewalk

Too skinny for everyone to walk. Don't understand why one is wider than the other.

Flashing Sign

The sign does not work correctly on late start days. There should be more times that it is flashing.

Intersection

There are always cars that start beeping at cross walkers. The cross is too long and wide. Does not feel safe, might crash while crossing.

Figure 9.14. What We Didn't Like—excerpt from the Growing Up Boulder 15-Minute Neighborhood report generated by Casey Middle School Youth. Image credit: Growing Up Boulder

The Kids' Hood Book inspired a report generated by youth ages 11–12 at Casey Middle School in Boulder, Colorado, at the conclusion of a Growing Up Boulder 15-Minute Neighborhood Project to assess walkability and child-friendliness in the vicinity of the school. A university student generated a digital template for the report prior to a single 90-minute session in which the report was generated. Students began by critiquing the template, which resulted in minor changes to color and layout. Like *The Kids' Hood Book*, the first page of the report included an introduction to the youth, with photos and a brief statement about each participant's "favorite thing about Boulder." The youth then synthesized their main findings from the images and ideas that they had generated over the previous four weeks. To accomplish this, the project facilitators projected their computer workspace onto a white board, which allowed all of the youth to see, comment, and write on the white board to make modifications as they collaboratively created the report. In total, students identified four sections for the report:

- Who we are
- What we liked in our 15-minute neighborhood
- What we didn't like
- Recommendations

"What We Liked" (Figure 9.13) and "What We Didn't Like" (Figure 9.14) included images and words from the youth based on their earlier photography assessment work. The report was printed at the university, and the following week, youth shared report details with city staff from the transportation and community planning departments.[4]

For the "Dapto Dreaming" project in Australia, adult project leaders wrote a detailed report that could be used as a long-term reference by the developers who initiated the project, while students worked with adults to create *Dapto Dreaming: A Child Friendly Report about Dapto.* (See the project profile in Chapter 11.) Twelve fifth-grade students (ages 10–11) worked in a child-adult research team to analyze results from participatory place evaluation and visioning workshops with 150 kindergarten and fifth-grade students. They generated indicators for child friendliness that would guide subsequent design workshops for their neighborhood. The child-friendly report was organized in the following way:

- An introductory page and the eight child-friendly indicators
- Eight pages of drawings, images, quotes, and data that support each of the eight indicators (one page for each indicator and supporting ideas)
- A page highlighting dreams and wishes from the children
- A project description page
- A contributors page, including the names of the child and adult research team members

The report was shared with the neighborhood developers, as well as fellow students, school staff, community members, and city council at a celebratory event (Figure 9.15).

Figure 9.15. A child-generated report developed by 10- to 11-year-olds. Image credit: Karen Malone

4. More information about the 15-Minute Neighborhood Project as a whole and all project reports can be found at the Growing Up Boulder website. Growing Up Boulder. "15-Minute Neighborhoods." http://www.growingupboulder.org/15-minute-neighborhood.html. (Retrieved on August 4, 2017).

Articles and Newsletters Written by Young People

Children and youth can also share information about their participatory projects in agency and organization newsletters (Box 9.4). This is both a way to summarize final accomplishments and to draw attention to work that is underway. Newsletters can also be created by youth for youth, offering a small group of young people who are engaged in participatory design and planning a way to communicate with the larger population that they represent.

Sharing Information On-Line

Increasingly, information is shared online, such as program websites. For communities with internet access, this is an effective way to report project outcomes and provide a lasting record

---

Box 9.4. **Sharing Project Experiences:** Youth Written Article in a Municipal Newsletter

This page is extracted from *Log Steps: The Official Newsletter of the Junior Ranger Program*. After a youth engagement process for open space planning (see Chapter 11), youth wrote this article about their experiences. The newsletter was mailed to about 100 Junior Rangers and their families and was also posted on their website.

Log Steps   Session I/II * [June 1-July 2]

Youth Engagement in OSMP

- Crew 2 -

The City of Boulder Open Space and Mountain Parks (OSMP) is developing a community vision for Boulder's open space in the North Trail Study Area (TSA). The plan aims to improve visitor experiences and increase trail sustainability while still conserving the area's natural, cultural, and agricultural resources. In an effort to engage Boulder's youth in the planning process, Crew 2 was selected to share their thoughts and recommendations during a planning workshop. We were asked to reflect and consider past OSMP experiences and identify things that could be changed to ensure the optimal hiking experience.

We felt honored that they came to us and gave us a chance to participate in the decision making process at such a young age. It was nice to have a day to think and reflect on our times with the crew, while you knew you were contributing to something real.

We learned how much time, detail, and effort goes into the planning process and took an active role discussing our recommendation for the North TSA.

The topics discussed ranged from mountain biking and leash laws to the need for detailed folding maps at the trail head. Tori and Deryn were incredibly responsive to our new ideas and we felt like our voices were being heard. We could teach them about new things that they hadn't considered before, like hammocking, an activity that involves a group of friends hiking to a particular spot and setting up hammocks to relax, listen to music, and enjoy nature.

Figure 9.16. Excerpt from a newsletter written by youth about their participation in a planning project. Image credit: City of Boulder, Open Space and Mountain Parks

that community partners can share and refer to and other communities can learn from. Website pages can feature a single project or compile a variety of reports.

Program Website. A website reaches many readers, and it can spread the influence of your work beyond your city's boundaries. It is a good place to archive all project images, artifacts, and reports for easy access by all of your partners. But creating and maintaining a website is time intensive. Make sure that you have enough staff time or a regular supply of volunteers and interns to keep your website up to date. A well designed website can showcase your program whereas a site that is out of date raises questions about whether your program remains active and effective. Many free website platforms allow you to create a high-functioning basic site that can showcase your work, including:

- A Home page that tells who you are and your mission or goals
- A page that lists staff, interns, partners and funders
- A page that describes current projects
- A page that describes any past projects and archives project reports
- Contact Us

If you are getting good press, share it—on the Home page or under a tab with a label like Resources or Publicity. Build in redundancy so the projects and reports are cross-referenced and easy to find.

There are many free and low-cost programs for building websites and hosting services. Search the web for the most popular website builders and web-page hosting services and their reviews. For a reasonable cost, a number of them allow you to upgrade site functions as you become more proficient or your needs expand.

Interactive websites are a means for youth and other members of a community to continue to input project information and comments.

One example is a website that both documents participatory workshops and allows further interaction on the topic of climate change: #Our ChangingClimate provides a "see, snap, share" interface for people to comment on observations of a changing climate (Figure 9.17). This website was also used as an engagement tool for youth in several cities of the United States to document their observations in participatory workshops and to learn about and take local actions to support community resilience.

Sharing Information through Video. Video information can complement written reports through print or online media. A short video that shows what young people did and enables them to share their ideas in their own words and their own voice, is a compelling way to reach diverse audiences. (See Chapter 5 for participatory video-making with young people.) Brief video segments of different steps in a project can be the most effective way to record exactly how activities were conducted. Videos also can be used to share details and allow children's own voices and emotions to convey their ideas in a compelling way.

Reports Generated by Adults

Before you sit down to assemble a report about project accomplishments, carefully consider its purpose and audience. Ask the stakeholders who will receive the report what they need.

Comprehensive reports provide a detailed description of all project partners, participants, and methods as well as data analysis and interpretation. Comprehensive reports are an important means of accurately capturing the project process and compiling information in one place. This is important, not only as a reference for project partners, but also for those who might be interested in developing a similar process. The results of the data analysis often are relevant beyond the boundaries of a single project. For example, if teens have developed recommendations

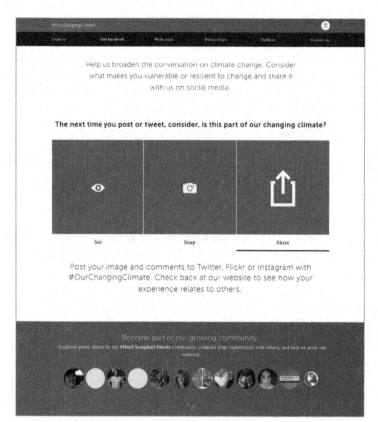

Figure 9.17. #OurChanging Climate's "see, snap, share" interactive interface. Image credit: N. Claire Napawan, Sheryl-Ann Simpson, Brett Snyder, #OurChangingClimate

for teen-friendly design features for a redeveloped park, many of their ideas may be relevant for future parks as well. A comprehensive report takes time to prepare, and the report writer should be identified early on in the project's timeline with sufficient time to prepare this document at the end of the project.

At-a-Glance or Summary reports provide a brief description of participants, main activities, and the major themes that emerged from young people's work. Shorter reports can present the most salient themes but may not present all data collected. This type of report saves time for both writers and readers and serves city officials or project funders who are interested in the basics of the project and actions taken rather than a detailed report. Shorter reports can also be printed in poster or handout form for distribution at meetings or conferences.

Project partners may desire more than one report format and produce a comprehensive report for staff who are tasked with applying project results and an At-a-Glance hand-out for wider awareness.[5]

Record keeping for reports. A complete and accurate record of your program's work gives credibility and helps you answer questions about past work quickly. It also makes report writing much easier if records have been kept in an accessible format from the beginning. Some project facilitators like to keep a journal where they record observations, reflections, striking experiences, and statements by children and participating adults. A journal can preserve a treasure trove of material to mine later for reports and other publications. Or you can record all data into project logs (See Forms 9.1 and 9.2).

---

5. Growing Up Boulder's reports are archived on their website, where you can find examples of both shorter summary reports and comprehensive reports. http://www.growingup boulder.org/all-projects.html

Develop a systematic way to store all project materials and artifacts, including notes, photographs, and digital scans of children's drawings and writings. Label images and other material with the name of the project, date, location, names of people in the picture when this is significant, and name of the photographer, artist, or author. Use children's names only when confidentiality rules allow, but note age and sex. Also note when an image is connected to a permissions form from a child, parent, or photographer that gives you the right to reproduce the image or that limits or withholds this right. You may also want to label images by theme so that you can use the search function on a computer for keywords such as "model making" or "public speaking"

Growing Up Boulder coordinators use an Artifact Entry Log to record all activities with young people, partners, and members of the community (Form 9.1). "Artifacts" include any item produced as a part of the project, including drawings, written works, photographs, presentation slides, models, or video-recorded performances. For each activity that a project includes, the recorder makes note of basic information such as the date, duration, location, and people present, and briefly describes the activity, the themes and ideas that emerged, and reflections. At the end of a project, all of this information can be condensed into a Project Summary Log, which gives an overview of a project at a glance and conveniently feeds into a report text (Form 9.2).

Reporting Back to Young People

One of the ethical principles of participatory work with children and youth is that adults inform them about how their ideas are used and reasons for outcomes. (See Chapter 3.) This chapter has already covered visual ways to present project results that can be quickly understood by children as well as adults. Posters, pictomaps,

drawings, and other visual representations of how city agency staff and designers intend to use young people's ideas can be shared by program staff, teachers, or staff in out-of-school organizations who work with young participants, to ensure that they know that their ideas were heard. Sometimes, however, there is a long time lag between young people's activities and the assimilation of their recommendations into city plans or the development of a school ground or other site. By the time plans are finalized, original participants may have graduated or dispersed.

When just one or a few groups of children are involved in a project, one of the quickest and most effective ways to report back is for city staff or representatives of a design firm to visit these groups to explain how they are applying young participants' suggestions. This also provides a way to get another round of feedback from young people. Do young people believe that current design plans align with their priorities?

Roger Hart noted that children are commonly only involved in the early stage of generating a conceptual design, but that as a final design takes form under the influence of technical requirements, regulations, budgets, and other constraints, interim decisions are made by professionals.[6] He argued that if children continue to be involved at key points in design decision-making, the final product is more likely to reflect their vision and needs, young people learn about the complexity of construction processes, and they are less likely to conclude that their role was tokenistic. When Wake and Eames evaluated the construction of a new school building for an

6. Roger Hart, *Children's Participation* (London: Earthscan Publications, 1997), 44. For a discussion of this point in the context of a schoolground greening project, see Angela Kreutz, Victoria Derr, and Louise Chawla. "Fluid or fixed? Processes that facilitate or constrain a sense of inclusion in participatory schoolyard and park design." *Landscape Journal* 37, no. 1 (2018).

7. Susan J. Wake and Chris Eames, Developing an "ecology of learning" within a school sustainability co-design project with children in New Zealand. *Local Environment* 18, no. 3 (2013): 305–322.

Artifact Entry Log

Project Name: _____   Name of Person Completing Log: _____

Session # or Title _____   Date of Session _____

Duration of Session   _____

Location of Session   _____

Type of Artifact(s)
Generated in this
Session   _____

Ages and Grades
of Children Involved   _____

Location where
Artifacts are Stored
and/or Saved
Electronically   _____

Description of
Activity   _____

Ideas that Emerged
from the Process   _____

Reflections and
Observations about
the Process   _____

Actions to take
before the next
session(s)   _____

Form 9.1. A sample artifact entry log. Image credit: Growing Up Boulder

eco-classroom that was designed with student involvement, they found that the problem of maintaining continuing communication as children graduated from class to class was resolved by creating a twelve-student "working party" that regularly met with the architect as the construction process proceeded.[7] This not only provided a continuing dialogue, but students in the working party produced a newsletter to keep the rest of the school up to date about the project and went into classes to report on the work underway.

Another way to report back is a letter addressed to young participants by a city official

Project Summary Log, page 1
[Project Name]

Dates of Project ....

Goal(s) of
Project ....

Youth Partners &
(Optional) Youth
Names ....

Ages and Grades
of Children Involved ....

Notable Student
Characteristics ....
(e.g., % English language learners, % with a disability, etc.)

Project
Coordinator &
Staff ....

Project Partners
Adult Names &
Roles ....

Other Adults
& Their Roles
(photographer,
experts, etc.) ....

By the numbers:
# of children
# of adult facilitators
in attendance at events
of sessions with children
duration of each session ....

Form 9.2. A sample project summary log. Image credit: Growing Up Boulder   *(Form 9.2 continued on the next page)*

or designer. For example, after the City of Boulder completed its Comprehensive Plan in 2010, children and teens who provided input received a formal letter from the Director of Community Planning and Sustainability, thanking them for their contributions and listing ways that their ideas were integrated into the final plan.

Young people themselves requested this type of response. They noted that they rarely received anything from the post office, and for digital natives, a piece of official snail mail was an exciting innovation.

(Form 9.2 continued)

Project Summary Log, page 2
[Project Name]

Brief Title or
Description
of Individual
Sessions in this
Project

Themes
Emerging from
Project

Artifacts
Collected

(e.g., writing, drawings, presentations, photos—and filepath location where each artifact is stored or saved on the computer)

Name and Role of
Person Completing
this Form

Date of Form
Completion

10

Reflection and Evaluation

C hapter 2 of this book noted that one of the principles for sustaining programs is to reflect and adapt. Reflection occurs during a continuum of processes: ongoing observations about what works best and what could be changed during the everyday implementation of projects; scheduled times for review and discussion among program leaders, project facilitators, partners, and young people; assessments conducted with the support of outside evaluators; and systematic processes of evaluation research to investigate whether lessons learned from your program may be relevant for wider audiences. This chapter primarily considers the first two steps along this continuum: creating a culture of reflection to notice what works better and worse during day-to-day activities, relative to program objectives; and scheduling regular occasions for people to share their observations and discuss implications for moving forward. In this way evaluation and reflection occur at every step as a project unfolds: and they can be built into participatory processes so that young people play active roles in assessment. You may never need to go beyond these steps of everyday reflection and group reviews; but in the event that you need to involve an external evaluator or you want to document your program's outcomes through evaluation research, this chapter's concluding section offers suggestions.

Evaluation is commonly divided into two types.[1] *Formative evaluation* takes place while a project is being planned or implemented, with

the aim of improving performance. Because it focuses on the quality of a program's processes, it is sometimes called process evaluation. It is usually done internally by program staff and other stakeholders for their own use, to promote continuous project improvement and refine goals and strategies. *Summative evaluation* is usually done at the end of a project or at a scheduled point in the life of a program to determine whether goals have been met. Because it focuses on outcomes, it is sometimes called product evaluation. It is typically done by external evaluators for the use of funders and administrators.

This chapter emphasizes formative evaluation, consistent with this book's focus on good practices in the everyday operations of a participatory program. At their best, however, formative and summative evaluations are complementary because process and product cannot be separated. To understand whether processes are effective, it is helpful to look at outcomes; and to know whether outcomes are likely, it is necessary to understand the content and quality

1. Michael Scriven, "The method of evaluation." *Perspectives of Curriculum Evaluation*, ed. Ralph Winfred Tyler, Robert Mills Gagne and Michael Scriven (Chicago: Rand McNally, 1967), 39–83. For resources on evaluation, see evaluation toolbox.net.au.

of processes. Therefore, the sections that follow share tools for assessing both processes and outcomes as projects unfold.

Reflection and Evaluation with Adult Stakeholders

On a day-to-day basis, reflection is happening whenever project facilitators observe how participants are responding. Is this activity working as intended? What do people say and do? Are young people focused and engaged? Excited? Drifting away? Why are they responding this way? Do teachers act as if they find the activity meaningful? Do volunteers appear prepared and confident? Record your observations in field notes, journals or project logs (see suggestions for record keeping in Chapter 9). If people express how they feel during the activity or what they are learning, capture their words. This is the front line of evaluation.

Reflection is also happening whenever program staff and volunteers sit down together to share their observations and discuss what is working well and what could be done better. Could this activity be adapted to be more successful? Is it meeting partner's needs? The needs of young people and their families? What steps should follow?

Drawing on his experience with the Growing Up in Cities program of UNESCO, David Driskell provides recommendations to create a receptive context for these meetings:[2]

- Provide a positive and supportive environment. Reassure people that their views matter and they can say what they think without risk.

- Criticize constructively. Begin evaluation activities by first discussing successes. What worked well? What did we achieve? Then move on to areas for improvement.

- Foster creativity. Reflection can be enlivened by role playing, drawings, interviews, and games that explore how a project is proceeding and how it could be done differently. You can ask different individuals or teams to take charge of a group reflection session and invite them to introduce different evaluation tools or develop their own.

- Accept criticism. Encourage people to look for some validity in every criticism and try to understand its cause. Communicate appreciation for a diversity of perspectives.

Document the suggestions that come out of reflection sessions and identify actions that need to be taken, who will follow up, and how they will inform the rest of the group. Let people know that they are welcome to advocate different approaches to improve an activity or event; but in this case, it can be helpful to list the advantages and disadvantages of different approaches. Then test the ideas and see what works.

Sometimes it is helpful to schedule time for staff and volunteers to write down individual reflections. With prompts, people can be asked to focus on discrete activities or broader aspects of a program's operation and direction. This can be accomplished during meetings, or people can be asked to bring in their writing to share. Doing this ensures that everyone's voice will be heard. Simple prompts that work well include: What did you do? How did it go? How do you know? Responses are usually recorded in 3 columns, one for each question. People can add their answers to a collaborative online document, or they can write them on a whiteboard or large sheet of paper.[3]

From time to time, it is a good idea to revisit whether program operations reflect guiding principles. Group meetings provide an oppor-

---

2. David Driskell, *Creating Better Cities with Children and Youth* (London: Earthscan Publications, 2002), 173–175.

3. For more information on reflective practices, see: Dannelle D. Stevens and Joanne E. Cooper, *Journal Keeping: How to Use Reflective Writing for Learning, Teaching, Professional Insight, and Positive Change* (Sterling, VA: Stylus Publishing, Inc., 2009).

tunity to ask the questions that thread through Chapter 3 on "The Ethics of Participation," such as whether a project embodies a climate of respect among all partners or involves a genuine sharing of influence and voice between adults and young people. You may want to use the "Conditions of Effective Projects for Children's Participation" (Box 3.2) as a checklist for self-examination, or if you are working with teens or older youth, the "Wingspread Declaration of Principles for Youth Participation in Community Research and Evaluation" (Box 3.4). If you created your own set of principles for good practice in collaboration with children and youth, use this list for your review. Consider, also, whether these principles penetrate all five dimensions of your program's functioning: normative, structural, operational, physical, and attitudinal (Chapter 3). If you plan to systematically compare your goals with actual outcomes, you may want to create a worksheet like the example shown in Table 10.2.[4]

The processes of analyzing material gathered during participatory activities and writing reports, presented in Chapter 9, form natural occasions for reflection. They allow you to compare outcomes achieved with intentions. How well do the achievements described in reports align with goals? How can problematic results be addressed? What steps could be taken to make programs and places more responsive to young people's needs? At the same time, material from your field notes, journals, and project logs can bring reports to life with descriptions of what happened during an activity or participants' statements about how they felt or what they learned.

Scheduling Times for Written and Oral Reflections

Because the Growing Up Boulder (GUB) program is a partnership between a university center, school district, city agencies, schools, and other community organizations, program coordinators created a formal process to check in with partners at the end of each project. They developed a short questionnaire that includes a few open-ended questions for reflection about what went well and whether Growing Up Boulder and its partners need to adjust course. (See Form 10.1.) At the end of each project in schools, teachers are also asked to write up and share their reflections about what went well and what could be improved.

Volunteers are an essential part of many participatory projects with children and youth. Their views should be valued whenever people gather to reflect on how a project is proceeding. Because Growing Up Boulder regularly uses undergraduate design students as project interns and volunteers, it also needs to know how well a project serves their needs for learning and development. Therefore, each student is asked to write a short reflection paper at the end of his or her project involvement. (See Form 10.2.) Volunteers are freely giving their time, and if they have good experiences, they are more likely to stay or come back and encourage their friends to participate. If interns are getting academic credit for their work, it is essential to be able to demonstrate that their time with you was well spent.

---

4. For useful guides to frameworks and activities for evaluating participatory projects with young people, see: www.betterevaluation.org/en/themes/evaluation_and_children; Irene Gujit, *Participatory Approaches—Methodological Briefs: Impact Evaluation No. 5.* (Florence: UNICEF Office of Research, 2014), https://www.unicef-irc.org/publications/pdf/brief_5_participatoryapproaches_eng.pdf. (Retrieved January 8, 2018); Vicky Johnson, Robert Nurick, Karen Baker and Rajni Shivakotee, *Children and Young People's Participation (CYPP) Training Workshop Guide* (London/Hove: Child Hope/Development Focus, 2013), https://www.childhope.org.uk/wp-content/uploads/2013/05/Child Hope-CYPP-Toolkit-FINAL.pdf; Perpetua Kirby and Sara Bryson, *Measuring the Magic? Evaluating and Researching Young People's Participation in Decision Making.* (London: Carnegie Young People Initiative, 2002), www.yacwa.org.au/wp-content-uploads/2016/09/2643_MeasuretheMagic_001.pdf; Gerison Lansdown and Claire O'Kane, *Toolkit for Monitoring and Evaluating Children's Participation.* (Save the Children, 2014), https://resourcecentre.savethechildren.net/document-collections/toolkit-monitoring-and-evaluating-childrens-participation; *My Environmental Education Evaluation Research Assistant* (MEERA), http://www.meera.snre.umich.edu.

Growing Up Boulder
Partner Reflection

Partner Organization _____

Staff Member(s) Completing This Sheet _____

Growing Up Boulder works with many partners throughout Boulder. Each partner is different; each has its own approach to working in the community. In order for us to determine what works best for each of our partners, we ask that you complete the following questions. Your reflections will shape our future work and the ways in which we work together.

Please complete this form in whatever way is best (with a bulleted list, narrative, etc.). And, thank you!

1. What has worked/is working well? What specific things did/do you appreciate about our partnership? What types of engagement have you found effective? What kinds of methods? What modes of communication have worked well (content, style, in-person, emails, reporting)?

2. What could be improved? Or, what could we do on our end that would raise our shared work to an even higher level?

3. Is there anything else you would like to share?

Form 10.1. Sample partner reflection sheet. Image credit: Growing Up Boulder

Growing Up Boulder
Volunteer Reflection

Reflection Due Date _____

Thank you for volunteering to work with young people this semester. We really appreciate your time and energy. Please send a one page reflection to [insert name and email address of volunteer supervisor] by the due date listed above. You may want to consider the following questions as you write your reflection.

1. What have you gained from your volunteering experience with Growing Up Boulder this semester?

2. What was/were the most enjoyable part(s) of your volunteer experience?

3. What did you learn about working with young people?

4. What did you learn about yourself?

5. Was there any aspect of volunteering that was challenging? What did you learn from this? How did you feel supported? How could you have been more supported?

6. How can you apply what you have learned to your studies or future career goals?

7. Would you recommend that Growing Up Boulder change any aspect of its process with volunteers?

When you submit your reflection, please state whether you are interested in continuing to volunteer with us. If so, please write your email at the end of the reflection.

Form 10.2. Sample volunteer reflection sheet. Image credit: Growing Up Boulder

The Most Significant Change Technique

The Most Significant Change technique was introduced to monitor a rural development program in Bangladesh, but it has proved useful in a variety of urban as well as rural settings.[5] It

5. Jessica Dart and Rick Davies. "A dialogical, story-based evaluation tool: The Most Significant Change technique." *American Journal of Evaluation*, 24, no. 2 (2003): 137–155.

involves the collection of people's stories about changes that they have experienced as a result of a program and participatory evaluations of these stories (Box 10.1). It has been widely applied with adults, including program staff, staff in partner organizations, and community members that a program serves, but it asks the type of self-reflective question that adolescents can respond to as well.

Box 10.1. **The Most Significant Change Technique**

The Most Significant Change (MSC) technique can be used to monitor short-term impacts from program activities as well as evaluate longer-term program outcomes. It enables stakeholders to identify impacts that matter to them and participate in analyzing story material. In the process, unexpected as well as intended changes may emerge. The technique involves ten steps, which are described in detail in the online guide referenced below, written by Rick Davies, who created the method for international development projects, and Jess Dart, who extended its application to program settings in Australia.

Designing the process and establishing the context

1. **Get started.** Find champions who are excited by the possibilities of this technique, train facilitators, and begin by piloting it on a small scale to see how it needs to be adapted to best fit your organization.

2. **Define domains of change.** Domains of change are broad categories that can be used to sort stories. They should be deliberately fuzzy to allow people to decide the changes that matter most to them within each category. For example, if your program hopes to achieve beneficial changes in individuals, communities, your program's own way of functioning, processes for city decision-making, and city policies, then each of these areas becomes a domain of change. If your program is not large and complex, you may let domains emerge from the stories that people provide. Three to five domains are a manageable number for story collection and discussion.

3. **Define the reporting period.** More frequent story collection, such as every three months, encourages a focus on short-term changes and increases the time committed to the process, but also enables staff to learn more quickly how to use the process and adapt program activities more quickly in response. Less frequent use, such as once a year, highlights longer term outcomes.

Fundamental steps in the process

4. **Collect significant change stories.** Begin by explaining how the story will be used and obtain the respondent's consent. Ask whether a person wants his or her name included in the story. If you later want to publish the story or use it in any public setting, get the story teller's permission. Stories are invited through questions that have the following general form:

(Box 10.1 continued on the next page)

Looking back over [specified time period, such as "the last three months" or "the past year"], what do you think was the most significant change in [a loosely named domain of change, such as "children's lives in this community," "students' lives," or "participants' relationships with their city"] as a result of this program?

People usually volunteer positive changes, but let them know that they can talk about changes of any kind, positive or negative. You may want to ask separately about "changes that reflect an area where the program could be improved."

For every story, record who collected it, when, a basic account of what happened, and the significance of events to the story teller. Respondents who write fluently may want to write down their own stories. If staff interview individuals and take notes, they should read back the story to make sure they have captured its essence according to the story teller. If capturing the story in the respondent's own words is important, tape record it and transcribe it. When staff become used to this technique, encourage them to also record unsolicited change stories that people tell. Appendix 1 in the guide referenced below includes Sample Story Collection forms.

5. **Review the stories.** The stories are reviewed at progressive levels of an organization, usually beginning with staff who work directly with participants and who know their lives best. The reviewers, who should be different from the story writers, sit down together with a pile of stories. If there are many stories, they may already be divided up into different domains of change, or the reviewers' first step may be to categorize the stories

into the domains that emerge. Everybody reads the stories (out loud if practical, because this brings the stories to life). For each domain of change, the group discusses the following question:

"From among all these significant changes, what do you think was the most significant change of all?"

This process requires that people articulate the changes that matter most to them as well as the story tellers, and thus clarify their core values and whether they reflect participants' values and needs. After the group identifies the criteria for its choices, the reasons for selecting each story are documented and attached to the story. (If people are about evenly split in their choice, more than one story may be chosen.)

To help ensure that lessons learned from the stories will be incorporated into the program's implementation, you can ask the reviewers to offer recommendations for action.

When there are many layers in a program, this process continues up the hierarchy. For example, in an international development program, the first review may be done by committees of field staff, who then pass all the stories they select to program administrators, who also go through a similar process of selection and discussion and then pass their work on to donors.

6. **Provide stakeholders with regular feedback about the review process.** This needs to be a transparent process for all stakeholders, including the story tellers. Therefore, it is important to relay back how stories were selected and the criteria used. People can be informed in meetings

or through newsletters, letters, reports, posters, or even dramatic re-enactments.

Optional steps

7. **Verify the stories.** If the people who select stories are not familiar with the events described, they may want to visit the sites where those events took place and gather more detail from more people.

8. **Quantify changes.** Keep all of the stories that were initially generated in Step 4, as you may want to count how often a particular type of change is described. You may also want to collect quantitative information about a change. For example, if a teacher said that children in her class became comfortable speaking to public groups, how many children had this opportunity?

9. **Conduct a secondary analysis of all the stories.** A secondary analysis can involve either an in-depth look at the content of all the stories or asking questions about the process such as who the stories represent, whose stories are being selected, and how the stories are being used.

10. **Revise the MSC process.** As you use the technique over time, you are likely to adapt it based on day-to-day reflections about what works best and what could be done better.[1]

1. The following references provide examples of the application of MSC in different settings and practical advice for implementing each of the steps: Jessica Dart and Rick Davies. A dialogical, story-based evaluation tool: The Most Significant Change technique. *American Journal of Evaluation*, 24, no. 2 (2003): 137–155; Rick Davies and Jess Dart. *The 'Most Significant Change' (MSC) Technique: A Guide to Its Use,* 2005. Available at www.betterevaluatioon.org/resources/guides/most_significant_change.

Pre- and Post-Photographs

Don't forget the potential power of pre- and post-intervention photographs as an evaluation tool. Chapter 4 recommended photographing a project site before activities begin, not only to document site conditions, but also to prepare for pre- and post-comparisons. When changes are dramatic, photographs can be worth a thousand words. Consider, for example, Figures 10.1 and 10.2, which show the school ground in London, Canada, that is featured in a program profile in Chapter 11, before and after participatory activities to turn it into an area for nature play.

Figure 10.1. School ground in London, Ontario, Canada, before participatory design and redevelopment. Photo credit: Janet Loebach

Figure 10.2. The same school ground after it was turned into an area for nature play. Photo credit: Janet Loebach

Children and Youth as Evaluators

Children's right to express their views in all matters that affect them—as stated in Article 12 of the United Nations Convention on the Rights of the Child—extends to their views about participatory processes.[6] Many of the methods in this book that enable young people to evaluate the communities where they live can be turned inward to involve them in assessing the programs that engage them. By turning the focus of inquiry on your program, you can invite young people to share how they experience activities and how your program impacts their lives—using interviews, focus groups, questionnaires, drawings, writing, collage, role playing, photography, video, and many other methods described in this book. Because these methods have been covered in other chapters, this section will only introduce a few resources and strategies that have been specifically designed to engage children and youth in evaluating the programs that serve them. These strategies build on a long tradition of participatory evaluation with adults with the aim of hearing from all the stakeholders in a program,[7] as well as the tradition of participatory monitoring and evaluation for communities in international development programs.[8]

In her book *Youth Participatory Evaluation*, Kim Sabo Flores provides step-by-step instructions for mentoring teens and young adults in evaluating programs.[9] Guided by the Wingspread Declaration of Principles for Youth Participation in Community Research and Evaluation,[10] she describes how to develop a team of youth evaluators, help them write an evaluation plan, train them as interviewers, focus group facilitators, survey designers, and journal keepers, and teach them how to analyze and present the information they gather. She also shows young evaluators how to use improvisational theater as a way to engage other youth in expressing how they experience their communities and institutions. (For more information on training young people in these skills, see Chapters 5 and 6.) [11]

Questionnaires

Questionnaires are a rapid way for all child and youth participants to indicate both how they feel about a project or program and how well it is meeting their needs. A simple questionnaire, such as the K-W-L method, can provide rapid feedback after a single project session or group of sessions (Box 10.2). Based on years of practice and research to understand critical features of programs that support positive youth development and community change, Linda Camino, Shepherd Zeldin, and their colleagues created *Youth and Adult Leaders for Program Excellence*, a guide to intergenerational program assessment that includes a workbook and questionnaires.[12] The four questionnaires include: a Youth

6. UNICEF, "Convention on the Rights of the Child." UNICEF.org. http://www.unicef.org/crc. (Retrieved September 16, 2017).

7. Elizabeth Whitmore, ed., *Understanding and Practicing Participatory Evaluation*. New Directions for Evaluation, Volume 80. (San Francisco, CA: Jossey-Bass, 1998).

8. Marisol Estrella and John Gaventa, *Who Counts Reality? Participatory Monitoring and Evaluation*. IDS Working Paper 70. (Institute of Development Studies, University of Sussex Learning from Change, 1998). Available at www.ids.ac.uk/publication/who-counts-reality-participatory-monitoring-and-evaluation-a-literature-review.

9. Kim Sabo Flores, *Youth Participatory Evaluation* (San Francisco: Jossey-Bass, 2008).

10. You can find the Wingspread Declaration in Chapter 3 of this book and at: Wingspread Symposium. *Wingspread Declaration of Principles for Youth Participation in Community Research and Evaluation*. University of Michigan. ssw.umich.edu/sites/default/files/documents/research/projects/youth-and-community/SymposiumII.pdf. (Retrieved September 23, 2016).

11. Ways to support and sustain research by young people, whether it focuses on community issues or program evaluation, are also covered in Melvin Delgado, *Designs and Methods for Youth-Led Research* (Thousand Oaks, CA: Sage Publications, 2006).

12. Linda Camino, Shepherd Zeldin, Carrie Mook, and Cailin O'Connor, *Youth and Adult Leaders for Program Excellence: A Practical Guide for Program Assessment and Ac-*

Box 10.2. **Session Feedback**

There are many ways to ask for feedback after a single session with young people. One is the K-W-L assessment—in which young people reflect on "what I Know," "what I Want to know," and "what I Learned."[1] This is a helpful reflection in providing feedback from the day but also for planning content for future lessons, and methods for future projects. This method can be adapted as an outdoor photography reflection, in which students reflect on a single question, such as "Today I Learned. . .", jot their responses on a prepared paper, and have their photograph taken with the paper at a relevant landmark. When students at an elementary school studied an adjoining park before proposing park improvements, they used this method. They took photos of themselves on the day they learned that residents had illegally dumped non-native koi fish into the park pond. They also took pictures of themselves in special places in the park and schoolground that they wanted to preserve.

1. Donna M. Ogle, "KWL: A teaching model that develops active reading of expository text." *The Reading Teacher* 39, no. 6 (1986): 564–570.

Table 10.1 The K-W-L Method of reflecting on a single activity. Examples from student responses are from a lesson about the natural history of a park that would be redesigned.

What I Know	What I Want to Know	What I Learned
Everybody loves the lake.	How long the lake will be here?	There was not always a lake here.
It used to be a farm.	How old is the park?	It once got covered in algae.
There are too many weeds and litter.	When will the park be done?	The fish (koi) in the pond were illegally put there.
About 10 years ago a lot of fish died.	Are we able to clean up the water?	In 2003, the pond was green and full of poop.
		The solar panels in the lake mix the water around.

Engagement Tool that youth and program staff and volunteers fill out to assess the quality of relationships between adults and youth; an Organizational Support for Youth Engagement Tool that adults and youth both fill out to indicate how youth are involved in decision-making, how well the program supports them, and outcomes from their engagement; and two Program Activity and Assessment Tools—one for youth and one for children under 12. The tools are based on general principles of successful programs for young people's civic engagement through activities such as volunteering, organizing, and

tion Planning (Community Youth Connection, University of Wisconsin Madison, 2004). Available at fyi.uwex.edu /youthadultpartnership./yalpe-workbook.

participation in governance. Not all of the questions may be relevant to your program, but many apply to participatory initiatives broadly, such as "Are your thoughts, ideas, and suggestions listened to and taken seriously by all?" Users can add questions tailored to individual program goals.

Because Growing Up Boulder is inspired by the Child Friendly Cities principles of UNICEF, its coordinators created a short set of questions to ask all participating children at the outset and end of a project, beginning with a few questions adapted from the Child Friendly Cities toolkit, which includes assessments of young people's opportunities for participation and citizenship.[13] (See Chapter 6.) When children are beginning readers, the questions are read out loud to the group. Because empowering children to see themselves as agents of constructive change in their city is one of the program's core goals, the questionnaire asks children about their knowledge, attitudes, and behaviors related to city decision-making and civic processes. (See Forms 10.3 and 10.4.) It often includes one or two open-ended questions at the bottom, such as: What was your favorite part? What was most challenging? What could Growing Up Boulder do differently in the future? Growing Up Boulder has students use their unique student ID numbers so that pre- and post-project surveys may be paired, while also allowing for anonymity of student responses.

In comparing pre- and post-project questionnaire results, coordinators noticed that when city staff engaged with children in face-to-face idea sharing at some point during a project, there

was a big increase in the number of children who said that they believed that their city government listened to them and valued their views, in contrast to children who never had any direct engagement with city staff. On a project-by-project basis, questionnaire sample sizes are likely to be small, but nevertheless, results can still reveal trends and provide occasions for reflection.

Open-ended questions, such as "what was your favorite part of this project," reveal young people's experiences from participatory processes in their own words. You may also want to add specific content questions that help you understand what students learned during a particular project, such as, "What did you learn about the needs of older people in the park?" These questions can also be used as catalysts for group discussions (Chapter 6).

If young children cannot fully express themselves in writing, you may want to ask them orally one-on-one or in small groups and note down their answers. An alternative is to have enough assistants to help each child communicate in writing. Although oral questions may

---

13. UNICEF, 2011. *Child Friendly Cities Assessment Toolkit* Child Friendly Cities.org. http://childfriendlycities.org/research/final-toolkit-2011/. (Retrieved September 30, 2017).

Form 10.3. Sample pre-project questionnaire. Image credit: Growing Up Boulder

Pre-Project Questionnaire

Questions	Yes, Always 5 ☺	Usually 4 ☺	Sometimes 3 😐	Not Usually 2 ☹	Never 1 ☹
1. I have a voice in city issues that matter to me					
2. I can help improve my city by sharing my opinion and ideas.					
3. It is important for young people to be involved in city decisions.					
4. I like to volunteer or help out in my community.					
5. Adults listen to what kids have to say in my community.					
6. I understand what happens to ideas that I share with the city.					

Post-Project Questionnaire

Questions	Yes, Always 5 ☺	Usually 4 🙂	Sometimes 3 😐	Not Usually 2 🙁	Never 1 ☹
1. After working on this project, I know that I have a voice in city issues that matter to me.					
2. After working on this project, I believe I can help improve my city by sharing my opinions and ideas.					
3. After working on this project, I feel it is important for young people to be involved in city decisions.					
4. After working on this project, I would like to volunteer or help out in my community.					
5. After working on this project, I know that adults listen to what kids have to say.					
6. After working on this project, I understand what happens to ideas that I share with the city.					

Form 10.4. Sample post-project questionnaire. Image credit: Growing Up Boulder

be easier, if you present them to a group, they privilege the few who are more outgoing. Written responses give everyone a voice, and are particularly useful if you do not want some children influencing what others say.

Evaluation Exercises with Children and Youth

When Jason Hart and his colleagues were asked to evaluate community development projects in Kenya, Ecuador, and India for Plan International, an organization with a strong commitment to children's rights, they included children as key informants.[14] Drawing on the tradition of participatory monitoring and evaluation,[15] his team

created a toolbox of methods, based on their belief that a range of approaches are required to build a rounded picture of the impact of a project on children's lives. They engaged with each group of children for several days, in two-hour blocks of time. Two of their methods, individual interviews with representative children and child-led walks, have already been covered in this book. (See Chapters 6 and 7.) Other exercises that they developed are described in Box 10.3. In addition to these evaluation activities with children, Hart and his colleagues conducted focus groups with Plan field staff, community volunteers, and parents to understand the changes they had seen in children as a result of Plan projects, as well as benefits at a family and community level. They also invited adults to share concerns about negative impacts that they might have witnessed. For example, parents sometimes expressed concern that the time their children spent on participatory activities was taken away from their schoolwork or chores.

---

14. Jason Hart, Jesse Newman and Lisanne Ackermann, *Children Changing their World: Understanding and Evaluating Children's Participation in Development* (Woking, Surrey, UK: Plan International, 2004).

15. Estrella and Gaventa, *Whose Reality Counts?*

Box 10.3. **Participatory Monitoring and Evaluation Tools for Plan International**

Project Timelines

Using large sheets of paper, or even sticks and stones laid on the ground, children draw a timeline that covers the length of a project's implementation in their community and then locate major activities and events along the line. The timeline becomes a basis for discussing how they experienced different points in the project's history and how events impacted them and their community.

Analysis of change

In small groups that may be divided between boys and girls or older and younger children, children discuss changes that they have experienced as a result of project participation. They may be prompted to consider whether participation has helped them overcome challenges and whether they have gained new knowledge and skills or

larger social networks. Invite them to share negative consequences too. Record their thoughts on flip-chart paper. Small groups can report back to the whole group.

In Delhi, India, children did a variation of this activity. They listed types of people who were most important to them in their daily lives. They then discussed ways in which their relationships with these people had changed as a result of their involvement in the project, and also how they themselves had changed as individuals.

Role plays

Children may have fun acting out major changes that they identify. They can be asked to act out aspects of their lives before the project, and then what they are doing differently now.[1]

---

1. Hart et al., *Children Changing their World*.

Also working in the tradition of participatory monitoring and evaluation, Robert Nurick and Vicky Johnson adapted methods meant for adult community members for use by young people.[16] They invited young people to define their own indicators of success and score projects against these indicators. Like Hart and his colleagues, they involved young participants in creating a horizontal timeline of project events, and then asked each young person to draw above it his "confidence line" that showed his level of self-confidence at different points on the timeline. This question can be tailored to project goals. For example, a girl could be asked to draw her level of confidence that she can influence conditions for biking and walking in the city, if this was a project objective. As the line rises and

falls, she explains what happened at each point in the project that affected her level of confidence. Nurick and Johnson also applied the "H" method to assessments with young people. (See Box 10.4.)

If you serve as an advisor to a child-run organization for environmental action or community development, you may find the evaluation methods created by Roger Hart, Jasmine Rajbhandary, and Chandrika Katiwada for the Children's Clubs of Nepal useful.[17] They were designed for adults to lead club members in documenting how their clubs function, if they operate

---

16. Robert Nurick and Vicky Johnson, "Putting child rights and participatory monitoring and evaluation with children into practice." *PLA Notes* 42 (2001): 39–44.

17. Roger Hart, Jasmine Rajbhandary, and Chandrika Katiwada, "Mirrors of ourselves: Critical self reflection on group work by the Children's Clubs of Nepal." In *Steps to Engaging Young Children in Research*, Volume 1: The Guide, ed. Vicky Johnson, Roger Hart and Jennifer Colwell (Education Research Centre, University of Brighton, 2014), 85–91. Available at https://bernardvanleer.org/publications-reports /steps-engaging-young-children-research-volume-1-guide.

inclusively and democratically, and if they fairly serve the needs of girls and boys, younger and older children. Once the activities have been introduced, club members can continue to use them for self-monitoring.

Because some of the Plan International sites where Jason Hart and his colleagues worked included children's clubs, their evaluation included the following exercise:[18]

18. Hart et al., *Children Changing their World*, 43.

Imagine that I want to set up my own club back in my country and I don't know where to start. Can you make a list for me of the things that are important for running my club? I want to know about the rules to have, how we should treat each other, how decisions should be made, what sort of relationship with adults we should have in the club.

Children discussed their lists in small groups and then together. They also considered how

---

Box 10.4. The "H" Method of Program Evaluation

Susan Guy and Andrew Inglis developed the "H" method of program evaluation for adult communities, but Robert Nurick and Vicky Johnson showed that it can effectively serve adolescents and youth as well.[1]

Materials: A large sheet of paper pinned to a wall, one marker and about twelve post-it notes for each participant.

1. To get the "H" dimensions right, fold the paper in half length-wise, then in half width-wise, and then in half again width-wise. Unfold the paper and with a marker, draw a large "H" along the fold lines, omitting the center vertical line.

2. Write a question for discussion in the top center. It could be, for example, "How well has this project helped you learn new skills?" At the left end of the horizontal line write "0," "not at all well," or draw a sad face. At the right end, write "10," "extremely well," or a smiling face.

3. Give each person a marker and ask participants to place their individual score somewhere along the horizontal line.

1. Susan Guy and Adrew Inglis, "Tips for trainers." *PLA Notes* 34 (1999): 84–87. (Retrieved September 30, 2017 from https://pubs.iied.org/pdfs/6150IIED.pdf.); Nurick and Johnson, "Putting child rights and participatory monitoring and evaluation with children into practice."

4. Give each person three post-it notes (they can ask for more if they want) and ask participants to write negative reasons for their score, or why they did not give the program the maximum possible score. Write one reason per note.

5. Ask participants to stick their notes on the left side of the H-form. The facilitator labels this column "negative reasons."

6. Give each person three more post-it notes and ask them to write down positive reasons—why they did not give the program a zero score. After people stick these notes on the right side of the H-form, label this column "positive reasons."

7. Ask participants to simply read out their negative and positive reasons, with clarification if necessary but without going into any discussion at this point.

8. Ask the group as a whole to decide on a group score. This is an opportunity for an open discussion. Write the score that the group agrees to in large numbers above the horizontal line.

9. You could then ask the group to list ways in which the program could be improved. This could be done by listing suggestions below the horizontal line, or by giving each person more post-it notes to write

---

(Box 10.4 continued on the next page)

(Box 10.4 continued)

suggestions individually and stick their notes in this area.

10. The group score, negative and positive reasons, and suggestions can be copied out neatly on a clean H-form and photographed to include in an evaluation report, or typed up as a figure.

This method can be adapted to evaluate places in your city, too. For example, the question posed could be, "How well do parks in your neighborhood serve teens," or "How safe do you feel in the downtown business district?"

Figure 10.3. A sample template for the H Method. Young people place sticky notes on different sections of the H to express their thoughts about an evaluation question. They place X marks or sticky dots along the 0–10 axis (center) to vote.

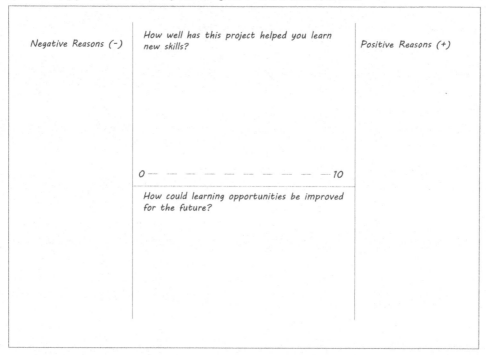

their own club compared with their ideal. This exercise could be adapted to any setting where you want to understand young people's views about ideal democratic practices, and how current realities compare.[19]

Child and youth evaluation is so important that it can form a project by itself. This was the focus when Growing Up Boulder collaborated with the Department of Open Space and Mountain Parks to ask young people to evaluate their preferred means and methods of participation, asking them *how* they preferred to be involved

19. For additional tools for engaging young people in participatory evaluation, see: Lea Esterhuizen, "Child led data collection." Save the Children Sweden, n.d. https://resourcecentre. savethechildren.net/node/5901/pdf/5901.pdf. (Retrieved September 30, 2017); Meg Gawler, *Useful Tools for Engaging Young People in Participatory Evaluation.* UNICEF, 2005, https://issuu.com/learneasy/docs/tools-for-participatory -evaluation. (Retrieved September 30, 2017); Shep Zeldin,

Libby Bestul and Jane Powers, *Youth-Adult Partnerships in Evaluation* (Ithaca, NY: ACT for Youth Center of Excellence, Cornell University, 2012), www.actforyouth.net/youth _development/evaluation/ype.cfm (Retrieved September 30, 2017);

in open space planning. In a focus group, twelve Junior Rangers aged 14 to 17 were asked if they wanted a year-round voice in Open Space planning and to explore the idea of a Teen Advisory Board. The Junior Rangers were enthusiastic about having a year-round voice, and suggested that an advisory board should meet once or twice a month with the priorities of meeting new people, making friends, doing teamwork, and applying technology as an outreach tool to connect with other children and youth in the community. Thirty elementary school students aged 8 to 9 attended a two-day workshop to learn about Open Space and Mountain Parks and its planning process and suggest how to include the voices of children their age. Through a combination of small group brain-storming and large group discussions, they recommended engaging children in planning activities in familiar spaces like schools, parks, the downtown business district, the library, and community centers. For how input should be collected, they wanted formal structures that used multiple creative and open-ended methods and built cooperative and trusting relationships.

Working with External Evaluators

You can productively continue with the types of evaluation activities described above for the length of your program's life, progressively building on lessons learned and refining what works. You only need to work with professional evaluators if your funder requires it, or if members of your organization agree that it would strengthen your program if you could talk about outcomes with more authority. As the opening of this chapter noted, external evaluators are usually brought in at the end of a project or mid-point in the implementation of an ambitious project, with a focus on outcomes.

"Old style" models of evaluation are sometimes still useful under conditions in which an external evaluator comes in to measure predetermined indicators of outcomes for the purpose of accountability. Too often, however, this approach is limited. The external evaluator may fail to understand a community's context and culture well, take time to establish rapport and trust with respondents, or measure outcomes that matter most for front-line staff and volunteers and the people they serve.[20] A more effective approach is for program staff and an outside professional to serve as co-evaluators.

This is known as the tradition of "empowerment evaluation,"[21] and it better fits the participatory culture promoted by this book. In this case, an external evaluator serves as a resource person to help you and other program stakeholders design processes of self-evaluation that will best serve your needs. Through collaborative activities, the evaluator helps stakeholders assess a program's strengths and weaknesses, articulate goals, plan strategies to move forward, and determine the evidence required to document outcomes, usually through a combination of qualitative and quantitative measures. Some outcomes may be tracked by your program staff, but, for others, you may need to rely on the professional evaluator's skills in data collection and analysis. In this case, in-house tracking and external documentation complement each other; and the results are likely to be viewed as more trustworthy because you worked with an impartial professional.

Some external evaluators are skilled in Appreciative Inquiry, a form of planning and evaluation that builds on an organization's or community's positive potential.[22] It is an assets-based approach that asks questions such

20. Jo Boyden and Judith Ennew, eds. *Children in Focus—A Manual for Participatory Research with Children* (Stockholm: Rädda Barnen, Swedish Save the Children, 1997).
21. David M. Fetterman, *Foundations of Empowerment Evaluation* (Thousand Oaks, CA: Sage Publications, 2001); David M. Fetterman, Shakeh Kaftarian, and Abraham Wandersman, *Empowerment Evaluation* (Thousand Oaks, CA: Sage Publications, 1995).
22. David Cooperrider and Diana Whitney, *Appreciative Inquiry* (San Francisco: Berrett-Koehler Publishers, 2005);

as: What works well here? What did we do best in the past and in our current work? What has been most life enriching? Often using interviews, storytelling, and visual media, people exchange significant experiences, imagine how they could create future collaborations based on their strengths, and then commit to actions toward this vision. Because participatory projects with young people aim to create more life-enhancing conditions, this approach is likely to be compatible with project goals.

Sabo Flores cautions that practices of participatory evaluation, including empowerment evaluation, have commonly been blind to the importance of involving young people in reviewing the programs that serve them.[23] In looking for an evaluator, talk to others in similar programs who have worked with a consultant, and check the references of anyone they recommend. Ask to see copies of previous reports that the consultants have written and ask for evidence that they know how to work with youth and the type of communities that you serve. Discuss your philosophies and styles of working and make sure they are compatible. Engage outside experts who share your values and practice the same ethical principles in interactions with children, staff, and other stakeholders that you seek to embody in your program's day-to-day operations.

If you are working with an evaluator, he or she is likely to lead you through an analysis similar to the worksheet shown in Table 10.2. It lists the groups that you are seeking to serve, the outcomes that you hope to achieve for each group, indicators that could be used to measure each outcome, and where you can find this information. A professional evaluator can also help you develop new forms of documentation where there are gaps.

Whereas your goals represent what you want to achieve through a project, indicators are specific outcome measures that can reflect changes over time. The best indicators are valid in the sense that they measure what they claim to measure, verifiable because they can be checked, sensitive to changes, accurate, comparable because they can be used accurately at more than one point in time, and meaningful to all.[24] They should also be easy to collect and use.

A comprehensive evaluation covers three levels of a program's functioning.[25] *Monitoring* draws on the type of quantitative record keeping illustrated by the Project Artifact Log shown in Chapter 9. It summarizes basic data about a project's delivery relative to its goals. For example, if a project intended to engage students in all grades in an elementary school during an academic year, did this happen? How many students did it reach at each grade level? How many hours of activities were delivered in each grade? Record what happened without value judgments.

Another level of functioning is the *quality of delivery*. This involves the processes of self-reflection about what works best and what could be improved that this chapter has emphasized. Value judgements are intrinsic to this aspect of assessment. The most difficult level to document is *effectiveness in achieving outcomes*. Therefore it is the most expensive, where outside financing for an external evaluator's help will likely be needed.

Some outcomes that you will want to measure are tangible. For example, if you worked with students to understand what would make biking to school more attractive to them, has the city added crossing lines on the way to school and has the school district installed bike racks as students suggested? Some outcomes can be observed and counted. Has the number of cyclists to school increased after two years of the project's implementation? Many important outcomes, however, are more difficult to measure,

Appreciate Inquiry Commons, http://www.appreciative inquiry.case.edu.

23. Sabo Flores, *Youth Participatory Evaluation.*

24. Boyden and Ennew, *Children in Focus.*

25. National Commission on Resources for Youth, *Evaluating Youth Participation* (New York: Author, 1982).

Table 10.2. **Aligning Outcome and Evaluation Measures**

This example draws from work by program coordinators and a doctoral student, Stephen Sommer, to develop an evaluation plan for Growing Up Boulder. This example is from a single project on making model plans for affordable and child-friendly multifamily housing.

Outcome Identification and Measurement Worksheet

Groups your project serves	Desired outcomes	Indicators	Sources of documentation
Third grade students	Students learn about urban planning and design	# of classroom hours spent on this project Student work incorporates professional planning and design considerations	Project logs Staff analysis of student writing, models, PPTs
	Students gain public speaking skills	Students competently express themselves before community members and public officials	Videotapes of student presentations
	Students believe that their ideas matter to city government	Students express increased belief that they can influence city decision-making	Pre- and post-project student questionnaires
Third grade teachers	Teachers increase their capacity to engage students in learning related to urban planning	Teachers help prepare and present project lessons They see benefits for student learning and want to continue with future projects	Project logs Teacher reflection papers Debriefing meeting
Undergraduate design students	Design students learn to work with community clients in participatory ways	Studio hours spent on project Hours of direct contact with third graders	Studio syllabus Student reflection papers
	They gain greater awareness about children's community needs	Child-friendly ideas appear in design student drawings and models In studio juries, design students give rationale for child-friendly elements in their work	Staff analysis of student drawings and models Studio faculty observations Studio faculty debriefing meeting
City Department of Planning & City Housing Office	City staff gain new child-friendly planning & design ideas	Staff express benefits from project and want to continue with future projects	Partner reflection sheets
	City plans become more responsive to children's needs	Child-friendly ideas appear in city plans and drawings	Staff review of city plans Debriefing meeting

such as whether a project increased students' sense of efficacy to make changes in their environment or trust in city government. For this purpose, you will need to find someone who can advise you about measures of children's sense of environmental efficacy and trust in government, and how to make valid and statistically appropriate comparisons of measures before and after project implementation.

As you consider what you might realistically expect to achieve through your program, it can be helpful to look at outcomes associated with similar programs. In the year 2000, leaders of the Growing Up in Cities program of UNESCO and the Childwatch International Research Network convened in Oslo, Norway, in a symposium on "Children's Participation in Community Settings" to seek consensus on likely outcomes from programs based on children's right to participate in community decision-making.[26] The outcomes that they generated are listed in Box 10.5, under three areas of impact: changes that well-run programs are likely to promote in participating children, children's communities, and the organizations that serve children. When Plan International convened experts in children's participation in England and commissioned a literature review regarding children's participation in community development,[27] the same three areas of impact emerged. In addition, a fourth area was identified: changes in families. Parents and other family members may come to see their children in new ways, endowed with rights to a voice in decisions that affect them and more capable than previously recognized. In cultures where the most valued behavior in children may be obedience to elders, an important outcome may be for families to give children more social freedom and scope for action and self-expression, especially in the case of girls. Perpetua Kirby and Sara Bryson also found support for a range of

benefits in their review of research on young people's participation in public decision-making.[28]

General lists of outcomes like these can form useful points of departure for your staff and stakeholders, but external evaluators can help you identify the outcomes that are most important and relevant to you, and what you can reasonably hope to document based on your practices and available measures. They can help you translate general outcomes into specific measurable indicators and identify information sources. You can do this kind of analysis without an external evaluator, but collecting data like this requires a greater commitment of time and resources than most programs can afford on their own, and the results will have greater credibility if they come from a professional who has no vested interest in your program.

Along a continuum from everyday reflection to a formal external evaluation, evaluation merges into research when your goal is not just to assess your individual project or program, but to apply systematic methods to generate knowledge that may be useful in other settings. If you ask broad questions about whether and why your project changes people's feelings, beliefs, knowledge, behavior, and skills, you begin to move beyond the type of evaluation that can be conducted largely in-house for in-house use to the field of evaluation research where results will also interest others in similar contexts. At this point, you need to work with someone trained in research skills, who knows what has previously been done to investigate questions like yours and how experience from past studies could be applied to make the investigation of your program's outcomes as valid and meaningful as possible. Evaluation research can also look for connections and cause-and-effect relationships between different levels of evaluation, because changes in people's feelings, beliefs, knowledge, behaviors, or skills (*outcome effectiveness*) are only likely if people have been engaged in relevant activities for extended periods of time (*monitoring*) and

---

26. Louise Chawla, "Evaluating children's participation: Seeking areas of consensus." Special issue on Children's participation—Evaluating effectiveness. *PLA Notes* 42 (2001): 9–13.

27. Outcomes identified by the literature review are summarized in Hart et al., *Children Changing their World*.

28. Kirby and Bryson, *Measuring the Magic?*

Box 10.5. Expected Outcomes from Ethical and Effective Practices of Child Participation

For children themselves:

- more positive sense of self
- increased sense of competence
- greater sensitivity to the perspectives and needs of others
- greater tolerance and sense of fairness
- increased understanding of democratic values and behaviors
- preparation for a lifelong pattern of participation
- new social networks
- new skills
- enjoyment

For the organizations that serve children:

- program and policy development that is sensitive to children's priorities
- the establishment of processes for participation

- increased commitment to children's rights
- innovation

For children's communities:

- public education regarding children's rights
- more positive public attitudes and relationships to children
- increased social capital
- improved quality of life

This list of outcomes is designed to correspond with "Conditions of Effective Projects for Children's Participation" identified at the same symposium (Box 3.2). When programs are ethically and strategically designed, it is reasonable to expect these outcomes.[1]

---

1. Louise Chawla, "Evaluating children's participation: seeking areas of consensus." PLA notes 42, no. 9 (2001): 13.

---

activities were conducted competently (*quality of delivery*).[29]

If you believe that your program may have significant effects that you want to understand better and that may inform others, see if you can interest researchers at a local university in what you are doing. If they have a record of research on community participation or young people's civic engagement, this is more important than the department they come from, which could be urban planning, education, geography, or other fields. Ask if they practice participatory research or participatory action research. Action research seeks to go beyond the generation of knowledge, or the verification of theories, to also improve the conditions of people's lives.[30] Many of the studies referenced throughout this book come out of this research tradition, as it is compatible with the goals of Growing Up Boulder and other programs that this book features.

People who practice action research engage in an iterative "action research spiral" that consists of planning for an action, taking action, observing results, reflecting on the results, and then

---

29. For reviews of environmental program features that are associated with positive changes in young people's environmental knowledge, beliefs and behaviors, see: Louise Chawla and Victoria Derr, "The development of conservation behaviors in childhood and youth." *The Oxford Handbook of Environmental and Conservation Psychology*, ed. Susan D. Clayton (Oxford University Press, 2012), 527–555; Marc J. Stern, Robert B. Powell, and Dawn Hill. "Environmental education program evaluation in the new millennium." *Journal of Environmental Education*, 20, no. 5 (2014): 581–611.

30. Sara Kindon, Rachel Pain, and Mike Kesby, eds., *Participatory Action Research Approaches and Methods: Connecting People, Participation and Place* (London, Routledge, 2007).

beginning this sequence again with a revised plan.[31] At the scale of research about a project or program, it mirrors the iterative processes of planning, acting, observing, reflecting, and replanning that characterize everyday operations in programs that practice self-reflection.

Whether you aim to cultivate a culture of reflection in your day-to-day work, or to engage in evaluation research about broad questions, you are committed to a spiral of continuously adapting and refining your practices as you learn from experience.

31. Stephen Kemmis and Robin McTaggart, *The Action Research Planner*, 3rd edition (Victoria: Deakin University Press, 1988).

11

"Real change involves opening the minds to rich and achievable alternatives."[1]

Putting It Together and Taking Action

Up to this point, this book has presented a multitude of individual methods to engage young people in studying their communities, exploring environmental challenges and possibilities, generating ideas to make places function better, and celebrating actions taken. Wherever you work and whatever your goals may be for participatory planning and design, we hope that you have found methods that you can adapt to your needs. In practice, few initiatives involve just one method or just one organization. If you work in a partnership with other groups, you are likely to use more than one method; and the methods you choose will be more successful if they reflect the shared goals and strategies of all partners and unfold within a structure that enables people to work together in a sustained way, learn from each other, listen to young people, and take responsive action. (See Chapter 2 for recommendations on how to assemble partnerships and create structures for ongoing learning and implementation.)

This chapter features ways to put multiple methods together within partnerships that are committed to action. It presents brief profiles of projects that focus on specific goals to improve urban environments for young people. These profiles cross the world from Canada to the continental United States, The Netherlands, South Africa, India, Australia, and Puerto Rico. They cover relatively small settings such as a schoolyard and a hospital ward, as well as larger scales: a neighborhood, a constellation of neigh-

borhoods, a beach, a wide expanse of open space, a network of city streets and pathways. Some involved children for just one or two sessions, others over a period of weeks or a year. Some were backed by large budgets and some relied largely on local ingenuity. All involved multiple partners. (See Table 11.1) Just as each location in the world is unique, so is each participatory project as it adapts to its context. Nevertheless, whatever the conditions of your own work may be, we hope you find examples here that suggest how you can put diverse partners and methods together and take action.

What these projects share is that adult leaders and facilitators listened authentically to the young participants and treated them as valued guides to create more child-friendly places. They used multiple methods so that young people could evaluate existing places, identify resources that need protection, and envision improvements. They engaged young people in dialogue and collaboration with each other and with adults. Along the way, partners developed

---

1. Colin Ward, as quoted on 179 in: Myrna Margulies Breitbart, "Inciting desire, ignoring boundaries and making space." *Education, Childhood and Anarchism: Talking Colin Ward*, ed. C. Burke and K. Jones (Abingdon: Routledge, 2014), 175–184.

Table 11.1. Summary of Case Studies

Project	Location	Approach	Methods	Actions
Schoolyard Design	Ontario, Canada	Design education Design + Build	Air quality and heat analysis Interviews Behavior mapping Precedent research Design workshops	Schoolyard greening Playground enhancement
Hospital Settings	KwaZulu-Natal and Gauteng Provinces, South Africa	Participatory action research	Drawing Collage Murals Puppets Video Booklet	Site-specific changes in programming and space use Training health professionals and nonprofit organization staff in participatory practices with children
Child Friendly Neighborhood Design	New South Wales, Australia	Participatory action research Participatory design	Interviews Surveys Field trips Design workshops	Neighborhood pathway and playground
Safe Communities	Bhopal and Mumbai, India	Participatory action research	Surveys Observations Focus groups Transect walks Mapping Drawing Interviews	Development of Safe Community Models that guide site-specific priorities for action
Great Neighborhoods	Boulder, Colorado, USA	Participatory planning Design education	Drawing Field trips Model making Presentations and dialogue Child-friendly cities assessment	Informing municipal strategic housing plan and comprehensive plan
Play Routes	The Hague / Tilburg / Zwijndrecht, The Netherlands	Participatory research Design workshops	Guided walking tours Mapping Design workshops	Play routes in three communities
Public Space Design	San Juan, Puerto Rico	Participatory design Design + Build	Photography Design workshop Participatory construction	Construction of three beach-front spaces
Open Space + Parks Planning	Boulder, Colorado, USA	Participatory planning	Drawing Field Trips Photovoice Co-Design graphic facilitation	Increased access to nature Changes to signage Increased long-term youth participation in open-space planning

capacity to shape the environment in democratic ways that gave attention to the needs of young people and the possibilities of their place. Attention like this to the needs of the emerging generation is a condition for social resilience, and attention to the dynamics of their place, a requirement for environmental sustainability.

As the first chapter of this book observed, the United Nations Convention on the Rights of the Child recognizes children as citizens of the present who bring important perspectives to decision-making, and not just citizens-in-the-making for the future. Yet children are, at the same time, both. Therefore, when they participate, it is important for them to feel that it is not an empty formality, but that they are heard and their ideas matter. (See Chapter 3 on the ethics of participation.) Work with children shows that they value being consulted, collaborating with others on enjoyable activities, and feeling heard as intrinsic benefits;[2] but for children to develop a sense of agency as citizens who can reflect meaningfully about their environment and work together with others to create better cities, it is also important that they see some ideas realized in action.[3] Therefore the project profiles in this chapter present different ways of taking action.

In his chapter on "Making Change Happen" in *Creating Better Cities with Children and Youth*, Driskell notes that the implementation of ideas takes three basic forms: physical improvements to the environment, education and changes in people's awareness about young people's capabilities and needs, and changes in policies and institutional frameworks for decision-making.[4]

This chapter shows that these different forms of change often overlap. In all of the projects featured here, young people learned more about their environment and their own capacities for individual and collective action at the same time as their adult partners learned about the value of working with young people and how to see the environment through their eyes. In each case, important goals were for partnership members to gain experience in how to work with young people and to learn the value of doing so. Across projects, groups who gained this experience included designers, design students, teachers, other professionals, staff in institutions or nonprofit organizations, government officials, and developers. Moving on to physical changes was also central to the projects in Canada and Puerto Rico, which resulted in community design-builds, and to the neighborhood development process in Australia. The Open Space and Mountain Parks trail study and Great Neighborhoods project, that involved partnerships between the City of Boulder, Growing Up Boulder, and other community organizations, led to changes in city-planning policies, with the expectation that physical changes will follow.

When colleagues who helped revive the Growing Up in Cities program of UNESCO reflected on effective strategies to lead projects from the participatory generation of ideas to the implementation of physical changes or new policies, they emphasized the importance of building broad networks and aligning goals with partners' priorities.[5] They recommended organizing these networks simultaneously from the bottom up and the top down by bringing together partners who work at every level: front-line organizations that engage directly with children and youth, parents, other local allies, and community leaders at the local level; city officials, funding

---

2. Louise Chawla, "Participation as capacity building for active citizenship." *Les Atheliers de l'Ethique*, 4, no. 1 (2009): 69–75. Accessed online at www.creum.umontreal.ca/spip.php?article1064; Roger Hart, *Children's Participation*. London: Earthscan Publications, 1997.

3. Louise Chawla and Victoria Derr, "The development of conservation behaviors in childhood and youth." In *The Oxford Handbook of Environmental and Conservation Psychology*, ed. Susan D. Clayton (Oxford: Oxford University Press, 2012).

4. David Driskell, *Creating Better Cities with Children and Youth: A Manual for Participation* (London: Earthscan Publications, 2002).

5. Louise Chawla, Natasha Blanchet-Cohen, Nilda Cosco, David Driskell, Jill Kruger, Karen Malone, Robin Moore, and Barry Percy-Smith. "Don't just listen-Do something! Lessons learned about governance from the Growing Up in Cities Project." *Children Youth and Environments* 15, no. 2 (2005): 53–88.

organizations, and media people at higher levels; and where relevant, people with influence at regional, national and even international levels. In the project examples that follow, you will find partners who cross all of these levels.

Networks like these create a framework to implement an action strategy of dividing youth priorities into three categories: changes that young people and their community can accomplish on their own, public obligations that the government needs to fulfill, and goals that require support from outside organizations or donors. In this way, no matter how complex higher-level actions may be, or how long delayed, each community can take its own steps to make immediate visible changes. (For the ethics of moving from planning to action, see Chapter 3.)

If you run into barriers in seeking to implement change, treat young people as partners in this part of your project too. They understand that everything that they imagine may not be possible in reality, and like you, they can learn from constraints as well as successes.[6] As the Growing Up in Cities program unfolded, several axioms for action emerged, including taking time to discuss the participatory process itself.[7] Research on the development of democratic behaviors indicates that opportunities to reflect on civic values and processes, and to hear different experiences and perspectives, is an important practice of citizenship in itself.[8]

---

6. Roger Hart, *Children's Participation* (London: Earthscan Publication, 1997); Kreutz, Angela, Victoria Derr, and Louise Chawla. "Fluid or fixed? Processes that facilitate or constrain a sense of inclusion in participatory schoolyard and park design." *Landscape Journal* 37, no. 1 (2018).

7. Chawla, "Participation as capacity building for active citizenship."

8. Judith Torney-Purta, Rainer Lehmann, Hans Oswald, and Wolfram Schultz. "Citizenship and education in 28 countries: Civic knowledge and engagement at age 14." *Amsterdam: IEA* (2001).

Participatory Schoolyard Design:
London, Ontario, Canada

With Janet Loebach

• •

At a Glance

Project Lead: Janet Loebach, Thrive Design Consulting

Location: Blessed Sacrament Elementary School, London, Ontario, Canada

Partners: London District Catholic School Board, ReForest London, City of London, school staff and community members, Department of Geography at the University of Western Ontario

Goals: Participatory design of natural play spaces, reducing air pollution, community awareness and capacity building for local environmental action

Participant Age Range: 5–14 years

Timeframe: Three years, including air quality testing both pre- and post- participatory redesign

Methods

- Pre- and post-testing air quality
- Thermal imaging
- Site measurements and scaled base plans
- Site inventory and assets mapping
- Interviews with users (students and staff)
- Behavior mapping
- Identifying opportunities and constraints
- Concept drawings
- Advanced design work (scaled drawings with plant palettes)
- Model building
- Presentations
- Costing
- Prioritizing
- Community Build

• •

Project Overview

This project began with a focus on air quality and health of children attending an urban school in the City of London, Ontario, Canada. The school was located next to a road with very high volumes of traffic, and the adjacent schoolyard area was deemed off-limits to students due to concerns related to the car traffic and air quality. The school approached Janet Loebach, of Thrive Design Consulting, to develop a design solution to minimize these hazards and improve the quality of the space. Janet recognized the opportunity of greening a school ground as a means of improving local air quality. The school administrators agreed that this was an area of interest and approved the project. Children are more vulnerable to the effects of air pollution, with greater incidence of asthma in areas with high air pollution.[9] By combining the study of air quality and potential health improvement with schoolyard greening, the school was able to obtain funding that included a participatory design process which would integrate the study of air quality with landscape design.

Project Implementation

The project began with initial assessments of air quality and heat islands and found that the most-concentrated air pollutants were within 150 meters of the roadway—the majority of the schoolyard fell within this zone. At the time, Janet was a Ph.D. student in the Human Environments Analysis Laboratory (HEALab) at the University of Western Ontario. The HEALab

Figure 11.1. Urban heat image. Light areas show areas of higher urban heat; darker areas show lower temperatures associated with vegetation. Image courtesy: Janet Loebach

Figure 11.2. Urban heat image. Youth demonstrated the contrast between body temperature (dark areas) and the heat of concrete (light areas). Image courtesy: Janet Loebach

Director brought in additional university students and loaned particulate meters to assess air quality with the elementary students. This created a focal area where vegetation might create a buffer zone to trap pollutants between the roadway and school play areas. In addition, students from the geography department's Climate Lab assisted elementary students in the use of thermal cameras to see the influences of hard surfaces versus vegetation on ground temperatures (Figures 11.1 and 11.2).

The participatory design process involved two stages—understanding the design process and designing—followed by a community design-build.

9. H. Ross Anderson, Graziella Favarato, and Richard W. Atkinson. "Long-term exposure to air pollution and the incidence of asthma: meta-analysis of cohort studies." *Air Quality, Atmosphere & Health* 6, no. 1 (2013): 47–56; Katherine K. Nishimura, Joshua M. Galanter, Lindsey A. Roth, Sam S. Oh, Neeta Thakur, Elizabeth A. Nguyen, Shannon Thyne et al. "Early-life air pollution and asthma risk in minority children. The GALA II and SAGE II studies." *American Journal of Respiratory and Critical Care Medicine* 188, no. 3 (2013): 309–318; Michael Guarnieri, and John R. Balmes. "Outdoor air pollution and asthma." *The Lancet* 383, no. 9928 (2014): 1581–1592.

Box 11.1. **What We Need to Know**

Space considerations when designing

- How much area do we have?
- What are our space limits?
- Seasonal and weather considerations
- Will the space be used year-round?
- What weather conditions do we need to think about?
- Do we need a structure for different climates (e.g., rain, sun)?
- Layout of the environment?
- What type of environment is needed?
- What type of design should be made for this type of land?
- Overall look: What should go where?

- What will look visually appealing?
- Will our design be unique (in visual appearance)?
- What should (or should not) be included in the space?
- What do we need to add or take away?
- Do we want more pavement than greenery?
- Should we take out pavement because it gives off heat?
- What equipment is needed for children to enjoy sports?
- Seating needed?
- Storage needed?

Stage 1: Understanding the design process

This initial stage introduced students to the design process. Students were introduced to the project by learning that they would be the primary designers and had a responsibility to both users and maintainers of the site. This stage also introduced students to the design process—what it is, who designs, and what are the steps in the design process. Facilitators asked students to identify what designers need to know, and how they can find this information. Students brainstormed ideas and grouped them into categories: what they need to know about *users and clients*, the *space/environment*, and *constraints and resources*.

One of the first democratic processes was to determine a project name and "design firm" identity as a class. Students used an iterative voting process and agreed upon the project name Green Direction. Then students broke into firms —groups of three to four members—who would work through the design process as a team and ultimately generate a proposed design plan. Each firm received a binder for notes to record their design process and a sketchbook for each student in the firm. Each firm then also chose its design firm name.

Stage 2: Designing

Assessment

In the design phase, students began by researching questions they had identified in the "what we need to know" brainstorming process of Stage 1 (Box 11.1). They then proceeded to map the existing conditions of the playground. Students learned to draw scaled base maps to show the existing configuration of the site. They also used a site inventory and mapping checklist to develop an amenities map (Box 11.2; Figure 11.3 and 11.4).

After completing base maps and inventories, students conducted behavior mapping exercises (see Chapter 4) in order to highlight places where children of different ages and interests played. Students noted conditions that

Figure 11.3. Students developed base maps and inventories of existing conditions as a way to learn about and evaluate the existing school grounds. Photo credit: Janet Loebach

Figure 11.4. The base map provided just enough outline of buildings and landscape features for students to add in their own observations. Photo credit: Janet Loebach

BEHAVIOUR MAPPING EXERCISE
BLESSED SACRAMENT

Names: Megan, George
Weather: Pa Cloudy/Windy
Date: Thursday April 26 2012

☐ morning recess
☑ afternoon recess

OBSERVATION	ACTIVITY	#	WHO GENDER	GRADE
1	playing soccer	2	girls	gr. 5
		4	boys	gr. 5
2	standing & talking	3	girls	gr. 1
3	climbing	1	boy	gr. 3
1 ⚡	Duck tape tag	4	girls	gr 4/5
2 ⚡	Skipping	4	girls	gr.1
3 ⚡	Playing with chalk	2	girls	Kindergarten
4 ⚡	talking	2	girls	gr 3
5 ⚡	Playing war	7	Boys	girls gr 3-4

* Alot of girls were playing games or talking and boys playing war or running games.
* Noticed that the little kids play in the west tarmack area!

Box 11.2. **Site Inventory and Mapping Checklist**

✓ Existing facilities/resources (basketball nets, soccer fields, play structures)

✓ Places for active game playing

✓ Places for quiet activities or hanging out

✓ Living things (trees, grass, gardens, shrubs, plants, flowers)

✓ Natural materials or landscape forms (boulders, hills, ditches)

✓ Places where trash or leaves collect

✓ Places where water collects after a rain

✓ Hot places

✓ Cold places

✓ Windy places

✓ Sunny places

✓ Shady places

✓ Places to enter and exit the school grounds

✓ Your favorite place (and why)

supported or inhibited play and highlighted any areas of conflict related to the social or physical environment (Figures 11.5 and 11.6).

They then turned to generating interview questions to understand different users' interests for a redesigned schoolyard. They developed three basic interview questions: How do you use the schoolyard now? What would you like to be able to do in the schoolyard? What natural things might you like to see?

Each firm was assigned one class of students, one teacher, and one staff member for their interviews. Each firm then reported back what they had learned to all the design firms in

Figure 11.5. Sample behavior mapping exercise: the data sheet was used to record date and time of day, as well as play activities by gender, grade, and location on the map. Image credit: Janet Loebach

Figure 11.6. Sample behavior map: students recorded their observation codes onto the base map based on observations recorded on the data sheet (Figure 11.5). Image credit: Janet Loebach

the class. From these evaluations, the students as a whole chose priorities for creating their own designs that included the needs of students, teachers, and staff at the school.

Design Research

After their assessments, students studied "good places to play" and model "natural areas" for school grounds in order to generate ideas for their own school redesign. Through the use of precedent study and computer research, they explored habitat gardens, plants native to southwestern Ontario, and usage of plants for different purposes. Students developed a Materials Palette of plants and landscape materials, including deciduous and coniferous trees, native perennial plants, types of ground cover, and surface materials. All materials in the palette had an associated unit cost; students were responsible for creating a design that would meet the $15,000 target budget.

Conceptual Design

Once research was completed to understand the site, users, and suitable materials, students began developing concept drawings for their school's greening. Concept drawings were then developed into scaled base drawings, using the initial base maps they had generated. Students then made three-dimensional models (Chapter 5) to represent their final designs.

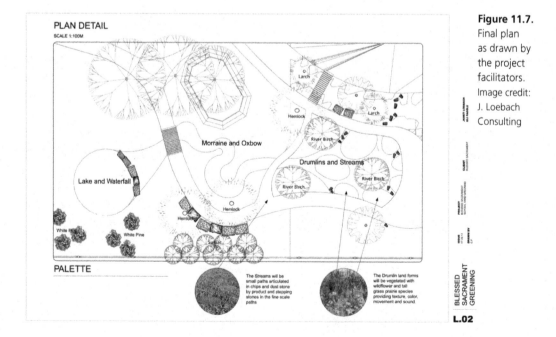

Figure 11.7. Final plan as drawn by the project facilitators. Image credit: J. Loebach Consulting

The design firms presented their designs to one another, providing details of their drawings, priorities, and rationale for their design choices. Janet then facilitated discussions with the students to synthesize ideas from the presented designs and establish priorities for the final site design. Janet worked with colleague Eli Paddle, a registered landscape architect, to prepare drawings of a merged design which reflected the collective priorities and ideas of the students. Janet and Eli brought the design plan back to the students for feedback. This helped generate a final plan that considered users as well as budgets. Site plans for the final merged design were generated by Eli Paddle with J. Loebach Consulting (Figures 11.7 and 11.8).

Stage 3: Construction

After large sections of asphalt were removed, planting beds and pathways were installed with the help of school-board personnel and local contractors. Students from various classes participated in most stages of the construction including the planting of more than 25 trees and large shrubs around the site, prepping beds for planting, and distributing mulch. The entire

school community was then invited to participate in a Community Build Day to assist with the final planting of small shrubs and flowers and cleaning up all planting beds. Students and community members volunteered to continue watering and caring for the garden.

Students created a structure to continue this program indefinitely, ensuring a tangible, ongoing connection between students and the new greened space. The program includes a Green Shirt program in which students don a green shirt at recess time and act as garden supervisors, ensuring all plants are protected and healthy, pulling weeds, and picking up any garbage. Project leaders and students decided to give the plantings time to mature before measuring the post-installation air quality and thermal indices.

Project Strengths and Reflection

One of the strengths of this process was the authentic decision-making power that students had and the associated responsibilities that came with it, including researching and costing. The project used multiple methods to assess the site, understand users, and learn about the design process. This provided multiple means for students to

Figure 11.8. Rendering to show anticipated playground design. Image credit: J. Loebach Consulting

PERSPECTIVE VIEW

BLESSED SACRAMENT GREENING

L.02

learn about design and strengthened the design outcomes. Such a comprehensive process requires time and commitment among facilitators, teachers, and students. However, it was easy to connect the project to a wide range of curricular topics and goals. For example, conducting field measurements of the site and translating these to scaled base plans fit well with the math curriculum. Writing a script to describe their firm's proposed design, and then verbally presenting this material to their peers, tied into language and communication goals within the curriculum. In the process, students moved beyond their own ideas and wishes for the site in order to establish priorities for all the school's users.

School staff supported the project in multiple ways, including facilitating student focus groups within their classrooms, participating in the staff interviews about their own use and wishes for the space, and allowing their students to participate in planting and watering activities. Parents in the community supported the project during the Community Build Day, as well as after completion of the planting by setting up a volunteer group to water and care for the garden during the summer months. Several municipal staff, including from Planning and Children's Services, volunteered their time to help facilitate the in-class participatory design process. Several local contractors also donated labor time and materials to the greening project. Project leaders reflected that if they were to do the project again, they would devote more time to developing short- and long-term maintenance plans for the school grounds, including ways to involve students of all ages, beyond those that were consistently involved in the design process. While a maintenance plan was not part of the design process and curriculum, the school did develop one on their own to address this need in the following year.

This project demonstrated that when children are given the right tools and support, they are more than capable of developing and articulating interesting and appropriate designs. Consistent with other participatory projects,

children's designs reflected not only their own wishes but also the needs and interests of others in the school community. Students continue to be protective of the space and show interest in its upkeep and continued development.

Designing a Child-Friendly Hospital: Phila Impilo!, KwaZulu-Natal and Gauteng Provinces, South Africa

With Jill Kruger

At a Glance

Project Lead: Jill Kruger, University of Johannesburg

Location: KwaZulu-Natal and Gauteng Provinces, South Africa

Major Partners: Oxfam International; Children's HIV Association, UK and KwaZulu-Natal; Street-Wise; United Nations High Commission for Refugees; King George V Hospital in Durban; King George V Hospital School; Durban University of Technology Television School; Great Ormond Street Hospital in London; African Centre for Arts, Culture and Heritage Studies, Department of Anthropology, UNISA; University of KwaZulu-Natal; Lesley University; Children, Youth and Environments Center for Research and Design, University of Colorado.

Goal: To identify children's recommendations for best hospital practices in healing

Participant Age Range: Children aged 6–13 and health professionals

Timeframe: Two weeks to pilot a model process in 2008, followed by intensive training in hospitals and nonprofit organizations with public health missions in 2008–2009. Dissemination through video, print, and integration of program modules in medical schools, nursing schools, and a university course on child rights continued through 2016.

Methods

- Themed drawings
- Collage
- Tree of Life mural
- Sock puppets
- Composite fabric painting

· ·

Project Overview

For some children with serious or chronic illnesses, a hospital becomes their home away from home. Being sick and distant from family is difficult enough without feeling helpless as well. The Phila Impilo! program of South Africa began as a way to transform large urban hospitals into places that express children's unique identities and agency; but its methods can be applied in any setting where children need protection and care and adults see children as partners who can contribute to their own healing and the well-being of others.

Phila Impilo! means Live Life! in isiZulu, one of the primary languages of the provinces of KwaZulu-Natal and Gauteng in South Africa, where the program was implemented. It began with a series of workshops over a two-week period with 26 children aged 6 through 13 years in King George V Hospital in Durban. (It has since been renamed Inkosi Dinuzulu Hospital in honor of the last Zulu king to command regiments in the battle against colonialism). All of the children had infectious TB or TB/HIV co-infections, and they had been in the hospital for periods that ranged from a few weeks to more than a year. Many were hospitalized for a second or third time. The workshops were followed by a process of advocacy, awareness training, and education to share the children's experiences and recommendations with health professionals who worked with similar patients throughout the provinces. For this purpose, a 26-minute DVD was created that showed views of the workshop and shared insights from the children and health

professionals,[10] and a colorful accompanying 64-page booklet was published.[11] This material presented factual information and participatory tools to facilitate a change in approach in health-care settings for children, while the images of the children and their drawings and words were intended to elicit a change of heart to encourage health professionals to relate to children with empathy and open communication. These materials were shared in conferences and training workshops for health professionals, and, as the Phila Impilo! approach was adopted, the program was piloted in five state hospitals and by four nongovernmental organizations that delivered health (and other) services to children in very resource-poor and rural areas, to ensure that its methods could be applied under a variety of conditions.

For the Durban pilot phase, caregiver and child consents were obtained at the beginning and end of the workshops and to approve the launch of the training video and booklet. Official approval was granted for Phila Impilo! to be introduced at King George V Hospital. The medical officer for the children's ward assigned the porch alongside the ward as a workspace. The project director and a facilitator with an arts background began by visiting the children in their hospital school to establish rapport and relationships of trust. Four other facilitators were selected to assist the program, and everyone trained together in a three-day workshop on child participation and communicative arts methods. The facilitators at the hospital also shared a working session before each day's interaction with the young patients. Two nurses joined the children's workshops to monitor their health and well-being, and the children's medical

---

10. Jill Kruger, *Phila Impilo! Live Life! Ways to Healing* DVD. (Overport, South Africa: Young Insights for Planning, 2008.) Available as a free download at http://www.open.edu/open-learncreate/mod/oucontent/view.php?id=53626. (Retrieved July 16, 2017).

11. Ibid.

officer regularly came by and shared some of the activities.

Because they rank low in hierarchies of power in South African society and are widely expected to show respect for adults, children in a number of South African cultures are careful to never appear critical of adults' decisions and actions, no matter how much they may be hurt by adult insensitivity, unkindness, or abuse. Therefore, Phila Impilo! facilitators asked the children about general themes rather than specific personal experiences and invited them to communicate through the medium of puppets. In groups, they agreed on key positive and negative experiences and desired services.

In the workshops, children shared that they felt stressed when caregivers and health professionals failed to give them information about their illness and condition, medical treatments, or how long they would stay in the hospital. At night, they found the vast ward space and unlocked doors frightening. Many came from difficult home situations and had lost a parent to illness or violence, so they needed counseling and comfort for these traumas and losses as well as for their own illness. They missed the autonomy and responsibility that they used to enjoy at home, and they missed school life, which gave them the honored role of "pupil" in their community.

In the hospital, they wanted places to play indoors and outdoors, toys to play with, safe and clean hospital spaces, and clean clothes. They wanted to be able to open windows for fresh air and views, and opportunities to feel the warmth of the sun when it was cool and trees to sit under when it was hot. They wanted to be able to keep some personal belongings, such as their own drawing materials, and hang photos of their families around their bed. If they were well enough, they wanted to go on excursions off the hospital grounds, with occasional weekend visits home. They wanted a hospital shop where they could buy toiletries and snacks, and pocket money for the children who didn't get money from home.

Project Implementation

Children's Workshops

The children were divided into mixed-sex small groups by age and did their activities around group tables in a shared room. At the beginning of the program, they agreed on rules to work together harmoniously and signed the list of rules with their handprints. (See Chapter 3.) Each workshop included a beginning ritual for mutual greeting, an end-of-the-day ritual for passing strength around a circle, games, and songs to share solidarity, fun, and caring. Each child also did a one-on-one interview with a facilitator in addition to the group activities. Workshops engaged the children in the following activities.

Themed drawings.

- Identity drawing with a mirror: Each child was given a small pocket mirror to paste on cardboard, and children drew the people and objects that they valued in their lives around their mirror (Chapter 5, Figure 5.12).

- The happiest day of my life

- The best person in my life

- The best person in this hospital

- Things I'm sad about in hospitals

- Things I'm scared of in hospitals

- *Umoya* (wind) letters: Children wrote notes and drew pictures for beloved adults, many of whom had died. Together they hung their letters on a clothesline outside and watched as the wind carried their words and images to their loved ones' spirits.

When the children shared their drawings about "the happiest day of my life," "the best person in my life," and "the best person in this hospital," they identified sources of happiness and resilience that suggested life-affirming experiences that could be integrated into the hospital program. Their drawings and discussions about

Figure 11.9. The children created collages reflecting their personal strengths. Photo credit: Julie Manegold

"things I'm sad about in hospitals" and "things I'm scared of in hospitals" indicated aspects of hospital life that required adjustment.

Collage. Children cut out magazine pictures and pasted them on a flexible sheet of cardboard "to express the beauty that lies in my heart and in my soul." Then they wrote or talked about the images they chose (Figure 11.9).

Tree of Life mural. One of the facilitators made a large tree out of flexible cardboard to hang at the back of the hospital playroom. Children cut out green leaves and strips of paper for bark. On the bark pieces, they wrote their problems and illnesses and then attached these papers to the trunk. On the leaves, they wrote their suggestions for ways to make their treatment as comfortable and effective as possible and attached them to the branches (Figure 11.10).

Puppet friends. The children, with staff assisting them as needed, made sock puppets by sewing plastic "eyes" on colorful socks. By speaking through their puppets, they could talk about feelings and issues they may have felt hesitant to communicate personally (Figure 11.11). (See Chapter 6 for a more extended description of this method.)

Figure 11.10. Tree of Life mural showing problems (bark) and suggestions for addressing these (leaves). Photo credit: Julie Manegold

Figure 11.11. A sample puppet friend. Photo credit: Jill Kruger

Composite fabric painting. After the other workshops ended, eight of the older children made a large fabric painting of the children's best and worst hospital experiences. The painting also included services and facilities the children would like to have in hospitals. All images were labeled (Figure 11.12).

Figure 11.12. Creating the composite fabric painting about hospital experiences and beneficial services and facilities. Photo credit: Monde Magida

The facilitators assembled each child's drawings, descriptions, and collages into an art book, with the cardboard collage as the front cover and identity drawing as the back cover. Each child was given this book to keep and share with family.

Project Dissemination and Training

The Phila Impilo! DVD was launched at a public showing in Durban in January 2008, where the children were given certificates of appreciation for their participation. Two parents whose children had died came to collect the DVD and certificate in their child's memory. The DVD subsequently screened on national television and at an international film festival in Ghana. As the children requested, the composite fabric painting was given to the government of KwaZulu-Natal Province.

Since its introduction, Phila Impilo! materials and its participatory approach have been shared with hospital and clinic staff and nongovernmental organizations with public health missions through many training workshops and public events, extending its use to new urban areas and rural clinics, and beyond KwaZulu-Natal and Gauteng Provinces to the North West Province and the Western Cape Province in South Africa. This has involved translating the material into isiXhosa and Setswana,

from its original format in isiZulu and English. At training workshops, participants are asked to develop at least two ways to redesign their setting or introduce new services to make their approach more "child friendly." At the University of Cape Town, the program was included in a five-day course on child rights and child law for health and allied professionals, and at the University of Fort Hare and University of Kwa-Zulu Natal, in courses for nurses and other health-care professionals. The International Children's Palliative Care Network distributed the DVD across Africa as part of a Palliative Care for Children Toolkit.

The program has reached international audiences through conferences on TB and AIDS and through the inclusion of materials in courses around the world at institutions such as the Open University and the Birmingham International School of Education in the United Kingdom and Western Sydney University in Australia. The publications and online access cited in this program profile have also given the program international visibility. From the beginning, the goal of Phila Impilo! was to create a model program as the basis for film and print materials that could be incorporated into staff training in any setting where children need protection and care, and to integrate program modules into university courses for the education of nurses and other professionals.

Lessons Learned

- Training professionals to do things in a different, participatory way with children and to view children as "partners in health" involves encouraging a "heart change"—not just learning new information for the head. Children's own voices and stories are the most direct way to reach the heart.

- Take training to places of need. Locate programs to promote new skills on home ground where people can apply learning directly to their environment and raise practical issues of implementation. This encourages organizations to own their processes of change.

- Encourage organizations to vary methods according to their own context and needs. Provide broad guidelines for action but let people customize the process.
- Staff from different positions in a hospital system need to participate in training workshops together.
- Working in hospital settings requires large investments of time at the front end to negotiate complicated systems and relationships. The content, presentation, and timing of training sessions, as well as follow-up support, need to be tailored to each new context.
- Lobbying to encourage changes in official policies requires cooperation over extended periods of time. Schedules for project delivery need to accommodate these timelines.

A complete listing of publications about this project can be found at the end of Chapter 11.

Designing a Child-Friendly Neighborhood:
Dapto Dreaming,
New South Wales, Australia

With Karen Malone

At a Glance

Project Lead: Karen Malone, Western Sydney University

Location: Brooks Reach Neighborhood, City of Dapto, New South Wales, Australia

Partners: Stockland urban developers, Dapto Public School, University of Wollongong, local indigenous advisors, play consultant and artist,

Stockton landscape architect, local community members, city council

Goals: To identify a place-based, child-friendly neighborhood design for the Brooks Reach neighborhood in Dapto, a suburb of Wollongong in New South Wales, Australia

Participant Age Range: Children aged 5–11 and their parents

Timeframe: Three months

Methods

- Drawings
- Surveys
- Photography
- Precedent photographs of other child-friendly designs
- Guided tours
- Mapping
- Focus groups
- Child-friendly report development
- Development of design recommendations
- Letter writing
- Celebration event for children, community, city council, and Stockland developers

Project Overview

As part of her work to establish child-friendly cities in the Asia-Pacific region, Karen Malone had been in discussion for many years with urban developers about the importance of planning communities with children in mind. After Karen gave a series of workshops to urban planners and developers, the urban developer Stockland identified funding to support the design of a child-friendly neighborhood in West Dapto, New South Wales, Australia, as an exemplar for other communities. To accomplish this, a team was composed to facilitate a series of child-friendly community research workshops with children and residents in the Dapto community. Participation drew from previous work with the UNESCO Asia-Pacific Growing Up in Cities, Child-Friendly Asia-Pacific, and UNICEF Child-Friendly Cities partnerships. Methods were based on Growing Up in Cities (GUIC) child-based indicators of environmental quality and the toolkit produced by the GUIC team.[12] The Dapto participatory process was organized into two phases: one in which 150 kindergarten and fifth-grade school children contributed their ideas to playground and streetscape design, and a second in which a team of 12 of the fifth graders worked with adult researchers to analyze data, generate a list of child-friendly indicators, and write a child-friendly report (which provided images, words, and simple language to summarize the project, see Chapter 9). This smaller group also went on to develop design recommendations for a playground and an adventure pathway, which would serve to connect an old neighborhood to the newly planned one. This pathway was designed with the support of a play consultant and artist, local indigenous advisors, Stockland staff, and a Stockland landscape architect.

Throughout the project, facilitators guided children to focus on the existing positive attributes of their community as well as areas for improvement. Ideas were shared at a celebration event that included community members, city council, and Stockland developers.[13] In the workshops, children said they liked the friendly people, parks and playgrounds, and natural places in their existing neighborhoods. Parks, playgrounds, and natural areas were also many children's favorite places, along with outdoor community facilities such as the skatepark and swimming pool. Children said they disliked speeding cars, dangerous people, and the streets. Fifth grade girls were worried about getting lost and not knowing how to be safe in their neighborhoods. While 66% of chil-

dren identified playgrounds or schools as places "especially for children," 13% also believed that wild or natural spaces were for children. Key recommendations capitalized on this nature connection for the playground design: children recommended a play space rife with nature and unique features, including a long slide down a steep hill, trees, a connection to an Aboriginal "scar tree" (Box 11.5), and many loose materials. The pathway was similarly creative with a primary route, alternative side routes or stepping-off points, sculptural and natural elements, and child-friendly signs (in terms of height and content). The pathway was also conceived as a space for placemaking, where children could add elements, sculptures, or trees, over time. The playground was completed in 2012, and in 2013 Stockland Developers and the research team were awarded the 2013 Planning Institute of Australia's Project of the Year and Child and Youth Planning Award.[14]

Project Implementation

Children's Research Workshops

Kindergarten Children. Thirty kindergarteners (5–6 years old) were engaged in two sessions. In the first, they described how they felt about and experienced their local place through a combination of drawings and survey interviews with adult researchers (Box 11.3, Figure 11.13) (See Chapter 6 for the full survey). Following the initial drawings and interviews, children collectively discussed where they go and what they do in their neighborhoods as a focus group with adults. In the second session, children "dreamed" about how a child-friendly community would look and feel in Dapto (Box 11.3).

Grade Five Children. All fifth graders (10–11 years old) participated in three sessions: i) an "independent mobility" survey—to understand the

---

12. Karen Malone, project lead, was part of the initial GUIC team for Australia. The toolkit referenced here is Driskell, *Creating Better Cities with Children and Youth.*

13. Karen Malone, *Designing and Dreaming a Child Friendly Neighborhood for Brooks Reach, Dapto* (University of Western Sydney, Bankstown, NSW, Australia, 2011).

14. Karen Malone, "Child friendly cities: A model." *Designing Cities with Children and Young People: Beyond Playgrounds and Skate Parks,* ed. Kate Bishop and Linda Corkery (New York: Routledge, 2017), 11–23.

Box 11.3. **Drawing and Survey Methods for Kindergarten and Fifth Grade**

In order to understand how they perceived their existing neighborhood, children drew and discussed the child friendliness of both their existing and imagined future neighborhood as follows:

Drawing and Survey Interviews

1. Children were instructed to "Draw a picture of your town or local area and include all your favorite places and places you don't like."

Figure 11.13. Kindergarten children drew pictures of favorite and disliked places in their town prior to interviews about these places. Photo credit: Karen Malone

2. Each child discussed their drawing with an adult researcher and the adult made notes on the drawing as the child spoke.

3. The adult researcher also had a list of survey questions that they completed as they spoke with the children. This included asking about places children like and dislike in their neighborhoods, favorite places, and places that children feel are especially for them (See Survey Sample in Chapter 6).

My Dreams for a Child-Friendly Community

4. In this method, children drew a picture of their "dream place" which was to include "all the things that would make a great place for children."

5. Each child then discussed his or her drawing with an adult researcher who made notes on the drawing.[1]

_____

1. Malone, *Designing and Dreaming a Child Friendly Neighborhood for Brooks Reach, Dapto.*

---

extent that children move about their town without adult supervision; ii) a photography session in which children took pictures of their local area using disposable cameras over a single weekend; and iii) a dreaming session to imagine how the new urban development would be child friendly.

The independent mobility survey was based on surveys that have been conducted around the world to understand children's ability to move about their town on their own—whether they bike or scooter or walk, the distances and locations children travel alone or with friends, and any perceived barriers to independently exploring their neighborhood.[15] In this survey,

children were asked how they got to school and with whom they traveled to school. Parents were asked about what they allow their children to do in terms of independent mobility, the reasons for these allowances or restrictions, neighborhood perceptions, and if children used a mobile phone (Box 11.4).

For the photography sessions, children were sent home with disposable cameras and an open-ended instruction to document their lives in their

_____

15. Independent mobility is a widely studied topic because it has declined much recently and because it is linked to

social, cognitive, and physical wellbeing. See, for example, a comprehensive study from the Institute for Physical Activity and Nutrition Research at Deakin University in Australia: A. Carver , J. Veitch, J. Salmon, C. Hume, A. Timperio, and D. Crawford. "Children's independent mobility—is it influenced by parents' perceptions of safety." Melbourne: Centre for Physical Activity and Nutrition Research (2010).

Box 11.4. **Children's Independent Mobility Survey**

Surveys were given to both fifth-grade children and their parents in order to understand how, when, where, and how frequently children move about their neighborhood on their own (See Chapter 6). Independent mobility is associated with social, cognitive, and physical wellbeing, and is often limited by traffic and car-dominated developments.

The survey included the following types of questions:

Children:

- How did you get to school today?
- Who did you travel to school with today?

Parents:

- What do you allow your children to do (e.g., cross main roads, go out alone, cycle on main roads, travel on buses)?
- What reasons do you have for limiting your child's independent mobility (e.g., traffic danger, strangers, bullying, structured time, better car access)?
- Do you perceive other adults in your neighborhood as looking out for their children?
- Does your child have a mobile phone? Does it give you confidence?[1]

_____

1. Malone, *Designing and Dreaming a Child Friendly Neighborhood for Brooks Reach, Dapto.*

community. The instructions were intentionally open so that children would take pictures of what they found important, without the influence of adult perspectives.

Similar to the kindergarteners, in the dreaming session, children were asked to imagine a child-friendly neighborhood, draw a picture of it, and share this with the adult facilitators (Box 11.3).[16]

Children's Design Workshops

A smaller group of fifth graders (twelve in total) went on to participate in five participatory design workshops, held every Friday for two hours at the school and at the Brooks Reach neighborhood site. In addition to the children, this team also included University of Wollongong researchers, a play consultant, two indigenous advisors, Stockland staff, and the Stockland landscape architect. In this stage, children and adults worked together toward three goals to develop children's ideas for a child-friendly neighborhood:

i) Analyzing data from research workshops and developing a list of child-friendly indicators (Figure 11.14)

ii) Developing a series of design recommendations for a neighborhood play space and pathway. Recommendations focused on key design elements and conceptual themes.

iii) Exploration of a potential walkable/adventure pathway between the old and new neighborhoods. This pathway was named the Emu Adventure Pathway.

The child-adult team worked collaboratively to develop a "Child Friendly" Dapto Report,[17] which included photos, children's voices and ideas, and child-friendly wording of the analysis from children's research workshops (Chapter 9). To support development of these recommendations, the team employed the use of drawings, guided tours, photography, mapping, and focus groups. In guided tours, children led the Stock-

_____

16. Ibid.

17. *Dapto Dreaming, A Child Friendly Report about Dapto.* Unpublished report.

Figure 11.14. Indicators of child friendliness were developed to guide children's workshops and recommendations for the new neighborhood design. Image credit: Karen Malone

Indicator or Theme	Icon	Comments from Children about Why These Indicators are Important
A place that supports play and has a playground		"To let children have fun." "So children don't just sit on the lounge and get unfit. So they could be running around." "So people can develop their climbing skills and have fun."
A place that keeps and protects nature		"Saves old trees. Keeps our heritage." "Keep scar trees and indigenous things." "To keep animals and plants from extinction and let animals have freedom and feel safe."
A place where we create communities		"Have street parties, where people can get together, be nice neighbors, share ideas." "Create a good atmosphere, socialize, and make new friends - communal gardens."
A place that allows you to be active		"It can be fun and children will be healthy and a good weight." "Let kids run free." "It can be fun."
A place that promotes learning		"To teach kids to respect the environment, like at our school we have a green team." "People don't throw rubbish, play safe, and learn to look after the environment."
A place that is safe and clean		"No pollution keeps us, animals, and plants safe so there should be no litter." "So no animals or people step on needles or pins and other sharp objects." "Keep us healthy and nature healthy."
A place that values children		"The future lies in our hands, so if you don't educate us, the future generation, to look after the community, it will be a bad place."
A place that has pathways		"Keep safe and so you don't step on nature." "Have pathways so you don't have to be worried about being hurt or run over by cars and motorbikes."

land landscape architect and Aboriginal custodians of the local area around the future play space. (See Chapter 7 for a general discussion of Child-Led Tours.) Children could ask questions about the sites' history as well as about the development process (Figure 11.15). This allowed all participants to consider the site and its future as a play space. Children then selected images from a collage of thirty play types while keeping in mind the child-friendly indicators (Figure 11.14). To develop the pathway, the group projected a Google map of the entire site onto a smartboard and children identified routes they

Figure 11.15. Children and project facilitators discussed the site on a guided tour. Photo credit: Karen Malone

thought would be safe, fun, and logical between the old and new neighborhoods. The children examined and discussed a wide range of pathway types by examining photographs of precedent pathways from other cities. They discussed pathway issues such as safety, traffic, efficiency versus adventure, risk taking and creating, and wayfinding. In the pathways sessions children also discussed placemaking within an Australian context, which led to a number of specific recommendations for the pathway (Box 11.5).[18] In the final stage of this workshop, each child wrote a letter to the Stockland staff in which they personally recommended the elements they felt represented child friendliness and should be included in the Brooks Reach neighborhood development.

18. Malone, *Designing and Dreaming a Child Friendly Neighborhood for Brooks Reach, Dapto.*

> ●
>
> #### Box 11.5. **Celebrating Place-Based Features**
>
> In the design of the child-friendly pathway, children "expressed the desire for a pathway that keeps, protects, and enables them to engage in nature" (Malone 2011, p. 37). They also wanted visibility, clear and colorful signage for wayfinding, and to identify means of celebrating Australian heritage. As one example of this, they were fascinated with a local "scar tree." Scarred trees are relict trees that the Aboriginal people used to sustainably harvest a section of wood from a tree without killing it. Aborigines would harvest this wood for canoes, water carriers, or to mark an area for spiritual significance. In this same sense, children recommended placing Aboriginal artworks along the pathway—for example, using Emu footprints as a stencil to mark the path.[1]
>
> ---
>
> 1. *Malone, Designing and Dreaming a Child Friendly Neighborhood for Brooks Reach, Dapto.*
>
> ●

Celebration Event and Outcomes

A celebration event was held for children, adult facilitators, community members, and Stockland staff to hear young people's ideas and visions. After three months, the developers returned with initial plans. Nearly one year later, many children who had participated returned to the Brooks Reach site for a "turning of the soil" ceremony to initiate playground development.[19] Wearing high-visibility jackets and hard hats the children were interviewed for the local TV station news that evening, and the event, with one of the young children serving as commentator, was broadcast live on the local radio. The development won awards that highlighted this approach to child-centered urban planning. Stockland also generated a guide for all staff that included the value of listening to community and, in particular, children at all their greenfield sites.

A complete listing of publications about this project can be found at the end of Chapter 11.

Promoting Safe Communities: Bhopal and Mumbai, India

With Sudeshna Chatterjee

● ●

At a Glance

Project Lead: Sudeshna Chatterjee, Action for Children's Environments

Location: Six poor, urban communities in five city wards in Bhopal, India; and three in two city wards in Mumbai, India.

Partners: Action for Children's Environments (ACE); UNICEF India; Committed Communities Development Trust (CCDT), Pratham Mumbai Education Initiative (PMEI), and Youth for Unity and Voluntary Action (YUVA) in Mumbai; Aarambh, Eka, and Muskaan in Bhopal.

---

19. Malone, "Child friendly cities: A model."

Goals: To create a Safe Community Model to mainstream the protection concerns of children in high-risk urban areas into city and community development

Participant Age Range: Young people aged 7–19 and adult volunteers

Timeframe: About six months for the participatory evaluation in each community; three years for the evaluations in all nine communities, the development of safe community models, and implementation of pilot projects and action priorities

Methods

- Household surveys
- Systematic observations
- Focus group discussions
- Transect walks
- Mapping safe and unsafe spaces on neighborhood aerial maps
- Integration of mapping data on a digital platform using GIS
- Map drawings of homes
- Interviews
- Issue-based case studies

Project Overview

India is one of the world's most rapidly urbanizing countries. One in six people in Indian cities live in slums and informal settlements,[20] which typically lack basic services like water, sanitation, and electricity. For children, city life presents many social and environmental threats to their healthy development. Guided by the Sustainable Development Goals of the United Nations,[21] which include safe housing and public

spaces for all, and the New Urban Agenda of UN Habitat III,[22] which calls for participatory and people-centered approaches to urbanization, the Indian nonprofit Action for Children's Environments led a consortium of local partners through a participatory process to identify protective strategies for children in high-risk urban areas. It aimed to conceptualize what the protection of children required in terms relevant to each community, develop child-specific indicators of children's wellbeing and disadvantage, and involve local children in community mapping, program development, and monitoring change.

The program involves three phases. In the first phase, children in slums and squatter settlements in Bhopal and Mumbai work alongside local adult volunteers and nonprofit organization facilitators to map their community and identify threats to children's safety and conditions that promoted safety. In the second phase, everyone works together to develop a Safe Community Model to increase children's safety. In the third phase, the model is adopted for implementation (a process currently underway). To describe these processes, this program profile focuses on the work in Mumbai.

The three sites in Mumbai were selected because they represented conditions in which many of the city's children live.[23] In Mumbai, 54% of the population lives in slums or squatter conditions, crowded into 9% of the city's land.[24] One program site, Lallubhai Compound, consisted of high-rise flats built to house the poor displaced from other slums as part of the city's

20. Office of the Registrar General & Census Commissioner, India. "2011 Census Data." Ministry of Home Affairs, Government of India, www.censusindia.gov.in/2011-Common /CensusData2011.html. (Retrieved January 5, 2018).

21. United Nations, "Sustainable Development Goals: 17 Goals to Transform our World." United Nations.org. http://

www.un.org/sustainabledevelopment/sustainable-develop ment-goals/. (Retrieved April 5, 2017).

22. United Nations, *Habitat III: The New Urban Agenda.* Habitat III. habitat3.org/the-new-urban-agenda. (Retrieved April 5, 2017).

23. Sudeshna Chatterjee, "Making children matter in slum transformations," *Journal of Urban Design* 20, no. 4 (2015): 479–506.

24. Mizra Arif Beg. "Demolitions throw Mumbai's poor onto the streets." The Citizen.org. http://www.thecitizen.in /index.php/NewsDetail/index/1/4247/Demolitions-Throw -Mumbais-Poor-onto-the-Streets. (Retrieved December 27, 2017).

Figure 11.16. On a transect walk, children demonstrated how they scaled a wall to access the local dump-yard for play. Photo credit: Sudeshna Chatterjee

rehabilitation and resettlement program. Residents owned their flats and had piped water and in-house toilets; but garbage was collected irregularly, and only 8 of the 26 buildings had working elevators. There were many empty floors and many empty, vandalized shops at ground level. The two other locations, Rafi Nagar and Shivaji Nagar, were slums at risk of flooding and fires, with inadequate public toilet facilities. In Rafi Nagar, half of the households had no security of tenure and the child labor rate was 82%. People in Shivaji Nagar were less physically and socially vulnerable, with more than half the population in regular employment and all of the children attending school.

All of the communities lacked safe play spaces. Children played in the streets and any available open patch of land (Figure 11.16). In Rafi Nagar, this included a nearby dumping ground, and in Lallubhai Compound, the banks of a large drainage ditch. Because of dangers of traffic and fights outdoors, parents kept young children indoors, and in Lallubhai Compound, children who lived above the fourth floor rarely played on the grounds. The compound had three playgrounds, but none of them were safe because of hazards from garbage and flooding. On the positive side, children expressed that they felt safe when they had trusted and familiar adults nearby and when they could enjoy spaces together with friends.

Mapping Safety Risks and Resources

In each location, 20–40 adolescent researchers aged 10–19 years were recruited to work with adult volunteers and nonprofit organization facilitators to document local safety conditions for children. For mapping safe and unsafe spaces, children under ten years were also involved. They investigated conditions for three age groups: less than 10 years, 10–14 years, and 15–18 years. Over a period of six months, they applied the following methods.

Housing surveys. Facilitators trained separate groups of adult volunteers and adolescent researchers to administer a questionnaire to 10% of the community households, minus households with no children aged 0–18 years. The adolescent-administered questionnaire covered housing, utility services, play and recreation, child labor, and systems of government and community protection. The adult-administered questionnaire gathered a family profile and asked about social safety nets, health, the neighborhood environment, education, participation, and conflict-resolution mechanisms. Facilitators divided the area up geographically and accompanied each young person for the first few interviews to answer questions about administration and ensure quality.

Systematic observations

Home observations. Using a clipboard and checklist, adolescent researchers visited 100 homes in each location to identify physical features and use of space that could be harmful to children's health, privacy, and learning at home. Adult facilitators helped each young person become familiar with the questionnaire instrument and went along on the first few house visits to ensure that the young researcher was comfortable with the process and to check on quality. Adolescents also carried a small notebook to record their perspectives and any questions that needed clarification; in some cases, they also carried a camera.

Neighborhood observations. Using a similar checklist procedure, adolescents formed small groups to observe their neighborhood environment, including streets and public spaces, garbage disposal systems, sanitation facilities, water collection points, street lighting, fire safety, transportation, and schools. Each group was assigned a different aspect of the community to observe and document. They could supplement the checklist with photographs and informal interviews with service providers and users. To check the consistency of the information and get viewpoints about neighborhood conditions from the three age groups, this checklist was administered repeatedly in different parts of the community and at different points in time. Groups of men and women volunteers participated in separate groups. Facilitators helped the young researchers maintain activity logs for the visits that they made to different sites and documented their observations on base maps.

Safe/unsafe spaces. Based on the house and neighborhood observations, and consulting the other methods used, children in all three age groups worked to map safe and unsafe spaces in their community. Each age group involved 20 to 24 children, in groups of no more than 12 at a time, with equal representation of boys and girls, with the goal of a sample of 60–72 children. The children used colored markers, sticky pads, pens, and pencils to label a community base map, plac-

Figure 11.17. Children mapped safe and unsafe spaces in their communities. Photo credit: Sudeshna Chatterjee

ing green and red dots on safe and unsafe spaces (Figure 11.17). Facilitators recorded their discussions and the data generated.

Transect walks

A subsample of 36 children was divided into three groups by age, with six boys and six girls in each group. In advance, facilitators prepared a list of the safe and unsafe spaces that children marked on the base maps. They then accompanied each group on a child-led walk through the community (Figure 11.16). As the children walked, they took photographs of safe and unsafe spaces which facilitators helped them annotate.

Focus group discussions

After the walks, the children returned to their centers with photographs and stories and had group discussions about their walks and the places they visited. In each group, a facilitator explained the purpose of the discussion and how the information collected would be used. Children were encouraged to discuss the issues that the photographs raised.

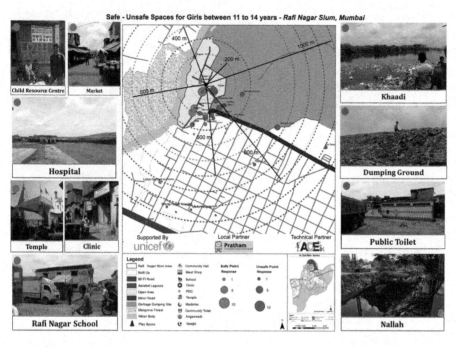

Figure 11.18. Photographs from transect walks and mapping activities were combined to show spatial locations of safe and unsafe spaces in the neighborhoods. Image credit: Sudeshna Chatterjee

The transect walks and focus groups helped to validate the data gathered from the mapping of safe and unsafe spaces. The map data was then integrated on a GIS platform by ACE for further analysis (Figure 11.18).

Maps of homes

As many of the emergent issues of child safety and abuse were directly linked to the habitability of homes, children were asked to draw maps of their huts or flats to explore issues such as density and overcrowding, cooking practices, toilet access, and privacy. This method was chosen because it was as unobtrusive as possible with respect to the private domain of the home.

Interviews

Many key informant interviews were conducted within the community to piece together the history of the settlement and verify the ownership of homes. Experts were also interviewed by ACE to understand the politics of service delivery and local governance in slums of Mumbai.

Issue-based case studies

Once the first phase of data was analyzed, it was apparent that some protection issues were not adequately captured, such as child abuse and child labor. Some of the local nonprofit organization partners who regularly worked on these issues developed case studies to highlight the depth and dimensions of these issues.

Developing a Safe Community Model

The participatory methods used during the first phase of the program were designed to empower communities to realistically assess their own environments in order to identify sources of vulnerability and strength: knowledge that is crucial to any prevention-based safe community model. During the second phase in 2017, the results of the participatory evaluation were connected to theory and research related to risk and resilience in child development in order to create a model, or plan, for how program partners and government at the local, district, and city-wide level can work together effectively to create safe communities for children.

The model is based on the principle that conditions for child protection need to be understood as a system that extends from the family and home, to the local community, to policies and decisions made at the level of the ward, district, and city as a whole. All of these levels affect children's physical environment, their social and economic opportunities, and the political and legal system that governs their lives. Therefore, a major goal of the model is to plan how these different levels can be brought together in an integrated way to improve safety for children.

During initial program planning, nonprofit organization partners, child and adolescent representatives from the selected sites in Mumbai and Bhopal, and representatives from the District Child Protection Unit and UNICEF India drafted indicators of protective factors that are essential for positive developmental outcomes for children. The indicators help identify priority areas for program design and policy action and form a framework to monitor progress. For example, one of the indicators for safe play spaces is "availability and accessibility of spaces for play, games and sports within the ward and neighborhood level."

Implications for action proposed in the Safe Community Model for Mumbai communities include:

Gaining access to specific funds

- Communities will demand funds from the Gender Budget of the Greater Mumbai municipal corporation and other relevant slum redevelopment budgets to develop community-designed and -built play spaces

- Local councilors (elected representatives) will raise demand in Ward Committee meetings for safer play spaces within slum communities and seek the release of funds for this purpose

Based on the results of the participatory evaluation of each community, a community-specific safety model, or plan for action, is created at each site.

Implementing and Monitoring the Model

The focus of program work shifted to this third phase of implementing and monitoring the community models in 2018, but recommendations for action began to emerge during the participatory mapping in phase one. Nonprofit organization partners who run child resource centers in each community are already piloting some of these ideas. These recommendations for action include:

- Outreach to parents to introduce techniques for positive parenting

- Raising awareness in children about how to keep themselves safe in their home, neighborhood, and community

- Empowering children to participate in neighborhood groups and stay away from risky behaviors

- Empowering the community to demand basic services from government at the ward, district, and city level, including basic protection services, safer and accessible schools, health centers in adequate numbers, and centers for addiction treatment.

- Motivating communities to design and build small play spaces throughout the local area with funding support from the local councilor's fund and ward office and municipal corporation budgets, and to take responsibility for their maintenance

The development and implementation of the safe community models is based in the belief that for families to create protective environments for their children, they must exist in communities that provide support and opportunities for families and children.[25]

---

25. ACE, "Promoting safe communities: Improving child protection in slums through a convergent approach in Mumbai and Bhopal." Action for Children's Environments. http://acetrust.net/project/promoting-safe-communities/. (Retrieved April 6, 2017).

Great Neighborhoods:
Young People's Perspectives for a Comprehensive Housing Strategy, Boulder, Colorado, United States

● ●

At a Glance

Project Leads: Mara Mintzer, Victoria Derr, and Flaminia Martufi, Growing Up Boulder; Michael Tavel, Senior Instructor, University of Colorado Environmental Design Program

Location: Boulder, Colorado

Partners: City of Boulder Community Planning, Housing and Sustainability Department; Whittier International Elementary School teachers and third-grade students; Boulder High School's Advancement via Individual Determination (AVID) Program teacher and ninth grade students; University of Colorado Environmental Design Program; University of Colorado architect; Boulder City Council; Boulder Planning Board.

Goals: To understand young people's views on making a child-friendly neighborhood in the context of the city's needs for increased density and affordable housing; to inform Boulder's Housing Strategy.

Participant Age Range: Children aged 8–16

Timeframe: One year of planning and implementation. Several years to inform the housing strategy

Methods

● Drawings

● Presentations and films about exemplary neighborhoods, green building, and green cities

● Field trips, with photo-framing

● Independent research

● Reflection writing

● Model making

● Presentations to city staff and officials

● Dialogue with university undergraduates, university architects, and city staff

● Child-friendly cities assessment

● ●

Project Overview

In 2013, the City of Boulder began preparing its Comprehensive Housing Strategy to address the need for higher density, affordable housing primarily for middle-income residents within the city. At the time, the city's Executive Director of Community Planning, Housing, and Sustainability and GUB Executive Committee member David Driskell wondered: "What would dense, affordable, child-friendly housing look like?" Thus was launched a year-long initiative, the "Great Neighborhoods" project (from 2013–2014) to explore this question with children, ages 8–16, to integrate young people's perspectives into a semester-long undergraduate planning studio focused on this same question, and to share these perspectives during the year and beyond with Boulder City Council members and Boulder's Planning Board members.[26]

This project utilized many methods shared in this book, including drawing, model making, learning from experts, and presentations to community members and city leaders. This project also highlights the value of training professionals in participatory processes and in engaging with young people as a part of their professional practice. Housing Strategy goals created in 2014 included those to inform family-friendly higher density housing for the Boulder Valley Comprehensive Plan update in 2015–2016. Integration of the housing strategy into long-term plans continues. This project thus also emphasizes the importance of sustained advocacy for the

---

26. This case study was derived in part from an article by Victoria Derr and Ildikó G. Kovács. "How participatory processes impact children and contribute to planning: a case study of neighborhood design from Boulder, Colorado, USA." *Journal of Urbanism: International Research on Placemaking and Urban Sustainability* 10, no. 1 (2017): 29–48. https://doi.org/10.1080/17549175.2015.1111925.

integration of young people's perspectives into long-term planning projects.

Project Implementation

The engagement strategy was conceptualized by leaders of the child- and youth- friendly city initiative, Growing Up Boulder, and a university faculty member who would be teaching the undergraduate planning studio. They chose to focus on a single site so that it would provide an intelligible scale for primary and secondary students while also being large enough to consider integration of housing into the larger urban system. The site chosen included forty acres of land for redevelopment as well as twenty acres of a riparian corridor along the Boulder Creek. This site included both city and university land and a mix of existing housing including university student and family housing, single family homes, and apartments. Further from the site but within the primary school catchment were also a mobile home park, a large apartment complex, cohousing, and public housing. Both primary and secondary school students lived in all these housing types (including university and single-family housing).[27]

Engagement was developed such that intensive involvement of primary and secondary students would occur in the fall semester followed by strategic integration of young people into an undergraduate planning studio in the spring.

Just as the project was about to begin in September 2013, Boulder experienced a 1000-year rain event throughout the city, and a 100-year flood along the Boulder Creek. Many Boulder residents were temporarily or permanently displaced by this event, with the community impacted flooding and debris, home damage and property loss. Families who lived in university housing in the project site were evacuated but allowed to return to their homes.

This experience shaped students' interest in flood mitigation and home protection as a part of this project.[28]

Young People as Experts on their Neighborhoods

In keeping with Growing Up Boulder's approach to beginning with children as experts, children and youth were asked to create a drawing of their home, its surroundings, and their favorite nearby places. They were asked to add additional places or drawings to represent their school, after-school, and weekend activities and to draw the routes they traveled and their modes of transportation (e.g., foot, bicycle, scooter, bus, or car). After completing their drawings, students then shared their drawings with each other and shared the types of housing they live in. Almost immediately, young people began to see that there were diverse types of housing in the city to support different families' needs.

Young People Developing Planning Competence

Interactive Presentation. Growing Up Boulder introduced the topic of density through an interactive presentation tailored to each age group (primary and secondary). This presentation introduced the ideas of density and affordable housing, gave visual examples of varying housing types, building heights, configurations of yards, shared green spaces, and housing types and styles from around the world. Each group then developed a definition of dense, affordable housing in their own words.[29]

Field Trips with Photography. Primary school students walked to an award-winning affordable infill development.[30] They learned about

---

27. Derr and Kovács, "How participatory processes impact children and contribute to planning."

28. Ibid.

29. Ibid.

30. Urban Land Institute (ULI). "Red Oak Park – 2012 Global Award for Excellence Winner." Urban Land Institute .org. http://uli.org/global-awards-for-excellence/red-oak

Figure 11.19. Primary school students visited a model housing development as a way to learn about features of neighborhood design. Photo credit: Growing Up Boulder

ceptualizing design ideas for their child-friendly neighborhood.[33]

Young People Synthesizing and Sharing their Ideas

Models. Primary school children each worked as a class to construct a single classroom model, creating a total of three. The students determined appropriate materials (through in-class research and classroom visits from experts), established design details such as features, colors, and materials, and collaboratively built their model of a dense, affordable housing site specific to the city of Boulder. Models were constructed from art supplies and recycled and repurposed materials, and some features were labeled (Figure 11.20, see also Chapter 5, Figure 5.25).

some of the features of this development from the property manager and took photographs to identify features of the development that they liked and did not like (Figure 11.19). (See Chapter 7 for a discussion of this method.) Secondary school students visited the university housing site that was identified as the project site for the planning studio and also used photo-framing to discuss aspects of the existing housing they liked or would change. Because of the flood and time restrictions that resulted, primary school students were not able to visit the project site as a class, though most students were familiar with it and some lived there.[31]

Digital Presentations. Primary school classes (three total) and the secondary school students prepared digital presentations using Power-Point or Prezi software. Classes were broken into groups to conduct research and prepare recommendations for housing, mixed-use features (commercial development and services integrated with housing), landscape, and transportation. These presentations were given to city staff members, city council members, school administrators, university faculty, and community members in the classrooms of the students.[34]

Guest Lectures and Films. Both groups of students watched a film, which included exemplary neighborhood design from Europe and the United States.[32] Primary school students also learned from visiting architects, engineers, and flood mitigation specialists. These experts visited the classroom in the early stages of children con-

Reflection Essays. All students were asked to reflect on their favorite aspect of the project and what they would change about the project's implementation. Primary school students also reflected on what they learned about designing dense, affordable housing, what makes a child-friendly community, and their greatest challenges during this project and how they overcame them.[35]

-park-2012-global-award-for-excellence-winner (Retrieved December 7, 2014.)

31. Derr and Kovács, "How participatory processes impact children and contribute to planning."

32. Timothy Beatley, *The Nature of Cities* (Boulder, CO: Throughline Productions, 2008).

33. Derr and Kovács, "How participatory processes impact children and contribute to planning."

34. Ibid

35. Ibid.

Figure 11.20. Model neighborhoods were developed using repurposed and recycled materials, including juice containers, straws, and cardboard boxes. Photo credit: Growing Up Boulder

Child-Friendly City Assessments. Both age groups of students also completed a pre- and post-project assessment using a subset of three questions (Box 11.6) from the *Child-Friendly Cities and Communities Assessment Toolkit.*[36] Pretests were administered on the first day of the project, and post-tests were give after the final presentations.[37] After project completion, these results were analyzed using statistical tests.[38]

Undergraduate Planning Studio

Undergraduate students began their semester by visiting both the primary and secondary school students' classrooms to hear the presentations students had given to the community and to ask questions about young people's perspectives on good neighborhoods. The university students then went through a similar process of learning about neighborhood design, exploring precedents, and developing design concepts. Undergraduates then shared their preliminary ideas with students in the primary school classrooms and with secondary students visiting the cam-

> ### Box 11.6. **Child-Friendly City Assessments**
>
> Children and youth were asked three questions derived from the *Child-Friendly Cities and Communities Assessment Toolkit* (Chapter 6). For each question, they could respond "never true," "sometimes true," "mostly true," or "does not apply." Young people responded to these questions at the outset of the project and the week following their presentations to city officials.
>
> "I help with projects to change my community"
>
> "I am involved in planning or decisions for the community"
>
> "The government (city council, mayor, etc.) asks me my opinions about my life or my community"

pus studio (Figure 11.21). Through a series of design reviews and dialogues, the undergraduates learned from young people, planners, city officials, and university architects, and developed master plans and detailed design features, such as housing designs, street treatments, or parks and green spaces that responded to young people's ideas (Figure 11.22). In addition to a gallery-style formal review during the semester

---

36. IRC/CERG, *Child-Friendly Cities and Communities Assessment Toolkit.* ChildWatch International Research Network. http://www.childwatch.uio.no/projects/activities/child -friendly-cities-and-communities-research-project/final toolkit2011.html. (Retrieved June 6, 2014).

37. Derr and Kovács, "How participatory processes impact children and contribute to planning."

38. Ibid.

Figure 11.21. Secondary students visited the university design studio to provide feedback and suggest revisions to master plans and design concepts.
Photo credit: Lynn M. Lickteig

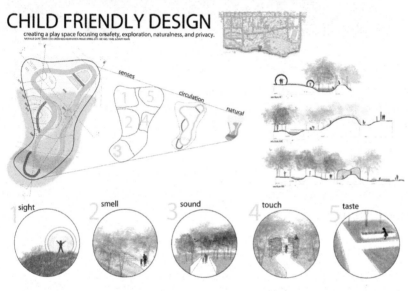

Figure 11.22. One of the university students conceptualized a design that would facilitate play spaces that promoted safety, exploration, nature, and privacy. Image credit: Nathalie Doyle

which included young people and adult partners, a subset of university students presented these ideas to approximately twenty city representatives the following fall, including officials from Boulder's housing division, community planning department, planning board, and design board to promote integration of young people's ideas into the Comprehensive Housing Strategy.[39]

Project Outcomes

Fostering Sustainability

Young people defined child-friendly cities as places where residents can play, access nature, use healthy modes of transportation, and have access to social spaces, both commercial and public. Both groups of students emphasized that they wanted to be integrated into city life, not separate from it. One of the outcomes from this project was the extent that young people integrated sustainability into their thinking and design recommendations (Box 11.7). This was true of both primary and secondary students, with some young people pushing the environmental design students to think harder about how they could better incorporate sustainability into their designs. Young people thought holistically about the city, integrating a broad range of sustainable and natural features into their recommendations. Children created innovative solutions to flood mitigation, and wanted to see wild spaces for animals, fruit trees, gardens, and natural play spaces woven into car-free zones.

---

39. Ibid.

Box 11.7. **Young People Promote Sustainability**

Environmental Sustainability	Energy efficiency, sustainable transportation (biking, walking, limited car use)
Social Sustainability	Meeting the needs of diverse people
	Promoting shared social spaces
	Including retail and housing close together so people can more readily access basic needs
	Pedestrian and bicycle friendly design
	Being friendly and treating each other well
Economic Sustainability	Considering building material and land costs in affordability
	Considering reduced utility bills because of more efficient energy use[1]

1. Derr and Kovács, "How participatory processes impact children and contribute to planning."

Integrating Ideas into the Comprehensive Housing Strategy

One of the challenges for engaging young people in long-term planning initiatives, such as Boulder's housing strategy and comprehensive plan, is that it is hard for young people to see immediate results of their work. In the Great Neighborhoods project, the undergraduate planning studio helped ameliorate this because young people did see their ideas integrated into plans and designs within the same academic year that they had developed them. However, the city's strategy for increased density and affordable housing takes much longer in its development. Initial goals for the housing strategy were approved by city council in 2014; action plans and working groups were developed in 2015 and 2016; and implementation was planned for 2017. While this high-level planning occurs, it was difficult to identify exact ways that young people's ideas were incorporated into the housing strategy. However, the initial six goals do respond to young people's ideas by recommending a balance of housing types within every neighborhood in the city and by creating 15-minute neighborhoods. Both of these goals outline details that

align with many of young people's suggestions, including new developments that incorporate diverse housing types, sizes, and prices, with opportunities for shopping, support services, public facilities, pedestrian connections, parks, libraries, and schools integrated into the neighborhood.[40] In addition, the Boulder Valley Comprehensive Plan was updated in 2015–2016. A number of the sustainability features that young people requested are articulated and added throughout the comprehensive plan, including specifics for bike and multi-modal infrastructure, energy efficiency, conservation, increased public space, and integration of art throughout public spaces. The housing policy within the comprehensive plan calls for considering embodied energy in existing buildings and strengthens the intention for diverse housing mixes to preserve and enhance housing choices. To reduce automobile use, the plan also includes specific revisions to add Neighborhood Centers as localized gathering places that provide everyday goods and

40. City of Boulder, "Housing Boulder (Comprehensive Housing Strategy)." https://bouldercolorado.gov/city-council /comprehensive-housing-strategy-housing-boulder. (Retrieved September 16, 2017).

services that are easily accessible by foot, bicycle, or public transit.[41]

For long-term planning processes such as this case, it is important to communicate timelines and processes to young people—so that they know how their ideas can be integrated—and to identify ways to correspond with young people even years down the road as plans are finalized. (See Chapter 9.) The role of adult facilitators also becomes important in longer-term projects: in this capacity, project leaders often need to continue to check in with community planners to ensure continuity, especially if staffing changes occur within city offices.[42]

Fostering Community

Malika Bose and her colleagues suggest that while many academics place value on tangible outcomes, such as master plans or design-builds, communities can place equal or sometimes greater value on dialogues and connections fostered through participatory design processes, wherein safe spaces are created for "diverse citizenry to come together with university partners to think about their futures and plan their own destiny."[43] This was also a value listed by many community members engaged in this project, including the young people themselves, teachers and school administrators, city staff, city council members, and planning and design board members.[44] Nearly two years later, as the housing

policy continued to be debated within the community, one of the city councilmen asked, somewhat playfully, if Growing Up Boulder could do the Great Neighborhoods project again. Like many city staff, he appreciated the thoughtful and educated perspectives young people gave to thinking inclusively and sustainably about housing.

Training Professionals

One of the goals of this project was to train emerging professionals—environmental design students—in the practices of participatory planning, to train undergraduate students in applied problem-solving and reflective practice, and to support them in communicating with people who hold diverse views.[45] This was particularly important because one of the limitations of participatory planning is often that professionals do not understand participation (and how it differs from simple consultations), and they often do not have the training or understanding of children as competent individuals who can share their views of the world in a constructive way.[46] Undergraduate students learned much in their perspectives about young people's ability to contribute in meaningful ways. Some students were transformed while others were enriched in their thinking about specific aspects of design (Box 11.8). All master plans specifically integrated young people's ideas, including increased nature and play spaces, street safety features, and better access to the creek (Figure 11.22).

A complete listing of publications about this project can be found at the end of Chapter 11.

41. City of Boulder, *Boulder Valley Comprehensive Plan (BVCP) Study Session on Scenarios and Housing Prototypes, Land Use Definitions, and Key Policy Choices.* Aug. 25, 2016. https://bouldercolorado.gov/bvcp/focus-areas. (Retrieved September 16, 2017).

42. This volume provides a nice discussion about advocacy and ethics in participatory practice: Sara Kindon, Rachel Pain, and Mike Kesby, eds., *Participatory Action Research Approaches and Methods: Connecting People, Participation and Place.* (Abingdon: Routledge, 2007).

43. Page 16 in Mallika Bose and Paula Horrigan, "Why community matters," *Community matters: Service-Learning in Engaged Design and Planning,* ed. Mallika Bose, Paula Horrigan, Cheryl Doble and Sigmund C. Shipp (Abingdon: Routledge, 2014), 1–21.

44. Victoria Derr, "Integrating community engagement and children's voices into design and planning education." *CoDesign* 11, no. 2 (2015): 119–133.

45. Ibid.

46. Sofia Cele and Danielle van der Burgt, "Participation, consultation, confusion: professionals' understandings of children's participation in physical planning." *Children's Geographies* 13, no. 1 (2015): 14–29; Julie Rudner. "Educating future planners about working with children and young people." *Social Inclusion* 5, no. 3 (2017): 195–206.

Box 11.8. **Young People's Influence on Design and Designers**

Children and youth's ideas influenced the undergraduate students' designs. The concrete and specific details young people offered through their recommendations helped many of the design students make better, informed plans. These ideas helped undergraduates to focus on their users' needs and interests:

> What we heard from the kids was that they wanted a safe neighborhood where they could go from one friend's house to another without having to cross streets, so from that, we created a block with buildings grouped so that you'd have to cross gathering areas such as parks and plazas [instead of streets].

> They don't like walking on the creek path because bikes fly by, and also. . . they didn't want to cross busy roads, and so we ended up putting the majority of the family housing south of the main road so they could be in closer proximity to the creek. And crosswalks on the creek path, with changes in materiality, so the bikers would know kids are crossing here.[1]

Some students' thinking was completely transformed in the process. These students went from thinking that young people would have "nothing to offer," to seeing that they had many creative and practical ideas that helped make a better plan:

> The praxis semester has changed how I think about things. At first I thought, 'What are we going to be able to learn from third graders building toilet-paper-tube models?', but it was so cool seeing through their eyes what this all means. I could tell they care a lot about their community and the future of it. It was really cool getting their perspective on things. They changed the way we were thinking about designing. It is hard to break away from the norms of how we've been designing. Working with the kids has helped us to do this.[2]

---

1. Victoria Derr, "Integrating community engagement and children's voices into design and planning education," 10.
2. Ibid.

Move Around and Play
The Hague, The Netherlands

With Marjan Ketner and Marjan Verboeket

At a Glance

Project Lead: Marjan Ketner and Marjan Verboeket, Speelwijk design firm, The Netherlands

Location: Segbroek, an inner-city district of The Hague, Stokhasselt and Vogelbuurt, two suburban districts of Tilburg and Zwijndrecht.

Partners

City of The Hague: City Department of Education, Culture and Welfare; City Department of Public Services; Housing Corporation: Staedion;

Public Elementary Schools the Klimop and the Toermalijn

City of Tilburg: City Department of Culture and Welfare; City Department of Public Services; Housing Corporation: Wonen Breeburg; Public Elementary Schools the Regenboog and the de Lochtenbergh; Islamic Elementary School Aboe el-Chayr; NGO Jantje Beton, dedicated to promoting and protecting outdoor play

City of Zwijndrecht: City Department of Spatial Development; City Department of Public Services; Public Elementary School the Twee Wieken and a Christian Elementary School

Goals: To design child-friendly public spaces where children can play outside and move about their neighborhoods safely. To design formal and informal spaces for play, including safe streets, public squares, and green spaces

Participant Age Range: Children aged 7–12

Timeframe: 8–12 months per project

Methods

- Mapping children's existing routes
- Guided walking tours of neighborhood
- Applying Kevin Lynch's Image of the City elements for mapping and design
- Community workshops

Figure 11.23. Guided tours helped identify questions such as "where can children safely cross the street?" and "how do children use urban amenities for play?" Photo credit: Speelwijk

Project Overview

Recognizing that a child-friendly neighborhood provides freedom of movement and integrated play spaces beyond playgrounds, designers from Speelwijk engaged children in a playful exploration of three neighborhoods of the Netherlands. The goal of participation was to understand where children go, to explore these places together and learn about routes and points of orientation that exist within the neighborhood, and to design small-scale interventions to increase children's access to play areas and the visibility of their walking routes. To accomplish this, the design team involved children in guided walking tours, mapped existing walking routes, and engaged residents in a collaborative design workshop. Design interventions served to create or enhance walking routes that are inviting to children, stimulate movement, and trigger their play and imagination.

Project Implementation

Guided Walks

In each city, children led researchers on guided walks. (See Chapter 7 for discussion of child-led walking tours). They began by working with children in a neighborhood school and looking at maps in the classroom to understand the routes

they take to school and the areas where children are able to independently roam. This mapping was used to identify routes for the guided walking tours.

Children were asked a series of questions along the tour route, including:

- Where do you go?
- Where do you cross the street?
- How do you play along the way?
- Which trees do you climb?
- Where do you hide?
- What streets do you avoid? Why?

Walking together, children explored these questions, played games, and recorded observations and experiences (Figure 11.23). Observations included the natural play elements children found and used along the routes, comments made by the children (such as, "we do not like rubbish"), informal routes or shortcuts children know or took on the walk, the ways that children have for avoiding cars in their walking routes, ways children interact with and play with urban elements (such as railings), and the orientation points that children have for navigating their neighborhood.

Mapping with Kevin Lynch's Image of the City

Drawing from Kevin Lynch's groundbreaking work in *The Image of the City*,[47] in which he identifies elements that people use to construct "mental maps" which help them navigate and understand the city, children were asked to iden-

47. Kevin Lynch, *The Image of the City*. (Cambridge, MA: MIT Press, 1960).

tify locations of the five elements that they use to get around their neighborhood (Figure 11.24, Box 11.9).

Children were asked to use these five elements to describe their experiences of their neighborhoods. They were asked specific questions about these elements, such as:

- Which paths do children typically use in their neighborhood?

Box 11.9. **Kevin Lynch's Five Elements of the City**

- **Paths.** Paths are the spaces along which people usually move. These may be streets, sidewalks, transit lines, or waterways. For many people, the paths they regularly take form their primary image of the city because this is the space they normally move along, see, and experience.

- **Edges.** Edges are a kind of linear boundary between two different types of spaces. They form a line between different kinds of spaces. Edges may be walls, a shoreline, or the boundary along a development. Edges may serve as a barrier to movement within the city.

- **Districts.** Districts are sections of the city that people can recognize being "inside of," in which there is a distinguishable physical character to the place. Defined

districts vary by city and the extent of their presence may depend on the city's design, character, and history.

- **Nodes.** Nodes are junction points within the city, often comprised of a convergence of different paths or traffic routes. They can be considered concentrations from which people and movement radiate outwards, such as a street corner or a square.

- **Landmarks.** Landmarks provide reference points and help people find their way within the city. These can be a building, a sign, a store, a flag, or a prominent physical feature, such as a mountain. These are used more frequently by people who live in or travel through a place often.[1]

---

1. Lynch, *The Image of the City.*

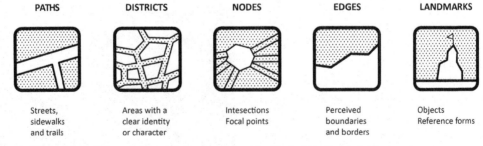

PATHS	DISTRICTS	NODES	EDGES	LANDMARKS
Streets, sidewalks and trails	Areas with a clear identity or character	Intesections Focal points	Perceived boundaries and borders	Objects Reference forms

Figure 11.24. Five navigational elements children identified within their neighborhoods (based on Kevin Lynch's *The Image of the City*). Image credit: Speelwijk

Figure 11.25. Children annotated maps to show places they play, routes, and landmarks. Photo credit: Speelwijk

- What do children perceive as borders for their play?
- Which areas have a clear identity for children (e.g., playgrounds or sports fields)?
- Are there intersections children use to determine their routes?
- Which buildings (or other landmarks) do children use for orientation?

As children responded to these questions, they placed simple flags with icons representing the five elements onto a neighborhood map. They also jotted notes about the elements that helped characterize the collective experience of children navigating their neighborhoods (Figure 11.25).

Residents' Workshops for Design Interventions

After these initial guided walks, observations, and mapping activities, children and residents were involved in workshops to develop ideas for how to make the city's image more vivid and memorable for children. In the workshop phase, children and families examined photographs of possible walking route interventions and made small scale models of ways to enhance the neighborhood.

The workshops served multiple purposes. First, residents were informed (in some cases by the children themselves) about the findings obtained from the guided walks. Second, children and residents were invited to share their knowledge, feelings, and ideas for child-friendly neighborhood routes and places. Participants were asked to first mark spots on the map with their opinions (positive and negative) about routes and spaces within the neighborhood, and then to generate new ideas for the area (Figure 11.26). Finally, children and residents examined the proposed route concepts and interventions for different areas (Figure 11.27). Children customized and completed semi-finished design frames for nodes, paths, and edges that Speelwijk had proposed.

Figure 11.26. In workshops, children and families generated new ideas for areas by drawing their ideas and adding them to neighborhood maps. Photo credit: Speelwijk

Figure 11.27. Children and families voted on a series of proposed routes and design concepts. Photo credit: Speelwijk

Figure 11.28. Tilburg Stokhasselt: Flags and "play-marks" indicate direction along children's walking route in a neighborhood with very few discernable landmarks otherwise. Photo credit: Speelwijk

Figure 11.29. Tilburg Stokhasselt: Electric boxes were used by children during the guided tours as navigational and play objects (See Chapter 2). These were then painted to purposefully indicate play routes and alert motorists to children's presence. Photo credit: Speelwijk

The workshops used visual communication and 3D presentations as much as possible. This helped to connect children from all ages and backgrounds who were attending the workshops.

Design Realization

In Tilburg Stokhasselt, a large suburban neighborhood with a mix of low- and high-rise housing with green spaces intermixed, the design concept was to create a play network rather than a single route. This would enhance navigation through what children perceived as a labyrinth of similar housing, with few landmarks otherwise to help them find their way. Footpaths would be placed along strips of grass with colorful flags and play marks that would indicate directions (Figure 11.28). Graffiti art was added to existing electricity boxes in order to alert motorists to children's play and walking routes in nodes of the neighborhood (Figure 11.29). (Also see Chapter 2, Figure 2.1 and 2.2 for before and after photographs of this.) A play network was designed to activate the edges along high-rise buildings, placing play tunnels, picnic tables, and small bridges in the green spaces on this edge (Figure 11.30). Finally, colorful and playful fencing was added along specific crossings of major roads. These fences would direct children to a safe crossing destinations and alert motorists.

Figure 11.30. Tilburg Stokhasselt: Colorful play routes designate safe walking routes for children, such as these bright orange metal tunnels. Photo credit: Speelwijk

In Segbroek, an inner-city neighborhood of The Hague with high density but low-rise buildings and few green spaces, "play carpets" were added along children's existing routes to add play and movement areas in the neighborhood. Three play carpets were developed. The first was a running track with a winner's "stage of honor" (Figure 11.31) and a city wallpaper of co-created graffiti art to add color to low-rise buildings. The second was a colorful walking labyrinth, and the third was a "big slide" that connected an upper park space to a lower walking route.

Similar to Den Haag Sebroek, play routes became the design concept for Zwijndrecht Vogelbuurt, a low-rise suburban neighborhood

Figure 11.31. "Play carpet 1": a running track to enliven and add color to dense housing with few play spaces. Photo credit: Speelwijk

Figure 11.32. The running track (Figure 11.31) was inspired by a walking tour in which children ran through narrow corridors. Photo credit: Speelwijk

with few existing play spaces for children. The central zone of movement passed through a car-free zone of the neighborhood, so the design team used the edges as zones to activate play, incorporating small balance zones, hopscotch, and spontaneous play parklets (Figure 11.33).

Design-Build with Children to Revive Remnant Public Spaces, San Juan, Puerto Rico

With Omayra Rivera Crespo and Yazmín M. Crespo Claudio

Figure 11.33. Zwijndrecht Vogelbuurt: One of the balance zones along an edge of the neighborhood. Photo credit: Speelwijk

• •

At a Glance

Project Leads: Omayra Rivera Crespo, Yazmín M. Crespo, Irvis González, and Andrea Bauzá, who compose taller Creando Sin Encargos

Location: La Perla, San Juan, Puerto Rico

Partners: Students from the four architecture and design schools in Puerto Rico—University of Puerto Rico, Polytechnic University of Puerto Rico, Pontifical Catholic University of Puerto Rico, and the School of Visual Arts and Design in Old San Juan; three international architecture collectives: Todo por la Praxis from Madrid, Spain, Arquitectura Expandida from Bogotá, Colombia, and FG Studio from New York, U.S.A.

Goals: To work with local children to identify remnants or forgotten spaces in the community of La Perla, and carry out architectural interventions to turn them into inviting spaces for public use

Participant Age Range: Children aged 7–11; undergraduate architecture students; design professors and professionals

Timeframe: One day for the photographic scavenger hunt exercise and one week for the design-build workshop

Methods

- A photographic scavenger hunt of public spaces and activities

- Photograph exhibition

- Design workshop
- Construction

Project Overview

Taller Creando Sin Encargos (tCSE) is an architecture collective formed by four Puerto Rican professors of architecture who share an interest in rehabilitating remnant urban spaces in collaboration with low-income communities and grassroots organizations. The collective organizes participatory design-build workshops that demonstrate how communities can make meaningful improvements to their environment and resourcefully reuse recycled materials.[48] In this project in La Perla, children were a core part of a larger team that included undergraduate architecture students. La Perla, located between the wall of the old city and the Atlantic Ocean, is a community in Old San Juan that was built in the 19th century by workers who came for jobs in the district's slaughterhouse. In 2013, when tCSE led this workshop, the majority of residents were women and children.

Project Implementation

In the months prior to the workshop, tCSE helped adult community members design a Museum of the History of La Perla in their community center, as part of the National Exhibition of San Juan. In the process, the collective learned about different sectors of La Perla, their people, and their stories, and established a strong relationship with the community. Community leaders then assisted the collective in identifying twelve children who represented each sector of La Perla to participate in the scavenger hunt and workshop. The children were boys and girls from ages 7 through 11.

---

48. In a design-build project, the same individual or group does both design and construction.

Photographic Scavenger Hunt

The children of La Perla move through their community with confidence and creativity, exploring every corner and converting ruined structures into their clubhouses. The beach and ocean are their playground. Therefore, they were well prepared to take pictures of their favorite and not-so-popular spaces in this place they knew intimately. On a Sunday morning, two weeks before the design-build workshop, the children were given disposable cameras and a list of prompts to guide their scavenger hunt through La Perla to find examples of different types of places and design elements. (See the list of questions in Box 11.10.) The objective was to discover the sectors of La Perla through their eyes. They set off in teams on the same day, returning four hours later with their pictures (Figure 11.34).

Figure 11.34. The children evaluated La Perla on their photographic scavenger hunt.
Photo credits: taller Creando Sin Encargos

Box 11.10. **Scavenger Hunt Prompts**

1. Take a photo of yourself
2. Take a photo of your street
3. Take a photo of your favorite place in the neighborhood
4. Take a photo of the place you least like in the neighborhood
5. Take a photo of the place where you would like to play but you cannot
6. Take a photo of the place where you meet with your friends
7. Take a photo of where you like to sit
8. Take a photo of the place where you like to see the sea
9. Take a photo of the road you take to go play
10. Take a photo of your favorite object, toy, or game
11. Take a photo of the door or window that you like
12. Take a photo of the staircase you like most
13. Take a photo of your favorite part of the wall
14. Take a photo of a street sign or element that identifies a sector of your community
15. Take a photo of something representative of your community (what it identifies or does differently)

Photograph Exhibition

To pay for developing the pictures, tCSE organized brunch in an arts organization in Old San Juan, where friends, students, and members of the community donated money. The collective selected images for a photograph exhibit at La Perla Community Center, ensuring that every child had at least one picture included. Based on the photographs and conversations with the children, the collective identified five sites for potential interventions—one in each sector of La Perla. With the help of the collective, the children and university students suggested possible uses for these spaces and how they could be transformed.

On the first day of the workshop, everyone began by viewing the exhibit, and the children presented their photographs (Figure 11.35). Their pictures showed the cultural life of La Perla as well as its spaces, and the children's self-confident knowledge of their community. At the end, members of tCSE handed each child a full-size print of one of the child's photographs.

Figure 11.35. Children hung their scavenger hunt photographs at the start of the design workshop. Photo credit: taller Creando Sin Encargos

Design Workshop

For the workshop Collective Architectures, students from each university divided into five groups to work on the five selected spaces. These groups had three days to develop their ideas. The children joined the groups and actively

Figure 11.36. The stairway that doubled as a section of an amphitheater. Photo credit: taller Creando Sin Encargos

Figure 11.37. Measuring the foundation for Luigi's Stair. Photo credit: taller Creando Sin Encargos

Figure 11.38. Luigi's Stair, completed. Photo credit: taller Creando Sin Encargos

shared ideas. On the fourth day, a design jury convened, composed of the three architectural collectives that visited from Madrid, Bogotá, and New York, along with professors of architecture and members of the community. The jury selected three projects for construction, all along the beachfront.

Construction

During construction, the children were hands-on helpers with simple building methods and painting. The projects designed and built were:

- A staircase to reach the sea in the sector of San Miguel, that doubled as part of an amphitheater where people could sit to watch the sea (Figure 11.36)

- A stair named the Surfer's Ladder that descended to part of the beach popular with surfers, along with a bench and a stand for surfboards at the bottom. It was dedicated to Luigi, a local surfer, and therefore people called it Luigi's Stair. (Figures 11.37 and 11.38).

- Restoration of a ruined structure to become a clubhouse for children named

Vista Mar. The children who came there named themselves "Los Gallitos," the little roosters. (Figures 11.39-11.42)

Construction work with children had to find a balance between durability—which takes adult construction experience and skills—and flexibility to enable children to participate as much as possible. In the case of the staircase/amphitheater, the children selected the colors of each step and helped with painting. They chose wooden pallets to be used as a continuation of the amphitheater seating area and helped tie the ropes

Figure 11.39. Structure before renovation as Club Vista Mar. Photo credit: taller Creando Sin Encargos

Figure 11.40. Club Vista Mar during construction. Photo credit: taller Creando Sin Encargos

Figure 11.41. The finished clubhouse. Photo credit: taller Creando Sin Encargos

Figure 11.42. The clubhouse design added opportunities for active play and climbing. Photo credit: taller Creando Sin Encargos

that became a large hammock. For the clubhouse, they designed a mural, helped paint it, and decided on the furniture, such as benches and bike racks. In the case of Luigi's Stair, they helped lay the foundations and assemble the sitting area.

This project demonstrates how a community can use participatory design methods, creativity, and low-cost recycled materials to turn little-used public spaces into useful attractions. It also affirms children's knowledge of their community, their ability to contribute valuable design ideas for all ages, and their right to spaces of their own. As this book is written, four years after the workshop, Luigi's Stair and the nearby bench still receive regular use. After using Club Vista Mar for about two years, the children have moved on to new gathering places.

Lessons Learned

- The permanence of a design intervention is not necessarily achieved through a lasting material construction. It happens when local residents appropriate a space as their own and generate activities that assure that it receives continuous use.

- Community spaces are dynamic and should be expected to change as people turn them to new uses. The design-build workshop encourages communities to take processes of change into their own hands.

- It would be ideal if the design-build collective could return to their sites of intervention six to eight months later to witness changes made by the community and assess how structures withstand use.

- To preserve the work done, community leaders (including adult community members with construction experience who participated in the building process) can develop a calendar for the maintenance of a space and draw up an agreement for how adults and children can care for this space together.

- Children's wisdom about their communities should never be underestimated. By participating in design-build processes from the beginning to end, they find new meanings in the recovered spaces and their sense of belonging grows.

- Participatory processes with children can be more important and rich than the final product itself. It is significant that the children see that they can do things for their community and that they learn new ways to create things.

- Important relationships can develop between the children, designers, and university students. With the children's guidance, the professionals and architecture students can reimagine meanings and possibilities for spaces, and the children can be inspired with new aspirations. In La Perla, for example, some children discovered that some of the architecture students came from backgrounds without money, like themselves, but they were achieving success through a combination of scholarships and part-time jobs. This enlarged the children's sense of possibilities for themselves.

For more information about workshops organized by taller Creando Sin Encargos, including more photos from this project, see their website at: https://tallercreandosinencargos.tumblr.com.

Open Space Planning,
Boulder, Colorado, United States

With Deryn Wagner and Halice Ruppi

At a Glance

Project Leads: Victoria Derr and Mara Mintzer, Growing Up Boulder; Deryn Wagner and Halice Ruppi, City of Boulder Open Space and Mountain Parks

Location: Boulder, Colorado, USA

Partners: Boulder Journey School teachers and students; City of Boulder Open Space and Mountain Parks (OSMP) leadership, interpretive staff, and members of the board of trustees; OSMP Junior Rangers; Boulder children and families; Architect Simon Bialobroda.

Goals: To identify ways to improve visitor experiences, increase environmental sustainability of trails and visitor infrastructure, and conserve natural, cultural, and agricultural resources in

7,700 acres of open space land in the "North Trail Study Area."

Participant Age Range: 3–17

Timeframe: 4 months to one year

Methods

- Field trips
- Drawing
- Bug costumes and bug book
- Photovoice
- Co-design for Ideal Vision
- Focus group to develop and prioritize recommendations
- Keep, change, add mapping activity
- Community event

Project Overview

In 2015, Growing Up Boulder and the City of Boulder's Open Space and Mountain Parks department partnered to engage children and youth in their North Trail Study Area. This planning process sought to identify strategies and actions to improve visitor experiences and increase sustainability of the physical environment and visitor infrastructure while conserving natural, cultural, and agricultural resources. Children aged 3–17 participated in engagement approaches. The goal was to experiment with a variety of methods to support engagement in open space planning while also informing a particular planning process for the north portion of open space properties.[49]

Three different groups participated in open spacing planning: i) Boulder Journey School—a preschool based on the Reggio Emilia approach

---

49. This case study was derived in part from an article published in: Victoria Derr, Halice Ruppi, and Deryn Wagner. "Honoring voices, inspiring futures: Young people's engagement in open space planning." *Children, Youth and Environments* 26, no. 2 (2016): 128–144.

to early childhood education,[50] ii) Open Space and Mountain Parks Junior Ranger program—which employs teenagers, aged 14–17, for summer service on OSMP lands, and iii) a Family Day, an open public event.

Engagement resulted in several consistent themes: desires for direct access and experience of nature, nature protection, nature interpretation and education, and issues with the city beyond the scope of OSMP planning. OSMP integrated many specific ideas from young people into their plan and also communicated back to the community and young people themselves how this work was integrated: through websites, press releases, public meetings, and letters to young people.[51] In addition, the city parks department responded to Junior Rangers' interest in "parks for teens" by initiating a subsequent planning process to better understand teens' desires for parks and play (Figures 4.6, 4.7, and 9.9).

Project Implementation

The methods employed for young people's participation varied across age groups. Each is described separately here. However, the results were compiled into a single report, which presented both specific details unique to a particular age group as well as over-arching themes.

Boulder Journey School

Preschool students at Boulder Journey School (BJS) explored insects as a major theme of study during the academic year, prior to the start of the North Trail Study Area planning initiation. BJS is based on the philosophy of Reggio Emilia, which honors children's own modes of expression and promotes active citizenship and a "pedagogy of listening."[52] As part of their insect investi-

Figure 11.43. Children drew the insects they observed on their school grounds, as in this praying mantis. Their enthusiasm for learning about these insects became the inspiration for further exploration into city parks. Image credit: Boulder Journey School

gations, students explored their outdoor playground, finding and observing praying mantises and butterflies (Figure 11.43); took field trips to local parks and natural areas; and researched insect body parts. In addition, teachers projected human-sized insect shadows onto their classroom wall so that students could experience the difference in scale between small insects and much larger humans. From this, children began considering how to enter natural spaces "so as not to scare the bugs." The result was child-designed costumes that integrated the biology they had learned, as a way to make themselves "less scary" to the invertebrates in natural parks.

When it came time for open space planning, they were interested in thinking about how recreation might impact invertebrate habitat ("the bug's homes") and to explore opportunities for nature play at Wonderland Lake, which was situated at the edge of the park. In this phase, BJS students learned about insects from the OSMP education staff (Figure 11.44). After a walk to the lake in the hot sun, students verbally shared ideas about what they liked and what they would change from their experiences. Back in the classroom, two children drew from their experiences to write and illustrate a "Bug Care Book," which described safe ways to find and hold bugs (Figure 11.45).

50. Ellen Lynn Hall and Jennifer Kofkin Rudkin, *Seen and Heard: Children's Rights in Early Childhood Education.* (New York: Teachers College Press, 2011).

51. Derr, Ruppi, and Wagner. "Honoring voices, inspiring futures."

52. Ibid.

Figure 11.44. Young children learned a bug song prior to exploring insect habitat. Photo credit: Victoria Derr

HOW TO HOLD BUGS

1. BriDGe FiNGer. YOU HOLD THE BUG AND MAKE A BRiDGe FOR THE BUG.

2. THAT ONe IS GOOD ABOUT THE FINGer. BeCAUSe IF IT WANTS TO BOUNCE IT CAN JUST TurN arounD AND BOUNCe.

3. FLAT, SO THeY CAN CLIMB or SLIDe arounD.

BeCAUSe THeY CAN MOVe arounD WITH A LOT OF SPACe TO CrAWL

Figure 11.45. To develop the bug care book, children developed storylines and illustrated the book with a combination of pictures and drawings. Image credit: Boulder Journey School

Junior Rangers

OSMP has employed teenagers in its Junior Ranger program since 1965. The youth corps approach has been to join service, learning, team building, and dialogue skills while building awareness and appreciation for open space and resource management. Prior to this engagement process, however, the Junior Rangers had not engaged with the planning side of open space management. Two crews participated in a six-hour workshop during their summer employment. The workshops introduced students to the planning process as well as the importance of young people's participation in this process. Junior Rangers met at the same Wonderland Lake facility and used photovoice to evaluate broadly what they liked and did not like about the open space (Chapter 7). The photovoice images were projected during the workshop and youth shared their thoughts with each other. After a short lunch break, they participated in a co-design visioning process (Chapter 8). In one session, co-design was facilitated by one of the project leads; in the second case, it was facilitated by a community-based architect (Figure 11.46). In

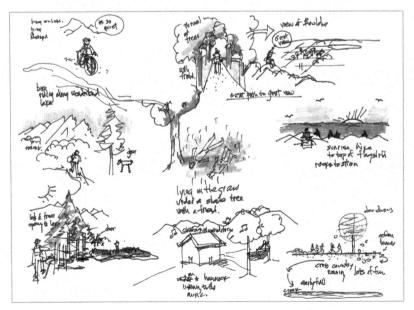

Figure 11.46. In the co-design process, Junior Rangers shared their visions of an ideal day in open space. Illustration credit: Simon Bialobroda

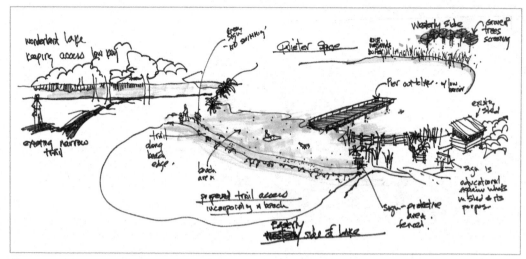

Figure 11.47. As a result of the co-design process, Junior Rangers also collectively discussed how open space could be redesigned to accommodate different types of user experiences. Illustration credit: Simon Bialobroda

the co-design process of the second workshop, Junior Rangers began discussing accessibility to Wonderland Lake based on some of their observations of social trails and lack of access. Junior Rangers had differing viewpoints about how the lake should be used, and so they participated in an impromptu design charrette to reimagine what the lake access should look like so it could meet the needs and interests of different users while also protecting the plants and animals at the lake (Figure 11.47).

In the final phase of this workshop, Junior Rangers developed recommendations for open space through a focus group discussion (Figure 11.48). (See Chapter 6 for the focus group method.) They brainstormed a wide range of recommendations, drawing from the photovoice and co-design discussions and then used sticky

Figure 11.49. To prioritize recommendations during the focus group, Junior Rangers were each given three sticky dots to vote for their top three choices. Photo credit: Victoria Derr

Figure 11.48. Junior Rangers developed recommendations through a focus group discussion. (See Chapter 6). Photo credit: Victoria Derr

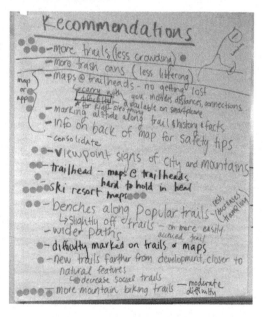

In the future, I would like _More trees and wild life_

in the North TSA because _There more to see_ .

Draw your vision here:

First Name: Age: _8_

Figure 11.50. Many visitors to the Family Day wanted to see wildlife habitat protected and enhanced. Image credit: Growing Up Boulder

dots to select their top three priorities (Figure 11.49).

To reach additional Junior Ranger crews while also respecting the time Junior Rangers needed for other work, project facilitators also took these recommendations to three additional crews. Each crew participated in a one-hour workshop in which they reviewed and discussed the previous crews' recommendations and then selected their own priorities.

Like Boulder Journey School, which values a "pedagogy of listening," the intentional focus on dialogue and consensus building of the Junior Ranger program was an asset to participation. Crew members respectfully listened and took seriously their role in contributing to the planning process.

Family Day

The family day was a several hours long event held on a Saturday at Wonderland Lake. The event was comprised of wildlife education stations that showcased unique species, such as ringtails and fossil history from the North Trail Study Area, as well as two engagement activities. The first activity was a drawing activity with the prompt, "In the future, I would like _____ in the North TSA because _____. Draw your vision here" (Figure 11.50). Open Space planning staff were particularly interested in the "because _____" prompt so that they could know participants' motivation for recommending a particular idea. This was important because sometimes it is not possible to integrate exactly what everyone wants; however, if the staff understood particular reasons or functions, they could think about how they might address this.

A second activity was a "Keep, Change, Add" mapping station. This station contained maps of the study area in various scales along with colored sticky dots and sticky notes. Participants could place color-coded dots in areas where they would like to "keep," "change," or "add" a specific aspect of the landscape. They could also leave more details about what they want to keep, change, or add, and *why*.

Ways the City Weighed Junior Ranger Input

Growing Up Boulder staff compiled results from all ages and participants into a report, which was shared with all OSMP staff, board members, and the general public. OSMP staff used the results from this process to inform their development of draft planning scenarios that the Open Space Board of Trustees, Boulder City Council, and general public could comment on. The draft and final plans included many of the improvements suggested by children and youth.[53]

Communicating Final Outcomes

Because the planning process extended beyond the engagement process, project facilitators wanted to ensure that young people would know their ideas were taken seriously. A variety of communication strategies were used to communicate outcomes to participants and the general public, including:

- Scenarios Letter to Junior Rangers (Box 11.11).
- Annotations of the plan
- Updates on website
- Additional community outreach events

When project facilitators asked Junior Rangers how they wanted OSMP to communicate with them about the plan, they said they would like to receive letters through the mail; they mentioned that they did not receive letters very often, but would like to. OSMP and GUB staff developed a letter to communicate all the ways the Junior Rangers' ideas were incorporated into the draft scenarios (and eventual final plan), which included eleven distinct ideas from children and youth (Box 11.11).[54] Among the additions to the plan were physical and regulatory improvements that supported young people's interest in direct interactions with nature and a balance between recreation and nature protection.[55]

A complete listing of publications about this project can be found at the end of Chapter 11.

---

53. Derr, Ruppi, Wagner. "Honoring voices"

54. Ibid.
55. Ibid.

Box 11.11. **Open Space and Mountain Parks Letter to Junior Rangers**

Dear Junior Ranger,

Open Space and Mountain Parks (OSMP) and Growing Up Boulder (GUB) really want to thank you and all the Junior Ranger crew members and crew leads who shared ideas about the North Trail Study Area (North TSA)! We were inspired and energized by your participation. Your unique perspective on resource management and recreation and your ability to dialogue around different viewpoints were impressive! We hope the stewardship values you developed as a Junior Ranger extend past your employment, and that you stay involved in the community planning process for the North TSA.

If you have more thoughts, you can comment online anytime at www.NorthTSA.org.

Thanks also to members of the 2014–2015 Youth Opportunities Advisory Board and the families, individuals, and children who attended Family Day. Input from young people has already been so valuable in shaping this planning process, and we wanted to share some of those successes with you.

You might remember that we got your input early in the planning process so we could incorporate that into potential solutions. A couple months later, we've got four draft scenarios—or options—ready for your review. Early next year, we'll narrow these different solutions down into an actual plan. For now, we've integrated your ideas, interests from the larger community, and science about our special resources into some options for the community to consider. The table below shows how we've included ideas from young people so far. There's more to come, though, so stay tuned!

Examples of how youth ideas have been included in draft scenarios:

Ideas from Young People	Translation into Draft Scenarios
More opportunities for interaction with water, like enhanced lake access, sand play, boardwalks, and clear trail access	All scenarios for Wonderland Lake would: Build a pier for fishing and wildlife viewing, Add two gathering areas in the shade by the waterfront, and Improve primary beach access on the peninsula. In addition, one scenario also considers enhancing access into the cattail marsh in Wonderland Lake, maybe with a floating pier. In all scenarios, water access would also be provided at the Fourmile Canyon Creek Bridge and Boulder Valley Ranch pond.
More trees for shelter and shade	New gathering areas on the Wonderland Lake peninsula would take advantage of shade from existing trees. In one scenario, a shelter would be built at the Wonderland Lake trailhead to provide a shaded meeting place.
Additional trails for hiking and biking (single track, moderate difficulty)	Lots of new or improved trails are considered in all scenarios, including mountain bike trails

(Box 11.11 continued on the following page)

(Box 11.11 continued)

Protecting and increasing chances to see wildlife, especially insects	The pier at Wonderland Lake would increase chances of seeing birds, fish, insects, and other critters—while still protecting them in their natural habitat.
	In other places like the North Foothills, wildlife habitat is either protected or enhanced in each scenario through trail alignments and other means.
More rocks for climbing	Access to Fourmile Canyon Creek near the bridge would allow for some fun climbing.
Improved access to information, both trail details and interpretive, that can be taken along on hiking trails (either mobile app or paper)	All scenarios consider ways to share stories about special resources throughout the North TSA. Staff would develop more detailed ideas for that once the North TSA Plan is finalized next year.
Signage changes (fewer overall, positive tone, educational)	Staff recognizes the need to address signs, which would happen once the plan is finalized next year.
Attention to social trails (prevention and evaluation)	All scenarios explore ways of addressing social trails—either through closing or formalizing them.
A wide range of perspectives about dogs in open space (from no dogs, to stricter limits, to more relaxed policies)	Every scenario presents a different way of managing dogs in order to balance the number and types of experiences that visitors can have with or without dogs.
Provision of drinking water sources at popular trailheads	Different ways to upgrade trailheads and expand amenities are explored under all scenarios.
Overall maintenance (trails, non-native invasive plants)	OSMP is committed to ongoing maintenance, no matter the scenario. Ways of improving trail sustainability and decreasing invasive weeds are also included in each scenario.

You might feel we didn't capture your ideas perfectly. If so, will you let us know online at www.NorthTSA.org? Keep in mind, it doesn't mean we didn't hear you or get what you were trying to say. Some things aren't really in our control, or they may conflict with what we're allowed to do.

Regardless, we really appreciate your creative ideas and your help taking care of our trail system. Our discussions with youth helped staff see this part of the OSMP system through a different lens! Plus, the things we put into motion now will make our city what you want it to be in the future.

As a reminder, we've included a map of the North Trail Study Area. If you want to learn more about the draft scenarios, visit www.NorthTSA.org or attend our next community workshop on Monday, October 19. And watch out: we will keep challenging you to help us with planning projects because we value your voice! It is your city. Your views matter.

Warm regards,

The North TSA Team

Open Space and Mountain Parks + Growing Up Boulder

Resources

Resources for Phila Impilo!

Louise Chawla and Jill Kruger. "Phila Impilo! Live Life! Ways to healing for children in long-term hospital care." *Participatory Learning and Action*, 58 (2008): 128–133.

Jill Kruger. *Phila Impilo! Children Advocate Best Practices for Healing* (Overport, South Africa: Young Insights for Planning, 2008).

Jill Kruger, Thea de Wet, and Salim Vally. "Education for hospitalised children: Lessons from Phila Impilo." *Education as Change*, 16, no. 2 (2012): 269–282.

Resources for Dapto Dreaming

Karen Malone. "Child friendly cities: A model." *Designing Cities with Children and Young People: Beyond Playgrounds and Skate Parks*, ed. Kate Bishop and Linda Corkery (New York: Routledge, 2017), 11–23.

Karen Malone. "Children's place encounters: Place-based participatory research to design a child-friendly and sustainable urban development." *Geographies of Global Issues: Change and Threat* (2016): 1–30.

Karen Malone. "'Dapto dreaming': a place-based environmental education project supporting children to be agents of change." *Education in Times of Environmental Crises: Teaching Children to Be Agents of Change*, ed. Ken Winograd (New York: Routledge, 2016), 113–127.

Karen Malone. "'The future lies in our hands': children as researchers and environmental change agents in designing a child-friendly neighbourhood." *Local Environment*, *18*(3) (2013): 372–395.

Judith Wilks and Julie Rudner. "A voice for children and young people in the city." *Australian Journal of Environmental Education*, 29, no. 1 (2013): 1–17.

Karen Malone. *Dreaming and Designing a Child-friendly Neighbourhood for Brooks Reach, Dapto*, (Unpublished Report, 2011).

Resources for Great Neighborhoods

Victoria Derr. "Integrating community engagement and children's voices into design education and community planning." *Co-Design: The International Journal of CoCreation in Design and the Arts* 11, no. 2 (2015): 119–133. http://www.tandfonline.com/doi/full/10.1080/15710882.2015.1054842

Victoria Derr and Ildikó G. Kovács. "How participatory processes impact children and contribute to planning: A case study of neighbourhood design from Boulder, Colorado, USA." *Journal of Urbanism: International Research on Placemaking and Urban Sustainability* 10, no. 1 (2017): 29–48. DOI: 10.1080/17549175.2015.1111925. Published online in 2015.

Victoria Derr, Mara Mintzer, and Grayson O'Roark. *Great Green Neighborhoods*. A report submitted to Boulder City Council and Planning Boards. (Boulder, CO: Growing Up Boulder, 2014). Available from: http://www.growingupboulder.org/great-neighborhoods.html

Resources for Open Space Planning

Victoria Derr, Halice Ruppi, and Deryn Wagner. "Honoring voices, inspiring futures: Young people's engagement in open space planning." *Children, Youth and Environments* 26, no. 2 (2016): 128–144.

Victoria Derr. *Young People's Contributions to Open Space Planning*. Report submitted to City of Boulder: Open Space and Mountain Parks. September 21, 2015. Available from http://www.growingupboulder.org/osmp.html

"From the city perspective this is really what we are looking for, engaging people of all ages so that they see that their views, their perspectives, matter, but also that they engage in a coeducational process so that it is a dialogue rather than just coming and voicing my perspective, actually listening to the perspectives of others, and in the process maybe changing their perspective, and coming to a richer understanding of the complexity. . . of all the things that go into creating a community."[1]

12

Conclusion

As the diverse projects in this book reflect, there are many approaches and methods to actively engage children in the planning and design of sustainable cities. A key aspect, echoed across the chapters, is the importance of dialogue, of listening to the perspectives of others. As David Driskell's reflection (above) makes clear, this is important not only in validating young people's views, but also in helping all members of a community understand the complexity of the city, as a place with rich social and physical processes at play.

Chapter 2 began by introducing some of the important characteristics of young people's participation. We conclude this book by revisiting these characteristics, both through the methods and projects contained within this book, and children's comments themselves.

---

1. David Driskell, reflecting on one of Growing Up Boulder's projects, Great Neighborhoods (See Case Study, Chapter 11). David Driskell was the City of Boulder's Director of Community Planning, Housing, and Sustainability from 2009–2017. Here he is reflecting on the Great Neighborhoods project (Chapter 11), which engaged children (ages 8–16), university students, and the community in planning dense, affordable, child-friendly housing. This quote was obtained from an interview with David Driskell, as cited on page 126 in Victoria Derr, "Integrating community engagement and children's voices into design and planning education." *CoDesign*, 11, no. 2 (2015): 119–133.

Local and place-based. Without exception, the projects and methods presented in this book engage young people directly in the places where they live, play, and sometimes work. They ask young people to evaluate and share feelings about their everyday experiences and also to imagine future places and desires for community improvements. Whether a long-term hospital stay or a large public space, young people are experts in how they experience the world and can contribute tangible and realistic ideas toward many types of projects. In some cases, *place-based* means exploring the rich history and diversity of a place, as in the case of Burke Park's bioblitz (Chapter 7) or taller Creando Sin Encargos' playful installations along the beaches of San Juan. In others, it means reflecting on how policies impact young people's abilities to live well in their city, as in the case of teen moms or undocumented youth (Chapter 6).

Transparent. Transparency can be achieved through a wide range of formats during a project, with diverse ages coming together to communicate and listen (as discussed in Chapter 8). It can also be achieved by generating reports together with children (Chapter 9) and maintaining commitments to communicate project outcomes, even if they happen months or years later. Reports, posters, and letters are visible and tangible means to directly communicate with young people, families, and the community at large (Chapter 9).

Inclusive. Methods can often be tailored to foster greater inclusion, as in the case of the Treasure Hunt with young people with disabilities (Chapter 7) or the Latino Urbanism walk to engage Latinx youth in thinking about how culture is integrated into the city's fabric (Chapter 7). Providing diverse methods for participation can also foster inclusion, drawing on different strengths and interests among young people. While many young people prefer arts-based methods (Chapter 5), young people also gravitate toward surveys or interviews (Chapter 6) or field-based learning (Chapter 7). In addition, methods and processes that encourage self-expression support young people's understanding that their voices matter. This can be seen in the quote from an 8-year-old who liked making nicho boxes "because we got to express ourselves" and by the joyful exchange of letters from children in two Mexican towns (Chapter 5). Inclusive practices foster a sense that the city cares, as expressed by a teenager involved in a Boulder public space project: "I learned that my voice is important. Our community cares about its youth."[2]

Relevant. The cases in this book make clear there is no one-size-fits-all method for participation. Some projects may involve just a few primary partners, as in Ontario, Canada, or San Juan, Puerto Rico (Chapter 11). Others may involve many entities, including multiple schools, city staff and leaders, nonprofit organi-

zations, and community members, as in the case of Growing Up Boulder's open space planning process (Chapter 11). Even when projects start with just a few partners, they often grow over time, as more people become interested, see the relevance, or are invited to contribute.

Educational for all parties. While society tends to frame education as the passing of knowledge from adults to children, education in a participatory setting means that everyone learns from each other. Children learn from adult experts and city leaders (Chapter 8), from their peers, and from different age cohorts (Chapter 11). This is not always easy, as one boy reflected after a neighborhood design project: "My challenge was thinking of our design because everybody disagreed. I overcame this challenge by civil discourse."[3] Children also sometimes extend this thinking into the future. One of the children in the Dapto Dreaming project (Chapter 11) believed that "valuing children is important because we can pass on our education to future generations."[4] This view extends education not just between different parties but also across generations and into the future. The case studies in Chapter 11 show a wide range of ways that education happens within a participatory context.

We must emphasize here that adults also learn from children. Designers have found that children's thinking is refreshing and helps them view projects in new ways.[5] Some projects, such

---

2. Reflection gathered during the Boulder Civic Area "Park at the Core" design process.

3. Victoria Derr and Ildikó G. Kovács, "How participatory processes impact children and contribute to planning: a case study of neighborhood design from Boulder, Colorado, USA." *Journal of Urbanism: International Research on Placemaking and Urban Sustainability*, 10, no. 1 (2017): 29–48.
4. Page 124 in Karen Malone, "'Dapto dreaming': A place-based environmental education project supporting children to be agents of change." *Education in Times of Environmental Crisis: Teaching Children to be Agents of Change*, ed., Ken Winograd (New York, Routledge, 2016), 113–127.
5. Joanna Birch, Rosie Parnell, Maria Patsarika, and Maša Šorn, "Participating together: dialogic space for children and architects in the design process." *Children's Geographies*, 15, no. 2 (2017): 224–236; Angela Kreutz, Victoria Derr, and Louise Chawla. "Fluid or fixed? Processes that facilitate or constrain a sense of inclusion in participatory schoolyard

as Dapto Dreaming or the Move and Play projects in the Netherlands, intentionally seek to integrate children's views into a design. However, even when children are part of planning projects that extend to the whole city, such as a large public space, small details stick with adults, sometimes many years later, influencing their thinking not only for a single project, but also as they think about the city into the future.[6]

Sustainable. Many models of sustainability support opportunities for direct engagement and action so that young people can learn a sense of responsibility and see opportunities for being engaged and active stewards of their communities. Junior Rangers expressed this sentiment in a thank you letter after their day of participation in open space planning (Chapter 11):

> . . . We felt honored that they came to us and gave us a chance to participate in the decision-making process at such a young age. . . It was nice to have a day to think and reflect. . . while you knew you were contributing to something real. We learned how much *time, detail, and effort* goes into the planning process and took an active role discussing our recommendations for the North TSA. . . We felt like our voices were being heard.[7]

Sustainability also includes people seeing themselves as a part of a community, promoting social equity, and thinking about how their actions impact each other and the planet. From walks that explore Latino Urbanism to democratic education that fosters a sense of service (Chapter 7), we see a range of methods that sup-

port the holistic thinking of education for sustainability. Young people often speak of wanting to care for others, as reflected in the resilience mural, which included food gardens for the homeless[8] (Chapter 5), or in the Dapto Dreaming project, where children's "dreams and wishes" for a child-friendly neighborhood included money for the poor and that "everyone should have a home."[9]

No matter the focus, young people often advocate for the protection and enhancement of nature. Sometimes this is an intentional focus, as in the case of schoolyard design in Ontario, Canada, but sometimes this emerges from the process itself. Children involved in neighborhood planning projects in Boulder and Dapto reflected this thinking, advocating for places that "keep and protect nature" (Chapter 11). In planning for Boulder's Civic Area, one 9-year-old thought, "maybe we could have a greenhouse library where the books could be about plants." Another suggested, "kids want to interact with nature and there's not a good way to do it. I think there should be bird feeders hung in the trees." Young people also emphasize the importance of fostering inclusive and welcoming places for people as well as nature (Figure 12.1).[10]

Voluntary. Chapter 3 highlights the ethical importance of voluntary participation. Young people should always be able to choose whether or not they participate, and how. Most children will engage some days more than others, and so it is also important to remember that children have the right to disengage and then re-engage. For some children, this may depend, at least in part, on the method. Most children will express favorites, as in this boy who participated in designing a dense, affordable, child-friendly

and park design." *Landscape Journal* 37, no. 1 (2018); Derr, "Integrating community engagement and children's voices into design and planning education"

6. Victoria Derr and Emily Tarantini, ""Because we are all people:" Outcomes and reflections from young people's participation in the planning and design of child-friendly public spaces." *Local Environment,* 21, no. 12 (2016): 1534–1556.

7. Victoria Derr, Halice Ruppi, and Deryn Wagner. "Honoring voices, inspiring futures: young people's engagement in open space planning." *Children, Youth and Environments* 26, no. 2 (2016): 128–144.

8. Victoria Derr, Yolanda Corona, and Tuline Gülgönen. "Children's perceptions of and engagement in urban resilience in the United States and Mexico." *Journal of Planning Education and Research* (2017): doi: 0739456X17723436.

9. Dapto Dreaming Child Friendly Report.

10. The treehouse model was originally featured in Derr and Tarantini, "Because we are all people."

Figure 12.1. Children developed models for an inclusive environment for a public space project along Boulder Creek, with tree houses for viewing nature and where everyone would feel welcome. Photo credit: Growing Up Boulder. (This image originally appeared in Derr and Tarantini, "Because we are all people.")

Figure 12.2. Children's playfulness. On a neighborhood walk, this boy held his nose in a playful gesture next to the dumpster while using the photo-framing method (Chapter 7). Photo credit: Darcy Varney Kitching

Figure 12.3. Children's playfulness. Later on the same walk (Figure 12.2), children took a break from evaluating the city to try out new play equipment they encountered along the way. Photo credit: Darcy Varney Kitching

neighborhood: "My favorite [part of the project] was when we made the Athens Court model because you got to share ideas and build the model and you had to cooperate because everybody helped."[11] No matter the methods, creating a safe and supportive environment, with choices and voluntary participation, is an essential aspect of participation.

Playful. While some methods, such as child- and youth-led walks (Chapters 7 and 11) are overtly playful, many methods provide opportunities to engage in creative expression, to enjoy each other, and to foster a lighthearted spirit to planning the city. James Rojas' City as Play method (Chapter 5), teenagers' Spatial Stories in Dublin (Chapter 7), Stanley King and Susan Chung's graphic facilitation (Chapter 8), and Kind and Samelving's Picto-Play icons (Chapter 5) are just some of the many ways that playful methods infuse participatory planning. Young people often bring this playfulness to the process themselves (Figure 12.2 and 12.3), while also recognizing the importance of helping shape their cities. The Great Neighborhoods case (Chapter 11) emphasizes the value of this playful perspective in helping designers and planners see the city with new eyes, too.

• • •

Ultimately, we hope this book shows that there are many paths to identifying and recording a community's strengths, expressing concerns, and promoting change. We have highlighted multiple means for young people to learn in collaborative settings, consider places from the perspectives of multiple users, and imagine and play with possibilities. This book shows how young people are citizens of today—not passive recipients of a future tomorrow—who deserve to be heard and have influence on the policies and places that shape their lives. When young people are engaged, they are inclusive in their thinking,

---

11. Derr, "Integrating community engagement and children's voices into design and planning education."

extending their ideas to people of other ages, abilities, ethnicities, and interests, as well as to other species and nature. Willem van Vliet, one of the founders of Growing Up Boulder, thus reasons that a city that is good for children is good for everyone.

When Kevin Lynch initiated the first Growing Up in Cities projects, the UN Convention on the Rights of the Child (CRC) had not yet been written. While his intention was for young people to be involved in informing urban policy and action, he found this challenging to accomplish. The CRC has provided new momentum, and a policy imperative, to engage young people in cities around the world. It is not always easy to accomplish this, sometimes taking years of searching for sympathetic allies and open doors as well as a lot of trial and error, but the burgeoning number of methods and projects in this book show just how widespread this idea has become.

We hope that the methods in this book show creative starting points for you to find your own direction—no matter how small, no matter the city conditions or cultures—to find possibilities for young people to contribute to their communities. When Growing Up in Cities was revived and its team of international colleagues were actively promoting many of the methods highlighted in this book, they thought dissemination of these approaches was akin to a dandelion flower's head: a means of blowing seeds all over the world, to let them be picked up where they may. We hope you find such a seed, emerging from cracked concrete or fertile soil, in your own communities, too.

Figure 12.4. The Growing Up in Cities project was like a dandelion head: its goal was to blow seeds of participation all over the world. Image credit: Emily Tarantini

References

8 80 Cities. *Building Better Cities with Young Children and Families.* The Hague, The Netherlands: Bernard van Leer Foundation, 2017.

ACE. *Promoting Safe Communities: Improving Child Protection in Slums through a Convergent Approach in Mumbai and Bhopal.* Action for Children's Environments. http://acetrust.net /project/promoting-safe-communities. (Retrieved January 2, 2017).

Alexander, Catherine, Natalie Beale, Mike Kesby, Sara Kindon, Julia McMillan, Rachel Pain, and Friederike Ziegler. "Participatory diagramming: A critical view from North East England." *Participatory Action Research Approaches and Methods: Connecting People, Participation and Place*, Ed. Sara Kindon, Rachel Pain, and Mike Kesby. Abingdon: Routledge, 2007, 112-121.

Alderson, Pricilla. *Young Children's Rights: Exploring Beliefs, Principles and Practices.* London: Jessica Kingsley, 2000.

Allegretti, Giovanni, Maria Andrea Luz da Silva, and Francisco Freitas. "Experiências participativas da juventude em Portugal." *O Público e O Privado*, no. 20 (2012): 153–205.

Ambresin, Anne-Emmanuel, Kristina Bennett, George C. Patton, Lena A. Sanci, and Susan M. Sawyer. "Assessment of youth-friendly health care: a systematic review of indicators drawn from young people's perspectives." *Journal of Adolescent Health*, 52, no. 6 (2013): 670–681.

Amsden, Jackie, and Rob VanWynsberghe. "Community mapping as a research tool with youth." *Action Research* 3, no. 4 (2005): 357–381.

Anderson, Sarah. *Bringing School to Life.* Lanham, MD: Rowman & Littlefield, 2017.

Anderson, Sarah. "Taking hands on civics to the street." *Community Works Journal.* Available online at https://communityworksinstitute.org /cwjonline/articles/articles-text/Anderson _civics.html. (Retrieved August 13, 2017).

Anderson, Sarah, and Anne Gurnee. "Our students as home-grown citizens." *Community Works Journal*, December 2016. https://medium.com /communityworksjournal/our-students-as -home-grown-citizens-democracy-is-not-fast -and-easy-362c09964c41. (Retrieved August 13, 2017).

Anderson, H. Ross, Graziella Favarato, and Richard W. Atkinson. "Long-term exposure to air pollution and the incidence of asthma: meta-analysis of cohort studies." *Air Quality, Atmosphere & Health* 6, no. 1 (2013): 47–56.

Appadurai, Arjun. "The right to research." *Globalisation, Societies and Education* 4, no. 2 (2006):167–177.

Appleton, Jay. *The Experience of Place.* London: John Wiley, 1975.

Arnstein, Sherry R. "A ladder of citizen participation." *American Institute of Planners Journal* 35, no. 4 (1969): 216–224.

Bagnoli, Anna, and Andrew Clark. "Focus groups with young people," *Journal of Youth Studies* 13, no. 1 (2010): 101–119.

Bandura, Albert. *Self-Efficacy.* New York: W. H. Freeman, 1997.

Bartlett, Sheridan. *Making Space for Children: Planning for Post-Disaster Reconstruction with Children and Their Families*. Chennai, India: Save the Children, 2007. cergnyc.org/files/2011/09 /Making-space-full-version-11.pdf. (Retrieved December 8, 2017).

Bartlett, Sheridan, Roger Hart, David Satterthwaite, Ximena de la Barra and Alfredo Missair. *Cities for Children*. London: Earthscan Publications, 1999.

Bartlett, Sheridan, and David Satterthwaite, eds. *Cities on a Finite Planet*. London: Routledge, 2016.

Bartosh, Sarah, and Victoria Derr. "The power of play in planning with immigrants." European Network of Child Friendly Cities. http://www .childinthecity.org/2016/02/18/the-power-of -play-in-planning-with-refugees/. (Retrieved September 24, 2017).

Beatley, Timothy. *The Nature of Cities*. Boulder, CO: Throughline Productions, 2008.

Beg, Mirza Arif. "Demolitions throw Mumbai's poor onto the streets." *The Citizen*. http://www .thecitizen.in/index.php/NewsDetail/index/1 /4247/Demolitions-Throw-Mumbais-Poor -onto-the-Streets. (Retrieved December 27, 2017).

Besenyi, Gina M., Paul Diehl, Benjamin Schooley, Brie M. Turner-McGrievy, Sara Wilcox, Sara, Sonja A. Wilhelm Stanis, and Andrew T. Kaczynski. "Development and testing of mobile technology for community park improvements." *Translational Behavioral Medicine* 6, no.4 (2016): 519–532.

Birch, Joanna, Rosie Parnell, Maria Patsarika, and Maša Šorn. "Participating together: dialogic space for children and architects in the design process." *Children's Geographies*, 15, no. 2 (2017): 224–236.

Blair, Johnny, Ronald Czaja, and Edward Blair. *Designing Surveys*. Thousand Oaks, CA: Sage Publications, 2013.

Blanchet Cohen, Natasha and Juan Torres. "Accreditation of child-friendly municipalities in Quebec: Opportunities for child participation." *Children, Youth and Environments* 25, no. 2 (2015): 16–32.

Bose, Mallika, and Paula Horrigan. "Why community matters." *Community Matters:*

Service-Learning in Engaged Design and Planning. Ed. Mallika Bose, Paula Horrigan, Cheryl Doble, and Sigmund C. Shipp. Abingdon: Routledge, 2014, 1–21.

Bourke, Jackie. ""No messing allowed": The enactment of childhood in urban public space from the perspective of the child." *Children, Youth and Environments* 24, no. 1 (2014): 25–52.

Bourke, Jackie and Dorothy Smith. "Spatial stories of Dublin's youth." Child in the City European Network, May 24, 2017. https://www.childinthe city.org/2017/05/24/spatial-stories-of-dublins -youth/ (Retrieved September 15, 2017).

Boyden, Jo and Judith Ennew, eds. *Children in Focus—A Manual for Participatory Research with Children* Stockholm: Rädda Barnen, Save the Children Sweden, 1997.

Breitbart, Myrna Margulies. "Inciting desire, ignoring boundaries and making space." *Education, Childhood and Anarchism: Talking Colin Ward*. Ed. Catherine Burke and Ken Jones. Abingdon: Routledge, 2014, 175–185.

Brower, Sidney, La Verne Gray, and Roger Stough. *Doll-Play as a Tool for Urban Designers*. Baltimore: Department of Planning, 1977.

Cahill, Caitlyn. "The road less traveled: Transcultural community building." *Transcultural Cities: Border-Crossing and Place-Making*. Ed. Jeffrey Hou. New York: Routledge, 2013, 195–206.

Camino, Linda, Shepherd Zeldin, Carrie Mook, and Cailin O'Connor. *Youth and Adult Leaders for Program Excellence: A Practical Guide for Program Assessment and Action Planning*. Community Youth Connection, University of Wisconsin Madison, 2004. https://fyi.uwex.edu /youthadultpartnership/yalpe-workbook/.

Campbell, Lindsay and Anne Wiesen, eds. *Restorative Commons*. General Technical Report NRS-P-39. Newtown Square, PA: USDA Forest Service, 2009.

Carroll, Penelope, and Karen Witten, "Children as urban design consultants: Children's audit of a central city square in Auckland, Aotearoa/ New Zealand." *Designing Cities with Children and Young People*. Ed. Kate Bishop and Linda Corkery. New York: Routledge, 2017, 105–118.

Carver, A., J. Veitch, J. Salmon, C. Hume, A. Timperio, and D. Crawford. "Children's independent mobility—is it influenced by parents' perceptions of safety?" Melbourne: Centre for Physical Activity and Nutrition Research, 2010.

Cele, Sofia, and Danielle van der Burgt."Participation, consultation, confusion: professionals' understandings of children's participation in physical planning." *Children's Geographies* 13, no. 1 (2015): 14–29.

CERG (Children's Environments Research Group). "Child Friendly Places." http://cergnyc.org /portfolio/child-friendly-places. (Retrieved January 11, 2018).

Chatterjee, Sudeshna. *Access to Play in Crisis: Synthesis of the Research in Six Countries.* IPA World (International Play Association), 2017.

Chatterjee, Sudeshna, "Making children matter in slum transformations," *Journal of Urban Design* 20, no. 4 (2015): 479–506.

Chatterjee, Sudeshna. "Children's friendship with place." *Children, Youth and Environments* 15, no.1 (2005): 1–26.

Chambers, Robert. *Participatory Workshops: A Sourcebook of 21 Sets of Ideas and Activities* London: Earthscan Publications, 2002.

Chatrakul Na Ayudhya, Uracha, Janet Smithson, and Susan Lewis. "Focus group methodology in a life course approach–individual accounts within a peer cohort group." *International Journal of Social Research Methodology*, 17, no. 2 (2014): 157–171.

Chawla, Louise. "Benefits of nature contact for children." *Journal of Planning Literature* 30, no. 4 (2015): 433–452.

Chawla, Louise. "Participation as capacity-building for active citizenship." *Les Ateliers de L'Ethique* 4, no. 1 (2009): 69–76.

Chawla, Louise, Ed. *Growing Up in an Urbanising World.* London: Earthscan Publications, 2002.

Chawla, Louise. "Evaluating children's participation: Seeking areas of consensus." Special issue on "Children's participation—Evaluating effectiveness." *PLA Notes* 42 (2001): 9–13.

Chawla, Louise, ed. Special issue on "Children's Participation—Evaluating Effectiveness." *PLA Notes* 42 (2001).

Chawla, Louise, Natasha Blanchet-Cohen, Nilda Cosco, David Driskell, Jill Kruger, Karen Malone, Robin Moore, and Barry Percy-Smith. "Don't just listen—do something!" *Children, Youth and Environments* 15, no. 2 (2005): 53–88.

Chawla, Louise, and Victoria Derr. "The development of conservation behaviors in childhood and youth." *Oxford Handbook of Environmental and Conservation Psychology.* Ed. Susan Clayton. New York: Oxford University Press, 2012, 527–555.

Chawla, Louise, and Willem van Vliet. "Children's rights to child friendly cities." *Handbook of Children's Rights*, Eds., M. Ruck, M. Peterson-Badali, and M. Freeman. New York: Routledge, 2017, 533–549.

City of Boulder. "Boulder Valley Comprehensive Plan (BVCP) Study Session on Scenarios and Housing Prototypes, Land Use Definitions, and Key Policy Choices." Aug. 25, 2016. https://bouldercolorado.gov/bvcp/focus-areas. (Retrieved September 16, 2017).

City of Boulder. "Housing Boulder (Comprehensive Housing Strategy)." https://bouldercolorado .gov/city-council/comprehensive-housing -strategy-housing-boulder. (Retrieved September 16, 2017).

Clark, Alison. "The mosaic approach and research with young children." *The Reality of Research with Children and Young People.* Ed. V. Lewis, M. Kellett, C. Robinson, S. Fraser and S. Ding. London: Sage Publications, 2004, 142–161.

Clark, Alison. "The mosaic approach." *Steps for Engaging Young Children in Research, Volume 2: The Researcher's Toolkit.* Ed. Vicky Johnson, Roger Hart, and Jennifer Colwell. Brighton, UK: Education Research Centre, University of Brighton, 2014, 143–146. Available at https://bernardvanleer.org/publications-reports /steps-engaging-young-children-research -volume-2-researcher-toolkit/. (Retrieved December 5, 2017).

Coates, Elizabeth. "I forgot the sky! Children's stories contained within their drawings." *International Journal of Early Years Education*, 10, no. 1 (2002): 21–35. Reprinted in *The Reality of Research with Children and Young People.* Ed. Vicky Lewis et al. Thousand Oaks, CA: Sage Publications, 2003, 5–26.

Cohen-Cruz, Jan. *Engaging Performances.* London: Routledge, 2010.

Colucci, Erminia, "Focus groups can be fun." *Qualitative Health Research* 17, no. 10 (2007): 1422–1433.

Cooperrider, David and Diana Whitney. *Appreciative Inquiry.* San Francisco: Berrett-Koehler Publishers, 2005.

Corbett, Jon, Giacomo Rambaldi, Peter Kyem, Dan Weiner, Rachel Olson, Julius Muchemi, Mike McCall, and Robert Chambers. "Overview: Mapping for change—the emergence of a new practice." *PLA Notes 54, Special Issue on Mapping for Change,* (2006): 13–19. https://www.iied.org/pla-54-mapping-for-change-practice-technologies-communication. (Retrieved January 8, 2018).

Corcoran, Peter Blaze, and Philip M. Osano. *Young People, Education, and Sustainable Development: Exploring Principles, Perspectives, and Praxis.* Wageningen, the Netherlands: Wageningen Academic Publishers, 2009.

Corona, Yolanda Caraveo, G. Quinteros-Sciurano, and M. Padilla Flores. "Relación epistolar entre niños de dos pueblos: Estructuras y estrategias del conocimiento." *Anuario de Investigación.* Mexico City: UAM-X, 2005, 614–635.

Cosco, Nilda, and Robin Moore, "Using behaviour mapping to investigate healthy outdoor environments for children and families." *Innovative Approaches to Researching Landscape and Health.* Ed. Catherine Ward Thompson, Peter Aspinall, and Simon Belm. London: Routledge, 2010, 33–72.

Cosco, Nilda, and Robin Moore. "Our neighbourhood is like that! Cultural richness and childhood identity in Boca-Barracas, Buenos Aires." *Growing Up in an Urbanising World.* Ed. Louise Chawla. London: Earthscan Publications, 2002, 35–56.

Cosco, Nilda, Robin Moore, and Mohammed Islam. "Behavior mapping." *Medicine and Science in Sports and Exercise* 42, no. 3 (2010): 513–519.

Cunningham, Chris J., Margaret A. Jones, and Rosemary Dillon. "Children and urban regional planning: Participation in the public consultation process through story writing." *Children's Geographies* 1, no. 2 (2003): 201–221.

Cushing, Debra Flanders, Emily Wexler Love, and Willem van Vliet. "Through the viewfinder: Using multimedia techniques to engage Latino youth in community planning." *Diálogos: Place-making in Latino Communities.* Ed., Michael Rios and Leonardo Vazquez London: Routledge, 2012, 172–185.

Damon, William. *The Moral Child.* New York: Free Press, 1988.

Dart, Jessica, and Rick Davies. "A dialogical, story-based evaluation tool: The Most Significant Change technique." *American Journal of Evaluation,* 24, no. 2 (2003): 137–155.

Davidoff, Paul. "Advocacy and pluralism in planning." *Journal of the American Institute of Planners* 31, no. 4 (1965): 331–338.

Davies, Rick and Jess Dart. *The 'Most Significant Change' (MSC) Technique: A Guide to Its Use,* 2005. https://www.betterevaluation.org/en/resources/guides/most_significant_change (Retrieved January 3, 2018).

Delgado, Melvin. *Community Practice and Urban Youth: Social Justice, Service-Learning and Civic Engagement.* New York: Routledge, 2015.

Delgado, Melvin. *Designs and Methods for Youth-Led Research.* Thousand Oaks, CA: Sage Publications, 2006.

Derr, Victoria. "Urban greenspaces as participatory learning laboratories." Special issue of *Urban Design and Planning,* titled *Built Environment Education and Participation of Children and Youth.* Ed. Angela Million, Rosie Parnell, and Thomas Coelen, (2017): http://www.icevirtuallibrary.com/doi/abs/10.1680/jurdp.17.00009.

Derr, Victoria. "Young people focus their lens on climate change." European Network of Child Friendly Cities, January 12, 2017. http://www.childinthecity.eu/2017/01/12/young-people-focus-their-lens-on-climate-change/. (Retrieved September 24, 2017).

Derr, Victoria. "Integrating community engagement and children's voices into design and planning education." *CoDesign* 11, no. 2 (2015): 119–133.

Derr, Victoria. "Children's sense of place in northern New Mexico." *Journal of Environmental Psychology* 22, no. 1 (2002): 125–137.

Derr, Victoria, Louise Chawla, and Illène Pevec. "Early childhood." *Urban Environmental Education Review*. Ed., Alex Russ and Marianne Krasny Ithaca, New York: Cornell University Press, 2017, 155–164.

Derr, Victoria, Louise Chawla, and Willem van Vliet. "Children as natural change agents: Child friendly cities as resilient cities." *Designing Cities with Children and Young People: Beyond Playgrounds and Skateparks*. Ed., Kate Bishop and Linda Corkery. New York: Routledge, 2017, 24–35.

Derr, Victoria, Yolanda Corona, and Tuline Gülgönen. "Children's perceptions of and engagement in urban resilience in the United States and Mexico." *Journal of Planning Education and Research* (2017): doi: 0739456X17723436.

Derr, Victoria, and Ildikó G. Kovács. "How participatory processes impact children and contribute to planning: a case study of neighborhood design from Boulder, Colorado, USA." *Journal of Urbanism: International Research on Placemaking and Urban Sustainability*, 10, no. 1 (2017): 29–48.

Derr, Victoria and Jeffery Morton. "Empowering young people through action on community environments." European Network of Child Friendly Cities, May 4, 2017. https://www.childinthecity.org/2017/05/04/empowering-young-people-through-action-on-community-environment/. (Retrieved August 21, 2017).

Derr, Victoria, Halice Ruppi, and Deryn Wagner. "Honoring voices, inspiring futures: Young people's engagement in open space planning." *Children, Youth and Environments* 26, no. 2 (2016): 128–144.

Derr, Victoria, and Emily Tarantini. ""Because we are all people:" Outcomes and reflections from young people's participation in the planning and design of child-friendly public spaces." *Local Environment: International Journal of Justice and Sustainability* 21, no. 12 (2016): 1534–1556.

Dewey, John. *The School and Society * The Child and the Curriculum*. Chicago: University of Chicago Press, 1991 (originally published in 1900 and 1902).

Doherty, Sean T., Patricia McKeever, Henna Aslam, Lindsay Stephens, and Nicole Yantzi. "Use of GPS tracking to interactively explore disabled children's mobility and accessibility patterns." *Children Youth and Environments* 24, no. 1 (2014): 1–24.

Driskell, David, and Neema Kudva. "Everyday ethics: framing youth participation in organizational practice." *Les Ateliers de l'Ethique*, 4, no. 1 (2009): 77–87.

Driskell, David. "Growing up in NYC: Reflections on two summers of action research." *Children, Youth and Environments* 17, no. 2 (2007): 472–783.

Driskell, David. *Creating Better Cities with Children and Youth: A Manual for Participation*. London: Earthscan Publications, 2002.

Epstein, Iris, Bonnie Stevens, Patricia McKeever, and Sylvain Baruchel. "Photo elicitation interview (PEI): Using photos to elicit children's perspectives." *International Journal of Qualitative Methods* 5, no. 3 (2006): 1–11.

Esterhuizen, Lea. *Child Led Data Collection*. Stockholm: Save the Children Sweden, https://resourcecentre.savethechildren.net/node/5901/pdf/5901.pdf. (Retrieved January 3, 2018).

Estrella, Marisol, and John Gaventa. *Who Counts Reality? Participatory Monitoring and Evaluation*. IDS Working Paper 70. Institute of Development Studies, University of Sussex Learning from Change, 1998. Available at www.ids.ac.uk/publication/who-counts-reality-participatory-monitoring-and-evaluation-a-literature-review.

Evans, Sheila. *PAR Guide: Promoting the Participation, Learning and Action of Young People*. Kingston, Jamaica: United Nations Children's Fund, 2004.

Fetterman, David M. *Foundations of Empowerment Evaluation*. Thousand Oaks, CA: Sage Publications, 2001.

Fetterman, David M. Shakeh Kaftarian, and Abraham Wandersman. *Empowerment Evaluation*. Thousand Oaks, CA: Sage Publications, 1995.

Field, Andy. "Lookout Interactive." Andy Field.com. http://andytfield.co.uk/project/lookout/ (Retrieved December 19, 2017).

Flanagan, Constance A. "Volunteerism, leadership, political socialization, and civic engagement." *Handbook of Adolescent Psychology*. Ed. R. M. Lerner and L. Steinberg, New York: John Wiley, 2004.

Flavelle, Alix. *Mapping our Land: A Guide to Making Your Own Maps of Communities and Traditional Lands*. Greenwich, CT: Lone Pine Foundation, 2002.

Fletcher, Sarah, Robin S. Cox, Leila Scannell, Cheryl Heykoop, Jennifer Tobin-Gurley, and Lori Peek. "Youth creating disaster recovery and resilience: A multi-site arts-based youth engagement research project." *Children, Youth And Environments* 26, no. 1 (2016): 148–163.

Fors, Hanna, and Anders Busse Nielsen. "Landscape laboratories: Sletten (DK)—offering residents spaces for activities between the garden and the woods." *'scape, The International Magazine for Landscape Architecture and Urbanism*, 15 (2016): 114–115.

Freeman, Claire, and Paul Tranter. *Children and their Urban Environment: Changing Worlds*. London: Earthscan Publications, 2011.

Gallagher, Kathleen, Rebecca Starkman, and Rachel Rhoades. "Performing counter-narratives and mining creative resilience: using applied theatre to theorize notions of youth resilience." *Journal of Youth Studies* 20, no. 2 (2017): 216–233.

Gallerani, David G., Gina M. Besenyi, Sonja A. Wilhelm Stanis, and Andrew T. Kaczynski. "We actually care and we want to make the parks better." *Preventive Medicine*, 95, (2017): S109–S114.

Garton, Nicholas. "Community remix: Hip hop architecture breaks down walls to build bridges." Madison 365, February 6, 2017. http://madison365.com/community-remix-hip-hop-architecture-breaks-walls-build-bridges/. (Retrieved September 18, 2017).

Gawler, Meg. *Useful Tools for Engaging Young People in Participatory Evaluation*. UNICEF, 2005, https://issuu.com/learneasy/docs/tools-for-participatory-evaluation. (Retrieved September 30, 2017).

Gehl, Jan. *Life between Buildings*. Washington, DC: Island Press, 2011 (originally published in 1971).

Gehl, Jan, and Birgitte Svarre. *How to Study Public Life*. Washington, DC: Island Press, 2013.

Gibson, William, and Andrew Brown. *Working with Qualitative Data*. Thousand Oaks, CA: Sage Publications, 2009.

Gigler, Björn-Sören, and Ballur, Savit, eds. *Closing the Feedback Loop: Can Technology Bridge the Accountability Gap?* Washington, DC: The World Bank, 2014.

Goodall, Jane. *With Love*. Vienna, VA: Jane Goodall Institute, 1994.

Gonzalez, Maya Christina. *I Know the River Loves Me / Yo Se Que el Rio Me Ama*. New York City: Lee & Low Books, Inc., 2012.

Gubrium, Aline, and Krista Harper. *Participatory Visual and Digital Methods*. Walnut Creek, CA: Left Coast Press, 2013.

Gujit, Irene. *Participatory Approaches—Methodological Briefs: Impact Evaluation No. 5*. Florence: UNICEF Office of Research, 2014, https://www.unicef-irc.org/publications/pdf/brief_5_participatoryapproaches_eng.pdf. (Retrieved January 8, 2018).

Guarnieri, Michael, and John R. Balmes. "Outdoor air pollution and asthma." *The Lancet* 383, no. 9928 (2014): 1581–1592.

Guy, Susan, and Andrew Inglis. "Tips for trainers." *PLA Notes* 34 (1999): 84–87.

Hall, Ellen Lynn, and Jennifer Kofkin Rudkin. *Seen and Heard: Children's Rights in Early Childhood Education*. New York/London, Canada: Teachers College Press/The Althouse Press, 2011.

Halvorsen, Kirsti Vindal. "Steps in the Plantain Project: The ideas, activities, and experiences of the Plantain Project, a scheme to safeguard children and their environment." *Children's Environments* (1995): 444–456.

Harrington, Sheila, ed. *Giving the Land a Voice: Mapping our Home Places*. Salt Spring Island, BC, Canada: Land Trust Alliance of British Columbia, 1999.

Hart, Jason, Jesse Newman, and Lisanne Ackermann. *Children Changing their World: Understanding and Evaluating Children's Participation in Development*. Woking, Surrey, UK: Plan International, 2004.

Hart, Roger. "Stepping back from 'The Ladder': Reflections on a model of participatory work with children." *Participation and Learning*. Ed. A. Reid, B. B. Jensen, J. Nikel and V. Simovska Guildford, UK, Springer, 2008, 19–31.

Hart, Roger. "The developing capacities of children to participate." *Stepping Forward: Children and Young People's Participation in the Development Process*, Ed., Victoria Johnson, Edda Ivan-Smith, Gill Gordon, Pat Pridmore, and Patta Scott. London: Intermediate Technology Publications, 1998.

Hart, Roger. *Children's Participation: The Theory and Practice of Involving Young Citizens in Community Development and Environmental Care*. London: Earthscan Publication, 1997.

Hart, Roger. *Children's Experience of Place*. New York: Irvington Publishers, 1979.

Hart, Roger, Jasmine Rajbhandary, and Chandrika Katiwada. "Mirrors of ourselves: Critical self reflection on group work by the Children's Clubs of Nepal." *Steps to Engaging Young Children in Research*, Volume 1: The Guide. Ed. Vicky Johnson, Roger Hart, and Jennifer Colwell. Education Research Centre, University of Brighton, 2014, 85–91. Available at https://bernardvanleer.org/publications-reports/steps-engaging-young-children-research-volume-1-guide.

Hartig, Terry, Richard Mitchell, Sjerp De Vries, and Howard Frumkin. "Nature and health." *Annual Review of Public Health* 35 (2014): 207–228.

Haynes, Katharine, and Thomas M. Tanner. "Empowering young people and strengthening resilience: Youth-centred participatory video as a tool for climate change adaptation and disaster risk reduction." *Children's Geographies* 13, no. 3 (2015): 357–371.

Hennink, Monique, Inge Hutter, and Ajay Bailey. *Qualitative Research Methods*. Thousand Oaks, CA: Sage Publications, 2011.

Higgins, Jane, Karen Nairn, and Judith Sligo. "Peer research with youth." *Participatory Action Research Approaches and Methods: Connecting People, Participation and Place*, Ed., Sara Kindon, Rachel Pain, and Mike Kesby. Abingdon: Routledge, 2007, 104–111.

Hill, Johanna. "Household mapping exercise in Nepal." *Steps to Engaging Young Children in Research, Volume 2: The Researcher Toolkit*. Ed. Vicky Johnson, Roger Hart, and Jennifer Colwell. Brighton, UK: Education Research Centre, University of Brighton, 2014, 78–82. Available at https://bernardvanleer.org/publications-reports/steps-engaging-young-children-research-volume-2-researcher-toolkit.

Hodgkin, Rachel, and Peter Newell. *Implementation Handbook on the Convention on the Rights of the Child*. New York: UNICEF, 1998.

Hoffman, Martin. *Empathy and Moral Development*. New York: Cambridge University Press, 2000.

Hoppe, Marilyn, Elizabeth Wells, Diane Morrison, Mary Gillmore, and Anthony Wilsdon. "Using focus groups to discuss sensitive topics with children." *Evaluation Review* 19, no. 1 (1995), 102–114.

Huber, Morgan, and Victora Derr. "Walking laboratories: Young people's experience of the street." European Network of Child Friendly Cities, April 28, 2016. http://www.childinthecity.org/2016/04/28/walking-laboratories-young-childrens-experience-of-the-street/. (Retrieved August 21, 2017).

Huckle, John, and Stephen Sterling, eds. *Education for Sustainability*. London: Earthscan Publications, 1996.

Hucko, Bruce. *Where There is No Name for Art: The Art of the Tewa Pueblo Children*. Santa Fe, New Mexico: School of American Research Press, 1996.

IRC/CERG. *Child-Friendly Cities and Communities Assessment Toolkit*. ChildWatch International Research Network. http://www.childwatch.uio.no/projects/activities/child-friendly-cities-and-communities-research-project/finaltoolkit2011.html. (Retrieved June 6, 2014).

Jenkin, Elena, Erin Wilson, Kevin Murfitt, Matthew Clarke, Robert Campain, and Lanie Stockman. *Inclusive Practice for Research with Children with Disability: A Guide*. Melbourne: Deakin University, 2015. http://www.voicesofchildrenwithdisability.com/wp-content/uploads/2015/03/DEA-Inclusive-Practice-Research_ACCESSIBLE.pdf. (Retrieved January 3, 2018).

Johnson, Vicky, Roger Hart, and Jennifer Colwell, eds. "Child-led group tours with children and adults." *Steps to Engaging Young Children in Research, Volume 2: The Researcher Toolkit*. Brighton, UK: Education Research Centre, University of Brighton, 2014. https://bernardvanleer.org/publications-reports/steps-engaging-young-children-research-volume-2

-researcher-toolkit. (Retrieved January 3, 2018).

Johnson, Vicky, Roger Hart, and Jennifer Colwell, eds. *Steps for Engaging Young Children in Research: Volume 1, The Guide.* (Brighton, UK: Education Research Centre, University of Brighton, 2004), 21–34. https://bernardvanleer.org/publications-reports/steps-engaging-young-children-research-volume-1-guide/. (Retrived January 3, 2018).

Johnson, Vicky, Robert Nurick, Karen Baker, and Rajni Shivakotee. *Children and Young People's Participation (CYPP) Training Workshop Guide* London/Hove: Child Hope/Development Focus, 2013. https://www.childhope.org.uk/wp-content/uploads/2013/05/Childhope-CYPP-Toolkit-FINAL.pdf. . (Retrieved January 3, 2018).

Johnson, Victoria, Joanna Hill and Edda Ivan-Smith. *Listening to Smaller Voices.* Chard Somerset, UK: ActionAid, 1995.

Kaplan, Matthew. *The Futures Festival: A Facilitator's Guide.* State College, PA: College of Agricultural Sciences–Cooperative Extension, Pennsylvania State University, 2001.

Kaplan, Matthew. *Side by Side: Exploring Your Neighborhood Through Intergenerational Activities.* Berkeley, CA: MIG Communications, 1994.

Kaplan, Matthew, and Alan Hatton-Yeo. *Intergenerational Forums.* Stoke-on-Trent, UK/University Park, PA: Beth Johnson Foundation/Penn State, 2008. http://aese.psu.edu/extension/intergenerational/program-areas/community-planning-visioning/intergenerational-unity-forums/intergenerational-forums.

Kaplan, Matthew, Frank Higdon, Nancy Crago, and Lucinda Robbins. "Futures festivals: An intergenerational strategy for promoting community participation." *Journal of Intergenerational Relationships* 2, no. 3–4 (2004): 119–146.

Kaplan, Stephen, and Rachel Kaplan. *The Experience of Nature: a Psychological Perspective.* Cambridge University Press, 1989.

Kaplan, Stephen, and Rachel Kaplan. "The visual environment: public participation in design and planning." *Journal of Social Issues* 45, no. 1 (1989): 59–86.

Kellett, Mary. *How to Develop Children as Researchers.* London: Paul Chapman Publishing, 2005.

Kemmis, Stephen, and Robin McTaggart. *The Action Research Planner*, 3rd edition. Melbourne: Deakin University Press, 1988.

Kind & Samenleving. "Picto-play 1.0." Kind & Samenleving.org. http://k-s.be/inspraak-participatie/picto-play-10-knip-en-plak-het-speelweefsel-bij-mekaar/picto-play-10-catalogus-en-handleiding/. (Retrieved September 24, 2017).

Kindon, Sara, Rachel Pain, and Mike Kesby, eds. *Participatory Action Research Approaches and Methods: Connecting People, Participation and Place.* London: Routledge, 2007.

King, Stanley, Merinda Conley, Bill Latimer, and Drew Ferrari. *Co-Design: A Process of Design for Participation.* New York: Van Nostrand Reinhold, 1989.

King, Stanley, and Susan Chung. *Youth Manual for Teachers and Youth Leaders.* http://youthmanual.blogspot.com/p/about-us.html. (Retrieved July 22, 2017).

Kinoshita, Isami. "Play maps in Japan." *Steps to Engaging Young Children in Research, Volume 2: The Researcher Toolkit.* Ed. Vicky Johnson, Roger Hart, and Jennifer Colwell Brighton, UK: Education Research Centre, University of Brighton, 2014, 78–82. https://bernardvanleer.org/publications-reports/steps-engaging-young-children-research-volume-2-researcher-toolkit.

Kinoshita, Isami. "Charting generational differences in conceptions and opportunities for play in a Japanese neighborhood." *Journal of Intergenerational Relationships* 7, no. 1 (2009): 53–77.

Kinoshita, Isami. "Three generations of play in Taishido." *Children's Environments Quarterly* 1, no. 4 (1984): 19–28.

Kinoshita, Isami, et al. *The Street Art Workshop.* Tokyo: Unpublished program report, 1992.

Kirby, Perpetua. *Involving Young Researchers: How to Enable Young People to Design and Conduct Research.* Layerthorpe, UK: York Publishing Services, 1999.

Kirby, Perpetua, and Sara Bryson. *Measuring the Magic? Evaluating and Researching Young People's Participation in Decision Making.* London: Carnegie Young People Initiative, 2002.

Kirshner, Ben. *Youth Activism in an Era of Educational Inequality.* New York University Press, 2015.

Kirshner, Ben, and Ellen Middaugh, eds. *#youth action: Becoming Political in the Digital Age.* Charlotte, NC: Information Age Publishing Inc, 2014.

Koester, M.. "On a mission: Creating a climate for rising 'C' levels in science education." Work in Progress. Kids Teaching Flood Resilience: https://www.kidsteachingfloodresilience.com/

Krasny, Marianne, and Keith Tidball. *Civic Ecology.* Cambridge, MA: MIT Press, 2015.

Kreutz, Angela. *Children and the Environment in an Australian Indigenous Community.* London: Routledge, 2015.

Kreutz, Angela, Victoria Derr, and Louise Chawla. "Fluid or fixed? Processes that facilitate or constrain a sense of inclusion in participatory schoolyard and park design." *Landscape Journal* 37, no. 1 (2018).

Krueger, Richard A., and Mary Anne Casey. *Focus Groups: A Practical Guide for Applied Research.* Thousand Oaks, CA: Sage Publications, 2014.

Kruger, Jill. *Phila Impilo! Live Life! Ways to Healing.* DVD. Overport, South Africa: Young Insights for Planning, 2008. Available as a free download at http://www.open.edu/openlearncreate /mod/oucontent/view.php?id=53626. (Retrieved July 16, 2017).

Kuper, Hannah, Frank Velthuizen, and Gwen Duffy. *PLAN International Guidelines for Consulting with Children and Young People with Disabilities,* 2016. https://plan-international.org /publications/guidelines-consulting-children -and-young-people-disabilities. (Retrieved January 3, 2018).

Lambert, Joe. *Digital Storytelling: Capturing Lives, Creating Community,* 2nd Edition. Berkeley, CA: Digital Diner Press, 2006.

Lansdown, Gerison. *The Evolving Capacities of the Child.* Florence, Italy: UNICEF Innocenti Research Centre, 2005.

Lansdown, Gerison, and Claire O'Kane, *Toolkit for Monitoring and Evaluating Children's Participation.* Save the Children, 2014. https://resource-centre.savethechildren.net/document -collections/toolkit-monitoring-and-evaluating -childrens-participation. (Retrieved September 15, 2017).

Liebenberg, Linda, Michael Ungar, and Linda Theron. "Using video observation and photo elicitation interviews to understand obscured processes in the lives of youth resilience." *Childhood* 21, no. 4 (2014): 532–547.

Linn, Karl. *Building Commons and Community.* New York: New Village Press, 2007.

Loukaitou-Sideris, Anastasia, and Athanasios Sideris. "What brings children to the park? Analysis and measurement of the variables affecting children's use of parks." *Journal of the American Planning Association* 76, no. 1 (2009): 89–107.

Lunch, Nick, and Chris Lunch. *Insights into Participatory Video: A Handbook for the Field.* InsightShare, 2006. http://insightshare.org /resources/insights-into-participatory-video -a-handbook-for-the-field/. (Retrieved March 10, 2017).

Lynch, Kevin. *Growing Up in Cities.* Cambridge, MA, MIT Press, 1977

Lynch, Kevin. *The Image of the City.* Cambridge, MA: MIT Press, 1960.

McCarthy, Julie, with Karla Galvão. *Enacting Participatory Development: Theatre-Based Techniques.* London: Earthscan Publications, 2004.

Madanipour, Ali, ed. *Whose Public Space? International Case Studies in Urban Design and Development.* Abingdon: Routledge, 2013.

Madrigal, Daniel, Alicia Salvater, Gardenia Casillas, Crystal Casillas, Irene Vera, Brenda Eskenazi, and Meredith Minkler. "Health in my community: Conducting and evaluating photovoice as a tool to promote environmental health and leadership among Latino/a youth." *Progress in Community Health Partnerships: Research, Education, and Action* 8, no. 3 (2014): 317–329.

Malone, Karen. "Child friendly cities: A model." *Designing Cities with Children and Young People: Beyond Playgrounds and Skate Parks.* Ed. Kate Bishop and Linda Corkery New York: Routledge, 2017, 11–23.

Malone, Karen. "'Dapto dreaming': A place-based environmental education project supporting children to be agents of change." *Education in Times of Environmental Crisis: Teaching Children to be Agents of Change.* Ed. Ken Winograd. New York: Routledge, 2016, 113–127.

Malone, Karen. "'The future lies in our hands': children as researchers and environmental change agents in designing a child-friendly neighbourhood." *Local Environment* 18, no. 3 (2013): 372–395.

Malone, Karen. *Designing and Dreaming a Child Friendly Neighborhood for Brooks Reach, Dapto*. University of Western Sydney, Bankstown, NSW, Australia, 2011.

Malone, Karen, Katina Dimoulias, Son Truong, and Kumara S.Ward. *Researching Children's Designs for a Child Friendly Play Space at Rouse Hill Town Centre* Sydney: Centre for Educational Research, University of Western Sydney, 2014.

Manzo, Lynne C., and Nathan Brightbill, "Toward a participatory ethics." *Participatory Action Research Approaches and Methods*. Ed. Sara Kindon, Rachel Pain and Mike Kesby London: Routledge, 2007, 33–40.

Marshall, Chelsea, Laura Lundy, and Karen Orr. *Child-Participatory Budgeting*. Belfast, Ireland: Centre for Children's Rights at Queens University, 2016. https://plan-international.org/publications/childparticipatory-budgeting. (Retrieved December 15, 2017).

Martusewicz, Rebecca A., Jeff Edmundson, and John Lupinacci. *Ecojustice Education: Toward Diverse, Democratic, and Sustainable Communities*, 2nd Edition. New York: Routledge, 2015.

Mehlmann, Marilyn, with Esböjrn Jorsäter, Alexander Mehlmann, and Olena Pometun. "Looking the Monster in the Eye: Drawing Comics for Sustainability." *EarthEd: Rethinking Education on a Changing Planet* Washington, D.C.: Island Press, 2017, 117–127.

Mertler, Craig A. *Action Research: Teachers as Researchers in the Classroom*. Thousand Oaks, CA: Sage Publications, 2008.

Mey, Günter, and Hartmut Günther, eds. *The Life Space of the Urban Child: Perspectives on Martha Muchow's Classic Study*. New Brunswick, NJ: Transaction Publishers, 2015.

Million, Angela. "Preparing children and young people for participation in planning and design." *Designing Cities with Children and Young People*. Ed. Kate Bishop and Linda Corkery New York: Routledge, 2017, 223–236.

Miraftab, Faranak, and Neema Kudva, eds. *Cities of the Global South Reader*. London: Routledge, 2015.

Mitchell, Claudia. *Doing Visual Research*. Thousand Oaks, CA: Sage Publications, 2011.

Moore, Robin C. *Childhood's Domain*. London: Croom Helm, 1986.

Moore, Robin C. "Collaborating with young people to assess their landscape values." *Ekistics* 47, no. 281 (1980): 128–135.

Moore, Robin C., with Allen Cooper. *Nature Play and Learning Places* Raleigh, NC/Reston, VA: Natural Learning Initiative/National Wildlife Federation, 2014.

Moore, Robin C. and Susan M. Goltsman. *Play for All Guidelines*, 2d edition. Berkeley, CA: MIG Communications, 1997.

Myers, Jr., Olin Eugene. *The Significance of Children and Animals: Social Development and Our Connections to Other Species*, 2nd edition. West Lafayette, IN: Purdue University Press, 2007.

Nallari, Anupama. 2014. "In-situ and child-led tours." *Steps to Engaging Young Children in Research, Volume 2: The Researcher Toolkit*. Ed. Vicky Johnson, Roger Hart, and Jennifer Colwell Brighton, UK: Education Research Centre, University of Brighton, 2014, 78–82, available at https://bernardvanleer.org/publications-reports/steps-engaging-young-children-research-volume-2-researcher-toolkit.

Napawan, N. Claire, Sheryl-Ann Simpson, and Brett Snyder. "Engaging youth in climate resilience planning with social media. Lessons from #OurChangingClimate." *Urban Planning* 2, no. 4 (2017): 51–63.

National Commission on Resources for Youth. *Evaluating Youth Participation*. New York: Author, 1982.

National Geographic. "Bioblitz." National Geographic.org. http://www.nationalgeographic.org/encyclopedia/bioblitz/. (Retrieved September 16, 2017).

The Nature Conservancy and The Cornell Lab. "Habitat Network," Powered by Yardmap. www.habitat.network. (Retrieved October 7, 2017).

Nelson, Bethany. "'I made myself': Playmaking as a pedagogy of change with urban youth." *RiDE:*

The Journal of Applied Theatre and Performance 16, no. 2 (2011): 157–172.

Nishimura, Katherine K. Joshua M. Galanter, Lindsey A. Roth, Sam S. Oh, Neeta Thakur, Elizabeth A. Nguyen, Shannon Thyne, et al. "Early-life air pollution and asthma risk in minority children. The GALA II and SAGE II studies." *American Journal of Respiratory and Critical Care Medicine* 188, no. 3 (2013): 309–318.

Nielsen, Anders Busse. "Landscape laboratories: Pocket woods for 21st century urban landscapes." *'scape, The International Magazine for Landscape Architecture and Urbanism*, 15 (2016): 103–109.

Ngunjiri, Eliud. "Viewpoint: Participatory methodologies: Double-edged swords." *Development in Practice* 8, no. 4 (1998): 466–470.

North American Association for Environmental Education. *Community Engagement: Guidelines for Excellence* (Washington, DC: NAAEE, 2017), http://naaee.org/eepro/resources/community-engagement-guidelines. (Retrieved anuary 8, 2018).

Nurick, Robert, and Vicky Johnson. "Putting child rights and participatory monitoring and evaluation with children into practice." *PLA Notes* 42 (2001): 39–44.

Ogle, Donna M. "KWL: A teaching model that develops active reading of expository text." *The Reading Teacher* 39, no. 6 (1986): 564–570.

Office of the Registrar General & Census Commissioner, India. "2011 Census Data." Ministry of Home Affairs, Government of India. www.censusindia.gov.in/2011-Common/Census Data2011.html. (Retrieved January 5, 2018).

O'Kane, Claire and Rita Panicker, "Body mapping." *Steps for Engaging Young Children in Research, Volume 2: The Researcher's Toolkit*. Ed. Vicky Johnson, Roger Hart and Jennifer Colwell Brighton, UK: Education Research Centre, University of Brighton, 2014, 115–118. https://bernardvanleer.org/publications-reports/steps-engaging-young-children-research-volume-2-researcher-toolkit/. (Retrieved December 8, 2017).

Osnes, Beth. *Performance for Resilience: Engaging Youth on Energy and Climate through Music,* *Movement, and Theatre.* Cham, Switzerland: Springer, 2017.

Owens, Patsy Eubanks, ed. *Youth Voices for Change: Opinions and Ideas for the Future of West Sacramento.* Center for Regional Change. University of California, 2010. http://artofregionalchange.ucdavis.edu/files/2010/Comicbook_size.pdf. (Retrieved November 14, 2017).

Parnell, Rosie. "Co-creative adventures in school design." *School Design Together.* Ed. Paul Woolner. London: Routledge, 2015, 123–137.

Percy-Smith, Barry, and Karen Malone. "Making children's participation in neighbourhood settings relevant to the everyday lives of young people." *PLA Notes* 42 (2001): 18–22.

Pevec, Illène. *Growing a Life.* New York: New Village Press, 2016.

Phillips, Louise. "Social justice storytelling and young children's active citizenship." *Discourse: Studies in the Cultural Politics of Education* 31, no. 3 (2010): 363–376.

Plan International. *Bamboo Shoots: A Training Manual on Child-Centred Community Development/Child-led Community Actions for Facilitators Working with Children and Youth Groups.* Bangkok, Thailand: Plan Asia Regional Office, 2010. https://plan-international.org/publications/bamboo-shoots. (Retrieved January 2, 2018).

Plastrik, Peter, Madeleine Taylor, and John Cleveland. *Connecting to Change the World: Harnessing the Power of Networks for Social Impact.* Washington, DC: Island Press, 2014.

Podestá Siri, Rossana. *Nuestros Pueblos de Hoy y de Siempre. El Mundo de las Niñas y Niños Nahuas de México a través de sus Propias Letras y Dibujos.* Universidad de Puebla, Mexico, 2002.

Program in Environmental Design. *10 Walks of Burke Park.* The University of Colorado, Boulder. https://www.colorado.edu/envd/10-walks-burke-park. (Retrieved December 27, 2017).

Pukar. "Youth and urban knowledge production." Pukar.org. http://www.pukar.org.in/youth-and-urban-knowledge-production/ (Retrieved September 24, 2017).

Ragan, Doug. "Using mapping to engage youth in planning and governance." (Unpublished paper, 2011).

Rambaldi, Giacomo, Jon Corbett, Rachel Olson, Mike McCall, Julius Muchemi, Peter Kwaku Kyem, Daniel Weiner, with Robert Chambers, Eds. *Participatory Learning and Action 54: Mapping for Change: Practice, Technologies and Communications*. International Institute for Environment and Development. https://www.iied.org/pla-54-mapping-for-change-practice-technologies-communication, 2006. (Retrieved January 3, 2018).

Ramezani, Samira, and Ismail Said. "Children's nominations of friendly places in an urban neighbourhood in Shiraz, Iran." *Children's Geographies* 11, no. 1 (2013): 7–27.

Research Connections. *Child Care and Early Education Research Connections*. The Regents of the University of Michigan. https://www.researchconnections.org. Retrieved December 27, 2017).

Rigolon, Alessandro, Victoria Derr, and Louise Chawla. "Green grounds for play and learning." *Handbook on Green Infrastructure*. Ed. Danielle Sinnett, Nick Smith, and Sarah Burgess Cheltenham, UK: Edward Elgar Publishers, 2015, 281–300.

Robert Wood Johnson Foundation. *Qualitative Research Guidelines Project*. www.qualres.org/HomeInfo-3631.html. (Retrieved December 5, 2017).

Rojas, James. *Interactive Planning Manual*. Growing Up Boulder.org. http://www.growingupboulder.org/uploads/1/3/3/5/13350974/interactive_planning_manual.pdf. (Retrieved on July 28, 2016).

Rojas, James. "Place It!" Talk given to Environmental Design Program, University of Colorado Boulder on September 22, 2014. Available at: https://vimeocom/106818561. (Retrieved on July 28, 2016).

Roosevelt, Eleanor. Remarks at the United Nations, March 27, 1953. Cited in Ellen Hall and Jennifer Kofkin Rudkin, *Seen and Heard: Children's Rights in Early Childhood Education*, New York/London, Ontario: Teachers College Press/The Althouse Press, 2011.

Rudner, Julie. "Educating future planners about working with children and young people." *Social Inclusion* 5, no. 3 (2017): 195–206.

Sabo Flores, Kim. *Youth Participatory Evaluation*. San Francisco: Jossey-Bass, 2008.

Sandland, Ralph, "A clash of conventions? Participation, power and the rights of disabled children." *Social Inclusion* 5, no 3 (2017): 93–103.

Sanoff, Henry. *Community Participation Methods in Design and Planning*. New York: John Wiley, 2000, 88–96.

Schultz, P. Wesley. "Inclusion with nature: The psychology of human-nature relations." *Psychology of Sustainable Development*. Ed. P. Schmunck and P. Schultz. Springer U.S, 2002, 61–78.

Schenk, Katie, and Jan Williamson. *Ethical Approaches to Gathering Information from Children and Adolescents in International Settings*. Washington, DC: Population Council, 2005.

Scriven, Michael. "The method of evaluation." *Perspectives of Curriculum Evaluation*. Ed. Ralph Winfred Tyler, Robert Mills Gagne and Michael Scriven. Chicago: Rand McNally, 1967.

Shkabatur, Jennifer. "Interactive community mapping: Between empowerment and effectiveness." *Closing the Feedback Loop: Can Technology Bridge the Accountability Gap?*. Ed. Björn-Sören Gigler and Savita Ballur. Washington, DC: The World Bank, 2014, 71–106.

Sintomer, Yves, Carsten Herzberg, and Giovanni Allegretti. *Participatory Budgeting Worldwide—Updated Version*, Dialog Global No. 25. Bonn, Germany: Global Civic Engagement, 2013.

Smith, Greg, and David Sobel. *Place- and Community-based Education in Schools*. New York: Routledge, 2010.

Sobel, David. *Place-Based Education*. Great Barrington, MA: The Orion Society, 2004.

Sobel, David. *Mapmaking with Children: Sense of Place Education in the Early Childhood Years*. Portsmouth, NH: Heinemann, 1998.

Sobel, David. *Children's Special Places: Exploring the Role of Forts, Dens, and Bush Houses in Middle Childhood*. Tucson, AZ: Zephyr Press, 1993 (republished by Wayne State University Press in 2002).

Stephens, Lindsay, Helen Scott, Henna Aslam, Nicole Yantzi, Nancy L. Young, Sue Ruddick, and Patricia McKeever. "The accessibility of elementary schools in Ontario, Canada: Not making the grade." *Children, Youth and Environments* 25, no. 2 (2015): 153–175.

Stern, Daniel. *The Interpersonal World of the Infant.* New York: Basic Books, 1985.

Stern, Marc J., Robert B. Powell, and Dawn Hill. "Environmental education program evaluation in the new millennium." *Journal of Environmental Education*, 20, no. 5 (2014): 581–611.

Stevens, Dannelle D., and Joanne E. Cooper. *Journal Keeping: How to Use Reflective Writing for Learning, Teaching, Professional Insight, and Positive Change.* Sterling, VA: Stylus Publishing, Inc., 2009.

Stone, Emma. *Consulting with Disabled Children and Young People*, Joseph Rowntree Foundation, 2001. https://www.jrf.orguk/report/consulting-disabled-children-and-young-people. (Retrieved January 3, 2018).

Stoopen, María Morfín, and Yolanda Corona Caraveo. *Nuestra Voz También Cuenta: Haz Que Se Escuche: Una Experiencia de Participación de Niñas, Niños y Adolescentes en el Municipio de Pachuca* (*Our voice also counts: make it heard*: *An experience of participation of children and adolescents in the Municipality of Pachuca*). Chapultepec, Cuernavaca, Morelos, Mexico: Grafimor S.A. de C.V., 2017.

StoryCenter. "Listen deeply, tell stories." StoryCenter.org. www.storycenter.org. (Retrieved September 24, 2017).

Sutton, Sharon, and Susan Kemp. "Children as partners in neighborhood placemaking: lessons from intergenerational design charrettes." *Journal of Environmental Psychology* 22, no. 1 (2002): 171–189.

Swart-Kruger, Jill. "Children in a South African squatter camp gain and lose a voice." *Growing Up in an Urbanising World.* Ed. Louise Chawla. London: Earthscan Publications, 2002, 111–133.

Tiburcio, Eleuterio Olarte, and Juana Zacarías Candelario. *Libros Cartoneros: Una Alternativa para la Integración a la Cultura Escrita.* Dirección General de Educación Indígena de la SEP. http://www.educacionyculturaaz.com/articulos-az/libros-cartoneros-una-alternativa-para-la-integracion-a-la-cultura-escrita. (Retrieved September 25, 2017).

Torney-Purta, Judith, Rainer Lehmann, Hans Oswald, and Wolfram Schultz. *Citizenship and Education in 28 Countries: Civic Knowledge and Engagement at Age 14.* Amsterdam: IEA, 2001.

Triandis, Harry C. *New Directions in Social Psychology: Individualism and Collectivism.* Boulder, CO: Westview Press, 1995.

Tufte, Edward. *The Visual Display of Quantitative Information.* Cheshire, CT: Graphics Press, 1983.

United Nations. *Agenda 21.* https://sustainable development.un.org/outcomedocuments/agenda21. (Retrieved June 29, 2016).

United Nations. *Convention on the Rights of Persons with Disabilities.* https://www.un.org/development/desa/disabilities/convention-on-the-rights-of-persons-with-disabilities.html. (Retrieved January 2, 2018).

United Nations. *The Habitat Agenda.* UN Conference on Sustainable Development, Habitat II. http://www.un-documents.net/hab-ag.htm. (Retrieved July 27, 2016).

United Nations. *Habitat III: The New Urban Agenda.* Habitat III. habitat3.org/the-new-urban-agenda. (Retrieved April 5, 2017).

United Nations. "Sustainable Development Goals: 17 Goals to Transform our World." http://www.un.org/sustainabledevelopment/sustainable-development-goals/. (Retrieved April 5, 2017).

United Nations. "World Population Prospects: The 2017 Revision." United Nations, Department of Economic and Social Affairs. https://esa.un.org/unpd/wpp/. (Retrieved December 27, 2017).

United Nations. "World Urbanization Prospects: The 2014 Revision." United Nations, Department of Economic and Social Affairs, Population Division. Custom data acquired via website. (Retrieved July 26, 2016).

United Nations. *World Urbanization Prospects: The 2005 Revision.* http://www.un.org/esa/population/publications/WUP2005/2005 WUP_FS1.pdf. (Retrieved July 26, 2016).

UNICEF, "Child Friendly Cities." http://www.child friendlycities.org. (Retrieved June 28, 2016).

UNICEF. "Convention on the Rights of the Child." http://www.unicef.org/crc (Retrieved June 29, 2016).

United Nations Committee on the Rights of the Child. *General Comment No. 19 on Public Budgeting for the Realization Of Children's Rights* (art. 4), CRC/C/GC/19, 2016.

United Nations Committee on the Rights of the Child, *General Comment No. 12: The Right of the Child to be Heard* (art. 12), CRC/C/GC/12, 2009.

UN-Habitat. *ICT, Urban Governance and Youth.* Nairobi: author, 2012.

Urban Land Institute (ULI). "Red Oak Park—2012 Global Award for Excellence Winner." Urban Land Institute.org. https://americas.uli.org /global-awards-for-excellence/red-oak-park -2012-global-award-for-excellence-winner/ (Retrieved December 7, 2014).

Wake, Susan. J., and Chris Eames. "Developing an "ecology of learning" within a school sustainability co-design project with children in New Zealand." *Local Environment* 18, no. 3 (2013): 305–322.

Wake, Susan J., and Qian Wang. "Developing the greenery: Results from a co-design project with landscape architects and schoolchildren in Auckland, New Zealand." *Fifty Years Later: Revisiting the Role of Architectural Science in Design and Practice: 50th International Conference of the Architectural Science Association.* Ed. J. Zuo, L. Daniel, V. Soebarto. University of Adelaide, 2016, 269–278.

Ward, Colin, and Anthony Fyson. *Streetwork: The Exploding School.* London: Routledge and Kegan Paul, 1973.

Wang, Caroline, and Mary Ann Burris. "Photovoice: Concept, methodology, and use for participatory assessment needs." *Health Education & Behavior* 24, no. 3 (1997): 369–387.

Whitmore, Elizabeth, ed. *Understanding and Practicing Participatory Evaluation.* New Directions for Evaluation, Volume 80. San Francisco, CA: Jossey-Bass, 1998.

Whyte, William Hollingsworth. *The Social Life of Small Urban Spaces.* New York: Project for Public Spaces, 1980.

Wilks, Judith. "Child-friendly cities: A place for active citizenship in geographical and environmental education." *International Research in Geographical and Environmental Education* 19, no. 1 (2010): 25–38.

Williams, Florence. *The Nature Fix.* New York: W. W. Norton, 2017

Wingspread Symposium. *Wingspread Declaration of Principles for Youth Participation in Community Research and Evaluation.* University of Michigan. ssw.umich.edu/sites/default/files /documents/research/projects/youth-and -community/SymposiumII.pdf. (Retrieved September 23, 2016).

Winograd, Ken, ed. *Education in Times of Environmental Crises: Teaching Children to be Agents of Change.* New York: Routledge, 2016

Wridt, Pamela. *The Kids' Hood Book: A Neighborhood Guidebook by the Students and Teachers of Stedman Elementary School.* In collaboration with Children, Youth and Environments Center for Research and Design at the University of Colorado. Unpublished report, Denver, Colorado, 2006.

Yeh, Lily. *Awakening Creativity: Dandelion School Blossoms.* Oakland, CA: New Village Press, 2011.

Younan, Diana, Catherin Tuvblad, Lianfa Li, Jun Wu, Fred Lurmann, Meredith Franklin, Kiros Berhane et al. "Environmental determinants of aggression in adolescents." *Journal of the American Academy of Child and Adolescent Psychiatry,* 55, no. 7 (2016): 591–601.

Zeldin, Shep, Libby Bestul, and Jane Powers. *Youth-Adult Partnerships in Evaluation.* Ithaca, NY: ACT for Youth Center of Excellence, Cornell University, 2012. www.actforyouth.net/youth _development/evaluation/ype.cfm (Retrieved September 30, 2017).

Index

Page references followed by *fig* indicate an illustrated figure; followed by *t* indicate a table; followed by *b* indicate a box.

About
the Authors

Victoria Derr is Assistant Professor of Environmental Studies at California State University Monterey Bay, where her teaching and research focus on the intersections between sustainable communities, place-based environmental education, and social justice. Victoria has engaged children, youth, and communities in participatory research in both rural and urban settings with tribal, Spanish land grant, recent immigrant, and international communities. From 2012–2016, she served as a co-coordinator of the child- and youth-friendly cities program, Growing Up Boulder, at the University of Colorado. Victoria holds a masters and doctorate from Yale University.

Louise Chawla is Professor Emerita in the Program in Environmental Design at the University of Colorado Boulder. With a masters in Education and Child Development from Bryn Mawr College and a doctorate in Environmental Psychology from City University of New York, her research areas are children and nature, children in cities, participatory planning and design, and the development of committed action for the environment. From 1996–2006, she served as International Coordinator of the Growing Up in Cities Program for UNESCO. Louise co-founded the Growing Up Boulder program and remains an active member of its Executive Committee.

Mara Mintzer is a co-founder and current Director of Growing Up Boulder, based at the University of Colorado Boulder's Community Engagement Design and Research Center. Previously, Mara was the director of a community school in California. She writes and presents internationally on the topic of engaging young people in planning and has designed and implemented a wide variety of programs for under-resourced children and families in New York and California. Mara received her bachelors from Brown University and her masters from Teachers College, Columbia University.